# THE UNCOMMITTED

# The Uncommitted
Alienated youth in American society

Kenneth Keniston

 A DELTA BOOK

A Delta Book
Published by Dell Publishing Co., Inc.
750 Third Avenue, New York, N.Y. 10017
Copyright © 1960, 1962, 1965 by Kenneth Keniston
All rights reserved
Delta® TM 755118, Dell Publishing Co., Inc.
Reprinted by arrangement with Harcourt, Brace & World, Inc.
Thirteenth Printing
Manufactured in the United States of America

Some of the material in this book is based on previously
published articles, and the author wishes to thank the
following for permission to use it: *The American Scholar;*
Basic Books and the American Academy of Arts and Sciences
("Social Change and Youth in America," in *Daedalus,* Winter
1962); *The Journal of Jewish Communal Service;* and Atherton
Press ("Inburn: An American Ishmael," in *The Study of Lives,*
R. W. White, Editor, 1963).

FOR MY FATHER

# ACKNOWLEDGMENTS

Three extraordinarily wise teachers have shaped the spirit and intent of this book: Henry A. Murray, David Riesman, and Erik H. Erikson. From Henry Murray, I learned something of the enriching complexity of human needs and imagination; Riesman increased my understanding of the power of social setting and social pressure to shape men's character and dreams; from Erikson, I gained greater insight into the interweaving of the developmental, the social, and the historical. All three of these teachers, I think, share the same fundamental aspiration: to do fuller justice to man's greatness as well as his sickness, to his variegated complexity as well as his simple-minded folly. I have tried to make this book reflect that aspiration.

I am also fortunate in having had many colleagues from whom I have learned immensely, in particular David Ricks and Robert Lifton. The case studies from which this book begins were made at the Annex to the Center for Research in Personality at Harvard, under the direction of Henry Murray, who at every stage supported and encouraged these studies of alienation. Much of the data on which these case histories are based was gathered by Henry Murray, David Ricks, Alden Wessman, Paul Gross, Theodore Kroeber, Arthur Couch, and others. To Couch I am especially indebted for his generosity in making available data from his Ph.D. thesis which added notably to my understanding of alienated students.

Other debts are equally outstanding. Talcott Parsons' analyses of American society have influenced my discussion of social fragmentation and family life, though I am aware he would disagree with many of my conclusions. Theodore Lidz's interpretations of family interaction and dynamics have provided a framework for my discussion of alienating families. My colleagues in the Department of Psychiatry in the Yale Medical School have also deepened my understanding of individual health and psychopathology. David Reisman and Robert J. Lifton commented on earlier drafts of this book; it is much improved from their suggestions.

This study has been generously supported by a variety of sources. A grant from the National Institute of Mental Health (M-1287; Henry A. Murray, project director) made possible the gathering of psychological data about alienated students. Support from the Laboratory of Human Relations of the Department of Social Relations at Harvard, from the Department of Psychiatry at Yale Medical School, and from the National Institute of Mental Health (Grant No. MH-0850801) made it possible for me to analyze this material. Earlier versions of all or part of several chapters have appeared in *The American Scholar, Daedalus,* the *Journal of Jewish Communal Service,* and the *Study of Lives* (New York: Atherton, 1963, edited by Robert W. White). Mrs. Alice Treat Altvater typed the manuscript with notable intelligence and skill.

Obviously, this study would have been impossible without the co-operation and candor of the many undergraduates, alienated and non-alienated, who volunteered to be research subjects; I have tried to show my gratitude by respecting their confidence. But my greatest debt is to my wife, Ellen, whose sensitivity, intelligence, and wise counsel have improved every page of this book.

K. K.

*New Haven, Conn.*
*October, 1964*

# Contents

*List of Figures*

THE UNCOMMITTED

# 1    The new alienation

Our age inspires scant enthusiasm. In the industrial West, and increasingly now in the uncommitted nations, ardor is lacking; instead men talk of their growing distance from each other, from their social order, from their work and play, and from the values and heroes which in a perhaps romanticized past seem to have given order, meaning, and coherence to their lives. Horatio Alger is replaced by Timon, Napoleon by Ishmael, and even Lincoln now seems pallid before the defiant images of hoods and beats. Increasingly, the vocabulary of social commentary is dominated by terms that characterize the sense of growing distance between men and their former objects of affection. Alienation, estrangement, disaffection, anomie, withdrawal, disengagement, separation, noninvolvement, apathy, indifference, and neutralism—all of these terms point to a sense of loss, a growing gap between men and their social world. The drift of our time is away from connection, relation, communion, and dialogue, and our intellectual concerns reflect this conviction. Alienation, once seen as imposed *on* men by an unjust economic system, is increasingly chosen *by* men as their basic stance toward society.

These tendencies can of course be exaggerated in individual cases. As many or more men and women now lead individually decent and humane lives as ever did. There are pockets of enthusiasm in every nation. Old values are clung to the more tenaciously by some as they are disregarded by others. And the growing sense of alienation brings reactions in the form of new efforts to reconstruct commitment. But other facts are equally incontrovertible, at least in America: that there has seldom been so great a confusion about what is valid and good; that more and more men and women question what their society offers them and asks in return; that hopeful visions of the future are increasingly rare. The prevailing images of our culture are images of disintegration, decay, and despair; our highest art involves the fragmentation and distortion of traditional realities; our best drama depicts suffering, misunderstanding, and breakdown; our worthiest novels are narratives of loneliness, searching, and unfulfillment; even our best music is, by earlier standards, dissonant, discordant, and inhuman. Judged by the values of past generations, our culture seems obsessed with breakdown, splintering, disintegration, and destruction. Ours is an age not of synthesis but of analysis, not of constructive hopes but of awful destructive potentials, not of commitment but of alienation.

Thus it happens that terms like alienation gain ever wider currency, for despite all their vagueness they seem to point to something characteristic of our time. We feel this "something" in the growing belief in the inherent alienation of man from man and from the universe, in our preoccupation with the rifts, traumas, and discontinuities of psychological development, in the increasingly problematical relationship between men and their society, in our concern over national purposes and the breakdown of established values, even in our wavering faith in the progressive drift of history. And we see alienation especially clearly in American youth, poised hesitantly on the threshold of an adult world which elicits little deep commitment. Despite the achievement of many of the traditional aspirations of our society, we commonly feel a vague disappointment that goals that promised so much have somehow meant so little real improvement in the quality of human life. Whatever the gains of our technological age, whatever the decrease in objective suffering and want, whatever the increase in our "opportunities" and "freedoms," many Americans are left with an in-articulate sense of loss, of unrelatedness and lack of connection.

The most common reaction to this sense of loss is to deplore it. Popular magazines decry the absence of decency and "goodness" in current literature, revivalists call for a return to the faith of older days, and "new" conservatives ask a re-awakening of a purer, harder, and more ascetic America. We blame the defection of Americans in Korea on the "softness" of American life, and encourage programs of physical fitness. We attempt to re-create a sense of national purpose by appointing a committee and publishing its report in an inexpensive paperback. We argue with our youth, pointing out their advantages and privileges, not understanding their reluctance to "fit" into American life. Intellectuals commonly believe that a solution to our problems will come from a "restatement" of our individual and collective purposes in some more convincing form than has yet been found, or from a "rededication" to goals which have lost their power to compel. And from art, we expect some new synthesis of which our society as a whole is not capable.

All of these reactions are, however, beside the point. One does not cure a depression by deploring it and pointing out the bright side of life; a paranoid delusion cannot be changed by rational arguments. Both conditions derive from problems which underlie their symptoms, and only by understanding these antecedent conditions can we begin to know how to effect cures. The sense of loss, confusion, and estrangement which besets many Americans today cannot be changed by remonstrations or arguments: most alienated Americans are already aware, for example, that the standard of living is rising; most already know that there are more long-playing records and quality paperbacks than ten years ago; and many already realize—sometimes all too well—that enormous opportunities and challenges confront them. Yet this knowledge is not always enough to produce a sense of commitment to American society. Rather than deplore alienation, we must try to understand its origins, to search out the factors in individual life, social process, and cultural history which underlie it; and we must ask, finally, whether alienation might not be applauded rather than deplored.

Alienation is not, of course, a uniquely modern or American phenomenon. In every era and society, at least a few exceptional individuals have spurned their societies; and from the ranks of the alienated in every age have come the misfits, malcontents, innovators, or revolutionaries who have changed their worlds the better to suit their discontents and idealisms. So it is only relatively that we can speak of a "new alienation." But by this term, I mean to suggest that the origins and forms of our modern alienations are new: first, that the roots of alienation in America lie in a new kind of society, and, second, that in such a society alienation characteristically takes the new form of rebellion without a cause, of rejection without a program, of refusal of what is without a vision of what should be. Furthermore, these two facts are closely connected, for our society systematically undermines the idealism and Utopian spirit from which alienation might gather purpose and innovating direction.

The novelty of our modern American situation is too little understood, even by those who are most concerned with alienation, anomie, estrangement, and disconnectedness. Most of the vocabulary of current social comment, including these very terms by which we characterize our modern discontents, originated in efforts to understand an earlier industrial society which no longer exists in America today. The term "alienation" itself trails clouds of nineteenth-century Marxism; and the recent "rediscovery" of the early writings of Marx has brought a revival of interest in the "alienation of the worker" in our society. Yet much of this discussion seems irrelevant to our modern situation. The alienation of the industrial worker from his labor is a relatively minor aspect of our modern alienation; and in any case, such workers constitute a fast-dwindling proportion of the population. The "new" alienation is, if not worse, at least different: it affects not only those at the bottom of society but those at the top, and it is not only imposed upon men *by* their society, but increasingly "chosen" by them as their dominant response *to* society. To understand what is "new" about alienation today, we must begin from an awareness of how far our society has come, for better or worse, from the early capitalism which first inspired Marx's creative indignation.

I will use the term "technological" to characterize the era in which we live. For all of its awkwardness, this term points to many of the essential characteristics of our society—its concern with "techniques," its glorification of "technical" competence, its systematic application of scientific knowledge to the problems of production and consumption. Other terms might do as well: ours is a "post-industrial" society, a mass society, a society of consumption, an organized society, and a specialized society. But however we label it, it is vastly different from the world of our grandparents; and we will fail to comprehend it with the concepts and values of their day. Indeed, the persistence of these concepts and values is one reason why we find modern alienation so puzzling: when most of us live in the material Utopia of a century ago, why should we feel estranged?

For some Americans, this question admits an apparently simple answer: for them, the material Utopia of the nineteenth century does not really exist. For the poor and unemployed and the rejected in our society, general material progress means little for it affects them little: they continue to be poor despite a television set to escape from their poverty. And in a psychological sense, it may be even harder to be poor in an affluent society than in an age when poverty is man's common lot. The rejected have no reason to embrace their society: it offers them little. For almost any American Negro, or for any unemployed worker whose job has been lost through automation, alienation makes good sense and requires no very complex explanation. Indeed, the only problem is to explain why such men are not *more* articulately alienated from our society than they are.

The alienation of the impoverished and the rejected rightly concerns us, but it does not puzzle us as much as the alienations of the average, affluent, adjusted American, nor the estrangements of the fortunate, talented, and privileged whom I will later discuss. What is "new" about our alienation is not that the "bottom" third of the population has little deep commitment to our society—many societies have been unable to command their rational allegiance—but that a sense of estrangement pervades the rest of our society, an alienation that has few apparent roots in poverty, exclusion, sickness, oppression, lack of choice and opportunity. This alienation is the more puzzling in that it seems to beset youth most heavily, yet by the standards of an earlier generation, youth "has the most to live for" and has been given "every possible advantage." How can we explain their alienation?

This book is an effort to begin to answer that question. I start with a study of a group of alienated young men, of how they came to be alienated, and of what it is about our society that alienates them. In these youths, alienation is more than a vague sense of estrangement—though it is that. It is also a way of life, an explicit rejection of the values and outlooks of American culture. These are young men whose alienation extends to virtually every encounter with their world, be it their society and history, their college and friends, or even themselves. Though they are rarely able to define alternatives to the conventional life of well-adjusted Americans, that life profoundly repels them. Yet these young men were born into comfort and affluence, given the best educations possible, endowed with high talent and healthy body, and they attend one of the country's most excellent and prestigious colleges. Their grievance against their society is based on no obvious deprivation, and their alienation cannot be explained by simple social hardship.

Because this is a study of the roots of alienation in a group of Americans who have no obvious reason to be alienated, it is also inevitably a study of the human toll of our technological society. In examining the lives of these college students, it will become clear that no merely psychological account will suffice to explain their estrangement. Despite the common threads in the backgrounds and pasts of these young men, they also share their membership in American society; and their alienation is a response not only to their idiosyncratic personal histories, but to the common facts,

stresses, demands, and estrangements of America today. They were
studied precisely because their alienation is extreme; and they differ
from typical Americans in a variety of other ways. But their alienation is nonetheless a reaction to very real social pressures,
stresses and strains that impinge upon the rest of us as well, and by
seeking its personal and social sources we may better come to understand our common plight.

There are two major traditions in studying a problem like alienation. The one, characteristically American, views it as a "personal"
problem, which of course it is for the alienated. A purely psychological account of alienation implies that its only causes lie in
individual life and "personal" pathology. Once we discover psychodynamics and distortions of development that "prevent" a
youth from committing himself to his adulthood and his society, we
have discovered all we need to know. Alienated youths themselves
often unwittingly support this view by their readiness to discuss
their childhoods, their intense interest in their own psychology, and
their articulate insight into the personal origins of their beliefs.
Like intelligent Americans in general, exposed and overexposed to
psychological thinking, they often tend to interpret their own behavior as "merely" a reaction to an unfortunate past.

The other tradition sees alienation as a social problem. This
tradition, rooted in European sociology but increasingly powerful
in America, views alienation as a reaction to the stresses, inconsistencies, or injustices in our social order. The alienated man is seen
as the inconscient victim of his society; his alienation is imposed
upon him by a tyrannical economic system, by politicians who ignore his interests, or by employers who exploit his labor. The role
of individual personality and personal pathology is largely ignored,
except as a symptom of social problems: the focus is on the "big
picture." In practice, however, a sociological approach to alienation can lead to very different evaluations of it. Those who start
from opposition to our social order naturally sympathize with its
victims and detractors. Those who are favorably impressed with
our society's stability, capacity for growth and change, and its high

degree of organization, view alienation as an inevitable and minor growing pain of a society whose benefits we should daily count. But in either case, the experience and life of the individual are of interest primarily as they reflect society.

Each of these traditions has limitations so obvious that they require little elaboration: put simply, the psychologist often misses the shaping social context of individual lives; the sociologist may not attend to the depth and richness of human experience. Yet merely to hyphenate these two traditions is not enough: "psychosocial," or "socio-psychological" approaches also require new ways of thinking, new concepts, new understandings of *how* men and society connect, and above all a new tolerance for complexity of explanation. It would be comforting to think we could find *the* cause of alienation in possessive mothers, the bureaucratization of modern man, or the decline of Utopia. It is confusing to begin to see that *all* these factors, and many others, are simultaneously involved. And confusion is compounded when we realize that each of these partial causes is itself interconnected with all of the others: that possessive mothers may be made more possessive by the limitations of their husband's jobs, that the decline of Utopia may be related to the quality of men's work. Faced with such real complexity, the search for causes must yield to a search for connections; and the primitive causal model of dominoes toppling each other to the end of the row must be supplanted by the concept of a centerless web, all of whose threads are related to, are influenced by, and influence, all of the others.

Only a view of man that recognizes and tries to do justice to this interrelated web of connections between the individual and society can cope with the actual complexity of life. Merely to list the social *and* psychological factors at work is not enough, unless we can also show how they are related to each other and why. Nor is it enough to show how personal predispositions ready men to become alienated from society, unless we can also show how their society first helps shape these personal predispositions. These are not simple tasks, for we lack both the theory and the vocabulary for them.

Moreover they involve us fully in the endless complexity of human behavior and social process, in ways of thinking that are strange, new, and difficult.

For all these reasons, I have not been able to pinpoint *the* cause or even the causes of alienation. I have not tried to choose between psychological and social factors as primary in producing alienation. And I have had to deal not with causal chains, but with persistent themes, embracing configurations, and continual interactions. Thus I cannot summarize my conclusions in a sentence or a paragraph, except to say that the new alienation is intimately bound up with the technological society in which we live, and we cannot understand alienation or our society without understanding both together.

An attempt to understand individuals in society must confront another inevitable problem: the biases, limitations, prejudices, and selectivities of the writer. An American observer of American society inevitably carries a heavy baggage of traditional American assumptions about life; and those who minimize or deny this imbeddedness in their social and cultural tradition are often its greatest victims. Moreover, the psychologist who tries to understand another individual carries an additional baggage, in the form of his own motivations, selective blindnesses, and favored hypotheses. The problem of "counter-transference"—the psychotherapist's conscious and unconscious emotional biases toward his patients—exists for the research psychologist as well. Even the decision to study a topic like alienation is a complexly motivated act.

Science is an effort to control the role of subjectivity in perception, interpretation, and explanation. But in the human sciences, this goal is hard to achieve. Even the rigorous experimentalist who studies rats and pigeons is likely to generalize in a most unscientific way about the behavior of human beings. In those unable to recognize their own prejudgments and assumptions, a narrow view of science can lead to preconception masquerading as "scientific fact," and to blindness to the unconscious selectivities which operate powerfully even in the interpretation of rigorously experimental data. Awareness of this problem and an intense fear of subjectivity often leads to the choice of "research problems" that are narrow and trivial. As the late psychoanalytic theorist David Rapaport put it, "The determined effort of our time to produce unassailably tested knowledge—an effort which is the midwife to a majority of the papers which fill our literature—too often ties us to piecemeal pursuits."

This problem cannot be finally solved. My own conviction is that the most truly scientific strategem in the study of man is a persistent effort to make conscious and explicit one's own motivations and preconceptions; and that the most objective students of society are those whose own values are most clearly stated, not those who claim that "as scientists" they have no values. The major effort of the student of man or society must always be to retain his own openness to his own presuppositions and to what he studies, so that he retains the capacity to be surprised by proving himself wrong. If the writer's preconceptions and values are made explicit, the reader is at least allowed to challenge these assumptions as stated and not required to ferret them out as imbedded in "objective" reporting and interpretation.

I have tried to do these things as best I could. I have attempted to make clear my psychological assumptions and my evaluations of American society. To anticipate a theme that runs throughout this book, I assume that the purpose of any society should be the greatest possible fulfillment of its individual members, and I believe that "fulfillment" usually requires the greatest possible integration of all aspects and potentials of the psyche. "Fulfillment" and "integration" are of course ideals which can never be totally achieved; but they provide a standard against which failures of human developments can be judged, and a goal to aspire to—though it can never be reached. The goal of psychological integration entails the balanced development and harmonious co-operation of many psychic potentials: men's basic needs and drives, their conscience and ethical sense, and their capacity for self-control and "rational" appraisal of experience. Societies can also be judged, I think, according to how much they promote and support such integration. And to anticipate once again, I will argue that American society exacts a heavy human toll as the price of its achievements by encouraging one-sided human development, by systematically splitting men's lives into parts, and by making wholeness hard to attain.

In analyzing how American society contributes to alienation, I have not tried to present a balanced picture. Books are written in context, and the context of this book is the conviction that the most powerful analyses of our society, like our most profound under-standings of human nature, are too often taken as apologies for the status quo. We commonly interpret them to mean that our society is basically sound and that those who cannot reconcile themselves to it would profit more from psychotherapy than from social re-form. I think we already hear enough from the pulpits of Academia as well as the megaphones of the mass media about the opportuni-ties, challenges, productivity, material standards, and achieve-ments of our society. We attend too superficially to the human price we pay for these achievements, rarely entertaining the thought that our society's accomplishments may have outrun its purposes, leaving us with outlived and outworn values. These themes, rather than the virtues of American society, are those I have stressed here.

The meanings of the term "alienation" are legion, and as this term has become more fashionable, it has become synonymous with whatever the writer believes to be the central evils of modern society. In the Appendix, I attempt to disentangle some of these distinct meanings, distinguishing between cosmic outcastness, historical loss, social stress, developmental estrangement, and indi-vidual alienation. In the pages to follow, I will start from a group of alienated individuals—that is, young men who reject what they see as the dominant values, roles, and institutions of their society. Such a rejection of society may take many different forms: the re-fusal of the delinquent or criminal to abide by social rules and laws, the withdrawal of the misanthropic and the psychotic, the protest of the reformer and the revolutionary. But in the students we will study, this rejection is primarily ideological: these are not delinquents, psychotics, or revolutionaries, but merely deeply disaffected young men.

The study of these students began a half-dozen years ago, when I began to realize that the outlooks of the alienated formed a coherent pattern, which I called the "alienation syndrome." Several years of research attempting to define and explore this syndrome systematically, working with more than two thousand students in all, will be reported in a separate monograph, *The Alienated Student.* Here I will discuss only one part of that research, a series of intensive, long-range psychological studies of alienated students. From a large group of undergraduate men, twelve were identified by psychological tests as extremely alienated. These were selected for special study, along with another group of twelve who were extremely non-alienated, and a third "control" group of students who were not extreme either way. All were asked to take part in a three-year study of their personal development.

For this study, all of the students wrote a lengthy autobiography and a statement of their basic values and "philosophy of life." All took the Thematic Apperception Test (T.A.T.), which consists of twenty cards, each showing an ambiguous picture, for each of which the research subjects are asked to make up a story. All the students also took part in a wide variety of psychological experiments, ranging from the systematic observation of five-man groups to studies of self-image, from investigations of moral values to research into personal identity. And all were repeatedly interviewed about matters autobiographical, philosophical, and experimental. For three academic years, most gave about two hours a week to the research.

The setting of this research clearly colored its results. All interviews and experiments were conducted in a private house, which, though partly converted to offices, retained a library, living room, dining room, and kitchen, and was furnished in a comfortable and "unscientific" manner. The students liked this setting and enjoyed the research; though they were paid for their time, most afterwards thought the experience would have been worthwhile without pay. These students also usually liked the psychologists who conducted the research, and frequently sought them out even when no research was involved. The psychologists, in their turn, tried to maintain an attitude of sympathetic neutrality with the students, who, learning their confidence was respected, spoke freely and openly to them.

The three-year span of the study provided time to know each student well, to develop hypotheses about his personality, past history, and style of life, and to check these hypotheses against the events and findings of later years. The students were affected and in some ways changed by their participation in the research project, for so much self-scrutiny pushed them toward greater frankness with themselves and with others. As the study progressed, many students were able to correct their own early errors of memory, to add new details to prior accounts, and even to offer hypotheses about the rationale of their own behavior. On graduation, each student had spent approximately two hundred hours in the research, and had provided hundreds of pages of information about himself, his beliefs, his past life, his family, his college life and development, his fantasies, his hopes and dreams.

This information provided the basis for the next six chapters. I approached each subject's records clinically: that is, I attempted to formulate the most complete picture possible of his development, his strengths, and his weaknesses. With my wife, a clinical psychologist, I worked over all material available for each student and ended, usually after several days, with a formulation of psychological development and present personality, a case history like that of Inburn in the following chapter. Little by little, a set of common themes in the lives of all alienated students began to emerge. We then turned to the *non*-alienated students, again proceeding case by case, attempting now to contrast the alienated with these committed and/or conformist youths. And finally, we studied the third or "control" group, who were neither alienated nor non-alienated, to make certain that our interpretations of the alienated distinguished them from more typical students.

I will not here discuss the extremely non-alienated students: they differ from the alienated in every respect to be noted in the following pages. Their style of life is committed or conformist, instrumental and practical; their ideologies are usually solidly and traditionally American; their past lives and families differ sharply from those of the alienated, and their fantasies are conventional, quiet, and happy. To be sure, all of the students studied, whether alienated or non-alienated, had points of similarity: all were intelligent, privileged young Americans who were attending Harvard College; and these facts alone involved further similarities. But the themes emphasized in the following pages are those which distinguish the two extreme groups. The middle group contrasted less sharply with the alienated, for in different form they had many of the same problems. In many ways, the themes of alienation discussed in the following chapters are a "writing large" of more muted themes in the lives of more typical students.

There were of course, enormous differences among the alienated students studied. There were students with great strength of character and personality, and there were others of extreme fragility. Some were committed to explicitly artistic careers, others had strong opportunistic and exploitative streaks, others were so preoccupied with fantasy life that they were virtually removed from contact with reality, and still others "used" alienation as a temporary maneuver in personal development. Elsewhere I have discussed these subtypes in detail; here, I will concentrate on the themes which unite these students.

To discuss each individual separately would have been extremely cumbersome: even the barest discussion of the major themes in one student's life will take all of Chapter 2. To present a similar summary of more than thirty other students would have been impossible. Furthermore, intensive clinical research involves a contract between researcher and subject whereby the researcher undertakes not to reveal the identity of the subject. In some cases, like the case of Inburn, the outward facts of life can be disguised so as to make recognition impossible; but the crucial events in the lives of other students are sometimes so idiosyncratic that any attempt to disguise them would either fail or distort crucial events. Thus, on grounds of both brevity and ethics, I have presented a composite case history in Chapters 3 to 6.

The alienated students who make up this composite are of course not typical of American youth. They were studied precisely *because* their alienation was extreme; and in addition, they were drawn from one of the most highly selected student bodies in America. Thus, their lives reflect both their intense alienation, and their talent, fortunate social position, and attendance at an "elite" college. Nor is their particular form of alienation—conscious, articulate, private, and ideological—the only, or perhaps even the dominant, variety of alienation in America today. One would find other varieties of alienation among reformers and revolutionaries, among delinquents, among homosexuals, among addicts, among the withdrawn, the apathetic, the indignant, even among the schizophrenic. The specialness of this group means that we cannot generalize in any simple way from these youths to others: in many respects, how these students deal with their estrangements, with the social stresses and historical losses which impinge upon their lives, is specific to them and perhaps to a relatively small group of talented and ideologically alienated students.

Yet there is a long tradition of studying the extreme to understand the typical: much of what we know in psychology was first learned by studying the especially distressed. And while the study of extremes should not lead to generalizations about the *behavior* of others who are not extreme, it can be used to understand the *problems and stresses* of more typical lives, and the *processes* by which others attempt to cope with these problems and stresses. The study of the alienated may therefore sharpen our eyes to some of the major pressures on American youth: having seen these pressures dramatically illustrated and reacted to by the alienated, we may be better able to discern the less extreme ways in which similar pressures shape the lives of less alienated youths. Indeed, I will argue that the major themes in the lives of these alienated youths are but extreme reactions to pressures that affect all young Americans, and that the alienated are responding not only to the idiosyncrasies of their individual pasts, but to dilemmas of upbringing, to social stresses, and to historical losses that affect their entire generation.

In some ways, the characteristics of these alienated students are especially well suited to revealing the roots of alienation among other Americans. For one, these young men have had superficially fortunate and privileged lives. Neither personal disability nor inferior social position, neither group prejudice nor cultural disadvantage, can simply explain their rejection of their society. Furthermore, they have done well in terms of many of their society's standards: their admission to Harvard College alone attests high achievement in high school, innate talent, and the fact that their parents could provide the cultural advantages indirectly helpful for admission to college and the financial support necessary to stay there for four years. Whatever their complaints about their society, these complaints cannot be explained away as simple reflections of obvious social injustice or personal misfortune. When these students reject their society they are reacting to disadvantages apparent even to the most talented, fortunate, and privileged.

Furthermore, the articulateness of these students is a help, for they are far more able to talk about their feelings, to voice their views of themselves and their world, than are most young men of their age. No one, however "verbal" or gifted, can hope to explicate *all* of the factors—individual, social, cultural, and historical— that affect his attitudes and his behavior; and these young men are no exception. But were we dealing with a group of less intelligence and less articulateness, we would find many more clichés and fewer original perceptions. As it is, these young men are often able to express perceptions of their society that less articulate youths may dimly feel but cannot voice.

The organization of this book parallels the development of my thinking about alienation. I started with studies of alienated students like the "American Ishmael," described in the next chapter. In the next five chapters I turn to a larger group of alienated youths, inquiring into the common psychological sources of their alienation, asking what constitutes an alienated ideology, way of life, personal history, and imagination, and noting how these themes come together to produce an alienated youth. Throughout the first half of this book, I am concerned with alienated individuals and with the psychology of alienation.

As the common characteristics of alienated individuals emerged, it became clear that alienation was not only an idiosyncratic stance toward the world, but also a diffuse reaction to a society and to a definition of conventional adulthood that was "alien" to the alienated. Their alienation could not be understood without also understanding what they were alienated from, the society that was alienating them. From alienated youth I therefore turned to alienating society, seeking the social sources of alienation. In this search I was above all guided by the major themes in the lives of alienated young men, seeking the stresses, dislocations, estrangements, and demands to which individual alienation is, in part, a reaction. And in a final chapter, I attempt to make clear my own vision of the kind of society that might lie beyond technology.

I have not tried to support my arguments with quotations or statistics (although after each chapter I have added a brief discussion of the sources of my remarks and often qualifications that I have omitted from the text). Rather, I have advanced speculations and interpretations about individuals and our society which might help explain why it inspires scant enthusiasm. If these speculations are wrong or these interpretations foolish or partial—as no doubt they often are—I would hope my errors would at least lead the reader to examine and articulate his own interpretations of our society. For the only point of which I am truly certain is that American society is changing so rapidly that our understanding of it, our assessment of it, and our goals for it desperately need re-evaluation. This is a worthy task, one even worth failing at.

# I  ALIENATED YOUTH

# An American Ishmael

Inburn's appearance in no way set him apart from other under-graduates. Tall, with blue eyes and sandy hair, he wore the uniform of his classmates: baggy corduroys, a button-down shirt, horn-rimmed glasses, and a tie more often than not slid down from the collar. He walked with something of a slouch, hands deep in his pockets, his eyes mostly fixed on the pavement as if he were deep in some private thought. From the cafeterias he frequented, one versed in the ways of the college might have surmised that he was of literary bent and, from the fact that he so often ate breakfast at one particular cafeteria at 11:00 A.M. (having overslept the dining hall's more Spartan hours), that he was given neither to regular hours nor to impeccable attendance of lectures. But these qualities did not distinguish him from a goodly proportion of his fellow sophomores.

Nor did he create an unusual impression on others. The opinion of a woman of fifty who knew him casually can perhaps stand as typical: "I rather liked him. He is thin and pleasant—perhaps not a decisive, strong-willed person, but always agreeable, never obvi-ously depressed, perhaps a little shy, as talkative as most men his age." A psychologist who knew him slightly commented, "He is a nice-looking fellow, with a deep voice that might go over well on the stage. He speaks hesitantly, but well despite pauses and hesita-

tions—more like written prose than ordinary speech." His manner
was polite, reserved, and even detached, which implied to some that
he was proud and condescending, and to others that he tended to
brood. Though he seldom looked directly at the person to whom he
was speaking, occasionally, when caught up in a topic, he would
gaze deeply and intently into his interlocutor's eyes, suggesting
deeper feelings than his outward manner expressed.

On the surface, his background and interests were also altogether unextraordinary. Like many of his classmates, he came from
a middle-class family outside of New England, and he had gone to
a good high school where he had graduated near the top of his
class and been editor of the school paper. His outstanding intelligence, however, did not distinguish him from his classmates, also of
high talent; and while his grades in his freshman year were slightly
uneven, they adequately reflected his ability and he made Dean's
List. His father was an executive with a large Detroit corporation;
and his mother, for a time a schoolteacher, had early abandoned
her career for domesticity. Inburn himself had been undecided for
a time as to his major, but had finally settled on English literature
as a field which combined his interest in writing and his superior
high school training in literature. Like other students of artistic interests, he had tried his hand at student dramatics and at writing, a
career he sometimes thought of following. He was a student in
good standing with the college authorities who had caused no one
any trouble and who would not be easily picked out in a crowd.

In the most public sides of Inburn's personality, then, there was
little to suggest what was the case: that he was deeply dissatisfied
with society, the world, and himself, that he almost completely rejected the institutional forms within which he was living, that he
would spend his first reading period for exams in platonic partner-
ship with a call girl whose memoirs he was ostensibly recording for
future use, and that, though he passed his exams, he would withdraw from the college never to return, heading instead on a motor-
cycle across the country to live with an "irredeemably dissolute"
high school friend in San Francisco. Despite his conventional sur-

face, indeed because of it, Inburn can stand as a prototypically alienated young man, separated by his own volition from the people, institutions, and beliefs which sustain most young men at his age in America, rejecting the forms by which most American men and women live, and condemned like the Biblical Ishmael by his past and like Melville's Ishmael by his own temper to live on the outskirts of society. In Inburn, we see alienation—the rejection of the roles, values, and institutions he sees as typical of adult American life—in unusually pure form; and the themes of his life can stand as introduction to and summary of parallel and comparable themes in the lives of others like him.

## An endless and featureless countryside

Like seventy other volunteers for a psychological research project, Inburn took a battery of paper-and-pencil tests, many of which were designed to measure alienated outlooks. He first came to our attention even before the questionnaires were scored, because of his mordant marginal comments on items that he considered stupid or irrelevant. He scored among the highest scores on every index we then had of alienation—on distrust, pessimism, resentment, anxiety, egocentricity, the sense of being an outsider, the rejection of conventional values, rejection of happiness as a goal, and a feeling of distance from others. And had other subsequently developed measures of alienation been available, he would have scored high on them—on subspection (the desire to look beneath appearances), self-contempt, interpersonal alienation, dislike of conventional social groups, the rejection of American culture, the view of the universe as an unstructured and meaningless chaos. But even more revealing than test scores are some of the individual statements which he marked "strongly agree," often with exclamation points added; taken together, they constitute a kind of credo of disaffiliation: "The idea of trying to adjust to society as now constituted fills me with horror." "There are sad and depressing times

when the whole world strikes the eye as a huge, heartless, impersonal machine, almost devoid of understanding, sympathy, and
mercy." "I sometimes feel that I am the plaything of forces beyond
my control." "I feel strongly how different I am even from some of
my closest friends." "I have very little in common with most of the
people I meet." "I don't think I'll ever find a woman who really
understands me." "I have very little self-confidence." "I usually try
to keep my thoughts to myself." "I sometimes wish I were a child
again."

Soon after, when Inburn was asked to write a statement of his
philosophy of life, he was unique among twenty-five students
chosen for intensive clinical study in that he wrote an allegory instead of a formal statement:

A group of men were motoring through an endless and featureless
countryside in a tightly closed car, with all the windows rolled up.
They reach a city, emerge from their vehicle, stretch their legs, and
look around. They have a two-weeks stay ahead of them; after that
they must move on into the wastes on the other side of the town, the
same as before they arrived.

"Well," I ask (being one of them), "what shall we do?" To all
our surprises, each wants to spend his time differently. . . . "Personally," say I, "I would like to see the sights of this place."

In this rather naïve allegory lies the ideal of my philosophy of
life. If human (i.e., *my*) existence is looked on as a short time spent
in a physical world with an inscrutable void on either side, it seems
that the time can be most profitably spent in accumulating the most
varied, the most valuable and most significant set of sense experiences it is possible to take in. . . .

. . . one must not see the same sights over-frequently. What experiences are most valuable to fill this sixty to seventy year interlude
are those that bring one into the closest contact with reality, with
the ground, the bedrock of sheer existence. This, of course, involves
living close to nature, outside of (or rather beneath) the superstructure of tin and shit and kite-paper man has built up to live in.

. . . Rather obviously, I am not practicing what I preach to any
extent at all now. I wouldn't be in this room writing this little essay
if I were. So far, all I do is insult myself by saying it's a fine idea, in

fact, it's the only idea in the universe, but you don't have the guts to put it into practice.

Inburn's statement is as noteworthy for what it excludes as for what it says. Unlike many other students, whose philosophies of life stress the importance of other people, Inburn mentions others only once, and then to state that he is different from them. Also unlike many of his classmates, he explicitly rejects the "superstructure" of society, and seeks above all the accumulation of sense experience, defined as that which will bring him into contact with "the bedrock of sheer existence."

Inburn's generally distrustful view of his fellow man was amplified when he was asked what harms and benefits he chiefly anticipated from his fellow men. He listed only "hostility, injustice, hypocrisy, slander, abuse." Asked whom he admired, he said "I never thought about it. Alexander maybe. Hemingway in Paris. Chopin," but asked whom he disliked, he responded with a long catalogue which begins "nearly everything, and everyone that's complacently middle-class," enumerates many specific examples, and concludes "I hate officious, supercilious, imperious, pompous, stupid, contented, or bigoted persons. I especially dislike opportunists." And asked what his chief satisfactions and ambitions were he said, "I don't think I'll ever have a main source of satisfaction. Only to live so that I may have the truest picture of the world possible when I die. You mean vaulting ambition? Nobody strives for ideals anymore. It's hard enough just to strive." And asked how he would reform the world if he could, he said, "This is an unfair question. I guess I'd like to have us all go back to the womb."

Here, then, is a young man whose every attitude fits an alienated pattern—full of distrust, he expects only harm from his fellow men; he has few admired figures, but many he dislikes; he sees life as a meaningless interlude whose chief aim is the accumulation of varied sense experiences. He rejects society and conventional institutions; though he has no definite plans for his life, he clearly wants something different from the conventional life which draws most of his classmates; he denies all ambition; and his facetious Utopia is the womb.


## More than a mere mother-and-only-child

Inburn's autobiography, written for the research project for which he had volunteered, begins to provide some clues as to the development of his alienation. Like one or two of the more literarily ambitious research subjects, he began his autobiography in the third person:

> He came screaming and red-faced into the world on a December night in 1938, loath to leave his insensible sanctuary. . . . It was in a hospital in St. Louis; his mother was a small, young woman and she never had a child again. His parents were both schoolteachers and poor, after the ravages of the depression. His mother was particularly good looking when she was young—black hair, a good nose, strikingly large eyes, a sensuous lip and a delicate yet hard, vibrant, vivacious body.

Inburn goes on to describe his mother's Greek immigrant parents, her mother "a simple, exuberant, and cruel woman," and her father, who ran a small restaurant, "a strong man, and strong-willed," "tireless, too tireless."

His further description of his mother is extremely detailed. Despite her immigrant parents, "she made herself socially to nearly every family in St. Louis" [sic]. "Her petite and much-in-demand bottom was between two worlds. . . . She dropped her restaurant-owner's daughter's bad manners and grossness, and made herself, completely, at the cost of a great emotional and psychological complexity." She was ambitious, she taught herself to play the piano beautifully (she even gave recitals), "she *would* read poetry (though she never wrote it), she *would* paint, she *would* play tennis on the bank president's private court, and with his son." Despite her parents' lack of sympathy with her educational goals, she worked her way through high school and college, finishing each in three years. Elsewhere, Inburn notes that his mother is at the extreme end of the temperament scale: "volatile, passionate, typically Mediterranean"; and he adds that she "has a delicate constitution and has been warned against severe mental as well as physical strains."

In contrast to his fulsome description of his mother, Inburn has little to say of his father. His father's family originally came from a farm in the Midwest, and Inburn's grandfather married his own brother's pregnant and cast-off girl friend, became a milkman in St. Louis, and was thereafter dominated by his wife, a "scolding, officious hypochondriac." The father's ancestry was primarily Welsh, with a mixture of German and Irish. Inburn's father showed early signs of intelligence and musical talent, and worked his way through high school and college, where he met his wife-to-be. As a child, he seems to have been dominated by his mother, the "scolding, officious hypochondriac," who forced him to work in the evenings for the family landlord, "an idea he has recalled with bitterness at times." Awarded a scholarship to an Eastern college, Inburn's father was unable to accept it because he had to help support his parents—a responsibility that included helping pay his older half-brother's debts. Inburn describes his father now as a "phlegmatic, deliberate, steady-minded Welshman," noting the extreme contrast with his mother. "Father is pretty much of a failure in his own eyes," he comments, adding, "He's done pretty well as far as the world is concerned, though." Elsewhere he calls his father "a pillar in the community," adding parenthetically, "(Small pillar. Small community)." He describes "a great distance" between himself and his father, noting rather unenthusiastically, "We are friendly, though, except when my Greek side is up and I become disgusted with him and he annoyed at me."

His parents married immediately after graduating from college and both worked as high school teachers, his father occasionally holding two jobs to supplement the family income. Inburn's account continues:

This, then, is the situation (one might say predicament) Inburn was born into. By 1938 his parents had saved enough money to have a house of their own . . . they hired an architect and had the place built just as they wanted. The father is acquiescent and the mother has excellent taste, and it came out beautifully.

The first memories Inburn has are of this house—door knobs, the carpeting, the bright yellow and white kitchen, the apple tree in the backyard, the plum trees in the field beyond. It was in a fairly undeveloped suburban section, staunchly middle class.

He was pretty as a child, a little plump, with his mother's eyes and grace and quite curly blond hair. Mama tells me [sic] proudly how often people stopped her on the street and exclaimed about him. The closest friend he had in preschool days was a girl his own age. . . . He had nearly no male companionship until he entered school in the first grade, a year early, and he was somewhat precocious (not alarmingly so). He seems to have been quite well adjusted, pretty well liked by everyone, quite well liked by his teachers. Although he showed some intelligence, he was not remarkable. He liked his dog, his home, radio programs, soccer ball, brick walls, the janitor at school, trees, mornings, green lawns, walking, playing with toys, having imaginary adventures with the boy across the street in the orchard behind his house.

But as with most children his age, the Second World War profoundly affected Inburn:

When he was five years old, his father went into the war; he was gone for four years. In these four years he and his mother had the most intimate of relationships. They were one. Every thought, every action of one could be anticipated by the other. Somehow it seemed more than a mere mother-and-only-child relationship. We were in complete spiritual and mental and physical harmony with each other. Sometimes she was even shy with me. It was a strange relationship.

This description is as remarkable for the element of fantasy it contains as it is for the undeniable facts it must refer to. Inburn emphasizes the fusion of mother and child, the completeness of their understanding, their total anticipation of each other's thoughts and actions, their oneness. But in fact, such oneness and fusion can seldom occur after the first year of life; thereafter, mother and child assume an increasing separateness which usually eventuates in the child's independence as an adult. That Inburn thus describes his relationship with his mother at ages five through nine thus suggests a strong element of wish, perhaps on the mother's side but certainly on Inburn's, that all separateness between him and her be obliterated.

The end of the war brought a double dislocation for Inburn: first, his father returned from the war, and second, immediately thereafter his father left teaching and moved with his family to a more lucrative and more bureaucratic position in a Detroit corporation, where he is now, in his son's words, "a kind of minor official." Inburn himself makes little of either of these facts; but without noting the connection, he dates several changes in his behavior from the age of nine or ten. Of his state of mind, he writes, "From about nine or ten on, he got to be very moody, thinking too much or reading the wrong kind of books. The moodiness was always well within himself, though, and he was seldom snappish, perverse, or irritable." Elsewhere, he dates the beginning of intermittent constipation from the same age. And in a supplement to his autobiography, when recounting his sexual development, he writes:

> I was disturbed when I was finally convinced that children came out of women. I didn't want to believe it. It seemed base and carnal at the time. . . . I thought that if people wished for children strongly enough they would just come. I was first enlightened by some slightly older boys (9-10?); later and more clear-headedly by my parents, though sketchily (14).

After the move to Detroit, Inburn's family continued to travel during summer vacations, which he recalls with pleasure. But also notes:

> But the summers away made it impossible for Inburn to play baseball. In that red-blooded American community baseball was a big thing. I was a little estranged from my fellows because of this.

Expanding on his subsequent relationships with his peers, he says:

I was accepted, but made people indignant towards me because
they felt I was not only superior to them but scornful of them. All
but one friendship pretty casual, red-blooded. Few quarrels. It didn't
matter that much. Frequent periods of extreme moodiness and solitariness. Disenchantment—estrangement.

In sum, his father's return and the family move to Detroit seem to
have been a turning point in Inburn's life, marking the beginning of
his moodiness, his constipation, his estrangement, and even coin-
ciding with his disgust at the "base and carnal" nature of birth. But
all of this is our surmise, for Inburn himself does not note the coin-
cidence of dates.

When he was fourteen, Inburn first became interested in girls,
describing himself as "struck dumb" by a girl "with eyes as blue as
his, and deeper, framed in a simple kerchief, staring into his face in
an autumn dusk." He continues,

Not long later sex reared its ugly head. He fell in with some of his
male contemporaries. And boys can be dirty. They can be vile. A
hundred times we talked about the girls at school, describing with
great vigor their proportions, or lack of them. Girls with breasts the
size of five-cent ice cream cones. . . .

He reports "excessive masturbation," accompanied by "great
clouds of guilt," and characterizes his major current feelings about
sex as "anxiety, shame, disgust." He has never had intercourse.

Inburn reports no further events of outward importance until he
was a junior in high school, when he met Hal, who played a major
role in the development of his outlook:

Hal was, and is, a cynical young man. Cynical, profound, skeptical,
sarcastic, highly intelligent, casual in his manner, yet intense in his
questioning. And he always questioned. His cynicism infected me; he
became my very good, my best friend, the best and closest I ever had.
What were we cynical about? You, for one thing, and ourselves, our
teachers, our world, cynical about the very act of existence. Or
rather, the fact of existence, for with us it was a passive experience.
We let time and values and actions pass over us like a wash, like a

coating of wax. We both had been raised as agnostics, but it was a mild sort of agnosticism, an unthought-about agnosticism. First of all we turned everybody's religion upside down and we shouted. We were roundly condemned, but Hal more, since he shouted more, and louder. That went by the board and we began on our contemporaries and on our society. We attacked everything, every person, every institution, with a bitter tooth. Our long secret conversations were rank with contempt. We were full of a magnificent disdain, and we fed it with all the knowledge we could get (and what wouldn't fit we disregarded)—Kafka, D. H. Lawrence, Hume, Rousseau, Voltaire, Shaw, Jung, Freud, Marx. We read voraciously, but not the right things, and not enough.

. . . Hal is gone now. He went to college in Berkeley for a while, but now he is apparently irredeemably dissolute. . . . And he just doesn't give a damn. There was a great rift between us when I went to the College. He thinks that it will ruin me, and now calls me a coward for not "finding out some things" on my own.

Maybe he's right. If he means I'm becoming more complacent, I must plead guilty. As far as I can see, we both want knowledge; we want to know about the underpinnings of existence. I'm trying to do it through the institutions of my society, the college, for example. Hal is trying to "find out some things" on his own.

And on this inconclusive note, Inburn ends his autobiography.

In what he tells us about his life, certain themes and facts stand out. First is the marked contrast between his two parents. His mother emerges as "Mediterranean," ambitious, energetic, high-strung, driving, volatile, passionate, and, in her son's eyes, sensuous and physically attractive. Even her family is characterized as strong, tireless, simple, exuberant, and cruel. But he suggests that she has paid a high price in "complexity" and a "delicate" constitution and psychology for her efforts in "making herself." Inburn's father, in contrast, comes from North European stock, and from a long line of men who were dominated by women. Recall how his chances for a better education were limited by having to pay his half-brother's debts. And consider his move from his first love, teaching, to a more lucrative job where he now considers himself "a failure in his own eyes" despite contrary community judgment. Without fully stating it, Inburn clearly implies his father's weakness vis-à-vis his mother's drive ("The father is acquiescent and the mother has excellent taste . . ."). Inburn obviously finds his mother's vivid sensuousness far more interesting than his father's phlegmatic and taciturn nature. All of this makes Inburn's father a man difficult to emulate; and we would anticipate that this fact, coupled with Inburn's unusual past relationship with his mother, would cause Inburn difficulty.

In addition, several events stand out as having crucial importance in Inburn's life. One is his romanticized idyl with his mother during the war. The absence of any child's father for three or four years would be important to his development; but for Inburn, its importance must have been accentuated by his unique, "more than a mere mother-and-only-child relationship" with her. His friendship with Hal, too, was crucial. Until he met Hal, Inburn's life seems little different on the surface from that of most young men his age, with "his moodiness . . . always well within himself"; Hal acted as a catalyst for Inburn's alienation. Thirdly, Inburn's initial unwillingness to accept the fact of birth, his inability to overcome his not unusual first reactions to sex, and his current anxious attitudes are also worth underlining. While many a young man in our society has difficulty in reconciling himself to the "facts of life," it is remarkable at the age of nineteen to list "anxiety, shame, and disgust" as the only three emotions which sex evokes. And finally, Inburn's relations with his peers follows a familiar pattern for an alienated young man. He was not good at the games which mattered in his "red-blooded" community, his fellows considered him scornful, and he felt "frequent periods of estrangement." Even when he became editor of the school paper with his friend Hal, the two of them "managed to ruin it in three months."

But so far, we know only as much about Inburn as he himself knows and is willing to tell us. To understand the underlying dynamics of his alienation, we must turn to the stories he told on the Thematic Apperception Test (T.A.T.), twenty cards with ambiguous pictures; for in these he gives us a deeper and less conscious picture of the way he views the world.


## The cat that swallowed the canary

Inburn's stories about older women add several new elements to the description of his mother in his autobiography. Confronted with a picture of a man, a woman, and a girl with books in her hand, he is reminded of D. H. Lawrence's book, *Sons and Mothers* [sic]. The older woman is described as "a rather possessive person," "obviously a strong figure," who feels "not quite like the cat that swallowed the canary but rather supercilious towards the girl and proud of her victories since the girl has . . . gone back to the family." Reminding himself of the play, *The Silver Cord,* he cannot decide whether the girl will be "finally engulfed by the mother at the end" or whether she would escape the mother's clutches. Or on a card which shows an older woman peering around a half-opened door, he describes a woman spying on a boy. He says several times that the woman is "some kind of odd member of the household," that there is an

> odd relationship between her and the boy. . . . There's something between them so they can't get close to each other. I said that there was something between them, but I didn't mean that, I mean there's *no* relationship between them because there's something blocking their getting closer to each other. She suspects on the part of the boy some monstrous and horrible act of some kind . . . something insidious and disgusting. Maybe it's some sexual act with himself, or maybe it's not that at all.

In the end, the boy, who, he tells us, is not doing anything wrong at all, begins "to wonder whether there's something monstrous that *she* commits . . . the boy would seriously consider looking in on her [in her room] sometime to find out . . . but he never does . . . nothing comes of it."

Another story again involves a similar bond between a man and a woman.

> . . . The girl . . . is a rather unstable character . . . she is violently in love with the boy and has more or less thrown herself at him. The boy has been sort of disturbed at this . . . and finally decided to play along . . . it wouldn't hurt—why not? . . . He would be just about to make a proposal that they go to bed with each other. She will undoubtedly agree, and if he can close his eyes just a little more and block out that rather unpleasant nose of hers, he'll be delighted because well, why not? And she'll be delighted because she thinks . . . this particular device will certainly bind him to her more strongly. . . . Afterwards . . . the boy again feels wretched. . . . He feels that it was something that shouldn't have been done . . . while he has no real affection for her other than a kind of— not a man-to-man relationship exactly, but just a kind of friendly, somewhat intellectual relationship. . . . Other than that he has no real desire for her, although he thinks she is a desirable girl . . . but then maybe he has known her from too early an age or something, but she's just grown up with the wrong relationship with him and nothing would ever be successful in that way. . . .

Here the woman is dominant and initiating, seeking with sex to bind the man to her, while he feels that "maybe he has known her from too early an age" for there to be anything but a platonic and "intellectual" friendship.

In another story, he tells of a man who has committed a minor transgression and who returns home to face his accusing mother.

> It's not important to anyone with any reasonable perspective on the situation. But both he and his mother have a funny perspective on the situation. Maybe something silly. . . . He will probably continue to do these things wrong again in the future and his mother will continue to rail at him until he's fifty years old, I imagine.

And, significantly, in trying to imagine an especially unpleasant treatment for one of his characters in another story, he recalls the scene in *East of Eden* where one brother takes the other and "pushes him . . . onto his mother, not in a sexual position but just makes them both fall to the floor and rub against each other, which is somehow an incredibly vile and loathsome thing to happen. . . ."

In all of these references to women, Inburn intertwines two related themes: the fear of domination and the fear of sexual closeness. His heroes are caught in "odd relationships" with their mothers or other women who dominate and control them, although at the same time the heroes remain bound because of their lack of "any reasonable perspective on the situation." Mothers are seen as "possessive" and "not quite like the cat that swallowed the canary, but . . ." Parallel with this is the peculiar nature of relationships between men and women, a "strangeness" which appears related to the ambivalent fear of sexual intimacy. Thus, the strange woman who spies on the boy suspects him among other things of some "monstrous" sexual act with himself; but in the end, the boy, instead of proclaiming his innocence or leaving, ends up considering spying on the older woman as well. Throughout these stories there is "something between" men and women which bars them from both intimacy and satisfactory sex, "something" related to their having known each other "from too early an age," perhaps something like the fear of the most "incredibly vile and loathsome thing," incest. Unconsciously, then, Inburn sees himself as bound to a possessive and even predatory mother, unable to break away from her, and at the same time both tantalized and horrified by the sexual connotations of closeness to her.

## The father, being absent . . .

Just as he says less of his father than of his mother in his autobiography, so in his T.A.T. stories Inburn has less to say of older men than of women. Characteristic of all his stories is his reference to the father of the girl with a possessive mother, of whom he notes, "The father, being absent, sort of leaves him out of my mind . . . he was rather inconsequential." And when he does tell stories involving older men, his tales are usually facetious or cynical. Thus, he tells a caustic story about Heaven in which it turns out that "Jehovah Himself is an incredibly ugly figure . . . regrettably the situation up there has been a little deceptively colored, . . . sold a little better than it is by the angelic ad men and the established church." Or again, to a picture of an older man who outstretches his hand over a prone figure, he tells of an "evil German doctor type" who gets boys under his mystical spell and eats them: "He's just an evil fellow through and through." And perhaps closest to his conscious image of potentially helpful older men is a story of a kindly teacher who understands and wants to help the hero: the young man

> thinks [the teacher] is a fine person and that there should be more like him. And yet somehow he is repelled by the picture of himself being like this, and he realizes that that's how it must be if he is to go along and follow along, drop in line, follow suit and so forth. . . . [The young man thinks of Marlowe and musical geniuses who died young, or] a man who lives with such vigor and strength and intensity that in twenty-five or thirty years he's burnt himself out and drops dead because he hasn't anything else to do. . . . He wonders whether an intenser life like that wouldn't be a better thing than just fobbing along course by course and day by day, the way the venerable and openly respectable [teacher] has done.

Inburn's anger at older males breaks through fully in only one story. He starts a facetious account of the president of Harvard College who on a pretext sneaks away from his wife to buy a pizza pie at a nearby tavern. The president is, however, set upon by a three-armed man who has been installing sewer connections, and "this dreadful three-armed man with a dirty sleeve on each arm of his jacket" rubs against him in the "incredibly vile and loathsome way" which, as we have seen earlier, Inburn associates with a son in a sexual position with his mother. When Inburn directly expresses aggression at a paternal figure, he does it in what he makes clear is the most disgusting and degrading way possible. But though this is the most direct instance, Inburn always sees to it that older men, when not omitted from the action, are debased, defiled, or ridiculed.

Paternal figures are not what they seem: the doctor is an evil hypnotist, Jehovah has been oversold by the heavenly ad men, the college president must sneak pizza pies and be vilely humiliated by the three-armed man from the sewer; and even the venerable teacher, for all of his understanding, turns out to be dull and pedestrian. But most important is Inburn's comment that "the father, being absent, sort of leaves him out of my mind."

## Existential pessimism

Many of Inburn's stories imply a kind of pessimistic existential world view, stressing the futility of endeavor, the intensification of life, the emptiness of love, and the desirable role of detached observer and commentator. In one story the hero, after a long and arduous climb up the inside of a dark tower, at last pushes open the windows.

> He looks out on the surrounding country and somehow he doesn't like the view very much. He doesn't think it's much of an accomplishment after all. He thought he would really get something out of it, but the country just looks farther away from the way it was on the ground. And there's no change in it; there's nothing he can see farther from his vantage point. So I'll just leave him there standing looking out of the window. . . .

The arduous effort has proved futile: the view is merely more distant.

In the story of the kindly teacher, Inburn has wondered whether it would not be better to "burn himself out" in twenty-five or thirty years rather than lead a dull, plodding life. On a card showing a man climbing a rope, his hero actually does die an early death: he is a circus acrobat in a land where there are

> nothing but side shows and other circuses. [The hero] is in the springtime of life, as many have undoubtedly said, free and free-limbed. He is strong and not only strong but proficient in acrobatics

and light, not a clumsy kind of strength but not delicate exactly either. He's refined his talents which are nearly entirely bodily. . . . There is no such thing as intellectualism in this delightful land. He is free from any foreboding thoughts but . . . here he is just before his death. After doing a stupendous trick from which he gets a great roar from the crowd . . . he falls off the rope, not meaning to . . . falls a long way down and kills himself with a smile on his face, . . . with no regrets on the way down. . . . Afterwards the crowd . . . does not gasp, is not horrified. . . . There is no great tension. . . . Things just go on as usual. They don't take him away at all. [The crowd envies him] because here is a man in the prime of youth, who is in tune with life, who can get up in the morning and sing and fall asleep at night without a wrinkle in his brow and has done this all his life—he's never known death or old age. And his life has been made more perfect by annihilation. . . . He will never know the infirmities of old age in all their various forms—in the mind, in the darkening sight and the creaking body. . . . And then the show is over, and people pour out into the little streets and passageways like a carnival has. And then things go on as usual.

Here Inburn extols a purely unreflective and physical existence, and recurs to his earlier value on dying at the height of life.

Another story stresses the same value in another way. Inburn tells of a pious boy who self-righteously keeps himself apart from the grossness, murderousness, and sensuality of the world.

But the boy has refined himself away to nothing, kept out of any sort of relations with people, . . . and for this reason he has got so far away from everything that he indeed is not living life as much as the people who are murdering. . . . It's better to murder, which is just an act, than to make no acts at all . . . it seems more desirable right now, if one must choose, to choose the part of those horrid old men in the background cutting other horrid old men up than to be the snotty, over-refined, completely ineffectual boy who is, in fact, wasting his life much more than the men in the background are.

The gratuitous act, even if it be murder, is better than no action at all.

Even the most optimistic and forward-looking of Inburn's stories has something of the same "existential" quality. His hero in one

story is said to be in some way "different" from his bum-
companions:

> Maybe some day he will be a kind of spokesman for this group of
> people. Maybe he'll write a book about them, or maybe he will try
> to portray them on the stage, or maybe he'll try to paint them. . . .
> He's different because he's not only a complete product of his times
> and his society and so forth but he's a man that doesn't come along
> very often, . . . a man who can understand the society that he's in,
> which is probably the greatest trick in the book, who can look at him-
> self in context and can understand completely what's going on, get it
> in the right perspective . . . understand why he is there, not in the
> great metaphysical and religious sense, but why the social forces have
> put him where he is. . . . At least he has this latent in him, the
> power to bring this out and put it down for others to understand.
> . . . And he will write a book . . . it'll be a good book, I imagine.
> . . . It's not a social criticism, it's not that he'll be making a plea.
> . . . He's not unhappy that these people don't have the best food in
> the world, that they have to sleep on the ground like that. It's not a
> matter of that; it's a judgmentless kind of interpretation and explana-
> tion rather than an emotional and sentimental Uncle Tom's Cabin
> business.

Here Inburn doubtless speaks of himself and his own best potential; and this story has an affirmativeness and hope lacking from all
the other nineteen. But even here he rejects "judgment," "social
criticism," "making a plea," and any "emotional and sentimental
Uncle Tom's Cabin business." In other words, morality has no
conscious place in his scheme of things.

Consonant with the lack of any inherent meaning or values in
life is Inburn's image of love. Long-range intimacy between two
people is never mentioned; and the act of sex is empty. In one
story, the hero is walking down a New York street:

> It was late in the afternoon, and in the afternoon those brown-
> stones take on a particularly remarkably intense russet color. It
> seems to stand out and glow, almost. . . . He noticed a girl . . .
> looking out the window on the second floor of one of the brown-
> stones . . . she happens to look at him, and he glances up at her

and, just by chance, their eyes meet naturally. And he stands there a
long minute, just looking up, oddly. And she doesn't divert her eyes,
and it's a kind of a very long instant that stays in one's mind. . . .
There's something about the whole scene that entrances them both.
. . . He keeps staring at the window. And in a few moments she appears below, behind the door which has got a kind of curtain in front
of it and an iron grill. And then she opens the door, and after a moment he crosses the street and goes up the steps . . . the polished
white steps. She's rather thin and not good looking, drab hair, and a
very cheap dress. . . . And without a word but "with eyes on the
double string" or whatever that quote is from Donne, they go up
the stairs to a . . . kind of single room. The shade is pulled down
and there's a very warm color on the window shade, even from the
inside.

. . . Finally, after all, they fall asleep. And he's awakened when
it's dark at night by the window shade flapping with some wind and
some rain coming in, and the cold air wakes him up. It doesn't wake
her. Now there's a light in the window shade, too, which is the street
light from outside shining in which is rather bright. . . . He gets
up, and dresses and doesn't do anything—leave a note, it would seem
a little ludicrous. He puts on his tie and coat and leaves. [The hero
eventually finds his way into a church, and the story ends.]

In this "nouvelle vague" story, Inburn makes his lovers silent;
neither is described except in externals; they have no relationship;
the man leaves the woman without saying good-bye; and throughout, the narrator is more interested in eyes, lights, architectural
details, and colors than in the man and woman.

All of these stories entail the same denial of meaning in life apart
from unreflective action, perception, and sensation. At worst, Inburn's heros are Raskolnikovs who would rather murder than do
nothing; intermediately, existential acrobats who die happy at the
acme of their flight, strangers who love and depart without speaking, or strivers whose efforts are futile; and even at best, observers
of their world who firmly refuse to judge, influence, or change it.
All of this is an elaboration in fantasy of his earlier, more intellectual assertion that as a stranger in a foreign city, his best plan is to
"see the sights" and to accumulate "the most varied, the most valu-

able, and most significant set of sense experiences it is possible to take in."

## The rage to re-enter

Inburn's autobiography begins with a description of him as "screaming and red-faced, loath to leave his insensible sanctuary." Here he states unequivocally what is the major theme of his life and the dominant motif of his T.A.T. stories: his longing to return to that first claustrum of security, his rage and desolation at being expelled, his continual sense thereafter of being a stranger in a foreign city. More than half of Inburn's stories contain some variant on the theme of being inside or outside, beginning with the first card, where he tells of a son of professional musicians who smashes his violin as a "violent rebellion." The father is restrained from "throwing him out in the street" because of "certain ties that he has—certain obligations to the family and the community," but the boy will thereafter be "an estranged member" of the family, and "he'll probably leave his family at an early age and won't be associated with them any more." In his second story, too, the central conflict is about the girl's leaving home and getting away from the mother who is "not quite like the cat that swallowed the canary, but . . ."

Having, as it were, introduced his main theme in a variation whereby the hero *chooses* rebellion and estrangement, Inburn states it in almost pure form in the third story. Here he tells of a student walking down the street at night on his way home from the library, where he has read a book which disturbed him. He stops in front of

an old grey house, one of those turn of the century jobs with a slate roof it and this phony Greek-revival business with all the pillars and the stuff in wood on the porch. He stops on the steps of the house. . . . He noticed one of the windows on either side of the door. The door was in the middle and there was a large window on either side. It was dark inside the little hallway. . . . He stood there looking at the window for ten or fifteen minutes, with this unusual, indescribable ding-batty he has in his hand . . . it could be any kind of odd piece of iron that he somehow picked up. And he stood there a long time, sort of standing there contemplating smashing the window. And if he could have just smashed it and gone away, throwing the thing through or just smashed it holding it in his hand, it would have been all right . . . he would have got whatever it was inside out of him. But he could not force himself to smash the damn thing. He stood there, as I say, for a long time, standing there very still and stiff with his arms down at his side and finally walked away, walked down the steps. . . . I remember in Herodotus the story of tying the woman's legs together just when she's beginning to be pregnant and then letting things go on as they did is probably the most exquisite torture that could be devised. Maybe this is the same sort of idea that he's got something enormous, monstrous inside of him, but he can't get it out. He could have got it out by smashing the window but he's still got it in him. . . .

In contrast to the two previous stories, in which his heroes sought to escape home and mother, here the hero tries to break his way back into a house. Unable to force an opening with the "ding-batty" in his hand, he is left with an "enormous, monstrous thing inside of him," which he associates with a child within his mother's womb. (Recall his facetious "I guess I'd have us all go back to the womb.") Note, too, the detail with which Inburn again describes the architecture of the house, emphasizing the windows and the central door, which parallel the hero's preoccupation with looking.

From this story alone we would have grounds for surmising that Inburn's "violent rebellion" and self-imposed estrangement over-lies a deeper wish to re-enter his "insensible sanctuary," and that his "estrangement" was not only chosen by him, but first forced upon him by a closed house which he cannot re-enter. In the primitive logic of fantasies and dreams, houses, wombs, maternal warmth, and women's bodies can stand for each other, and the configurations of the house façade parallel the regular symmetry of the face, the windows and eyes being for seeing from and into, the door being the mouth of entry. In such equations, to look into a window, to gaze into the eyes, to enter the door of the house, or to re-enter the surrounding warmth of a mother's arms become equivalent. So interpreted, Inburn's preoccupation with gazing, with perception, with architectural façades, and with claustral security are all facets of the same nuclear theme of regaining his "insensible sanctuary."

These interpretations are supported in other stories. Through them all runs the same preoccupation with seeing, gazing, and looking—especially with a kind of obsessive standing and staring into the eyes of another or the windows of a house. (Recall his first girl friend, "with eyes as blue as his, and deeper . . . staring into his face in an autumn dusk.") In the previously discussed story of the silent lovers, the descriptions of the façade of the house, of looking into the window and gazing into the girl's eyes, the account of the light that comes in the window—these narratively extraneous elements overpower the ostensibly central theme of the relation of man and woman. And in the end of that story, the hero again stands looking "much longer than he stood looking at the window" at the church which he finally enters. In this story, it is as if Inburn's seeking could finally be solaced neither by sex nor by looking, but by entering a church, whose secure walls have always signified enfolding asylum. And even Inburn's writer-hero embodies the highest form of perception, looking at the world around him and understanding it.

As counterpoint to these stories in which the hero is outside an enclosure looking in, Inburn tells three in which the hero manages to get inside and look out. In one previously mentioned, he is inside a

tower that goes very far up with a turret on it. . . . He enters through the door and finds darkness is throughout the place. It's a vertical maze: it goes up instead of spreads out. The tower, incidentally, has no windows except this one which is toward the very top, on the other side of the building from the door he entered by, so that he doesn't know it's there. He goes up and all is in darkness, and he is feeling his way around. Finally he works his way all through the day and the next night and gets to the top, gets into a final room where

there is a casement window, but he can't see it. It's closed, and there's
no light coming through. . . . [He] finally comes to the window
which he feels out and finally gets the handle of. . . . He's tired
and hungry and exhausted and covered with sweat. With this last bit
of force, he pushes open the two windows one with each hand, and
the bright light of the early morning streams in on him. . . . Facing the east, the window is, and he's blinded for a few minutes. . . .
The feeling he has on his skin and on his silk shirt is like climbing up
how many flights it is up that circular thing, the Statue of Liberty,
and finally looking out her head, out of one of those windows and
usually getting a cold from it. He looks out on the surrounding
country and doesn't like the view very much. He doesn't think it's
much of an accomplishment after all. . . .

Here the identification of the inside of a building and the inside of a
woman's body is explicit, though Inburn seems to suggest that his
obsessive search for a way back in is doomed to failure—the view
from within is really no better than the view outside. The scene
calls to mind the small child's wonder at his mother's height, his
curiosity about whether what she sees is different from what he
sees, and his fantasy that perhaps he could enter her body and see
through her eyes.

But in two other stories, the view from within is unqualifiedly
good. One story tells of

a cheerful presentation of Noah's Ark . . . the two little windows,
sort of homey portholes with curtains. There are two comical little
animals, in a pair, of course, looking out . . . —mammals who
have got a nice berth on the ark and they're enjoying the view. . . .
[He wonders why there is a smokestack in the picture.] . . . The
clouds would be all sorts of fantastic colors—purple. . . . The
water of course, would be blue and the ship would be all sorts of
colors. The animals would be brown, I imagine. They've been sailing
for a long time. And I suppose the most remarkable thing is that
they just keep sailing. They don't land anywhere. The water never
recedes, that's the most pleasant part about it.

Inburn's "cheerful presentation" here has "comical little animals"
looking out on the never-receding waters in a childhood idyl, happy

because there is no landing, no receding waters to break up the happy communion of son and mother. With its bright colors and "comical" animals, the story is reminiscent of a childhood fairy tale which covertly expresses the child's wish to sail away forever inside the life-filled Ark which represents the secure warmth of his mother's surrounding presence.

But perhaps the most remarkable portrayal of a full return to claustral security, coupled with gazing out, occurs on a blank card for which Inburn manufactured both picture and story:

> Well, the scene is rather dark, streaked with light. It's underwater, very warm water, although it's apparently a sea. . . . This missile most resembles a one-man submarine. It's propelled by a very un-bulky kind of machinery. It's just very simple, cigar-shaped, I suppose. . . . It's angling down toward the bottom right-hand corner of the card. . . . The water is uniformly dark . . . , since the surface is at this time considerably far above the top of the card.

> And inside this thing is a face which you can see. In a kind of window in front, a man is stretched out. Well, the thing is small. It's only about eight feet long, perhaps even shorter than that. He's on a cushion inside, a long cushion. His hands are at his sides. He's on his stomach with his chin not resting on anything but looking forward, looking out into the water. And although we can see the thing, it's very dark to him. He can see, oh, perhaps some of those small fish that glow but that's about all. That's the only thing that lights up, that lights up the scene. As I said, the water is very warm. This is hard to illustrate, but it's that, and heavy. . . . This thing was custom built for him, fitted for his size and height. And he does have controls . . . he can go up and down and to the left and to the right, though there's no change in speed.

> This is the fulfillment of something this young man has always inanely wanted to do since he was a very little boy. In fact, he pictured himself doing just this when he was perhaps seven or eight or nine or ten years old. . . . The idea occurred to him once when he was in his bedroom stretched out on his bed in this kind of position with his elbows up supporting him, and it was dark and very hot in the room. The room had grown slowly dark—he didn't notice the absence of light from the windows until it was all gone. And then this idea occurred to him, that of slipping through these heavy, silent, liquid seas in a very warm and utterly comfortable state. And he

was eating some crackers out of a box. . . . But this was a very pleasurable sort of thing.

As a matter of fact, in the picture the young man is . . . eating crackers from a small box, and falling down into the ocean. He didn't direct his life toward doing this because just sort of circumstances permitted it. He remembered his urge and had enough resources, enough leisure time to do this thing. He's probably not going to surface, just go down, down, and down. Somehow once he got into the water it became not the Atlantic Ocean or the Mediterranean but it was just *a* sea, *the* sea, with nothing on the surface, with no continents to go back to . . . and the place not being there from which he set off any more. . . . This is the kind of extended moment which he wouldn't mind going on with forever—which he probably will, just continuing down into the dark water. . . .

If Inburn was consciously searching for an analogy on the intra-uterine condition, on the symbiosis of mother and child, he would be hard pressed to find a better one. Even the age at which this fantasy first occurred to the hero is significant, for it was at "seven or eight or nine or ten" that his father returned to break the "oneness" of mother and son, and inevitably to awaken a powerful wish for this unity to be restored. And how better restore it than by re-entering that sanctuary from which, as Inburn had recently learned with revulsion, he had been born?

Thus, the central and unifying themes in Inburn's fantasy life center around the rage to re-enter the "insensible sanctuary" which he had with his mother. So intense is this wish that it surpasses the desire for a more adult intimacy with her or another woman, and is expressed symbolically as a craving to re-enter the body of the woman who bore and nurtured him. That such a re-entry and fusion is to be accomplished through the eyes, through looking, through the communion of a gaze, and through an (often obstructing) window is doubly understandable. The infant first perceives his mother when he gazes into her eyes while nursing; and thereafter, for most people, to "look deeply into someone's eyes" remains a symbol of that communion which anticipates and forever thereafter surpasses all mere speech. But also, for Inburn the eyes are the organ of the body farthest from that "base and carnal" place from which infants truly emerge; and for a young man who can identify himself with a "man from the sewer" and who feels only "anxiety, shame, and disgust" about sex, communion through the eyes is far less "vile" than that other communion which adult men and women can know, and by which men regain at least temporary sanctuary in women. Indeed, the story of the Greek-revival house with the hero's "indescribable ding-batty" in his hand, the tale of silent lovers in which the empty act of sex is followed by entering a church, the intrusive smokestack on Noah's ark, and even the cigar-shaped submarine itself, suggest that for Inburn his own sexuality is at times an irrelevant intrusion on his central fantasies about women.

## The outsider who would be inside

We now have learned enough of the central themes in Inburn's life to enable us to try to reconstruct the origins and current functions of his alienation. In any such reconstruction, it is well to keep in mind that the principle of parsimony seldom applies in explaining individual lives; rather, only when we have begun to understand the subtle interweaving of themes, the "overdetermination" of any single act, belief, or fantasy, and the multiple functions that every dream, wish, action, and philosophy serves, do we begin to understand something of an individual. Thus, even with the best of intentions the psychologist must continually oversimplify, and by singling out one set of alienated beliefs and outlooks for special explanation, I here oversimplify Inburn the more.

To begin with, the outward circumstances of Inburn's life provided a setting within which his alienation became more than casually possible. As an only child, he was undoubtedly destined to feel more intensely about his parents than would a child with siblings or an extended family to dissipate the concentration of his affections and angers. Further, his father's absence for the four crucial years of the war must inevitably have intensified his pre-existing feelings about his mother. And then, too, the son of a sec-ond-generation mother of Greek descent and a father of northern European stock is very likely to note a sharp temperamental con-trast between his two parents and their families. But these assured facts only provide a setting for the more central psychological events and fantasies which underlie Inburn's estrangement.

For further explanations, we must assume that Inburn's account of his parents is in many ways correct, at least as it describes their impact on him. His mother, as we have noted, emerges as a posses-sive, ambitious, driving woman, who, once she stopped teaching, devoted herself exclusively to domestic life. And at the same time, Inburn describes her as moody, passionate, highly sensuous, and physically attractive. The T.A.T. story in which a women seeks to bind an unwilling man to her through sex again suggests that In-burn sees his mother as not only possessive, but as emotionally seductive, seeking from her son a kind of emotional fulfillment he could not provide and unconsciously attempting to use her attrac-tiveness to bind him to her. Thus, even as a small child, Inburn probably felt torn between his dependency on his mother and his enjoyment of their extraordinary closeness on the one hand, and on the other her unwanted possessiveness and her unconscious needs that he be more to her than a son.

With a strong and vital husband, a possessive and seductive mother's effects on her son are usually limited; indeed, with such a husband, a woman is less likely in the first place to seek excessive fulfillment in her relationship with her children. But Inburn's fa-ther, at least as Inburn perceives him, was neither strong nor vital. "Taciturn," "phlegmatic," and "acquiescent," he had probably been better prepared by his own childhood for the role of the domi-nated than the dominant. Inburn also suggests that his father was disappointed with his own life, perhaps at least in part because he "acquiesced" to the extent of leaving his original vocation for a better-paying if less idealistic job. And finally, one can only wonder with what feelings the father could have greeted being denied an excellent education, struggling in the depression, or being taken away from his family, work, and country for four years during the war. In short, we have few grounds for believing that Inburn's father had qualities or zest enough to offset his mother's drive and sensuousness.

Even without Inburn's father's long absence during the war, such parents would have made for a rivalrous family triangle of singular intensity and equivocal outcome. More often than we generally acknowledge, husbands must struggle for their wives' affections with their children—and especially with only sons, who have but one rival between them and their mother's exclusive devotion to her child. And if the wife should come to find her husband dull or a failure in life, then the outcome is especially equivocal. But in Inburn's case, the wish to supplant his father must have been overwhelmingly reinforced by his father's sudden departure for the war. Few five-year-olds could resist the temptation unconsciously to consider such a four-year absence a token of their own triumph. We know something of the ensuing mother-son relationship from Inburn's idyllic account of his unique understanding with his mother; and we learn more from his T.A.T. stories in which the central relationships are peculiar intimacies between young men and women, with fathers and older men absent or somehow debased and scorned out of significant existence.

I have already noted the component of fantasy in Inburn's recollections of this idyl, which he endows with qualities more like those of an infant-mother symbiosis than those of a five-to-nine-year-old's relationship with his mother. Some of this he must of course have felt, perhaps encouraged by his mother's increased need of and responsiveness to him in her husband's absence. But some was clearly a fantasy, and time alone would have probably sufficed to break the illusion of perfect understanding and oneness. But his father's sudden return exacerbated, underlined, and made more traumatic Inburn's probably dawning awareness that he was less and less his Mama's pretty little child, and more and more a separate person, alone in crucial ways. It is from the age of nine or ten that he dates a variety of new feelings of moodiness and estrangement, and to the same age that his submarining hero traces his wish to slip forever downward in the deep warm sea. Again and again, Inburn as a college sophomore still expresses or symbolizes this overpowering wish for fusion with the maternal, for a blissful state without consciousness, for an "insensible sanctuary," in the last analysis, to be like a tiny infant in his mother's arms, who by gazing into her eyes enters her enveloping protection. What time and his increasing age had not accomplished in destroying the possibility of asylum, his father's return completed; thereafter, as it were, the waters had receded and the submarine was beached.

For most children, such a loss, which is after all universal, can be assimilated without excessive backward yearning because there are active pulls into a future seen as better than what must be abandoned. For a boy, such forces are usually embodied in his father, who by the mere fact of an admired existence implicitly teaches his son that it is worth while to grow up to be a man. When there is no such father, when the mother's excessive devotion to her son undermines her husband's relative worth in the son's eyes, or when the father considers himself a failure and thus implicitly denies that the son should become a man like him—then the son's incentives to leave gracefully his ties with his mother are diminished, and physiological growth goes unmatched by psychological readiness.

For Inburn, then, there was an especially great deal to lose and especially little reason to give it up. Once he had been the apple of his mother's eye, fused at least in fantasy to her answering gaze, the child with whom she had been so strangely intimate as to be shy; but in his desire to retain his claustral estate he had, without wishing it, lost it, ended with a possessive and sensuous mother on his hands, and been left without a father to boot. Small wonder that his father's return brought moodiness, brooding, and constipation, and that when during the same year he learned the facts of birth, they seemed "base and carnal" compared with his own developing fantasies of regaining his former sanctuary. Henceforth, Inburn was to consider himself an outcast, dreaming of an Eden from which he perhaps dimly recalled he came, forever comparing his exiled realities of a dominating, seductive mother and a taciturn, psychologically absent father with the cozy cabin in Noah's Ark and the down-slipping submarine in the warm sea.

But so far his inner feelings of estrangement were, he implies, "always well within himself," and he was "seldom snappish, perverse, or irritable." In the development of a more overt alienation, two further facts are crucial. The first is Inburn's sexual maturation and the accompanying psychological changes which he describes in his scornful account of "sex's ugly head" and the "dirtiness" and "vileness" of adolescent boys. Few boys in our culture, however enlightened their parentage, can pass through adolescence without further reassessing their closeness with their mothers; and for many, the acute fear of any sexual intimacy with anyone like her continues throughout life. But such fears, however normal a part of development for American men, can reach panic proportions in a youth who brings into adolescence an unresolved need to enter a woman not as a man but as a child seeking shelter. When these needs are coupled with a prior notion that sex and birth are base and carnal (undoubtedly transmitted in part by parents), deep anxieties about sex can last long into adulthood. And finally, if, as for Inburn, the prospect of becoming a man like one's father is deeply disconcerting and implicitly discouraged by mother and father alike, then the advent of manhood is even more disruptive. Adolescence must have further complicated Inburn's already tortuous relationship with his mother, adding to her possessiveness the new threat of that most "loathsome thing," incest.

In all young men and women the advent of adulthood releases immense new energies and potentials, which in most are centrally involved in establishing new intimacies with the opposite sex. This new learning is seldom smooth; but when it is severely blocked by unresolved needs and frustrations from the past, it takes but a

slight catalyst—and often no catalyst at all—to transform these
energies into rage, scorn, and aggression, often symbolically directed against those who have stood in the way of full adulthood. It
was Hal, then, who provided the second crucial fact, the catalyst
and vehicle for the transformation of Inburn's inward moodiness
into an open and scornful alienation. From Hal, or with his help
and encouragement, he learned cynicism, disdain, scorn, and contempt for the "superstructure of tin and shit and kite-paper" which
represented society to them. Hal became for Inburn a kind of anti-
social superego, so much so that Inburn puts his discontents with
college into Hal's mouth, and when he finally leaves college, it is
not to return to his parents, but to live with Hal and demonstrate
that he has not, in fact, become "complacent." Further, with Hal
he learned the vocabulary and logic of his instincts, culling from
the works of the most alienated writers of the last two alienated
centuries the diction of estrangement. The sense of alienation and
exile, the rage and frustration which might have found outlet in
delinquency in a youth of less intelligence, perceptiveness, and articulateness, in Inburn was aimed at targets sanctioned by usage
and made meaningful by their personal symbolism, and thus found
expression within a historical tradition. What had been contained
was now released, and Inburn became overtly alienated.

Inburn's alienation in word and deed thus serves multiple purposes. Most centrally, it rationalizes his felt condition as an outcast
from his first sanctuary: the feeling of exile is generalized, univer-
salized into the human condition, as in his tale of the travelers in
the endless and featureless countryside. Furthermore, by condemn-
ing the society and the forms of society from which he himself
came, Inburn states the partial truth that there is no sanctuary and
that he does not wish to return. And by attacking society and all its
authoritative concomitants, Inburn indirectly criticizes his father
and all he stands for: conventionality, being a "small pillar in a
small community," being "complacently middle-class," perhaps
even being a "failure in his own eyes." Inburn's grievance against

his father is a double one: his father disrupted Inburn's idyl with his mother, and probably more important, he was not strong enough to offer anything better than the mother-son intimacy which he disrupted. Inburn has accounts to render, and render them he does in his alienation.

# 3      The rejection of American culture

It could be argued that a variety of different kinds of people, with very different outlooks in other respects, and rather opposite motives could reject their society. There appears at first to be no cogent reason why repudiating American culture should entail any special views about the nature of the universe, the quality of truth, or human nature. But in fact the rejection of the dominant values, roles, and institutions of our society is far from an isolated attitude: among the students studied, alienation from American life was almost always a part of a more general alienated ideology, embracing not only attitudes towards the surrounding society, but towards the self, others, groups, even the structure of the universe and the nature of knowledge. I will turn later to some of the reasons why alienation is so pervasive and far-reaching an outlook. First, let us examine the main components of an alienated ideology.

## The distrustful eye

Central to alienation is a deep and pervasive mistrust of any and all commitments, be they to other people, to groups, to American culture, or even to the self. Most basic here is the distrust of other

people in general—a low and pessimistic view of human nature.
One student writes,

> I feel that man is interested only in himself. Human nature is at
> best self-centered, fickle, etc. This is to say that in man's interaction
> with other creatures possessing egos the self is foremost in all that
> we do and all that is called human nature by men. Others can be
> expected to react in their own best interests.

And the alienated react enthusiastically to questionnaire statements
like these:

> Experience in the ways of the world teaches us to be suspicious of
> the underlying motives of the general run of men.

> Nice as it may be to have faith in your fellow men, it does not pay
> off.

As might be expected from those who stress the evilness of human
nature, alienated students believe that human intimacy is fore-
doomed to failure and best avoided.

> Emotional commitments to others are usually the prelude to dis-
> illusion and disappointment.

> It is generally advisable to avoid close personal attachments to
> others.

Just as commitment to individuals seems undesirable, so even more
does any attachment to a group:

> "Teamwork" is the last refuge of mediocrity.

> The whole idea of "taking an active part in the life of the com-
> munity" leaves me cold.

Political and social activities seem especially undesirable or futile
to the alienated. One writes archly in his statement of basic values:

> I leave speculation about world affairs to our politicians; they are
> so completely inept at doing anything other than speculating. . . .

Political activity is like the games children play. . . . Whatever happens will not affect my thinking.

Even the prospect of an atomic war does not rouse the alienated subjects, although they mention it far more regularly than do most students. Rather, they accept atomic warfare in a spirit of resignation and even some gladness:

The modern world is going to hell, but since the race is doomed to die some day, I can't see that it makes much difference.

Another writes:

There is something wrong, I think when whole nations threaten each other for whole decades with ridiculously destructive weapons like two grammar-school bullies. I often doubt that man deserves to live; dogs do a better job of it and jellyfish better still.

One student ends his philosophy with a poem on the same theme:

Of course there will be a war eventually. Very eventually.
I'll let it bother me then.
In my lifetime trees will get scarce.
I would like to see more trees.

Along with this pessimistic rejection of any social, political, or "civic" commitment goes a repudiation of American culture in its more general forms. Alienated young men tend to be highly articulate about their reasons for disliking their national culture; and these reasons are completely apolitical. Thus, one writes:

America is the land of friendship, not of love. America is a paradise of pretenders; love cannot exist on pretense. America is a land of equalities; equals are friends and unequals are lovers. America worships machines, the machines of steel or the machines of the mind; love is of humans and machines are eunuchs. . . .

Another writes more prosaically:

I have come to experience horror at the good American way of life, namely, the comfortable, middle-class existence. . . . This seems boring to me.

A number reject "the American way of life" because it is material-
istic:

> Society as I see it stinks. . . . If by progress we mean that we are
> morally sound, spiritually uplifted, advanced in our appreciation *de
> rerum natura,* then I should say that we never even got far enough
> to say that we are regressing. Our society seems to be oriented to-
> wards Mammon, and to my mind this isn't good, . . . not as an
> end in itself.

Still another ground for repudiating this country lies in the standards of mass culture:

> American culture is trashy, cheap, and commercial.

> The standards of American society are tuned to the individual of
> average mental ability; to "conform" to thought in our society is to
> make oneself average. Its pleasures as shown in most of the popular
> arts are average also, and to me, dull.

One alienated student sums up for the rest when he notes:

> I have no feeling of relationship to an over-all American society
> defined in terms of success and security. These are not ideals that
> give me any pleasure.

The alienated rejection of commitment extends even to daily actions. With a special mixture of ambivalence and gloom, the alienated affirm that resoluteness is impossible:

> Second thoughts about things we have undertaken are only natu-
> ral: almost every endeavor has disadvantages which only become ap-
> parent once we are embarked on it.

And the alienated agree with a questionnaire statement like this:

> I make few commitments without some inner reservation or doubt
> about the wisdom of undertaking the responsibility or task.

Vacillation, hesitation, foot-dragging, and unwillingness are seen as the inevitable consequences of any demand for long-range commitments: the nature of life is such that we can never be sure, and that every choice precludes equally desirable alternatives.

On every level, then, the alienated refuse conventional commitments, seeing them as unprofitable, dangerous, futile, or merely uncertain and unpredictable. Not only do they repudiate those institutions they see as characteristic of our society, but the belief in goodness of human nature, the usefulness of group activities, and the possibility or utility of political and civic activities, closeness and intimacy with others, or even a resolute commitment to action or responsibility. The rejection of American society is but one part of a more global distrust of any commitment.

## Native existentialism

As of the time when they wrote their philosophies, only one or two of the alienated students had ever read any existentialist works, and none of these had more than a passing knowledge of existential thought. Yet these young men were for the most part inconscient existentialists, and when, later in their college careers, they were to come upon writers like Sartre, they would sometimes seize on existentialist thought with a sense of *déjà vu*. Their existentialism is pessimistic, gloomy, and foreboding, emphasizing the darkness, isolation, and meaninglessness of life.

> There are times when the world strikes the eye as a cruel and heartless place. . . .

> I don't think too many people really do find satisfaction in life. This probably means that there isn't too much satisfaction to be found. . . . Life is fairly grim . . . even my pleasure is a mournful sort. I start off believing that I'll never find much more satisfaction than I have now. This places me way ahead of many, many people, who never stop searching for happiness as long as they live.

Wise men know that there is more pain and misery in life than pleasure and delight.

Characteristically, the alienated not only insist on universal pessimism, but maintain that "only cows are contented"; like the subject just quoted, they usually feel somewhat superior to those who believe in and search for happiness.

Alienated pessimism, like most alienated outlooks, is intended not so much as a description of personal feeling as an assertion about the world. The alienated prefer to maintain that the world is a dark and gloomy place rather than to say simply that they are pessimistic. Psychologically, it is important that they see the world, the state of the universe, as *causing* and justifying their own pessimism. The same tendency to see the human condition, rather than their own personal psychology, as determining their outlook is also present in the alienated subjects' views about anxiety: they affirm that modern society, not their own neuroses, produces their apprehensiveness:

> Whether he admits it or not, every modern man is the helpless victim of one of the worst ailments of our time, neurotic anxiety.

> Every day the newspapers give fresh cause for apprehension: holdups, senseless murders, persecutions, preparations for war, prophecies of disaster.

The belief of alienated young men in the anxiety-producing nature of the universe goes beyond specific events: it extends to a conviction that the universe itself is basically empty and meaningless. As one subject writes:

> It is random, chaotic, stupid, and the way it is. Why sweat about what we can't control, or even explain. . . . No God, no determinism anyway—the Universe seems *dead*. Not friendly, not unfriendly, not fighting us, not helping. It sits, and man works, and he (man) doesn't realize his plight in the face of this fantastic joke, but he has to go on.

Several alienated questionnaire items express similar thoughts:

The notion that man and nature are governed by regular laws is
an illusion based on our insatiable desire for certainty.

Honesty compels us to admit that our lives are without any inherent regularity, purpose, or form.

In such a pessimistic, anxiety-provoking, and "dead" universe,
truth necessarily becomes subjective and even solipsistic. The alienated are true to the logic of their position, and almost to a man
accept the subjectivity and even the arbitrariness of their own
points of view. One writes:

I don't really believe what I write in this "philosophy"—that is, I
can't find any reason to believe it . . . any objective basis for accepting any set of values, any philosophy, etc., rather than any other
—if I say something "should be," it is just my own personal emotional reaction to the question.

Another expresses a similar version of "private truth":

I hold many beliefs regarding the "ideal life" which, though I believe in them completely, I know could never be adopted by man-
kind as a whole, nor would I want them to be. . . .

Whatever sense of meaning a man may have must inevitably then
be his own creation:

Because man is just a fairly miraculous accident, the only way
he can accept the fact that his life is slightly more meaningful than
that of a crab or a tapeworm is to carve some meaning out of it for
himself: i.e., make artificial goals which, while having no great
meaning, can satisfy him. . . . I have had to devise a clever reason
to retain my sanity.

There is no meaning in any particular person's presence here on
earth . . . unless each person manages to find some rationale for
his presence in his part of the world, life is otherwise meaningless.

Many of the alienated go on to note that they have yet to create
these "artificial goals" or a "rationales for [their] presence," and

the reasons for their lack of success are partly apparent from their distrust of all commitments, and from their further views of the human condition. Virtually all stress man's basic aloneness in the world, though some go on to allow the possibility of communication with others:

> . . . all men are lonely; and, in a sense, all men are alone from the day they are born until the day that they die. For no person can live another person's life; no person can, in the end, make another person's happiness. On the other hand, two people can find much joy in each other.

> In our relationships with other people we are confronted with a single sad fact: there is no communion, only rapport of a limited sort. When I say that I like another person, or when I am as physically close to him or her as possible, I do not experience any communion; I merely form an ever-changing image of that person in my own mind, one that is based on the evidence of the senses and the humor of the ego.

Men are inextricably separated from one another by their own subjectivity and ontological egocentricity. Isolation is their natural state, since no two men inhabit precisely the same world, and no two are creating the same meanings for their lives. When communion occurs, it is a miracle, the bittersweet encounter of basically lonely and separate souls.

Part of the difficulty in communication comes from the unreliability of appearances. Not only do the alienated generally agree with a statement like "Beneath the smiling face of man lies a bottomless pit of evil," but they affirm that all appearances are suspect, whether of men or institutions. Thus, nothing can be accepted at face value, every appearance is likely to be deceptive, and every surface conceals opposite potentials beneath it.

> Most people wear masks: we can never really know a man until we probe beneath the surface.

> I cannot take life as it comes: I must penetrate to the heart of it, see people stripped of their externals.

Even a commitment to things-as-they-seem is here distrusted.

In such a world, lacking inherent meaning or the possibility of genuine "communion" with others, the present moment necessarily assumes overwhelming importance. The alienated generally affirm that they have no long-range goals, and indeed believe it impossible to find or create such goals; instead they are "realists" of a special kind, whose ultimate philosophical justification for their acts is their own immediate feeling, mood, pleasure, or enjoyment. Long-range planning is impossible, given the uncertainty of the future and the likelihood that things will turn out badly; what remain are the needs of the moment, of the body, the senses, the heart, and the "humor of the ego."

Philosophically the core of this native existentialism is the denial of inherent meaning to man's life or the universe: in a universe without structure, regularity, or purpose, the center of whatever meaning can exist must inevitably be the solitary individual, isolated, gloomy, apprehensive, wary of appearances, and heeding primarily the needs of the moment. But psychologically the central theme is one of personal isolation and meaninglessness, and the composite picture which emerges is of a lonely man, surrounded by a universe he cannot understand and vaguely fears, peering uncertainly into a future that bodes him ill, separated, albeit reluctantly, from inspiriting communion with man, society, or the universe.

## Anger, scorn, and contempt

In principle, it might be possible for a youth to accept the world view so far outlined in a spirit of resignation and acceptance. One might agree with most of the alienated articles of faith and still feel grateful for the opportunity to *create* meaning in life, or for those moments of "transcendence," those miracles whereby men overcome their estranged lot. Indeed, such an acceptance is found among the more optimistic of existentialists, who accept man's existential outcastness as the enabling precondition for the exhilarat-

ing task of creating vital meaning, and thus find courage to accept
his Sisyphean life-tasks joyously. In principle, all of this might be
possible; but psychologically it is difficult, and factually we do not
find such an acceptance among these alienated young men. Their
reaction is far from stoical; on the contrary, they respond with anger, resentment, bitterness, scorn, and contempt.

Ideologically, their resentment is expressed in their belief that
hatred and contempt are inevitable and desirable. They respond
affirmatively on the questionnaires to Mencken's assertion that

> Every normal person is tempted at times to spit on his hands, hoist
> the black flag, and start slitting throats.

They believe that

> Worthy of praise is the man who hates the right people on the
> right grounds.

and they argue that

> Love and hate are inseparable. We often hate most those who are
> supposedly closest to us.

More immediately, they directly and indirectly acknowledge their
own angers:

> The mere sight of some people is enough to make you boil.

> I am often aware that I really loathe someone.

But the anger of the alienated is rarely expressed in outbursts
and direct attacks on others. Rather, it escapes in a somewhat fil-
tered and transmuted form, as an angry scorn and contempt for
others who do not see the world in the same light. Despite their
awareness of the subjectivity of their own interpretations of reality,
the alienated are humanly inconsistent in their intolerance of the
unalienated:

I am also very intolerant, both of people and social, political, and business organizations. Without giving reasons, I shall name such things as student councils, the military, narrow-minded people, and 99% of life in America.

People by and large appear fairly stupid to me. I meet very few people whom I consider as having any insight into life. . . . Under "insight into life" I might list: the fact of life's ultimate futility, the stupidity of taking any small area of life and its activities as being more important than any other, the ability to see more than one side of everything.

The alienated do not suffer fools gladly, and they consider most of their fellows stupid. Above all, they have contempt for those who "blind themselves" to the "realities" of existence by "pious optimism," shallow consolations, and the easy acceptance of the traditional verities of our society.

Alienated contempt is so pervasive that it extends to the self. True to their position, the alienated believe that

Unless a man is filled with revulsion, he cannot claim to self-knowledge.

and

Any man who has really known himself has good cause to be horrified.

More personally, they admit that

I am often filled with self-accusation and self-recriminations about things I have done or might have done.

In other words, distrust of human nature and unwillingness to accept appearances extends even to their own motives: the scorn which the alienated feel for most of their fellows is equaled by their contempt for themselves.

The ethical corollary of anger, scorn, and contempt is self-interest, and in the alienated we find a special form of egocentricity

which involves the need to use others for one's own purposes—and
the converse conviction that the same principle governs the actions
of one's fellows, even when these are disguised under some other
principle. The alienated *dis*agree with questionnaire statements like

> Happiness comes when a man puts self-interest aside and devotes
> himself to the welfare of others.

and agree with

> There are times when it is absolutely necessary to use other people
> as tools in the accomplishment of a purpose.

> A man should look out for himself *first;* if successful, he may be
> able eventually to be in a position to look out for others.

But the anger implicit in such statements is more apparent from
some of their philosophies:

> I have not a great deal of concern for the feelings of others, and I
> don't feel that they have any concern for mine. When individuals do,
> I usually tend to alienate them by taking advantage of them. . . .
> Man is responsible only to himself—he has, for example, the right to
> kill other humans, knowing the consequence of the law.

The same student says elsewhere

> To act on a moment's desire is a wonderful thing that most hu-
> mans have grown too frightened to do. Those people I enjoy are
> those who are still able to have fantasies and to act without considera-
> tion. There are very few such people that I have found.

This subject is extreme in the explicitness of his hostility ("the
right to kill other humans"), but through other philosophies runs
the same basic theme of self-interest in a self-interested world.

The anger of the alienated is not hard to understand. These are
young men who are unable to believe in what they consider the
consoling myths that support their fellows: they find the universe
and their own lives lacking in meaning and direction; they live in a

"dead" universe filled with self-seeking men who hide their motives from themselves. Furthermore, the alienated believe that most men cannot tolerate a true (alienated) view of things, but dishonestly hide behind platitudes and traditional axioms. The alienated feel doubly deprived—of the illusions which support other men and of the object of those illusions—certainty, meaning, communion, and purpose. It is hard to rejoice on learning that God is dead: more understandable is anger and rage at one's loss, and contempt for those who still believe in His existence. The alienated do not take the "discovery" of their existential outcastness lying down; theirs is neither resignation to nor enjoyment of their condition, but underlying fury at what they have lost, and resentment, especially at those who still maintain their illusions.


## The aesthetic quest

Finding out what the alienated are *against* is easy: they excel at scorn, derision, hostility, and contempt, and any statement opposing almost anything will elicit some agreement from them, providing it is worded in a derisive or scornful way. They are philosophers with hammers, and their favorite theoretical occupation is destruction, reduction, pointing out inconsistencies, chicaneries, hypocrisies, and rationalizations—whether in others or in themselves. But finding out what they are *for* is harder, partly because these young men are so wary of anything that might even approach Positive Thinking. Their distrust of any affirmation is apparent in their questionnaire responses, which show a strong tendency to oppose any statement of positive goal—even when, as is sometimes the case, they may partially agree with it. Thus, the effort to develop questionnaire scales to measure the *positive* values of the alienated were almost completely unsuccessful: they give no statement the benefit of the doubt, and quibble with the wording of every sentiment with an affirmative cast.

But beneath this distrust of affirmation lies another more fundamental reason for the apparent absence of positive values and goals among the alienated: few alienated young men *have* clear positive values, readily articulated goals, neatly describable life plans. Theirs is an ideology of opposition, and the world offers so many targets for their repudiation that they have little energy left for the development of affirmative values. Despite their emphasis on the personal creation of idiosyncratic meaning in life, many tell us they have yet to find such clear meaning, and they tend to suspect even their own best thoughts and deepest instincts. Like the young man who notes that he has had to "devise a clever reason to retain my sanity," they often implicitly derogate their own values and goals. Indeed, this is the perennial problem of the opponent and rebel against society—so much of his energy goes into opposition that he is often left without resources for construction, or even for articulation of the principles in whose name he opposes.

But if the alienated lack clear affirmative goals and values, they nonetheless share a common search in a similar direction; and if, at the age of nineteen or twenty, they have failed to articulate a coherent alternative to what they see as the mindless materialism which surrounds them, we must recall that few men, young or old, have found such alternatives. And we must examine their searching carefully for what they may reveal of their implicit values and strivings.

Some of these strivings can be inferred from what they oppose. Among their goals are honesty, direct confrontation with unpleasant truth, unflinching awareness of evil—implicit in their rejection of pretense, hypocrisy, self-blinding rationalizations, and self-serving defenses. Furthermore, from their emphasis on the moment, we can infer that these will not be young men who are devoted to long-range idealism, and that they will be forced to stay close to the present, to the short term, to the here-and-now. And from their denial of universal truth and emphasis on the egocentricity of human nature, we can safely predict that they will justify their values in terms of fundamentally selfish reasons—emphasizing their own needs, their own impulses, their own sensations and feelings.

To say more than this, we must look again at the philosophies and interviews of these young men, for here, sometimes clearly stated and sometimes hidden between the lines, can be discerned the outlines of their quest. One writes:

> I think there is but one endeavor, and that is the struggle for infinite awareness, for a total comprehension of all things and all events, of their origins, their evolutions, and their endings—the struggle to extend one's consciousness to the infinite limits of time and space, in all directions; a consciousness as large and eternal as the universe itself.
> I want to be God.
> By earthly standards this is often called blasphemous, or heroic or pretentious. . . . One must regard this not as an object within human attainment, but as an imperative, spoken by the infinite through the breath of life itself.

And another says,

> I want to circumscribe my life as little as possible. I do not want to narrow my horizons more than absolutely necessary. . . . I value my personal freedom very highly. I am capable of luxuriating in the thought of being able to do what I wish. . . . The most I would even want to do is somehow to express all, or some, of what I feel about life. I don't mean that I have any big feelings which I want to get down somehow; I only mean that I have a lot of little ones, which I would like to communicate to others, somehow. This is as far as I'll go toward describing my goals for my future life.

Or recall Inburn's statement:

> . . . the time [in life] can be most profitably spent in accumulating the most varied, the most valuable, and the most significant set of sense experiences it is possible to take in. . . . those that bring one into the closest contact with reality, with the ground, the bedrock of sheer existence.

Another young man, asked if despite his gloomy view of the world, he ever enjoyed life, answered:

> I find life quite enjoyable when savoring the experiences which it brings and recreating them in my mind. I like to plunge into it: solitary expeditions to Boston dives and street corners. . . . I even like pain: excruciating afternoons spent in exchanging hypocrisies with wealthy, snotty old ladies who have never heard the ancient truism about the similarity of human feces. Such episodes as these delight me; I frequently swell up with a wild frenzy. After tasting of life such as that I must find solitude. Then I can relive the episodes. The drunks cry again as they reveal their wretched childhoods, the artificial Beacon Hill accents reveal the shallowness and the basic insecurity of the Brahmins again, even better than in reality. It is then that life becomes meaningful. I don't know why. . . .

The same young man adds later, with characteristic alienated pessimism:

> I would like to be a creative writer. I doubt that I will succeed, however. As a second choice I would like to be a dairy farmer in Vermont.

Different as these statements appear, they have much in common. All place primary emphasis on experience and feeling, on the search for awareness and the cultivation of sentience and perceptiveness; they suggest the importance of solitude and solitary assimilation of experience; and they further emphasize the importance of expression of this experience.

These same themes recur in virtually all alienated young men. Almost to a man, they emphasize what I will call "aesthetic" goals and values. By "aesthetic" I do not necessarily mean specifically artistic (though many alienated subjects do aspire "somehow to express all, or some, of what I feel about life"), but rather those goals and values whose main temporal focus is in the present, whose primary source is the self, and whose chief aim is the development of sentience, awareness, expression, and feeling. So defined, aesthetic values are those which do not require a distant future for their attainment: they can be cultivated and enjoyed in the present; they require no psychic savings account with interest payable after many years; they involve activities which can be enjoyed for their own sake and not because they lead to some desirable future. Aesthetic values contrast sharply with instrumental values— that is, with values which stress the cultivation of present sacrifice and control for the sake of the future.

In such an outlook, reason must play a secondary role to feeling. One alienated subject writes:

> Feeling is the truest force at man's command. Through it he knows what he is really like.

Another, more emphatically, believes that

> Life without emotion, without passion, is merely another form of death (and springs, I believe, from fear). If you live with a passion, if you learn to feel strongly about things, if you are able to find yourself, then you will want to say so (in all probability). You will want to express yourself.

He later continues in the same vein:

> The only life worth living is a creative one, whether it is in the absolute (or traditional) sense of the artist (painter, writer, musician) or as a social worker or an engineer. . . . A businessman who wants to improve society can be creative.

But he immediately adds, "However, it is extremely unlikely."

In the struggle for emotion, passion, and feeling, the enemies are two: first, excessive rationality and self-control, and second, social pressures which limit independence. "Reason is not all that helpful an item" writes one; another speaks of "life-giving irrationality"; a third says, "I am definitely in favor of the spontaneous, and in an inexpressible opinion, opposed to reason." Though many admit that reason has its place, it is in Santayana's sense, as the harmonizer of the feelings: passion must remain at the center.

Society is harder to deal with for most of the alienated, and they place enormous value on independence and freedom, while admitting rather reluctantly that complete independence must be limited. Indeed, the only questionnaire about positive values on which alienated subjects scored higher than their classmates was one stressing "the independent spirit, free and alone."

One writes in his philosophy:

> The most important force in my philosophy of life is the desire to be a true individual, wholly independent from outside influences, both mental and physical.

Another, still more vehemently, says,

> For myself, society and others can go to Hell. If they have something worth while to say, I'll listen, but most often society has only a mold to force you into, destroying rather than creating.

The individualism of the alienated is not, then, the traditional American view of the individualist working for the good of society *within* society; mainly it is a solitary and lonely individualism of the outsider, the man who lives physically within his society but remains psychologically divorced from it. It is the individualism of what has been called "inner emigration," of those who though they remain physically in their own land, have left it spiritually.

The alienated accept and sometimes enjoy the image of themselves as outsiders. A special scale of statements based on Colin Wilson's excursion into the views of famous outsiders brought enthusiastic agreement from alienated subjects:

> I feel strongly how different I am from most people, even some of my closest friends.
>
> I will either be a colossal success or a colossal failure, nothing in between.
>
> I doubt if I will ever find a woman who really understands me.

There is no democratic acceptance of others here, no emphasis on the similarities which unite men, but a proud acknowledgment of the differences which divide the alienated from others. No modest success, but total success or total failure; no quiet understandings or even quiet desperation, but overt estrangement from the common lot of men.

And finally, an important part of the aesthetic quest is the refusal of conventional American definitions of success and achievement. I have already noted the antimaterialistic outlook of the alienated. Money is of little importance so long, as one says, "as my children don't have to beg"—and this young man is unusual in thinking about having children at all. Most reject material standards without qualification. As one says,

> Work that is work is stupid. The writing of an essay on a given piece of literature to be read by only one person is infinitely more worth while than being able to live on $15,000 a year. . . . Life is hardly long enough to spend four or eight years in training the result of which is to make money.

To a man, the alienated completed a sentence which began "Most work in America is . . ." with terms like "a rat race," "unrelieved routine," "monotonous." Just as the idea of "playing an active part in the life of the community" "leaves them cold," so does the idea of "climbing the ladder of success." They want none of it.

What they want instead is, as we have seen, hard for them to articulate: it has to do with awareness, passion, faithfulness to experience, with pleasure and immediacy, with "circumscribing my life as little as possible." It has to do with being an individual who stands solitary against his society, unmoved by it, retaining his freedom and autonomy whatever its pressures. And finally, for many it has to do with complexity of person, with being able to express what they feel about life, with creativity. Their philosophies are all different, and by assembling this composite picture I do not do full justice to their complexity or their individuality. But though they themselves stress their oppositions and repudiations of much of their world, we should not be deceived by their distrust of "Positive Thinking" into seeing only the negativism of their views. Like the young man whose summary of his philosophy follows, they are thinking deeply about what they stand for, and are beginning to articulate it:

> My notion of the great man is this: the man who is educated for solitude, who can stand himself alone, whose interests are so profound that he can entertain even himself, much less his friends. His personality is as complex as his deeds, and (what a relief!) no more. This man would be incapable of "baring his soul"—it is already obvious in the complexity of his actions.

## The refusal of American culture

We began from a definition of alienation as an explicit rejection of American society, and we have seen that rejection in several contexts: in agreement with statements like "the idea of adjusting to American society as now constituted fills me with horror"; in a rejection of active political and social involvements; and above all in the many statements which deny any "feeling of relationship with American society as a whole." Thus, the young men we are discussing clearly fit this initial definition of alienation by rejecting what they see as the dominant roles and institutions of their society.

But what is puzzling is that these youths share so many other outlooks apart from their rejection of their society. With almost monotonous regularity, these young men (who rarely know one another and form part of no group which might give them a common ideology) express essentially the same views about human nature, about intimacy, about the metaphysical structure of the universe, about the nature of philosophical truth, about the relative importance of the present, about the likelihood of future felicity, and so on. Yet there is no *a priori* reason why the rejection of American society should entail any one set of supporting or associated beliefs. In other eras and in other societies, the concomitants of alienation have been far from invariant. Men have rejected their society for a variety of reasons: because they had some ideal future society in mind (as with youthful socialist and communist revolutionaries the world over); because they harked back to some earlier social order, often romanticized, which they sought to re-create in the present (as with reactionary revolutionaries); or at times because they held in higher regard some non-material kingdom of the spirit for which the "real world" was but an anticipation, a purgatory, or a preparation. Men and women can refuse their allegiance to a society that asks too much of them or to one that asks too little; they can revolt against an order that promises only poverty and suffering when they aspire to better things, or against one where lowly birth, color, or race denies them opportunities afforded the more fortunate. If we were to survey alienations throughout history (or even in other sectors of American society), we would not find the unanimity of concurrent belief that we have seen in these students.

Why, then do these young men agree about so many other things in addition to the worthlessness of contemporary American society? One key difference between this and other alienations stands out: most rebels and revolutionaries rebel *in the name of* some higher principle or value which they hold more dear than the existing social order. But these young men do not. Historically, most of the alienated have concurrently served some positive goal in whose name they are estranged—be it the radical reconstruction of society, the restoration of ancient verities, the salvation of the soul, national sovereignty, abundance, or opportunity. But these young men find it hard to articulate any clear programs or objectives; and when they do, their values turn out to be private, "aesthetic," and often explicitly irrelevant to the vast majority of men. With these students, then, we are dealing with what we can call *"unprogram-matic alienation,"* rebellion without a cause, dissent without a fully articulated foundation.

In contrast with rebellions with a cause, unprogrammatic aliena-tion tends to be unselective—to take the entire culture as its target. To understand why this is, we must acknowledge that acts of rejec-tion spring from complex personal motives, some related to the now-forgotten frustrations of childhood, some to the difficulties of current living, some more directly and consciously to the inequities and evils of the society that is repudiated. A rebel often supports his rejection of society by that universal human potential which has been called "characterological anger": resentment, rage, and hos-tility which stem from early life and which are available, in all of us, to inspire and intensify our indignations, irritations, repudiations—and at best our creativity. Like "free-floating anxiety," such diffuse resentment tends to attach itself to any and all objects at hand—sometimes regardless of whether or not they merit anger—unless it is somehow channeled to a few specific and appropriate targets.

The social critic and the revolutionary are often men who have a great storehouse of this free-floating indignation, repudiation, and anger available to motivate their rebellion, and who at the same time have learned to express their anger in attacks against some aspect or all of their surrounding society. Criticism of one's society is, of course, not the only possibility for a deeply angry man: others express their inner frustrations in ritualistic conformity and rejection of those who deviate; others torment their intimates. Nor do I mean to imply that the criticism of society is to be deplored as nothing but the displacement of childhood angers; on the contrary, the world would be a poorer and more stagnant place without men who could appropriately mobilize their own private discontents to improve their society. But when in any society a large number of men and women have a deep reservoir of potential anger because of shared frustrations in the process of growing up, or because of com-mon frustrations in their current lives, or because of actual in-

equities in their social order, or (most often) because of all three
—then it takes little catalyst to direct this anger against the prevailing social order and, sometimes, to channel it into the effort to reconstruct society.

Given a program—a revolutionary ideology—diffuse characterological angers can be focused negatively on specific targets (what
the ideology points to as the *causes* of current frustrations) and
positively on specific goals (what the ideology specifies as its *objectives*). At best, diffuse anger can be transformed first into concrete
criticisms of actual evils and then into "aggressive" efforts to transform the society for the better. Indeed, it is partly the ability to
capture such collective angers which enables political leaders to
create revolutions, to make men risk death and hardship, take
chances with the future of civilization, and (at times) transform
their societies for the better. The same angers and resentment,
however, inevitably remain unfocused, diffuse, and free-floating
without a program or an ideology which pinpoints the problems to
be attacked, enumerates the areas in which the social order is in
need of change and those which are peripheral. With no criterion
for selecting *the* targets, everything becomes a potential target.
Without an articulate conception of what is desirable, energy which
might have been channeled into construction is available only for
rejection. The enemy is the entire status quo—not merely pernicious aspects of the social order which must be changed to permit
improvement, but the entire social and cultural ethos. And this is
precisely what unifies the ideologies of these alienated students—
their rejection not only of selected visible aspects of American society, but of the basic assumptions and values of traditional American culture as a whole.

In ordinary usage we think of "culture" as meaning primarily the
standards of taste, manners, art, and, in our own day, mass media;
"low standards of culture" are low standards of taste, of beauty, or
art; and "cultural" are those interests traditionally cultivated primarily by women in our society having to do with reading, flower

arranging, music, poetry, and so on. But anthropologists use "culture" in an extended, almost botanical sense, as the medium of values and assumptions within which an individual grows, flourishes, and dies. Standards of taste and cultivation are of course part of this surrounding environment, but more important are those usually implicit and unexamined assumptions about the nature of life, man, society, history, and the universe which are simply taken for granted by most members of a society. Thus, every viable culture has characteristic cultural configurations, guiding and unifying assumptions about itself and its members, notions of what it is to be a man or a woman, of the purposes of life, the relationship of man to himself, history, nature, and the invisible world. These assumptions are learned early in childhood as those "facts" of life without which existence would be unthinkable, as those ways of dealing with others, the impersonal environment, and oneself which are simply taken for granted.

Seen in these terms, then, what unifies the ideology of these alienated young men is their generalized refusal of American culture. As we will later see, this refusal of culture goes beyond matters of philosophy and belief, and extends deep into the personal lives of these youths. But even on the level of explicit values, virtually every alienated outlook can be seen as a rejection of (often unstated) American assumptions about life and the universe. Where Americans have traditionally lived for the future, and still sometimes see history as progressive, the alienated value the present and see history as retrograde, moving downward or backward. Whereas the individualism of most Americans has traditionally been tempered by an acute sensitivity to public opinion, that of the alienated is opposed to social pressure and is "realistic" in its emphasis on personal needs. The point-by-point contrast of an alienated ideology to this "traditional American ethos" can be best seen by simply taking the opposite of each alienated outlook; the result is a recognizable portrait of the traditional American world view.

| ALIENATED OUTLOOK | OPPOSITE ("American culture") |
|---|---|
| DISTRUST OF COMMITMENT: | COMMITMENT: |
| Low view of human nature | Human nature basically good |
| Repudiation of intimacy | Closeness, togetherness |
| Rejection of group activities | Team-work, social-mindedness |
| Futility of civic and political activities | Usefulness, need for civic and political activities |
| Rejection of American culture | Praise of democratic culture |
| Vacillation, hesitation to act | Resoluteness, decisiveness |
| PESSIMISTIC EXISTENTIALISM: | OPTIMISTIC "IDEALISM": |
| Pessimism about future | Optimism about future |
| Anxiety about world | Confidence about world |
| Universe chaotic, unstructured, meaningless | Universe orderly, structured, purposive |
| Truth subjective and arbitrary | Truth objective and necessary |
| Meaning "created" by individual | Meaning found in universe |
| Impossibility of "true" communication | Possibility of mutual understanding |
| Appearances usually misleading | Appearances trustworthy, taking at "face value" |
| Short-range personally centered values | Long-range universally grounded values |
| ANGER, SCORN, AND CONTEMPT: | FRIENDLINESS, RESPECT, AND ADMIRATION: |
| Justification and admission of resentment; rejection | Disapproval and denial of resentment; acceptance |
| Intolerance, scorn | Tolerance, respect |
| Self-contempt | Self-confidence |
| Egocentricity in egocentric world | Sociocentricity in friendly world |

| AESTHETIC QUEST: | ACHIEVEMENT GOALS: |
|---|---|
| Awareness, experience, sentience, "being" | Activity, manipulation, "doing" |
| Living for today | Saving for tomorrow |
| Self-expression and creativity | Instrumental work |
| Passion, emotion, feeling | Reason, self-control, self-discipline |
| Isolated individualism | Socialized individualism |
| Social outsider | Social participant |
| Rejection of "success" | Drive to succeed |

This contrast between alienated beliefs and their opposites makes clear the extent to which alienation constitutes a total reaction against values long associated with a characteristically American outlook. The opposites of alienated outlooks are those which students of American society have pointed to as the basic assumptions of our culture. What unifies the alienated outlook, then, is its point-by-point denial of each of these historical verities and their replacement by opposite notion.

This is not to say that every American today holds all of the beliefs I have labeled "traditionally American"; nor is it to assume that every one of these beliefs is clearly articulated and explicit in each of its adherents. "Culture" is most often taken for granted, imbedded in the structures of thought, usage, and language, and is articulated only in times of crisis, when—as in our Declaration of Independence—a new nation seeks to define its future identity, or when—as now—an old nation faces a profound questioning of the values which have supported it for generations. Indeed, the fact that the list of non-alienated values reads more like a mild caricature than an accurate description of our current outlook points to the recent weakening of our unquestioning and implicit acceptance of this world view. Without such widespread questioning, it would be difficult for these young men to sustain an ideology that is so fundamentally opposed to that of a majority of their fellows. It is probably only to the extent that lesser alienations are "in the air," part of the cultural climate of the times, that individuals can find their way to so total a repudiation.

For if we take alienated beliefs one by one, virtually all of them find some support in some current of modern thought. I have already noted the parallel between pessimistic existentialism and alienation, a parallel made more meaningful by the fact that existentialism, too, grows out of rejection of the traditional pieties of what Kierkegaard called "Sunday Christianity" and what Nietzsche saw as the life-denying blindness of bourgeois society. One can also find substantial support for many other alienated views: many schools of psychoanalysis would support their darker assertions about human nature, the inherency of destructiveness, and the fundamental nature of self-seeking. And distrust of appearances is not only a cardinal tenet of much depth psychology (which alerts us to the unfathomed impulses beneath our civilized rationalizations), but of Marxism (which shows class interest lurking beneath most statements about society), and even of philosophical analysis (which behind traditional philosophical questions discovers "misunderstandings" about the way in which words are normally used). Even the traditional American belief in the importance and efficacy of individual political participation is fading before the complexity of the problems which face our nation. In all these areas the alienated can find support and ammunition for their rejection of the traditional American world view—if only a few would follow them so far in their total rejection of this ethos, many would support them on individual points.

This interpretation of alienation as a refusal of traditional American culture is not, however, one that most alienated youths would accept, or that, if they accepted it, they would find relevant or meaningful. For them, alienation is not part of a deliberate effort to locate and systematically oppose the basic values of our culture, but rather a set of conclusions about life that grew relatively un-self-consciously out of their own experience, that appears to be confirmed by it, that makes sense of the way they experience the world. For all of its oppositional quality, and indeed perhaps because it so embracingly and comprehensively opposes that coherent, well-organized, and self-consistent world view traditionally associated with America, alienation is itself a coherent and consistent view of the world. The alienated are in general true to the logic of their position: denying universal truth, they accept that their own assertions are subjective and arbitrary; believing in the evilness of human nature in general, they accept self-contempt along with contempt for others; convinced of the difficulties of human communication, they point to their own isolation. For them, alienation is but an expression of an experience of life, of feelings, and of fantasies, which they cannot comprehend within traditional American culture.

# 4    Non-commitment as a way of life

That consistency and distinctiveness which we have uncovered in the ideology of the alienated cannot be found in a superficial survey of their daily behavior. To be sure, all of these young men were college students, and this fact alone gave a certain regularity to their lives—attending (or deciding to cut) classes, eating their meals in college dining halls, living in college residential houses. But these are the appointed activities of all college students, and in no way distinguish the alienated. In appearance and public manner, they do not differ from other students, apart, perhaps, from a mild predilection for "old clothes"—blue jeans and tattered jackets—which is shared by many but not all their classmates. They are a healthy group of young men, not disabled, infirm, or disadvantaged; they range from tall to short, from fat to thin, from handsome to homely. One once grew a rather scraggly beard and shaved it off soon after, but one brief beard out of twelve is about par for their classmates as a whole.

Seen in the college dining halls, walking to classes, or sitting in seminars and classrooms, these young men do not attract attention. An astute observer might comment that they seem to hold themselves slightly aloof from others at times, and suggest that they were shy or scornful or both; but another observer might be more impressed by their impetuous vehemence in other discussions and

find them actively involved with their fellows. To be more ingen-
ious in our search for alienated students, we might visit the campus
coffee houses at 11:00 P.M., the cafeteria that has a reputation as a
"beatnik" hangout, or the motocycle and racing car set in the college. In some of these places, we might occasionally find one or
two, but even then rather on the peripheries of the group.

A search through the college records would also yield little of
note. Like all the students in the college, these young men arrived
with test scores and school records which promised outstanding
performances and attested to exceptional intellectual abilities; their
academic achievements in college had been just about what was
predicted for them at the beginning of their freshman year: they are
neither "underachievers" nor "overachievers." And if we looked
into the formal facts of their family backgrounds, we would find
these ran the full gamut of possibilities in the college: average
parental income high, as at any private college; parents highly educated (a B.A. and usually graduate work for one or both); typically upper middle class in background, with a few aspiring young
men from working-class homes and a few from more upper-class
backgrounds. A slight disproportion of these subjects would mark
"no religion" when asked their religious affiliations, but this would
be more likely a result of alienation rather than a cause. Among
those who were most critical of American popular culture, there
would be very slightly more Jews than expected by chance, but the
difference is miniscule, and religion would not begin to account for
alienation.

A superficial survey of their daily activities would yield equally
few results. We might note that none of these young men were
engaged in varsity athletics, but their high-school records show
somewhat more interest in sports. We might comment on their predilection for the humanities as majors, or the fact that there is an
unusual concentration of alienated students at the college residence
known for being most bohemian; but all of these facts would be
readily expected from what we have learned of their broadly "aesthetic" interests. Despite their distrust of intimacy, they spend

about as much time with the opposite sex as do their classmates. And if, by chance, it should occur to us that a group of young men with so oppositional an outlook might have come into open conflict with the "authorities," a search through the college or local police records would yield little result.

In most outward and public respects, then, Inburn is representative of alienated young men in his "typicalness." We will later see that a more intensive look at the family backgrounds of these young men does indeed uncover special patterns of family relationship and history; but none of these can be related in this group to the usual sociological factors like social class, area of residence, religion, ethnic background, or death or divorce of parents. Quite possibly, were we to restudy these same young men when they were ten years older, we might find that they were doing very different kinds of things than their less alienated fellows. And were we to study the population at large, we would undoubtedly find a connection between social factors (e.g., low socio-economic status) and the amount of alienation present. But among these students, social and religious background have little to do with alienation.

Yet the alienated *are* different from their non-alienated classmates: they usually do the same things but they do them in a special way; they differ not in *what* they do but in *how* they do it. In early adulthood (and probably throughout life), alienation expresses itself most characteristically as a *style of life,* a special attitude brought to ordinary activities, a special relationship to the crucial events of one's life—rather than as any simply identifiable kind of behavior or set of activities. Whatever the alienated do, they do in an alienated way; and by examining their style, we may come to understand better what alienation involves.

## Intellectual passion

I have already noted that the grade averages of the alienated are about what they should be according to pre-admission predictions. As a group, the alienated tend to be, if anything, slightly

more able than their classmates, especially on I.Q. tests that measure "verbal" (as opposed to mathematical) aptitudes. And as a
consequence, more than half of them are honors candidates in a
college where about half of the student body maintains an honors
(B) average. But if we look behind these over-all averages, a
different picture begins to emerge. The extreme of this trend is one
alienated student who announced early in his college career that
getting good grades in college was "fantastically easy," and proceeded to take half again as many courses as required. At the end
of one term on this schedule, his grades were A, B, B, C, D, and E,
which gave him a B average for the four (highest) grades counted.
Another student interested in architecture mastered the material in
an advanced course in architectural engineering on his own, yet
failed completely the required prerequisite for the same course because he disliked the lecturer, text, course, and section man, and
consequently did none of his assignments. The course grade, because it was in addition to his required schedule, did not count on
his average.

These are extreme results of the characteristic intellectual style
of the alienated, a style which involves intensely passionate concentration on a few topics of particular personal importance, coupled
with a relative inability to do other work. The special topics which
excite the interest of these young men have three common characteristics: they are "far-out," unorthodox, esoteric, and unconventional; they bear a very close though symbolic relationship to the
psychic concerns of the young men; and they are seldom academically unimpeachable. One young man, much worried about his
ability to stand up under social pressures, became interested in the
"brainwashing" of American POW's in Korea, and in a few weeks
of total concentration managed to read and master practically
everything written on the topic. Another student, in the throes of a
conflict with his conventional parents, became interested in the development of criminal outlooks and for a time espoused the view
that criminals were merely those who did not conform to conventional middle-class notions of morality. Still other students, con-

cerned with their own fantasies and impulses, find in the study of psychoanalytic writings a way of structuring and organizing their thinking about themselves. The close connection between intellectual pursuit and personal concern is not always obvious to these young men—on the contrary, the obsessive quality of these interests often hides their more personal sources. But to an informed outside observer the connection is sometimes painfully clear.

Total intellectual passions are difficult to reconcile with college requirements, the more so since the timetable of these interests follows the vicissitudes of the psyche and not the established calendar of the academic year. Furthermore, the topics to which the alienated devote themselves are seldom academically respectable: they prefer Sartre to Kant, Ginsberg to the Elizabethan lyricists, and Wilhelm Reich to Pavlov. The assignment of a given writer in a course is often enough to kill any further interest in him among the alienated. One young man developed an intense interest in Shelley and Byron, and devoted many single-minded weeks to studying their work and their lives. But when they were assigned in a literature course, his interest disappeared and he found himself unable to do the assignments. Others react with a less extreme withdrawal of interest, or manage somehow tenuously to relate the requirements of their school work to their own interests; but all share the same predilection for topics at once personally meaningful and as distant as possible from the orthodoxies of the academic establishment.

The academic fate of students so disposed obviously depends in large part on the outlook of their college. In a college with detailed daily assignments and inflexible requirements, they will not prosper. Similarly, in any educational system where orthodoxy is strong, their oppositional streak will lead them into continual conflict with authoritative views and the authorities who support them. In understanding the academic successes of these students, it is important to recall that they attended a college noted for iconoclasm, heterogeneity, and laissez-faire attitude toward its undergraduates. Most of the courses available to these students offered them large freedom to tailor the course to their own needs: by choosing final exam questions on subjects close to their own intellectual passions and by writing term papers on such topics, they were often able to transform characterological necessity into an academic virtue. Even when they could not always do this, their successes in some areas canceled out their failures in others, to yield good over-all performance.

And when all is said and done, the alienated are in many ways extremely rewarding students to teach, partly because of the passion with which they approach any subject that fires their imagination, and partly because of their iconoclasm and questioning outlook. This iconoclasm appeals especially to the often harassed younger teachers on whom the burden of grading usually falls, because it expresses an oppositional streak which must be vigorously suppressed by those negotiating the perilous waters between Ph.D. and tenure. The alienated respond eagerly to challenging teaching; and when they are not challenged, alienated young men, who take the stated goals of most colleges cynically and dislike grades altogether, can approach the grading system with high calculation, doing just enough work to assure an honors grade, or carefully anticipating their likely grades to assure the desired over-all average. Like the student quoted above, many feel that getting grades is a matter of a system to outwit the "System," and that it is really "fantastically easy" if one is willing to make a few small compromises. And when the "heat is on" just before examinations, these students often have an extraordinary capacity for concentration, for completing a series of long-overdue term papers and simultaneously preparing for finals in long-neglected courses.

But for all their adequate if unconventional performance, these are not students who live happily in what must be, even in the most permissive college, a somewhat restrictive environment. As we might infer from their oppositional outlooks, they frequently attack their college, they despise any traces of "college spirit," and above all they question the merit and adequacy of their own participation in the educational process. Here again, the particular college they attended affected their outlook towards it, and probably, indirectly, toward many other things. For the alienated agreed with their classmates in finding their college unusually heterogeneous, unusually un-rigid, unusually free from pressures for conformity either among the students or from the faculty. At other colleges where the hand of student opinion was heavier, where there was a clear definition of the Big Man on Campus, the same young men would doubtless have taken the college itself as one of their primary targets, and might not have so fully developed that more generalized alienation we have seen in their philosophies. But this was seldom possible with these students: the college was so pluralistic and permissive that it tended to absorb and even encourage criticisms. So the discontents of these students could rarely be expended against their college; and when they were dissatisfied with their educations, as they often were, they most often tended to blame themselves. Of twelve alienated students, four withdrew from college before receiving their B.A.'s, and most of the rest seriously considered leaving at one time or another. Their reasons were instructive: they generally felt that they were not "getting what they should" from college; they often recognized that their inability to do assigned work with enthusiasm (if at all) meant they wasted much of their time; and most of them felt that they were seeking something which they had not begun to find in college. Self-blame predominated over blame of the college—as it does in most students who leave college in midstream. Though with one exception they did return after a year or two off, their year of working or wandering changed them relatively little in basic outlook, but merely convinced them that a B.A. was more worth having.

## The detached observer

The doubts of the alienated about the educational process extended to the extracurricular activities in which they took part. A number of the alienated were involved in such activities; a few held, for a time at least, responsible positions in college organizations—but in their choice of these activities, in the roles they sought out within them, and above all, in the mode of their participation, they retained their alienated style. Alienated students find any institutional involvement complicated and troubled: they are not "joiners," and any hint of pressure leads them quickly to withdraw. They studiously avoided athletic competition (though some had taken part in secondary school athletic competition and one, despite small stature, had been an excellent high-school football player); and they equally consistently eschewed all activities and organizations with any posible taint of "college spirit" or "boosterism." Instead, they found their way into activities where their humanistic or dramatic interests could be expressed.

Some of these activities were quintessentially fugitive, like helping to found the small literary magazines that flourish and quickly die on and around the campus. Others were necessarily short-lived because they were theatrical; taking part in the production of one of the fifty or so plays annually produced by undergraduates also suited the alienated style of total absorption in one passionate endeavor. Other activities were literary in more conventional ways: writing for or editing one of the more established journals published by students. But in each of these activities the alienated tended to bring a particular alienated style. In one case, a young man much interested in the theater always got himself into production positions which, though essential, were nonetheless solitary, and allowed him total autonomy. Another student soon established a bad reputation for himself by becoming intensely involved in the direction of several plays, and after persuading or cajoling others to accept his principles of interpretation, losing interest and withdrawing from the show. Still another wrote for a number of "little magazines" on the campus, but was never willing to become involved in the actual running of the magazines. Another accepted a responsible position on a publication, but failed to meet deadlines and produced half the usual number of issues. And most characteristic of all was the alienated student, elected to an important position in a national organization, who, soon after his inauguration, quit college without warning either to his fellow students or the college authorities—as if "success," commitment, and responsibility had been more than he could bear.

We might well have inferred the principle of their extracurricular activities from the philosophies of alienated students: they dislike and distrust institutional involvements and responsibilities, which make them feel trapped and restricted; they can seldom be happy when truly involved with a group, and only survive on its peripheries. This same principle may help explain why the alienated are not found among the "beatnik" groups on the campus. Almost to a man, they find such groups conformist, sterile, and "not serious"; they scorn those who belong to them. While they are often fascinated by the "beat" style of life, and while many of them may in their own way adopt its characteristics, they are in many ways *too* alienated to be "beatniks"—a stance which, after all, involves accepting an identity, a sense of solidarity, and a set of expectations about one's "beat" behavior.

What do the alienated do with their time, then? As we might expect from their philosophies, they spend much of it alone. They do not distinguish between work and play, and consequently cannot organize their lives around those schedules of "studying" and "goofing off" which many students use to discipline themselves. When the alienated "work," it is usually on some topic of passionate, even obsessional interest to them; they rarely work because they have to, but because they "need" to. Put more precisely, the compulsions which drive them are less often academic requirements than are those of their fellows, and more often inner psychic compulsions only tangentially related to the requirements of the institution. Similarly, their "leisure" activities often have much of the same driven quality, which makes the usual work-play distinctions irrelevant to them. Indeed, what they do when not studying is very similar in psychological meaning to their studies: in both, they try to intensify, deepen, and comprehend their experience.

This cult of experience is sometimes explicit in their philosophies, but its meanings are clearest when we see them in daily activ-

ities. For example, as a group, the alienated are wanderers, walk-
ers, and hitchhikers: when confronted with a major or even a
minor problem they are likely to "take off," sometimes for a long
midnight walk, sometimes for a few years—as with the young man
who precipitately left college after being elected to an important
office. "Taking off" may mean a voluntary leave of absence for a
year, hitchhiking across the country in an unintended imitation of
Kerouac (whom they have not read), a long walk along the river, a
three A.M. visit to the burning city dumps which seems to solace the
student's nameless rage and anger, an observer's visit to the slums
or the red-light district, not for gratification but for something else
which they find it hard to describe. But their descriptions of their
wanderings have much in common: in these solitary travels, many
find a kind of ecstatic and mystic union with Things, a Joycean
epiphany in which the universe is seen in the garish pennants of a
filling station, childhood memories recaptured by a sudden smell of
burning leaves, or a rapturous moment created by the way the light
of the setting sun falls through an archway onto the grass. It is as if
they were seeking some consoling contact with objects and things,
contact more immediate and embracing than afforded by daily experience, and as if only this contact could nourish and refresh
them.

In all of their wanderings, the alienated remain observers but not
participants—or rather, their participation consists of observation.
They extend the role of observer into other areas, and are fascinated by the bizarre, the unusual, the strange, and the deviant. Recall Inburn, who spent his period of preparation for examinations
recording the memoirs of a call girl. Or remember the student who
talks about his happy contacts with the drunks, bums, and Brahmin
ladies on Beacon Hill, whom he later recollects in tranquillity. Another student attached himself peripherally to a group of off-beat
writers who lived near the campus; he limited himself to observing
them and took no active part in their group, although their activities
and oddities obsessed him during many of his waking and sleeping
hours. Others approach the bizarre and the deviant more intellec-

tually, as with the student who made a long study of criminality, or others who became fascinated by psychosis and perused arcane volumes seeking to understand its significance. In all of these interests, the students are, despite their sideline position, deeply involved: they identify profoundly with the objects of their research at the same time that they seek to differentiate themselves from them.

Only rarely do the alienated shift from the role of observer to that of participant. A few youths tell us (rather proudly) that they drink to excess, and recount difficulties encountered in their binges. Others are fascinated, usually at a distance, by drugs, especially hallucinogenic drugs which promise passage through the "gates of perception" or "expansion of consciousness." Others are fascinated by the experience of psychosis, and wonder whether they understand what it would be like to be insane. Still others have indulged in minor thefts, not from need, but for the sake of the experience of stealing or, as one subject said, "to prove to myself that I didn't feel guilty." Excessive speed fascinates one or two with a history of speeding tickets. But in general, as college students, they focused on the perceptual rather than the active sides of experience; and, paradoxically for so oppositional a group of young men, they were not behavioral non-conformists. Indeed, the very intensity of their private search for unconventional perceptions and awareness probably lessened their need for public non-conformity.

Their oppositional stance is, however, fully expressed in one of their most characteristic activities: arguing. In intellectual discussions with their peers they are dominant, active, negative, and hostile, constantly interrupting and correcting their fellows, criticizing every point of view brought forward, and impressing their peers with their scornful, contemptuous attitudes. In such discussions, the opposition of the alienated sometimes goes beyond his convictions: he often opposes views with which he fully agrees, merely for the sake of argument. As an informal debater, he tends to be effective, partly because he is articulate and well informed, and perhaps mostly because his position of opposing what others say requires no positive coherent position to back it up. In one experimental situation, however, when alienated subjects were confronted with a single experienced and hostile antagonist who attacked *their* alienated views with great personal bitterness, the same students were thrown off balance and responded rather mildly. Only afterwards, when describing the discussion to a psychologist who did not witness it, did they fully vent their scorn, contempt, dislike, and derision of an assailant who had bested them. This suggests an important fact about the alienated—that they find it easiest to express their hostilities in a large group of people with an abstract topic of discussion; when confronted with only one other person who argues *ad hominem,* they conceal their immediate anger, but later lapse into a slow and enduring burn. On abstract subjects, and when not personally attacked, however, arguing is for the alienated an avocation that goes far beyond challenging views they disagree with: it is a characterological necessity, a part of their self-images; its goal sometimes seems to be more to make a statement about the kind of people they are than to convince anyone else of the rightness of their views.

## The overexamined life

I have so far emphasized the solitariness of alienated students—their tendency to avoid intimacies and involvements with groups or with people. As a group they spend less time with others, are less intimate with them, become less manifestly involved with groups than do many or most of their peers. To all but their closest friends and acquaintances these students are usually known as aloof and rather negativistic, somewhat scornful, unwilling to be drawn into the activities of others, perhaps condescending. Their acquaintances tend to know relatively little about them, and the alienated usually resist any attempts to break through their armored sense of privacy.

There is, however, another and contrasting side to most of these young men, a side which is very deeply if ambivalently involved with others despite outward appearances to the contrary, a side which prevents any simple characterization of them as aloof, shy, withdrawn, or indifferent to others. One characteristic type of involvement, seen frequently when such youths become research subjects, involves a simultaneous attraction to and fear of an admired person. One unusually insightful alienated student described his feeling about a graduate student whom he admired in these terms: "Whenever I am with him, he is so enthusiastic about what he is doing that I want to drop everything and follow in his footsteps. It sort of scares me." A similar pattern often emerged with research psychologists whom the alienated came to admire: they would very candidly discuss their worries and anxieties with such men—knowing their confidences would be respected—and seek advice on how to conduct their lives. But if the psychologist responded with anything that could be construed as advice, they would invariably attack it as irrelevant, lacking in understanding, and stupid. Yet paradoxically, despite their sometimes bitter attacks on the research project and on individual members in the project, the alienated seemed more deeply involved in it than most non-alienated students.

All of this suggests that with potentially emulable older men, the alienated are involved in a struggle *against* their own underlying admiration and desire to emulate, a struggle which they must maintain precisely because they are so overwhelmingly drawn to men who might serve as models for them. Underneath their public face of opposition and negativism, the alienated must often feel their central selves are too weak to tolerate admiration of another person without being totally absorbed by him.

Some of their contemporaries evoke this same mixture of admiration and consequent repudiation by the alienated. Other students who "know where they are headed" are most likely to arouse these feelings. The comments of the alienated about them tend to follow a similar line: on the one hand, they reluctantly admire the purposefulness and lack of vacillation in such young men; but on the

other, they deplore what they see as the conventionality, narrowness, and limitation of vision inherent in this purposefulness.
Toward other students who are alienated they have less equivocal
feelings: they heartily dislike and repudiate anyone else who is alienated, seeing his alienation as sham, hypocrisy, and a cover-up
for weakness. In this rejection of the like-minded it is not hard to
infer self-contempt: the motives they ascribe to their fellow alienated are those they most fear in themselves. And even in their fierce
rejection of the conventional and everyday, we might suspect some
fear of their own conventional or conformity-loving potentials.

But the most striking aspect of the involvement of the alienated
with others is its ruminative, even obsessional, quality. Virtually no
relationship of any duration escapes detailed analysis and examination from every point of view: the character of the other, his motives for liking or not liking the subject, the subject's own motives
for entering and continuing the relationship, the effects of the relationship on both parties, etc., etc., etc. Every human encounter has
for the alienated an ambivalent quality, so that no judgment can
ever be simple and unqualified. Every relationship ultimately becomes a question of identity, of whether to be or not to be like the
other person; and since identity is in these young men unsettled and
unsure, so are their encounters with others. The result is an overexamined life, wherein every hour spent in any kind of close contact with another demands at least equal time for analysis, questioning, searching for motives, meanings, and effects.

These characteristics are especially prominent with the opposite
sex. Rather surprisingly, given their repudiation of intimacy and
their agreement with statements like "I don't think I'll ever find a
woman who really understands me," the alienated differ not at all
from their classmates in the frequency with which they date and in
the amount and variety of their sexual experience. As with any
group of students, the range of this experience is wide, varying
from those who have rarely been out with a girl to those with intense passionate affairs of relatively long duration. Among the majority who as college students date fairly actively, there are several

different patterns, each involving intense and ambivalent attach-
ments coupled with much rumination about the relationship. One
pattern involves transient encounters with a series of girls, none of
whom are found satisfactory for any long-range relationship. If
such short-term affairs involve sexual relationships, the subject is
very likely to feel extremely guilty about them, believing with a
certain mixture of feelings that he ruthlessly exploited the girl.
Each new relationship is entered into with the highest of hopes, and
every break involves the same intense feeling of disillusionment
and even of betrayal—regardless of who initiates the break. Often,
such breaks are seen to involve a preferred rival, and the presence
of a more successful rival merely adds to the alienated student's
feeling of disillusion and defeat.

Another dating pattern involves a more prolonged relationship
with a girl described as extremely docile, dependent, passive, com-
pliant, and subservient. One young man describes "teaching" his
girl friends how to satisfy him sexually, and implies that his own
passivity limits the number of available partners. Another discusses in enthusiastic terms his fiancée's "total" dependence on
him, and makes no attempt to hide his enjoyment of his own sense
of superiority over her. In these cases, there appears to be little
reciprocity between the young man and his girl; the relationship is
premised on the availability of a girl who will never be challenging,
assertive, or aggressive, or even perhaps, never demand real intimacy.

The final alienated pattern of dating involves an intensely grati-
fying relationship with a girl who is somehow defined as "forbidden"—whether by virtue of her past, her religion, or merely the
student's parents' opposition. Such relationships tend to precipitate
violent quarrels and breaks between the student and his family, and
he clearly enjoys pitting himself against this segment of the world.
However deep and satisfying such relationships are to the students
themselves, they are invariably carried on in the shadow of the
disapproving family, and one sometimes wonders whether a shift of

family policy might not lead to the dissolution of the tie and the search for a new partner even less "suitable." Whatever the motives of the student, it is highly consistent with the alienated style to find someone whom an important part of his world defines as undesirable and to fall deeply in love with her.

In hearing these undergraduates talk about their girl friends and dates, one is again struck with the amount of ambivalence and examination of relationship that goes on. Their partners sometimes complain to them that they "pick them to pieces," and this is true. However much they may seek and occasionally find intimacy, it is threatening: they find it difficult to trust the object of their love unless she is either totally dependent on them, or else somehow defined as undesirable. Thus, their continual dissection of all relationships has a fearful quality, as if they needed continually to re-examine the trustworthiness of the other and reassure themselves that the relationship was not harming them. In all of their encounters, they retain the same agonizing combination of desire for closeness and fear of it; and the ways they deal with this ambivalence—the way they choose their potential intimates and the way they deal with those to whom they might be close—often merely serve to confirm their view that intimacy is the prelude to disappointment and disillusion.


## The fragmented self

If we ask how the alienated describe themselves and how they perform on psychological tests, we find a similar set of distinctive alienated qualities. In interviews as on questionnaires, the alienated make no bones about their own confusions, angers, anxieties, and problems. These are not young men who conceal their own unpleasant motives and fantasies from themselves or others: given a list of symptoms, worries, anxieties, and concerns, they will check all they possibly can, as if to boast of their superior honesty with themselves. They tell us that they are confused, anxious, nervous, irritable, hostile, angry, impulsive, depressed, and dejected. They say they are suspicious, lacking in will power, resentful, unfriendly, and jealous. They experience time as confused and disorganized, as the arena for decline and decay; consequently, they have few long-range plans. They question their ability to cope with life, they feel unfulfilled in their work and at the college, they say they are rarely themselves with other people; they describe themselves as philosophically confused and disoriented. Indeed, given any list of "socially undesirable" characteristics, the alienated affirm that they possess them. And on interviews, once the ice has been broken, they talk freely about their disturbing feelings, fantasies, and dreams; they sometimes worry aloud about their ultimate sanity; they ask reassurance as to their normality.

How are we to understand these results? One possibility is, of course, that the alienated are indeed incredibly disturbed young men, neurotic, apprehensive, and confused. And as we will see, there is some evidence to support this view. But at the same time, we must recall that most of our definitions of "mental health" (like most of the tests by which we try to measure it) are based on traditional American notions that the "mentally healthy" are those optimistic, practical, unapprehensive, "reasonable," forward-looking men and women who people our cultural Hall of Fame. Insofar as a young man rejects these definitions of the good life, he will (by definition) be "unhealthy" in the terms of his culture. Thus, at least a part of the appearance of mental unbalance in these young men may come from their rejection of the very premises by which mental health is usually defined.

A related factor in understanding the "mental unhealth" of the alienated is their relative lack of repression. Most "good adjustment" in America presupposes a "healthy" amount of repression, suppression, and denial of unpleasant thoughts, feelings, and fantasies—an "accentuation of the positive," a determined effort to see the bright side of things and of oneself and not to dwell on the sordid, unpleasant, hostile, or nasty side. Much of this repression, this "not noticing," is involuntary, for from an early age American children are usually taught to suppress their open complaints and direct aggressions, finding more suitable and sublimated expressions. Such feelings do not, of course, disappear, but they do in time tend to disappear from the consciousness of those who have them. In a youth who will not or cannot repress, such motives will be far more accessible to awareness, and therefore more available for reporting to psychologists and on personality questionnaires. Seen this way, the man or woman with great insight into his own motives—including the bad ones—will often appear more "neurotic" on tests than the man without awareness of precisely the same motives.

The alienated, then, whose lives are overexamined, who make a virtue, even a fetish, of complete and ruthless honesty with themselves about their most undesirable qualities, and for whom awareness and self-understanding are central goals, show up poorly on personality tests partly because they lack the ability to repress or the desire to put up a "good show." It is more important to them to admit—or to exaggerate—their problems and thus to retain their tenuous inner conviction of honesty with themselves and with others about themselves, than it is to appear "normal," a classification they despise. In psychological research one quickly learns to distrust "objective" test scores and look at behavior, for it often happens that an individual with extremely "healthy" test scores can be in reality far more disturbed than a man who checks all the symptoms but somehow copes with life.

We can explain away some of the appearance of poor psychological health in these young men by recognizing their awareness of and exaggeration of their symptoms, and perhaps by refusing, with them, to accept conventional views of "good mental health." Yet behaviorally this remains an unusually confused, disoriented, and unhappy group of young men. The defiant public face of scorn and opposition soon gives way to clear unhappiness, depression, self-doubt, and apprehensiveness. And beneath their assertions that "suffering is the primary source of wisdom" they are not totally reconciled to their discontents. Though they proclaim that unhappiness is the lot of any man honest enough to face reality and himself as he is, they find it hard to suppress their own suspicions that it may be something about *them* —rather than the human condition—that makes them so miserable.

To put their plight in a phrase, they suffer from what the psychoanalyst Erik Erikson has called "identity diffusion"—from an intense feeling of the precariousness and disunity of the self, from doubt about their own continuing capacity to "cope," coupled with a relentless search for some trustworthy foundation for selfhood. Their use of intellect is in the service of this quest for understanding and meaning for the sake of ultimate selfhood. Their dissatisfaction with their education is coextensive with an inability to find in college any solid sense of who they are and where they stand. The search for identity pervades their wandering, their seeking some renewing contact with Things, their simultaneous refusal of the identity of a "beatnik" and their need to define themselves as "one who opposes." And in their fear of being overwhelmed by their own admiration, in their scorn both for those who resemble them and for those who are different, in the wariness and distrustfulness with which they approach reciprocity and intimacy of any kind—in all these we can infer the same fragility of self.

Strong in opposition, these young men are weak in affirmation; unable to articulate or even to know what they stand for, they have little sense of self to stand on. For the achievement of identity requires in every young man and woman an implicit set of goals and standards—usually those provided by society—which tell him who he is, where he stands, whence he comes and whither he goes. Even those who find some principle in whose name they reject their society can find personal meaning in their allegiance to that principle and in solidarity with others who are faithful to it. But rebels without a cause can only stand against, not for; and even their opposition is diffuse and unspecific. The price they pay for this opposition, a price exacted by all societies (which must refuse sanctioned identity to their opponents), is inner confusion, disunity, and fragmentation. For this reason if for no other, it is far easier psychologically to be a revolutionary with a program than an alienated youth with only a vague set of rejections.

# 5         The alienating context

We now know something of what these alienated youths believe and how they live their daily lives, but we have little notion as yet of their personal pasts, of how they grew up, what their families were like, and how their alienation developed. To begin to understand these questions, we will examine what they tell us of their lives in their written autobiographies and in countless interviews. In any such examination, we must keep in mind that not everything an individual tells us about his past is necessarily the whole truth, and that often the most important truths are stated between the lines. Some of the facts and themes reported must be interpreted as attempts to *explain* the past rather than as actual facts, and still other reports turn out to be expressions of wish and desire rather than of personal history. But these distortions, exaggerations, and self-justifications are usually apparent when seen in the total context of information available—just as, for example, we have seen with Inburn that his account of his "oneness" with his mother up to age of nine must have contained a strong element of wish which distorted his recollection of the actual events. And even the most grossly distorted statement of fact is a meaningful psychological statement: a self-justifying phrase points to the area in which an individual feels in need of justification; a wish-distorted recollection underlines the intensity of the underlying wish.

With these qualifications—familiar to any reader of detective fiction—we can approach the accounts of alienated young men about their own lives, searching for some consistency, for unifying themes, for similarities. Some of the consistencies we find will be of little special significance: for example, we will find that these young men are very much concerned with defining their independent positions vis-à-vis their families, but this concern is almost universal among college men in our society and we can here assign it no special meaning. Or again, the alienated report almost to a man growing up in that suburban environment of ample houses, trees, and playmates which also characterizes the pasts of most of their classmates: it has little special value in helping us explain their alienation. Rather, we will be looking for those past experiences, family constellations, memories, and incidents which are shared by many or most of the alienated, but *not* to the same degree by their less alienated classmates, and most of all, for themes of life history which clearly distinguish this alienated group from those on the opposite end of the scale, the extremely committed or extremely conformist.

## The distant past

As a nation, America has tended to outgrow and forget its past, looking instead to its future, seen as ever better than what went before. Despite their repudiation of the American ethos, the alienated are no exception to the first part of this rule. Not one of them mentions spontaneously a past more distant than the grandparental generation; only one, of a distinguished and familiar American family, mentions his family genealogy, and when he does, it is to deplore the uses to which his maternal grandmother put it. The "distant" past is for these young men the generation of their parents' parents, and its exemplars are the old men and women whom these young men remember from their own childhoods. Without specific questioning, we would not have known that they were all at least third-generation Americans, and that most of them came from families so long established in this country that no one remembered (or cared) how many generations ago the first ancestors arrived on these shores.

But of grandparents and their generation, these young men have more to say, since they knew them as children; and what they say often has a surprisingly positive ring to it. One of the most extremely alienated writes of them:

> My mother's father was the most kind and honest man I've ever known. . . . As a child, I felt he was the best man in the world . . . and I think I wanted to be like him, in fact I'm almost certain.

Another comments:

> The most interesting member of our family was my great-uncle, an eccentric who has spent his life making recorders which though their quality is great he refuses to sell. He seems to have found a wonderful spiritual peace. I admire his strength in being able to create beauty whatever that creation's consequences must be.

Another writes, again of his mother's father:

> He was supposed to have been a brilliant man and to have been a prodigy in Europe. Eventually he gained such pre-eminence that men such as Erlich and Einstein counted him as their friend. He had an amazing variety of talents . . . a fantastic memory and ability to make friends. In some way my grandfather was my idol for many years and still is.

Other accounts of grandparents are less unqualifiedly favorable, but this generation still emerges as strong and heroic even in its vices. Recall Inburn's characterizations of his mother's immigrant family as "strongly," "strong-willed," "cruel," and "exuberant." And note the common qualities in this description:

> My mother was constantly fighting her mother, a Philadelphia society woman universally regarded as the definitive bitch of all

time. Mother's ears were filled with genealogy day and night, and not as a matter of beautiful tradition, but as a device that my grandmother used to assert her dominance.

He views his grandmother not merely as a nasty woman, but gives her the heroic vice of being "universally regarded as the definitive bitch of all time." Of his father's family, the same youth writes:

My father was oppressed by both parents, his mother being a celebrated musician and strong personality, and his father a rather domineering sportsman.

Another implies the same combination of strength and domination in this account of his father's family:

He was born of a family of eccentrics, all brilliant, but all endowed with an abiding hatred of the world. . . . [He] was brought up under a rigid discipline which was designed to make him into a strong man among what my grandfather lovingly termed "the piefluff of our age."

And even in this account of his parents' struggles to break away from the world they were born into, this young man suggests the power of their world:

They were descendants of immigrants of a poverty-stricken old world, of a rigid Orthodox Jewish background . . . trying to break with it all and establish new lives for themselves.

Whether they see their grandparents in a positive or negative light (and many see them surprisingly positively), the alienated view them as strong, even heroic, figures, in their brilliance, rigidity, domineeringness, or eccentricity. Part of this view may come from the fact they knew their grandparents when the latter were old, and perhaps now mistake that rigidity of character which comes with age for heroic strength. But we also know from other studies that when young men view their parents' parents in some particular way, they are usually reflecting their parents' own interpretations as well. Thus, it is likely that to our subjects' parents as well, the grandparental generation appeared strong, heroic, domineering, and rigid, sometimes admirable, sometimes tyrannical. For the fathers of these young men, the most emphasized quality in the previous generation is domineering strength, as with Inburn's account of how his father was dominated by his own mother, a "scolding, officious hypochondriac." Our subjects' mothers, on the other hand, seem to have seen their own fathers, at least, as more unequivocally admirable figures, a perception which is reflected in our subjects' accounts. Neither our subjects nor their mothers find this same strength in the subject's fathers.

## What Mother gave up

Chronologically, mothers inevitably come first: the infant develops an attachment and need for the person who mothers him which is as strong as his need for nourishment; without mothering, he will fail to thrive as surely as if he were deprived of food and drink. Psychologically, too, mothers come first in our society during a long period of our prolonged childhood; and it is from those who mother us that we first learn the quality of human love and support, and to them that we turn not only for physical care but for the solace and maternal comfort which is equally important. And in America, as in many other cultures, mothers often remain psychologically "first" in that they continue to represent one of the most fundamental possibilities of human relationship open even to an adult. Certainly for middle-class American college students, it is the rule to find that a young man's mother continues to play a more important role in his psychological development and fantasies than his father; only in exceptional cases, with exceptional fathers, do we find young men ultimately more concerned with their fathers than their mothers.

All of this is true for the alienated, and in itself does not adequately distinguish them from their fellows, except perhaps that it is even more true for the alienated: like Inburn, many of them hardly mention their fathers at all until prompted. But what further characterizes the alienated is the *special quality* of their feeling about their mothers.

For one, most of these students emphasize the renunciations and sacrifices their mothers have made in their marriages. Sometimes the subject feels that the mother abandoned a promising career for her marriage. This is implicit in Inburn's comment:

> She showed early talent as a pianist (again, completely through her own ambition), and indeed at one time gave solo recitals. . . . Nothing ever came of it.

And the same theme is more explicit in remarks by other subjects:

> When she was young, she had ambitions to be a writer, and she told me she hated to settle down to the dreary task of becoming a housewife, and she would have preferred to write. For her sake, I'm rather sorry she married.

Another raises the same question only to deny it:

> She spent a couple of years at a dramatic school and then worked as a secretary. . . . My mother thinks she could have been a good actress, but doesn't really regret having married my father.

And another reports this conversation with his mother:

> She said a few things like, "At this point I don't know whether I'd recommend marriage." She's got a big investment in marriage but . . . I think she meant that marriage for anyone with creative instincts, anybody who thinks he could do more on his own, that he owes it to himself not to get married.

The theme, then, is of a talented woman who gave up a great deal in order to marry. About their mother's talents, these young men are very articulate. One stresses his mother's intelligence:

Mother did much better than father in school . . . she soon learned to be independent and she was very much of a liberal. At college she was immensely witty and popular and managed to graduate *summa cum laude.*

But more commonly the subject emphasizes emotional and artistic qualities:

She is an extremely sensual, emotional person. . . . [She has] great personal magnetism, dynamic vibrant force, and energy. . . . She must have attention, she must be publicly praised; therefore she often makes herself look foolish, and it would be more so were it not for her great personal magnetism, energy, and attractiveness.

Inburn describes his mother in similar terms:

She was particularly good-looking when she was young. . . . She rose to an extraordinary position among her contemporaries . . . through sheer will and hard experience. . . .

Another emphasizes the artistic side of his mother:

My mother has what you might call an artist's temperament, romantic, often deeply moved by a work of art—sometimes music, sometimes literature.

In the frustration of these talents, it is usually these young men's fathers who are seen to have played a central role. Often as in earlier quotations, the blame on the father is implicit, but sometimes it is explicit:

I often feel sorry for her. She had an unhappy life ever since she married. [My father's] constant complaining, his nervousness, and his heavy drinking have upset us all, but particularly my mother, who once knew a different sort of life.

After [my birth], my mother became lonely for attention since my father's monomania to succeed gave her none. She became interested in dress design and now owns and runs a dress shop. . . . This allows her extremely acute and active mind to release its energy.

And the following young man's feelings about his mother can summarize the outlooks of most of the rest, with his combination of
regret at her unrealized talents and his implicit blame of his father:

> I have always been sentimental about my mother, and "Gee isn't
> it a pity" and all that. See, she never went to college. She got super-
> good marks in school, but she didn't get the scholarship she wanted,
> and she didn't go to college at all. She just stayed home, and home
> was this little town in Pennsylvania. So you have the feeling she's
> always been cramped. . . . Then she had my father to contend
> with. . . .

But for all of their special sympathy with their mothers' frustrations and undeveloped potential, these young men also emphasize
another side of their character, now placing it in the forefront, now
in the background. This is their mothers' dominance, possessiveness, and neuroticism. The young man just quoted said in another
context:

> She is a very high-strung person, and she has a neurotic walk.
> . . . Two years ago I felt quite suffocated in her presence. . . .
> She thinks I am a person who has run away from all the difficult
> things: the faith, the flag, my mother. This is a hard thing to bear,
> when your mother constantly accuses you of something you think is
> absurd.

Recall Inburn's statement:

> Mother is in poor health. She has a delicate constitution and has
> been warned against severe mental as well as physical strain.

Another young man says in the same vein:

> My mother has no known illnesses but she does not look very fit
> and suffers from tiredness and other minor discomforts.

By stressing "known illnesses," he seems to imply that his mother
may suffer from unknown ones, and by emphasizing her "tiredness

and other minor discomforts," that these may be neurotic in origin.

The possessiveness and dominance of these mothers is often discussed. One states the point succinctly: "My mother is affectionate and nagging," and goes on to describe her recent "nervous breakdown." Another writes somewhat caustically,

> Her only defect is that she refuses to face such realities or incongruities as drinking, sex, not getting married, majoring in psychology . . . and the like. Her careful watching over my career and my life in general has had little effect, much as water running off a duck's back.

Others imply their mothers' dominance most clearly in relationship to their fathers, usually by recounting some aspect of the family's history. Recall here Inburn's account of his family's new house: "The father is acquiescent and the mother has excellent taste, and it came out beautifully." Another subject notes that "It was due to her work solely that my father was able to pay his way through graduate school"—here the added word "solely" says much about the young man's view of his two parents. Another, whose mother has continued to work throughout her marriage, describes the situation this way:

> She worked and still does in the insurance business as a saleswoman. . . . She always paid the [private school] bills for the last four years, and expensive gifts have always come from her. She owns both cars in the family and has bought Father a greenhouse, a pond, and hundreds of dollars of perennials. I think she feels she has to make up for . . . not being the domestic sort.

Another gives this account of the early years of his parents' marriage:

> Mother says that when she married Dad . . . she made up his mind for him. . . . [After their marriage] Dad's aberrations frightened and disturbed her; she tried to curb him of his drinking, his habit of staying out late at night, and so on; and she succeeded. He still drinks today . . . but there are no more binges.

Such tales are characteristic of the way these young men view their mothers, both in relationship to their fathers and to their sons, our subjects. We cannot know for sure to what extent these accounts are accurate, how much they tell the full story. As we shall see when we study the fantasies of these alienated young men, their less conscious views of their mothers are more complicated. But at least as their sons consciously see them, these women emerge as credible human beings, frustrated in their own development (and who confide their frustrations in their son), talented, often emotional women who at the same time are difficult and neurotic, overpossessive and dominating with both sons and husbands. But what is perhaps most important is the *special sympathy* these young men feel for their mothers, even at the same time that they find them neurotic, nagging, and overpossessive. As with no one else, they feel a special identification with these women, a special regret at their mothers' unrealized potentials, a special suffering at their mothers' unhappinesses.

## Father's lost dreams

Like Inburn, most alienated young men tell us less about their fathers than about their mothers. This fact iself is of considerable importance, since most other students describe their fathers at somewhat greater length: it suggests that the fathers of these young men played a relatively unimportant conscious role in their sons' lives, and certainly that they played a less important role than did their wives. A second relevant fact about these fathers emerges from our discussion of grandparents: surprisingly often, our subjects' fathers are portrayed as having been dominated by overpowering parents in their own youths. We cannot be sure whether this assertion is accurate as fact; but it clearly points to the son's view of his father as a man who, from the start, has been dominated and dominatable.

We have already seen this theme in Inburn's discussion of his father, a man dominated by his mother, "acquiescent" with his wife, who gave up his first job choice, teaching, for a better-paying job where he now is "a failure in his own eyes." And in the implicit descriptions of their parents' relationship with each other, we have noted how alienated subjects describe their mothers as the more vigorous, decisive, and strong. But the most specific instance of Father's defeat by life comes in these subjects' accounts of their fathers' vocations. Here they emphasize the abandonment of early hopes and youthful dreams, and the attendant breaking of their fathers' spirits. One, speaking of the early years of his parents' marriage, describes it this way:

> Dad had just left his last job, and since all his friends were heading for Paris, he wanted to join them. He asked Mother to leave her job and come with him. She refused . . . she believed it would be wrong to leave [her parents] and she was afraid—afraid to leave her small, relatively insecure, but still her own, business. She was afraid of the unknown future in an unknown country . . . so he remained in this country, in New York, and the dreams of his youth, of the far places of the world, and his place in them, died. Although he seems to have reconciled himself to the loss of these particular hopes . . . I think that Mother's refusal hurt him deeply. There is a buried frustration, loss, bitterness, and disappointment in him, which creeps to the surface sometimes.

Another makes his father a double apostate:

> My father was a very competent artist as a child, and he wanted to become a painter, but he found the rigors of artistic life too much and he found he could more easily become a scholar; he adopted the course that insures success.

But even scholarship did not provide sufficient success, his son maintains, continuing:

> My father was a scholar of no mean ability. [He] acquired very young great fame. Like all young genius my father found his precociousness a curse. He found himself the curiosity of the society in

which he moved . . . occupied with speeches and dinner engage-
ments. Hungry for activity and accomplishment he became an apostate from the scholarly world and devoted himself to business ad-
ministration.

This young man is very explicit about his father's having "sold
out" his youthful (artistic) dreams for success, even more than
Inburn's scornful description of his father as a "small pillar" of a
"small community." Others merely imply the same sequence from
a career or potential career which might have been self-expressive
or creative to one which, despite remuneration and public esteem,
is viewed by the son as less worthy. Often the pressures are financial and familial. One young man, the eldest son in a very large
family, writes:

> My father left his teaching job and moved the whole family to
> Washington where he is now working for the Defense Department
> . . . gets paid quite a bit more. . . . [He] has never told me any-
> thing of this, but I imagine that the knowledge that [another] child
> was on the way precipitated his change to a new job.

These job changes are not in themselves at all unusual: on the
contrary, almost all of them were "up," to greater rewards, prestige, and responsibilities; and one can find similar job changes in
the histories of parents of many college students, alienated or not.
What is important about these shifts is the way they are seen by the
subjects—the tone of disappointment, the implication of "selling
out," the unseen presence of domestic pressure, and the stated or
unstated condescension of these young men for the present weakness of their fathers. The subjects imply, as we have seen, a certain
sympathy for the abandoned dreams of their fathers, and perhaps
for their image of the youthful fathers themselves; but toward their
fathers as they are *now,* they feel (or communicate) a lack of basic
respect. Their sympathy for their fathers is more attached to their
fantasy of what their fathers were like twenty-five years ago than to
anything their fathers are now.

As for their fathers now, these college students describe them with such singular consistency that it almost seems the same man is being described by the entire group, now with greater compassion, now with less. One of the more compassionate writes:

> My father is quite reserved. Either people feel uncomfortable because he will not commit himself personally to them, or else they get beyond this prisonlike exterior to the warm lonely man inside. Obviously, such a man finds it hard to show emotions, no matter how deeply felt, in public. It embarrasses him to reveal his insides to the world and he is afraid of being hurt.

Another begins by talking about his own drinking, which his mother considers excessive:

> [My drinking] worries my mother while my father rarely mentions it. He is very difficult to talk to—he has no desire to talk. . . . He wishes to enjoy his gardening [perennials] into which he has put most of his spare time. He does not care to enter society any further than our group of friends. . . . He is a man who believes in privacy and his own individual choices. I disagree with him in many things.

Or note the condescension in this description of another disinterested father:

> My father has always been more or less disinterested, except when an important decision or some breach of discipline came up. Recently, he has tried to become more of a friend or "Dad," but I am too independent and unemotional, and the result is always a miserable failure.

And still another presents the following description of his father:

> Some of the ways in which he treats my mother . . . suggest to me that there is something radically wrong with his way of treating loved ones. . . . [He] is quiet and moody . . . he had little to do with me throughout childhood, but despite his coldness he is unusually devoted to his children.

It would be a mistake to infer simply that these young men despise their fathers. In the descriptions quoted, most of them retain some understanding of what they see as their fathers' weakness, inability to express themselves, of their loneliness, and even of their love. One writes:

> I loved my father, though with the restraint and inhibition that arises, I think, from his having been away from home, and, more important, from his genuine inability to be relaxed and affectionate in our company. He doesn't love children, and whatever love he has for anyone is denied free expression, which is almost to say that it might as well not exist at all, at least to someone as spontaneous as my mother.

The main themes of all these descriptions are related terms like "unable to express himself," "withdrawn," "cold"—and yet at the same time these subjects sense (or perhaps wishfully imagine) some lost part of their fathers which wants to express itself, some vestige of the idealistic youths they imagine their fathers once were.

One way of putting the difference between the way the alienated feel about their mothers and their fathers is to note that their mothers' frustrations are seen as *imposed from without* (usually by marriage), and consequently their mothers are *not blamed* for the potentials they have sacrificed; their fathers, on the other hand, are seen to have *freely chosen or at least accepted* their lot in life (often because of their own weakness and the pressures of domesticity), so that they are *held responsible* for their failings—no matter how much these failings may arouse compassion along with scorn in their sons.

Most of these students are quite aware where their primary sympathy lies, and say as much:

> I respect my mother more than my father. I resemble my father physically, my mother temperamentally.

Another says:

My basic attitudes are more shared with my mother than with my father . . . I'm afraid that my father and I are very far apart in ideology, and a break is bound to come in a few years.

And yet about neither parent, nor their marriage, are most of these young men truly enthusiastic.

One writes:

I do not respect them. I feel they have submissively adopted the ideals which their success has forced upon them. . . . The only thing my parents have in common is their intelligence. My mother was a humanist, my father a scientist. My mother loved people, my father hated them for their weakness. . . .

And another, who has earlier contrasted his mother's artistic sensitivity and feeling with his father's insensitivity, summarizes nonetheless:

I like my parents equally well, which is really not a great deal. . . . My father, though he seems just as intelligent as my mother, is her opposite in temperament, and it's surprising that they get along so well with each other.

Psychologically, then, the young man who describes his family situation in early life as "a father far away and a mother close at hand" summarizes for most of the rest.

## Themes of early life

Many of the events in the early lives of the alienated differ but little from those of their classmates. They tell, like Inburn, of the houses where they lived as children, of playmates and early school recollections, of academic successes. But as a group, they emphasize certain themes and omit others, which permits us to say that they at least *recall* a somewhat different childhood than their less alienated contemporaries. Once again, we cannot be sure to what extent what they now recall gives us a true picture of their early lives and to what extent it is a reconstruction in the past of themes of the present: much of distant memory is determined not only by the actual events of the past but by the pressing needs of the moment. Thus, what they choose to recount of their early lives most probably combines actual event and later significance: they remember those events which symbolize, illustrate, and epitomize themes of enduring significance in their later lives.

Chronologically the first, and psychologically one of the foremost, of these themes is that of what psychoanalysts call "orality" —that is, the theme of consuming, being nurtured, eating, being cared for—and of the problems attendant on an "incorporative" relationship to one's environment. What unifies all these themes is that the subject remains relatively passive (like an infant being fed), and receives or seeks to receive his sustenance without any effort on his part, as a gift or gratuity (like food put before him on the table). Oral references are much more frequent in the autobiographies of the alienated than in those of most college students. For one, the first memories of these students—memories which are often of great thematic significance in an individual's life—often have to do explicitly with food. Some mention food aversions, some mention intestinal upsets, some mention feeding problems, and one even surmises that his voracious nursing produced breast cancer in his mother and required the removal of one of her breasts. Read symbolically, these memories emphasize the difficulties in an incorporative relationship more than the joys to be gained from one: few recall blissful moments of a full stomach, but many recall the pangs of gastritis.

A second related theme in these autobiographies is the predominance of women in early recollections. Recall here Inburn's assertion that his first playmate was a girl his age. Others describe a similar world without men, where mother, sisters, aunts, girl playmates, grandmothers, mothers' friends, and women teachers predominate, and where fathers, brothers, boy friends, and other males are almost completely absent. They recall happy or unhappy adventures with their mothers, but rarely with their fathers; their playmates as small children—or at least those they now choose to recall—appear to have been largely girls. In most cases, other information tells us that their fathers were often present throughout large periods of early childhood; but they are seldom mentioned. To be sure, most middle-class American boys grow up in a world in which women predominate as mothers or as teachers; but other non-alienated young men now *talk* about their childhood memories of their fathers, while these young men do not. Psychologically, this predominance of women is related to the "oral" themes mentioned: women are those who provide for small children without asking return, who nurture and cherish without seeking reward, whereas it is men who more often push to achievement and independence. The preponderance of women suggests again the importance to these youths as children of a relatively passive, dependent, incorporating role with nurturing women.

Related to this theme are more specific recollections of happy times alone with mother. Inburn's description of his four-year idyl with his mother, of their "more than a mother-and-only-child" relationship, is the most dramatic of these recollections; but others recount similar times albeit of shorter duration and intensity. One speaks of a happy vacation on Cape Cod with his mother when his father was away; others speak of adventures with their mothers. It is possible that our subjects' fathers were along on these expeditions, but if they were, the subjects do not mention it: Mother's presence made the difference. Again, these memories point to an unusually intense attachment of mother and son.

Of brothers and sisters, our subjects say relatively little. Inburn, an only child, responds "Sibling schmibling" when asked about brothers and sisters, and the rest might have answered the same. Three-quarters of the alienated students were only children like Inburn or else eldest sons (not an altogether surprising proportion, given the relative smallness of their middle-class, late-depression families), so in few cases were there older brothers with whom to compete for the role of most privileged male child. And even those with older brothers usually give little sign of strong rivalry. One writes of his brother, "He was maddeningly jealous as my parents favored me," and in all other cases, it appears that our subject was either the eldest or the favored male child in the family. This does not mean, of course, that these young men could have avoided competing with their brothers and sisters, but compared to non-alienated students they mention sibling rivalry little, and there is no reason to reject the inference that it was relatively unimportant. The central relationships discussed are between mother and son; beside Mother, other family members fade into insignificance.

Their recollections of school are almost invariably pleasant. Like most students in the college, perhaps even more than most, the alienated usually liked school, got along relatively well with their women schoolteachers, and did well, though rarely extraordinarily well. From an early age, they read a great deal, did their homework with relative ease, and soon found that their intellectual abilities enabled them to excel. This is, of course, commonplace for students at any selective college; what is more unusual is that these alienated students concentrated almost exclusively on their intellectual accomplishments as children. They rarely "ran with the gang" like their unalienated classmates. Occasionally, they mention their "lack of interest" in the gang life of their school classmates, or they emphasize that some minor disability (e.g., wearing glasses) made it "impossible" for them to play baseball, soccer, football, capture the flag, or whatever else their more athletic classmates were doing. But more often, they simply do not mention activities with other children, and it is only by comparing their autobiographies with those of other students that we realize the omission of this crucial element in the growing up of Americans. We cannot know for sure how they felt at the time about "not belonging" with the gang; but it would be consistent with what we know of them if we guessed that they did not mind greatly. Phrases like "a little shy," "retiring," "not gregarious" frequently crop up in their descriptions of themselves as children, which would imply that they were somewhat homebound and perhaps overly tied to their mothers, and that they really preferred (or thought they preferred) going home to read or play alone after school.

We might have anticipated that these intellectually rebellious and alienated young men would have been rebels as children, troublemakers at school, constantly at odds with the authorities, quarreling with their parents, hellions who ran with the gang. But the composite picture which emerges is quite different. Like Inburn, they were relatively solitary children, quite intellectual from an early age, boys who played largely alone or within their families, and certainly not troublemakers. Those few who tell of youthful misdeeds do so with such obvious pride that one suspects these recollections are more motivated by present alienation than by typical past events. The intellectuality of these youths even as children is especially important, for it was instead of, rather than in addition to, the gang activities which are most typical of young boys in our culture. From early in their school years, they must have learned to deal with life primarily with their minds, to use their imaginations rather than their fists to deal with their tensions, and to cultivate outlooks which could bear fruit in solitude. Like Inburn, they may have felt estranged at times and moody, but their moodiness was not "acted out," and remained "well within" themselves. This orientation toward ideas rather than action, toward inner solutions, persists into their adulthood.

## Adolescence and alienation

The early adolescences of alienated young men were marked by unusual turmoil. The advent of adult sexuality was not easy for them; nor did they effortlessly accept the sometimes gradual and sometimes sudden change in their parents' responses toward them. The forms this turmoil took were varied and diverse; but what distinguishes the alienated from others is that there are so *many* symptoms of inner upheaval.

Some of these young men responded to adolescence with an extreme asceticism which is relatively uncommon among American adolescents, though more familiar in Europe. One young man describes his stringent efforts to lose weight, to build himself up physically, to discipline his body, to prolong the intervals between urinating, to be helpful around the house, and to stop masturbating. Others talk of an intensified interest in books and ideas, with which they attempted to channel the flood of unfamiliar feelings. Others mention increased moodiness and a tendency to brood and introspect. Some began to do even better than before in their schoolwork, and rose to positions of intellectual predominance among their classmates, most of whom had become even more involved in athletics.

A small number of the alienated also began at this time a series of semi-delinquent escapades which eventually got them into trouble with the school or local authorities, to say nothing of their parents. One young man, whose father was president of the local school board, broke into an abandoned house and was arrested, much to the embarrassment of his father, to whom the police released him. Another tells of excessive drinking and speeding, and this time stresses his mother's reaction to his misbehavior. In such descriptions, the focal point is usually the parents' reaction rather than the misdeed itself, and a good part of the motivation for such delinquencies must have been to create embarrassment in these parents and to demonstrate tangibly the subject's emancipation from their control. In other young men with fewer intellectual resources and families of less social standing, the same misdeeds might have marked the beginning of a delinquent career; but these subjects had parents with a position in the community who could "bail them out" and prevent the severe public punishment that might have confirmed them in delinquency. Even more important, they soon learned that there were other, more effective ways of demonstrating their freedom from parental influence by using their intellectual talents.

Sexuality itself was an especially disturbing fact of life to these young men. Most had not been adequately prepared for its advent by their parents' instruction nor, more importantly, by their parents' implicit attitudes towards the physical and sexual; and for almost all, sex produced considerable guilt over masturbation, sexual fantasies, and illicit sexual activities. A few report conscious incestuous fantasies and/or dreams involving their mothers or sisters, which were immensely disturbing; and one had "sexual relations" with his younger sister for a few months. Others were preoccupied with invariably unsuccessful attempts to stop masturbating, whose failure left them with a weakened sense of their own capacity for self-control. A few began in their mid-teens to have active sexual relations with girls, but these experiences were rarely satisfactory, and usually left them feeling guilty or afraid. None of these facts, taken singly, is remarkable or even indicative of any unusual disturbance in our culture, where adolescence is more often upsetting than not. But what is remarkable is the amount of concern in these subjects, and the absence of any positive experiences which might have offset early fears and worries. Inburn is extreme when he lists only "anxiety, shame, and disgust" as his feelings about sex, but something of the same predominance of negative and anxious feelings exists in many other alienated subjects.

The sexual fantasies of the alienated both in early adolescence and later, as college students, also have a characteristic quality, one which recalls the emphasis on "orality" in early childhood. In their erotic fantasies, as in their actual sexual behavior, these young men have a strong predilection for situations in which they do not have to take the initiative, in which gratification comes to them without any effort on their part. One writes, "My major sexual fantasy consists in girls just coming to me with no effort on my part and seducing me." Others emphasize their "passivity" and lack of "aggressiveness" with girls:

When I go with a girl I am overly passive and this is the usual reason for the break between us which always seems to come.

Another notes:

If intercourse must result because of aggressive foreplay on the part of the boy, it is something I am incapable of doing.

And still another says, in the same vein:

My ideal partner would be an aggressive woman who would take the initiative in beginning preliminary activities to a certain extent.

I have earlier noted that as college students, the alienated go out with girls neither more nor less than any other group at college, and their amount of overt sexual experience in adolescence does not differ from the usual. What does differ, as seen in these quotations, is the unwillingness of these students to take the aggressive and initiating role nominally expected of men in our society: they prefer being seduced to conquering aggressively, and they seek out situations and relationships where this will occur. One writes:

I made a great deal of love to a woman twice my age about a year ago; she too disgusts me. . . . It seems to me that one of the most satisfactory things about the sex act is the tranquillity, the oblivion, that follows, and for this reason I am apt to turn my thoughts to the aftermath. . . .

Here the subject implies his own passivity with an older woman, the initiator of the affair, and enjoys not the sex act itself, but the total oblivion of its aftermath. Another expression of the same trend is seen in two young men who report disturbingly erotic feelings about small girls—where, again, adult sexuality would not be required—and two others, both with active heterosexual lives, who report occasional isolated homosexual episodes in college.

All of this may help explain why adolescence was a time of such turmoil for these young men, and why, even as young adults and despite considerable sexual experience, so few of them have made any kind of peace with their sexual natures. Our culture defines the male sex role as active and initiating, and these young men find passivity and "being done to" far more satisfactory than active "making." To be pushed by increasing age, changing physiology, and social expectations into a role which they are not only inwardly unprepared for but emotionally opposed to, is more than enough to explain their enduring discomfort.


## The release of alienation

We have so far found little mention of these students' common characteristic in college, their alienation. In their accounts of their lives until the age of about fifteen, one finds no wholesale repudiation of American culture. In middle adolescence, however, they report the freeing of their potential to become alienated, although there is no common set of events which makes the potential manifest. Inburn's case illustrates one pattern, in which his encounter with an extremely alienated classmate provided a dramatic catalyst for his pent-up and well-contained potential. Recall his description:

> His cynicism infected me. . . . First of all we turned everybody's religion upside down and we shouted. . . . That went by the board and we began on our contemporaries and on our society. We attacked everything, every person, every institution, with a bitter tooth. Our long secret conversations were rank with contempt. We were full of a magnificent disdain, and we fed it with all the knowledge we could get. . . .

No other subject found as clear a catalyst as Inburn's friend, but others followed a similar pattern on their own. Most often, the beginnings of alienation were gradual and without any apparent precipitating factor. One student writes:

> In high school, I became tired of most everything. Religion seemed nonsensical, and I stopped going to church. Among my not-so-honorable activities were: I first had sexual intercourse with a girl, I began to drink heavily, and I attempted suicide (not really intending to succeed). . . . During my senior year, I led a thoroughly profligate life.

Another dates the beginning of his "cosmopolitan feeling" to early high school:

> I began to feel cosmopolitan: I began to feel above these kids. I had my friends in St. Louis and my friends in New York; and these kids in high school were miserable little rustics, that's all. So I felt really removed. I began piling up books and making a big show of it, as well as just reading them. I never ceased spitting on the television set, and . . . I told them that if I had the chance I would spit on the flag. . . . And at each step I felt myself more alienated, more distinguished, in some ways, than the people I went to school with and fooled around with.

A subject who spent a year studying at an English secondary school attributes part of his feeling about America to this:

> I can't say that I dislike the American man but yet I would condemn him, simply because his humanity is atrophied. . . . I mean after England and my experience there, the American man somehow repulses me as silly if nothing else.

The frequent contrast between growing alienation and positions of school leadership often led to conflicts with school authorities, as well as a felt gap between public appearance and real self. Inburn writes, for example:

> I was elected editor [of the school paper] and Hal was feature editor. We ruined it in three months. We didn't meet deadlines, we wrote outrageous feature stories; we instilled subtle cynicism (sometimes not so subtle) into everything we wrote; we took the money for one issue and went out and got drunk with it. . . .

Another subject writes in a similar vein:

> [Toward the end of high school] I decided that it was about time for me to stop playing the outsider, and I'd play the game of being the insider. So I became head of organizations, and . . . we organized a little political party, and I became president of the school and editor of the newspaper and all kinds of things that made me look—

nobody really believed it—like a real good, solid high-school citizen.
. . . I always felt superior to this. I felt different from it. I supposed
it was a tremendous joke, and I would always play with the idea of
fooling people, of having at assembly somebody who wouldn't, you
know, play along and say nice things. . . . We were having a little
celebration in the school cafeteria, complete with wine. Well, wine's
illegal. I was the cause of it, and so . . . they threw me out of
school.

Another emphasizes his feelings of presenting a false façade to the
world:

I was again elected class president, though by this time I recognized it as a farcical honor. I used to think that if my classmates
really knew what a despicable creature I was they would never consider me for honors. . . . Apparently my junior-year classmates
were too stupid to realize what I was, for in the spring I was
awarded a medal which said that I best typified the boy in my class
who has the highest scholastic record, the best character (!) etc.
. . . There are other [honors] of which I am absolutely ashamed
—when I can stop laughing.

The overt rejection of American culture, then, developed late in
these young men, and was not a reflection of values held in their
homes but a reaction *against* these values and those of school and
community. To a man, they disliked whatever they sensed as the
prevailing values of their schools, whether it was the making of
"Christian gentlemen" in the case of one Eastern prep school, or
the informal cultivation of the "good guy" in the case of many high
schools. Though they often did very well in terms of these values
and outwardly conformed to them, inwardly they rebelled; and this
contrast between behavioral conformity and growing ideological rejection in turn led to increasing feelings of estrangement from the
majority of their fellows who took them at face value. Then, too,
the fact that alienation as an ideology developed in isolation, or at
most with one alienated friend, probably helped make it more
thorough-going, more pervasive, less tempered by argument and
confrontation with less alienated outlooks. In this respect, the alien-

ated are consistent with their past, with their lifelong tendency to work out their problems in private and intellectual terms, leaving active involvements with the outer world to others.

I have tried here to give a composite picture of what the alienated tell us of their families and their past, emphasizing those strands they share with each other though not to the same extent with other students their age. Such a picture of the outward events and settings of an individual's life is a prerequisite for any understanding of his development, since it provides the context, a milieu within which he grew and changed. But it is not enough: as important as these events (and perhaps more important in tracing psychic development) are the ways these events reverberated on the individual, the way he unconsciously perceived them, the psychological residues they left, the ways fragments from the past remain actual and active in the present. Before we can attempt a more general reconstruction of the development of alienation we must turn to information about the inner development of these young men.

# 6     The victor who lost

Long before the advent of psychology as a discipline, intuitive men and women have made inferences about each other on the basis of fantasy, imputing motives, wishes, and needs to others which these others were loath to admit. This process is not itself mysterious, though it has been systematized by psychology in the past half-century and is therefore no longer the special prerogative of the intuitive. But even without a knowledge of psychology or a vocabulary to express our perceptions and inferences, most of us are sometimes aware of fondness or hostility in others of which these others remain adamantly ignorant; and no special knowledge of dream symbolism was required for men to intuit that dreams were somehow portentous or expressive—though we have recently learned more about how and what they portend or express. A man who continually tells gloomy stories is, in the absence of contrary evidence, rightly assumed to be gloomy, no matter how much he may deny it; a man whose conversation always points a moral is correctly said to be concerned with moral problems, even should he publicly maintain that he is above such considerations. We are all amateur psychologists, for we must, in the process of growing up, learn to make inferences about others.

The principles a psychologist uses in making interpretations about the less conscious sides of personality are not fundamentally different from those used in everyday life. What differ are his systematic techniques for collecting information upon which to base such inferences, his systematic training in the principles by which such "interpretations" can be made, and his systematic knowledge of a special body of theory and fact which attunes him to what is most relevant, important, and indicative in the material he surveys. Psychoanalysis is of course the best-known technique for gathering information, making interpretations, and pointing out significances. But as a research technique, psychoanalysis has major limitations, related both to the vast amount of time it takes and to the requirement that its subjects accept the role of patients. As a result, other techniques more suited to research have developed for studying unconscious motivations.

One such technique is the encouragement and study of fantasy in what are usually called "projective tests." Among these is the test used with these alienated subjects, the Thematic Apperception Test (T.A.T.). The T.A.T. consists of twenty cards, each of which has a somewhat ambiguous picture on it. The subject is asked to make up an imaginative story about each picture, a tale with a beginning, a middle, and an ending; the psychologist administering the test occasionally asks for more information or encourages the subject to be as imaginative and "free" as possible. In these studies of alienated subjects, each student lay on a couch in a semi-darkened room, facing away from the psychologist who handed him the cards; in this situation, imagination tends to be richer and fuller than in a face-to-face setting. The result of the testing is twenty impromptu stories told to the ambiguous pictures, and these elicited fantasies provide a rich basis for inferences about the personality of the subject.

The principles by which such interpretations are made are fairly straightforward. Obviously, no single story can alone be the basis for valid conclusions: only when the same themes or similar figures reappear in several stories and make sense in context can one conclude that they indicate something important about the subject. One assumes that recurring characters in the stories express something about the subject's perceptions of the world around him, and that the recurring themes of his plots reveal the fundamental human situations which have been and continue to be of greatest importance to him. With young adults like the subjects studied here, one generally assumes, for example, that the characteristics ascribed to older women are related to his perceptions of his mother; and the central character or hero is usually a portrayal of some aspect of himself. And finally, one attempts to integrate inferences based on the T.A.T. with all other information available, whether it be studies of overt behavior, autobiographical information, other tests, or interviews. Consequently, in seeking the experiential referents of the stories told, one must use all one knows not only of psychological theories, but also of the facts of the narrator's life.

When studying a *group* of individuals like these alienated subjects, an additional step is required—namely, an effort to separate whatever, if anything, these subjects have in common from whatever is idiosyncratic and unique in each. Thus, in addition to careful studies of each individual (like that of Inburn), one looks for those themes that recur in most or all alienated subjects—those views of men, women, themselves, and human relations that appear consistently in their fantasies but not in those of the unalienated. Here, too, there is an imperative continually to relate common themes of fantasy to common themes of life history, trying at each step to understand how the milieu of these subjects affected their fantasies and how these fantasies in turn influenced the way they perceived and reacted to their milieu.

With these general principles in mind, we can now consider the fantasies of the alienated, attempting to trace through them the psychological development of these subjects.

## Lost Eden and the Serpent

Some fantasies have a special quality, a primitiveness, a strangeness, and an archetypal mood which sharply distinguishes them from more mundane imaginations. The experienced clinician recognizes such fantasies intuitively as somehow fundamental, central, and early in the life of the individual; and even the layman without clinical experience can usually sense the power, primitiveness, or archaic quality in these images and themes. If we try to analyze how it is we sense that these fantasies are different from others, we find that the subject himself often indirectly tells us so: he struggles for words in attempting to describe the images before him; he repeatedly uses analogies or imagery which suggest that his fantasy is at some level ineffable; he stresses that things "appear" this or that way, that it is "as if" something were the case, that the objects in his narrative "seem" to have this or that quality. In all of this, he suggests that he is operating at a level where things are not necessarily what they seem, where appearances and realities may be incongruent, and above all, at a level where he has the greatest difficulty in finding words to communicate what he feels. At other times, we recognize such primitive fantasies because they have a magical quality (often concealed in a humorous story), because things shift and change from one thing into another, because realistically impossible events are said to occur, and because the characters appear like the heros and villains of fairy tales rather than the people we know in our adult lives. Or again, other stories sound like ghost stories, filled with strange voices, mysterious presences, and objects that have indescribable claims on people.

Descriptively, what unites such fantasies is that they resemble those of small children; developmentally, what unites them is their origin in early childhood, often before experience is organized in adult verbal categories, and certainly before clear notions of causality and of the linkages between appearance and what we call adult reality are forged. When as adults we recall our childhoods vividly, it is usually via smells, tastes, emotions, and tactile feelings which often defy full verbal descriptions; or again, we may dimly re-experience a vague sense of dread or joy which we cannot communicate in our adult language. The child, after all, learns language tenuously and slowly, and for many years can adequately express only a small part of his feelings in words: indeed, there is good reason to believe that much of our verbal expressiveness as adults is purchased at the price of simply stopping having (or what is almost the same, stopping noticing) the experiences that we could never find words for. Thus when a young adult like any of these subjects, lying on a couch in a darkened room and telling stories about vague and amorphous pictures, has some fantasy or theme from his early life struck by the testing situation, he will often be unable to say precisely what it is he feels, and will grope for words, use analogies, tell fairy tales or ghost stories in the effort to communicate something of what has been evoked in him.

The extent to which young adults tell stories which have this archaic quality varies enormously. At one extreme are those youths, usually non-alienated, all of whose stories are realistic, descriptive, and often as proper and conventional in theme and moral as any tale from a woman's magazine. At the other extreme are these alienated subjects, who tell story after story with the same weird and compelling strangeness. Such archaic themes can mean very different things about an individual, depending on whether they appear to control him or whether he, as narrator, can control *them* in the interests of a finished and coherent tale. But whatever they show about the strength or weakness of the controlling ego, the presence of such themes indicate that he is, for better or worse, unusually open to that deepest stratum of personality wherein these images reside, and in all probability, again for better or worse, unusually affected as an adult by these archetypal themes and figures.

The first and deepest image in the psyche is that of the mother, and in their accounts of their lives, alienated young men have already suggested that their early relationships with their mothers were, and remain, of great importance to them. In their emphasis on the many difficulties they associate with an "oral" relationship—the food aversions, stomach upsets, and feeding problems—they also hint that they see this relationship as somehow troubled. In their fantasies, they confirm and amplify these themes, picturing an infantile Eden which has been lost, yet to which they unconsciously long to return.

The theme of an idyllic environment, carefree and bountiful, appears in a number of stories, sometimes involving direct references to Mother, sometimes stressing the gratuitous nature of all satisfaction. One such story, involving the mother directly, includes the following passage:

> The little boy is in his mother's arms. . . . She has picked him up and comforted him, and he loves this very much—how comforting, . . . how wonderful this mother kind of thing is, how wonderful . . . she loves him and she's there to take care of him. . . . He's always remembered the rest of his life how comforting it was to sit in his mother's arms. . . .

Or recall Inburn's happy idyl on Noah's Ark:

> . . . lighthearted scene . . . amusing and pleasant . . . Noah's Ark. . . . homey portholes with curtains. There are two comical-looking animals, in a pair of course, looking out . . . the female animal has come around and has come into the male animal's room so they can be together and look out of the window together . . . they just keep sailing. They don't land anywhere. The water never recedes, that's the most pleasant part about it.

And still others tell of bountiful harvest feasts among carefree workmen, emphasizing the unlimited plenty of food, and the fact that it is completely free.

But as in the autobiographies of these youths, references to idyllic and gratuitous plenty are less frequent than suggestions of the traumatic ending of such pleasures. Such stories characteristically involve separation from the source of supply, followed by starvation. One such story is again very direct in its reference to the young man's parents. The hero has been abroad, and returns sick to his parents:

> He looks very weak as though he hadn't been eating very much. . . . The mother was very concerned and she began to feed him as much as she could. [The boy nonetheless sickens and dies] . . . and the parents feel very bad for the rest of their lives, naturally, be-

cause this was their only son and they should have taken better care of him.

This story is reminiscent of a childhood fantasy of how sorry the parents will be if they do not take good care of their son. But most other stories with similar themes are less direct. One, for example, tells of a group of Arctic explorers:

> This group of men . . . have been shut off for several weeks from their supply sources. Their food is running quite low. . . . They're going slightly bats. . . . The food will run lower and lower . . . until all that's left is one man who now, a young fellow . . . has gone completely mad.

Other comparable tales suggest equally dramatic demises for the heroes, sometimes madness, sometimes starvation, sometimes accidental death. They share not only a common concern with separation from the source of limitless supply, but a common moral that he who becomes separated perishes in one way or another. Psychologically, they suggest that among the worst things that can happen to a young man is to lose his source of total and unconditional love, that the result is a kind of psychological death.

Given this view, a number of other stories follow with considerable unconscious logic—these are recurrent stories about "possessed" heroes seeking to make their way *back* to what they have lost. Often this early lost condition is symbolized by enveloping water, as in Inburn's tale of the descending submarine in the warm, enveloping water:

> . . . a sea, the sea, with nothing on the surface, with no continents to go back to. . . . This is the kind of extended moment which he wouldn't mind going on with forever—which he probably will, just continuing down into the dark water. . . .

Another subject expresses a kind of Hart Crane fantasy with this tale of a young man standing on a boat deck during a violent storm:

Half asleep, and being beaten by the rain and whatnot, standing there looking he begins to see a light in the sea . . . the light seemed warm and friendly in comparison to the storm; and the sea and the sound seemed to be calling to him, and he steps over the rail and goes into the sea in a state of trance and is drowned.

The mysterious past is sometimes symbolized, as in this story, by a calling voice which lures the hero to his death, a death which is somehow sweet nonetheless. In another such story, the hero is an artist, and the beckoning medium is not water, but air:

He attempts . . . somehow to find some kind of communication with the mysterious . . . he feels his soul swoon inside of him. He steps from his bed and he feels somehow as though someone is calling him, and he is happy at last because he has seemed to reach something. He feels almost like perhaps Icarus must have felt; he feels as though he can fly, and so he walks to the window . . . , and he steps out and he falls.

Another common variant on this same theme is the crazed effort to find a long lost dead one, almost always a woman. One young man makes his hero an old fisherman who sails his boat into the sea, into the place where a black gull, after whom his lost childhood sweetheart was named, has dived into the water. Others frequently tell of heroes who attempt to dig up the graves of their lost wives. In one, the hero is an old man who has been a recluse since his wife's death:

There are no lights on in his house. . . . They go in and find that he's not there. . . . Then, they, knowing that he constantly visited the graveyard, go up that way to see if they can find any clue to where he has gone. They find his body half submerged on top of her grave . . . as if he were trying to crawl into it. . . . He has buried himself on top of his wife's grave.

Another subject's hero, a German theologian, dreams he finds the graves of the "lost gods" of an earlier age:

He spends the rest of his time poring over more commentaries, . . . trying to find the source of his dream. But he didn't find them . . . his dream, as a consequence, is gone completely out of the sphere of ordinary experience.

Still other stories tell of amnesic heroes who search to recover lost identities, heroes blind from an early age who cannot forget their first visual memories, or actor heroes who become obsessed with the role of crying like children for their mothers and have "lost any sense of self." These stories are a catalogue of obsessions with the past: undertakers enamored of their female subjects, ghoulish grave robbers, insane and demented heroes passionately obsessed with the recovery of that which has been lost, detectives searching for lost people, lovers mourning for dead ones. All these stories point to an unconscious obsession with a lost relationship with the early mother, an inability to escape the pull of this dim memory, a continuing quest for some equivalent or substitute. The very primitiveness and vagueness of these stories, the continual presence of heroes who are said to be crazed, possessed, and insane, the recurrence of terms like "mysterious," "strange," "vague presence," and "weird," all point to the developmental earliness of their referents, to an era when all objects and people must have had something of the same strange, mysterious, uncomprehensible quality on which our adult experiences of the "uncanny" are ultimately based.

Every Eden has its serpent, and among the stories of these sophisticated and literate young men we find references to prehistoric monsters, powerful and unassailable male figures which have much of the same archaic and "weird" quality as do most of the foregoing stories. One student speaks explicitly of a serpent in a nightmarish and explicitly prehistoric tale: a caveman, swimming in a lake, hits a moose-like creature he finds in the water:

Normally . . . such a blow was sufficient to kill this mooselike animal. But this time it wasn't, and the animal caught hold of the boat with his huge antlers and tossed . . . the caveman . . . into the water. . . . The moose caught up with him and gave him a tremendous kick with one of its legs. [The caveman sinks, only to meet a sea-serpent "immense, perhaps forty feet long," which eventually traps him in a cave] . . . he could never cope with this thing in such a narrow space as the cave. And his fears were confirmed as the great serpent entered the nearly filled cavern and he strangled the caveman and killed him.

Another subject tells of a dragon which destroys the village's food supply by eating its crops, and when pursued, turns on its assailants and kills them to a man; another young man describes two strange buffalo-like creatures who fight to the death for the possession of food. (Note the repetitive concern with food and supplies.)

Others of these dangerous creatures are human beings described as strange and unreal. In one story, the revolutionist hero is assigned to kill the head of the counter-revolutionary forces; he comes upon him sleeping:

> He was big, he was large. . . . He swelled, he seemed to push out against the darkness. . . . He couldn't kill him. The man was too large. He couldn't possibly kill him, it would be impossible. . . . He was so large. . . .

Here the recurring emphasis on the bigness, the largeness, of the hero, the fact that he "seemed to" push out against the darkness gives the story an eerie quality.

Stories like these would raise the hackles of a pre-school child, but they are very unusual in college students. The primitiveness of the dangerous male characters and the implication of weirdness, strangeness, and past-ness of the action suggest that these archaic male figures correspond with an infantile image of the father as a powerful, destructive, food-and-supply-destroying assailant. The dragons and murderers portrayed in these stories are the same figures we meet in fairy tales, in myths, and in countless nightmares of small children (especially of boys who are unusually attached to their mothers and who resent their fathers): and like the image of an all-embracing maternal presence, they correspond with one side of the perception of parents by small children in our culture.

We must therefore resist any temptation to reconstruct a picture of our subject's *real* parents from these archaic images, or take them as representations of real individuals whose reflection can be found in the weird forms of these lost loves and invincible dragons. Such archaic fantasies as these exist in us all as children, and our question should not be where they originate, but why they persist into adulthood—why these figures, which in most young men disappear or become reconciled with other more "realistic" images, here remain in their infantile form and retain their immense power or awesome fearfulness. To answer this question, we must turn to other stories which revolve around later family rivalries.

## Young Oedipus and his Pyrrhic victory

Most observers of childhood behavior have come to take for granted that children go through a period of intensified rivalry for their parents' affections in early childhood. For a boy, this period begins when he becomes aware that he is a boy and that this means he is in some respects like his father and unlike his mother, and when his horizons widen enough to perceive that a special and privileged relationship exists between his parents in which he (as a child) is allowed little part. Some psychologists and psychiatrists place greatest emphasis on the broadly sexual content of these rivalries; others stress struggles for affection and exclusive attention; and others see issues of dependency and independence as the crux of the conflict. But all would usually agree that all these issues— childhood sexuality, exclusive affection, attention, dependence, and independence—can and usually do become involved in a small boy's feelings about his parents.

In oversimplified essence, these often fierce competitions and rivalries involve the child's painfully learning his "place" in the family: in the case of a boy, what it means is that he is a boy and not a girl; and in the case of both boys and girls, that because they are children and not parents, their parents have special rights and privileges with each other and over their children. Boys, on realizing that they are male like their fathers, often challenge their fathers' special privileges with their mothers, only gradually learning that they must grow up before they can claim exclusive possession of a member of the opposite sex. Furthermore, at about this stage in life, a child is likely to be torn between his own desires to remain an infant, passive and dependent on his mother, and his equally strong needs for independence and autonomy. Fathers are often, in our society, those who most vigorously push their sons towards "manly" independence, discouraging "babyish" and mother-dependent behavior, encouraging both wife and son to make the latter "stand on his own two feet." Such pressure is in fact pressure against the boy's infantile attachment to his mother, and is usually perceived as such by the boy, resulting in even more intense resentment of the father who seeks to attenuate the ties between mother and son. The resulting rivalries, jealousies, competitions (and the less-discussed but equally important loves, affiliations, and identifications) are usually lumped together under the name of the Oedipus complex.

We also know a good deal about how these normal conflicts of growing up are best resolved in our society. Ideally, the son comes to accept with relative equanimity his position both as a child in a family of adults and as a male in a family (and world) of two sexes. He little by little turns away from his mother toward his father, seeking to emulate those qualities that make his father admirable in his mother's eyes and which may therefore "rub off" on him to make him admirable; he very gradually abandons his dependence on his mother, accepting her more and more as merely one supporting and comforting person among others, and no longer the be-all and end-all of life. Once these difficult and basic lessons about gender and generation are learned, children in our society usually enter a period of greater tranquillity, which coincides with the early school years; and their new-found calm allows them to turn their full energies away from a now-stabilized and accepted position in the family toward the acquisition of those complex skills required for full membership in our society.

If all goes relatively well within the family, Oedipal conflicts are forgotten or, put more precisely, they are gradually dissolved into relatively clear conceptions of sex role and generational position. As a result, many adults find the violent feelings of early family rivalries theoretically plausible but difficult to recall concretely. Both the intensity of these original feelings and the amount of energy and time required to learn the lessons of family life and position mean that once these lessons are learned, the original conflicts are usually repressed and can be resuscitated only by special techniques like psychoanalysis. We see this repression in the fantasies of most non-alienated college students, who are usually at great pains to point out that rivalries between men are only apparent and easily resolved. T.A.T. cards which might suggest two men in conflict over a woman evoke strong denial that any such conflict could exist, or, if it exists, long endure. These young men have learned their early familial lessons well, have transformed open rivalry into friendly cooperation or mild, socially acceptable competition; stimuli that might elicit traces of former rivalries evoke polite yet firm denial.

This picture of the "typical" course and resolution of familial rivalries is not, however, a description of what alienated students appear to have undergone. Far from denying rivalry between men, they take it for granted, importing it into stories where the picture does not suggest it. Far from avoiding competition between two men for a woman, they see it everywhere, sometimes turning man-woman relationships or man-man relationships into competitive triangles. And far from abandoning their dependence on their mothers and turning towards admired fathers, they lust after their lost dependency and see potentially admirable men as underlyingly fraudulent or corrupt. These themes emerge repetitively, even monotonously, in the fantasies of alienated students. Most immediately striking is that so many stories are so overtly Oedipal, dealing so openly with a son's hostility to an older man who exploits his mother. For example, one young man, presented with a card showing a young man and an older woman, tells this melodramatic tale:

. . . the villain is going to foreclose the mortgage, and the old lady
is going to have to leave the property. She hasn't anywhere to go,
and no money. . . . The son . . . discovers that the villain has
been involved in crooked real estate dealings and that sort of thing,
and exposes him, and he's arrested, and they get their farm back.

Here the mere presence of a young man and an older woman is
enough to suggest a villain in the background, against whom the
son must defend the mother. Other stories tell of a youth whose
mistress is unfaithful to him (he kills her for it); a boss who propositions his employee's wife; a hero whose father mistreats his
mother, etc., etc. Heterosexual relationships are seen as inherently
triangular, involving two rivals for the affections of the same
woman. Even T.A.T. cards that depict two men together are sometimes seen to involve a conflict between the two men for a woman's
affections. The rivalries which most young men have resolved and
forgotten are here very close to the surface.

These conflicts have the same outcome in most stories, and it is
unexpected: the *younger* man usually wins. As in the melodrama
just cited, the younger man defeats the villain and protects his
mother. Again and again, the younger hero's aggression against his
rival is successful: the rival perishes, is exposed, is broken—
sometimes through the actions of the hero, sometimes by accident.
Consider this story, wherein the hero's boss has propositioned the
hero's wife just before a party:

[The employee] just goes completely wild, grabs the boss and
gives him a good swift punch in the mouth. The boss falls forward
. . . and falls on the cocktail glass, the long stem of which pierces
his chest and snuffs out his life. . . . He doesn't quite know what he
is doing, but he starts to return to his wife, does so in such a fashion
that he kills himself against a bridge abutment.

Here, largely by accident, the hero's rage destroys his rival, and
though the hero too succumbs, it is *not* because of the rival—a
point to which we will return. In another story, this time dealing

directly with father and son, the two have a "tremendous falling out":

> Arthur [the son] finally says, "Look, I hate your guts" . . . he saw that terrible look—finally all his father's pride broken down, this shell his father built. He felt that, in a sense, he had wounded him terribly. The next morning he . . . discovers that his father has had a stroke during the night—no reason for it. . . . He somehow has a feeling of responsibility. . . . His father won't die . . . [but] even when he returns, will be too proud to give in after what has been said. So that even though he didn't die, Arthur lost his father.

Here again, the hero's aggression is more effective than he consciously intends, and he destroys his father and their relationship forever. Again too, disaster befalls the hero (he loses his father), not because of his father's strength but because of his weakness.

Such stories might be interpreted as merely the statement of a wish on the subject's part that he had overcome his father in their struggle, a wish made stronger because the son in actual fact lost the struggle. But this interpretation fails: the son seldom portrays his father as a man strong enough to defend his rights or to vanquish his adversaries; furthermore, the son-hero almost never faces a human male adversary who does defeat him; and finally, when these heroes eventually meet their downfall, it is not at the hands of the father-figure, but by some extraneous force. The typical story involves, then, the hero's revolting, defeating his male adversary, and then being destroyed by some other force.

This theme is best seen in the surprising number of stories of political revolutionaries told by these apolitical students (and not to anywhere nearly the same extent by most other students). In one such story the youthful hero, Paul, one of a group of Communist intellectuals, assassinates the Minister of Internal Affairs:

> They will feel that they have done well and that the pressure is off, not realizing that the Minister has started a machine going

that no longer matters whether he heads it or not. Eventually Paul himself will be killed.

Here the assassination, though successful, is to no avail, and the hero-assassin himself is eventually killed. Another subject tells of a young Communist hero assigned to kill his own father, a "low-ranking civil official," who has found out information dangerous to the Party. The hero complies, only to be himself hunted down and killed by the Party. Another revolutionary is killed by his own men when he tries to restrain them from looting; another succeeds in his revolution only to see the revolutionary regime turn into a despotism worse than that which it replaced.

These stories of revolution are, paradoxically, cautionary tales. The revolutions and aggressions are almost invariably successful, but precisely *because of their success,* they are followed by some situation even worse than the one the hero sought to change. The implicit personal moral is "Don't try to revolt: I succeeded and look what happened to me." Less alienated students, in their rare tales of revolution, point different morals: revolutions fail because the forces they seek to overthrow are too powerful to be downed, or because the established order is really beneficent and well-intentioned. Such non-alienated fantasies suggest an acceptance of the strength and benignity of society and of the paternal presence that first epitomizes society to most American youngsters.

What do these alienated stories imply about the development of these young men? If we assume that they reflect indirectly the actual sequence of psychological events in these students' early lives, they imply that these subjects believe that they indeed succeeded in displacing, overthrowing, and replacing their prime rivals, but that their victory was Pyrrhic and that its sequel was an unanticipated disaster, a tyranny worse than that overthrown, a psychological equivalent to death. The full meaning of this unexpected and un-sought disaster can be inferred from the picture of older men and women in the fantasies of these young men.

## The real victor

Most children no doubt have at one time the same archaic conceptions of their parents we have seen in these subjects, and most young men in our society have passed through a period of intense rivalry within their families—indeed, in most of us, shadowy vestiges of these early images and conflicts persist in the deepest strata of our minds throughout life. But for the more fortunate, time and benign experience serve gradually to modify these archaic parents into more realistic ones, who retain less exaggerated versions of their qualities. The enveloping presence of the nurturing mother gives way gradually to a more realistically perceived woman who retains some of the same mothering qualities; the invincible and frightening male adversary shades gradually into a father who retains some of the strength and power of his predecessor. The archaic vision of the parents is not so much replaced or countered by these later conceptions as it is slowly *absorbed* in them, overlaid by them, gradually transmuted and transformed into progressively more and more realistic conceptions of the parents.

Once again, the development of these alienated young men departs from this ideal picture. They appear to have had little opportunity for a gradual modification of parental images, but to have abruptly discontinuous conceptions of early and later parents. This can be seen in their later more "realistic" images of both older women and older men. Women shift radically from being nurturing to being possessive, controlling, and destructive; men suddenly change from invincible monsters to broken, phony, and corrupted adults.

Virtually all alienated students manage somehow to suggest that women are active, possessive, and controlling, though the way they suggest it varies. Very often, women are seen as restraining men's sexuality or aggressiveness. In one story, the mother seeks to control her sons' dating:

She hopes to maintain a strong domineering relationship with respect to her sons' relationships. She only introduces her sons to those girls—of whom she approves . . . she tries to stop them from going on dates with young ladies. . . . [One of the sons is apprehended in serious conversation with a girl.] She gets very upset . . . after hearing the conversation [and] is coming into the room to cast the girl out of the home and take the son to task for disappointing his mother so.

Sometimes the same point is made with reference to a girl, as in the following story of a girl called Una whose aunt has brought her up to avoid boys. The aunt comes upon Una and a boy kissing:

She becomes furious, absolutely furious. Una is horrified that her aunt has broken in on her privacy like this. [The boy] is terribly embarrassed. . . . He leaves, of course, at that point. . . . Una does realize that [he] is well-meaning, has been good for her, but that it could never go on. . . .

In these stories, the mother or her surrogate stands between the hero and a sexual relationship. But in other tales, the woman is seen as preventing aggressive non-conformity. Consider the view of women and marriage contained in the following story of a young man who led a "wild life" before his marriage.

His fiancée made him promise . . . he'd settle down and get a permanent job somewhere. . . . So he got a job with a business company, but . . . he hated it. . . . They began to have small fights. . . . One day he comes home from work after . . . a particularly big fight the night before, and he finds her lying on the couch . . . he can't really feel any pulse . . . they pump her stomach. She lives. . . . [The husband reforms and works harder.]

In another story, the hero's mother tries to educate him to stay out of all the "roughhousing" that goes on; or recall Inburn's story of the mother who is "not quite like the cat that swallowed the canary but . . ."

One of the peculiar characteristics about such women is that they are portrayed as either right or victorious or both. These mothers, wives, and aunts *succeed* in blocking their charges from intimacy with the opposite sex; they manage to force reluctant men into conformist or unaggressive positions; and when their warnings are unheeded, it is usually to the hero's disadvantage, as in a story of a Kenya settler who wants to go fight the Mau Mau.

> Blanche, who is his wife, cautions him . . . she wants him almost any way. . . . She's asking him not to go because she has a strong feeling . . . she's going to lose him now, and he is going to leave now. . . . The Mau Maus have . . . been waiting . . . they kill him as he steps outside to get in the car.

In another story with a similar moral, the mother tries to make the son into a "menial" like his father:

> Jack wants to be an automobile mechanic. . . . His mother, however, would like him to follow in his father's footsteps: his father was a milkman. Although it may seem incredible that she would want him to follow such a menial occupation, she sees nothing unusual about it. . . .

The boy breaks away from his mother and home only to be drowned in a scuffle with a homosexual. The woman has her way; or if she does not, it is the man who suffers from not taking her advice.

The women in these stories are strong, controlling, and dominating, and their chief efforts are to make men *less* sexual, *less* aggressive, and *more* socially conforming than they want to be. In none of the stories are there the references to simple, mutually satisfying relationships between men and women which are found in the fantasies of other students. One reason for this omission appears in stories in which sexual relationships are fraught with prohibitions and overtones of incest. The following story, told by an only child, is typical of the more direct references to incest:

. . . She, a prostitute, picked him up . . . and they sleep together. He awakens in the morning before she does and gets up, dresses and —now sober— . . . a little sick when he looks down at her, he can recognize her as his sister who he hasn't seen in several years. . . .

Or recall Inburn's account of an "incredibly vile and loathesome thing," being pushed into a sexual position with one's mother. A parallel theme of impotence and fear, possibly for the same reasons, appears in stories like this one, told by the subject who had a brief sexual relationship with his younger sister in early adolescence:

He found this girl he was interested in . . . he wanted to marry her. . . . He never did much sexually—actually afraid to—but he thought everything would be okay when he got married. . . . [They marry] . . . he comes into the room and finds her asleep in a nightgown . . . it's very shocking in a way . . . very embarrassed now. . . . He really can't make up his mind what to do, but he finally realizes he could never do it, and he goes in the other room and sleeps.

Sexual relationships are but rarely consummated; the heroes are inhibited, impotent, or disillusioned. These feelings must reflect in part the subjects' image of women as opposing sexuality; but in another part, they undoubtedly refer to the equation of all women with their mothers and their consequent fears of incest.

Women as so far depicted are not deliberately destructive: however unpleasant, controlling, or possessive they may be, they do not deliberately harm others. But in a few extreme stories, there appears a related but more ominous picture of women as utterly destructive. Such stories point to the deepest and most threatening possibilities of the opposite sex. Consider this story about a celibate young priest:

. . . the priest is being presented as the husband to a goddess who is really a lizard, a lizard that's much larger than the priest, naturally and is obviously repulsive to him. . . . The thirteen men whose duty

it is to render the victims each month, in the middle of the month
. . . push him forward.

In the end, only the priest's celibacy saves him, which suggests the
narrator's view that only avoidance of sex will enable him to escape
the predations of women. Or listen to this story of sweet old Mrs.
Saffaro, who might be straight from *Arsenic and Old Lace*:

> . . . one day she suddenly decides that she has become tired of her
> husband. And so . . . she poisons him with arsenic in his tea. . . .
> She's very gentle in her manners, very kind in her voice, and she
> keeps cats, and feeds stray dogs, and gives the children candy. . . .
> The police send Gordon to investigate the case, . . . during which
> time she gives him a cup of tea. . . . Finally, he asks her if she has
> married—I mean murdered—her husband . . . and all of a sudden
> he feels rather strange and drops to the floor dead.

If this is the deepest layer of the post-Oedipal image of the mother,
these young men must feel enormous fear or anger at this controlling, destructive, and emasculating figure. We already have seen
something of this rage in Inburn, one of whose heroes has "something enormous, monstrous inside of himself, and he can't get it
out." Sometimes the hero's anger is clearly directed at the mother,
as in this story:

> . . . He's about to strangle his mother. . . . She looks blankly out
> the window because all is lost . . . in about three seconds he'll
> reach over with his rubber gloves and strangle her. . . . He just
> found out some information which makes him outraged at his
> mother. . . .

But just as often, it is a diffuse and nameless rage directed at all
things and people. One hero awakes to find that

> . . . there were just no human beings on the face of the earth. . . .
> [He] found himself supremely happy. This was what he had always
> desired and dreamed about. . . . [He] devoted the rest of his life to
> destroying all traces of mankind. He died alone many years later
> but a completely happy man.

In other stories the hero's anger is directed at a woman who turns out to be a prostitute and refuses to leave her trade for him, and in still others, heroes are angry at women who prove unfaithful.

Fathers and older men contrast sharply with this picture of mothers and older women. In some stories, the alienated are at pains simply to exclude the father from the action. Recall Inburn's "the father, being absent, sort of leaves him out of my mind . . . he was rather inconsequential." Another subject says of a father,

> . . . his father had more or less retired because he was a cripple or something and couldn't work—it doesn't matter. . . .

And still another points out that the hero's father is missing from a mother-son story because "his father had died when he was a very young man." Since all of the fathers of these young men were alive when their sons were in college, these statements must be read psychologically rather than literally, and must mean that in some important way, the father was seen as absent or unimportant in his son's life.

In the quotation above, the father is put out of action because he was a "cripple or something." The suggestion that the father is damaged recurs frequently in other stories. For example, in one story of the pioneer days of the West, the narrator explains,

> The father has become more or less an alcoholic . . . right now his father has gotten into a tavern brawl and been knifed, and they've tried to fix him now—repair him. . . . the boy . . . is wondering just what is the sense of all this pioneering when these things happen.

And in others, the father is similarly seen as "out of action" because of some inherent or acquired defect. As a consequence of men's disabilities, psychological or physical, it is women who initiate and act in these stories, and men who are acted *upon* by them. One subject, for example, presented with a card showing an older

and younger man standing together, tells a story of two men dominated by a woman whom the card does not picture. The two men
are physicists at a party sponsored by the wife of the college president, a woman who is a

> . . . social climber, a pusher, that sort of thing, and she thought it
> would be fun if she could have a dance. . . . The president reluc-
> tantly agreed to this. . . . The poor physicists are in misery over the
> idea . . . and yet of course they are obligated. . . .

Here again men are weak, unable to defend themselves against the
pressures of women.

In some alienated stories, men are initially presented as strong
and admirable. But even this turns out to be a mistake; they are
eventually exposed as weak, corrupt, dishonest, and fraudulent.
Consider Dr. Kruger, a dentist much admired in his community,
who claims he "throws himself into his work." Actually, the narrator reveals, Dr. Kruger gives his patients a mouthwash that
makes their teeth rot and thus assures himself a steady business.
But one day

> A strange visitor blindfolds him and takes him to the cemetery
> where he has him drill a hole in the earth and tap in a tombstone.
> The visitor says, "Here's your chance now, Doctor, to throw your-
> self into your work." Kruger was found dead the next morning,
> buried in the graveyard.

So Dr. Kruger, too, is exposed in the end. We should also recall
Inburn's tale about Jehovah presiding over the Last Judgment, and
the discovery of the judged that Jehovah is an "incredibly ugly
. . . person," and that the "situation up there has been a little
deceptively colored." Or in another, less facetious story, it is the
mother who exposes the father to her son:

> She told him that her husband had not been married to her, even
> when he was born . . . that in addition he had been involved . . .
> with a bootlegging racket and . . . in connection . . . he in effect
> caused a man to commit suicide by ruining him completely.

Men only *appear* admirable: underneath apparent strength and re-spectability lurks devious dishonesty and corruptness; apparently admirable men are, in Holden Caulfield's word, "phony."

If this be true, then it follows that paternal figures must be re-jected as models, a theme explicitly stated, for example, in Inburn's tale where his hero refuses to follow the teacher who "fobs along" day by day and course by course. In another comparable story, a bachelor uncle tries to help out his young nephew, but the boy

> always felt bad about this because he realized that his uncle was just trying to be kind, and yet he couldn't help sort of hating his uncle underneath it all because all he wanted was to be left alone. . . .

The uncle turns out to be something of a fool: not only does he fail to realize how the boy feels, but he thinks

> what a fine guy he's been, what a fine use he's put all his money to, and how superior he is to all his brothers and sisters.

Another subject has his hero reject the ideals of an older man be-cause the latter's ideals do not work. In his youth, the young hero, Clay,

> finds him . . . a romantic figure whom he comes close to worship-ing. He attempts . . . to hold up to the standards the older person has given him. . . . However, Clay finds the idealism that he has been told by the older person won't work. It makes conflicts with his practical life. . . . So he gradually abandons these ideas. . . . The older man dies . . . happily because he has the idea he has done one good thing for . . . this younger man.

Again, the older man dies foolishly, if tragically, little realizing that his idealism has long since been abandoned.

From these contrasting images of women and men we can now return to the question of why victorious rebels are so invariably defeated by some extraneous force which is the product of their revolution. Some small part of the recurrent mishaps which follow successful revolutions may perhaps be explained as an homage to the traditional piety that crime does not pay. But withal, these are not young men who feel compelled to point pious morals. A more important explanation must have to do with the family situation that followed their "victory" and made it hollow. What these young men most deeply long for is, as we have seen, total fusion with a maternal presence, and they must have made their "revolutions" in hopes that they could remove everyone who stood between them and their mothers. But though in some psychological sense they believe they succeeded in vanquishing their fathers—reducing them into the weak, damaged, phony and unemulable characters they now portray in their stories—they simultaneously lost the goal for which they strove. In place of the surrounding and comforting maternal presence, they won a mother who they now see, at best, as controlling and limiting, and at worst, as devouring and murderous. The intimacy they wanted with her was replaced by her stringent limitations on their initiative, by her possessiveness, by her efforts to make them unsexual, unaggressive, and conforming. And furthermore, by defeating their fathers, these youths lost the right of every boy to a father whom he can admire: instead they now see their fathers as psychologically absent, not worthy of respect or emulation, "phony" in their appearance of respectability, underlyingly weak, controlled by women. The real victors—those who retain the capacity to affect, move, and change the world around them—are women. Ironically, both father and son end up in the same boat, controlled by the same woman.

The implications of this family situation are far-reaching, and in the next chapter, in attempting a more total reconstruction of the ambience that has produced these alienated youths, we will explore them further. But for now we must remember that the picture of parents we have inferred is based on the fantasies of only one of the parties to the family drama, and as such is bound to be one-sided, perhaps even caricatured. Mothers who appear predatory to their sons may (usually do) have their own reasons for the way they behave; fathers who appear weak and phony may have opted for effectiveness in work rather than in an impossible family situation; and the lenses through which sons view their parents are invariably fogged by wish, irrationality, and the desire for self-justification. Furthermore, the images of parents we have discussed are in most cases truly unconscious. Consciously, these young men see their parents in a different, more understanding, and less immoderate way: they would be rightly indignant if we asserted that these unconscious images were their "real" views of their parents, and would probably disavow all recognition of the family drama we have speculatively reconstructed here. And they would in one sense at least be right, for all we know of imagination and fantasy suggests that it is never literal, that it always embroiders and elaborates and completes, that it is always more than a mere depiction of the real events to which it refers and from which it springs.

## The alienated self

In exploring the psychological development of these alienated youths through their fantasies, I have placed great emphasis on those themes that date from the early years of childhood. The reasons for such emphasis are several: for one, it is in earliest childhood, often before the beginnings of conscious memory, that the ground rules of later fantasy are often laid down. During these first years, the individual acquires a special sensitivity to some situations and an obliviousness to others which is likely to remain part of his makeup thereafter. Thus, if we search for the developmental referent of adult fantasies, we are often led back to these early years, to single events and recurrent situations that would explain the prevalence, the repetitiveness, and the content of the recurring fantasies in adulthood. Furthermore, in psychological research, fantasy is usually our best avenue to early life, which most young men have forgotten, and which, even if they recall, they remember only in fragmentary and distorted light. We can use the subject's own memory as a guide to our reconstruction of later years; but early life usually disappears from consciousness and is reconstructible only through fantasy.

In these young men, however, there is an additional reason for our emphasis on the dramas of early years: these dramas continue to have unusually great effects on their current lives and feelings. In other youths, it is more difficult to make informed inferences about childhood on the basis of fantasy, for current fantasies are not so comprehensively colored by themes dating from these early years. Instead, many—sometimes most—themes and characters have to do with the present or the anticipated future. But, in a special sense, the alienated still live in their pasts, and its traces color and even overwhelm their fantasies as young adults.

This emphasis on childhood, however, should not be construed to mean that the early events we have reconstructed irrevocably determined the later lives of these young men. For the alienated, this childhood past remains more "actual," more psychologically present, than for most; yet the courses of their lives cannot be said to be fixed or forced upon them by their childhoods. What is even more important than the past is how they have tried to come to terms with it, what has become of this past and what has become of them in the process of dealing with it. We must, therefore, look one final time at their fantasies, to see what they tell us of the current selves of our subjects.

The central point about these young men as students has already been made overwhelmingly clear: for them, the past remains overwhelmingly "present" in the present. Their views of the world are often monotonous in their depiction of a few simple childhood alternatives: that men are either weak and phony or (less likely) monsters; that women are either possessive and controlling or immensely comforting and nurturing; that all interpersonal situations are quintessentially rivalrous triangles. To be sure, given these basic themes, the alienated embroider them with richness, imagination, and often humor. But nonetheless, the alienated appear "stuck" on a relatively limited number of possibilities, and in that sense, "fixated" as young adults on the Oedipal drama and pre-Oedipal desires we have been able to infer.

The inability of these subjects to transcend and go beyond the past has to do, above all, with their inability to abandon the fantasy of their lost mothers. As we have seen, one part of the obsession with the past comes from the fear of renouncing what was or might have been best about it. But for at least some of these young men, there is more: they are also afraid of abandoning the past for fear of harming those they abandon. I have already noted that heroes who leave home or other sources of supply usually starve to death or meet a similar sad fate; but in other stories it is the women they neglect, fail to appreciate, or abandon who suffer and sometimes die. In one story, for example, the hero's wife supports him through school, but he neglects her and drinks up her money. She sickens from grief and dies, and he, overwhelmed by guilt, eventually dies in the gutter. In still another,

> Let's say that they had been lovers, and she had been carrying on with another man while pretending to be his girl friend. The man deserts her, and she kills herself. . . . She is lying there dead, and [he] is very unhappy about this. . . .

Even gross infidelity is here not sufficient grounds for desertion: to abandon one's first love under *any* circumstances often leads to irreparable harm to her. Crudely translated into familial terms, these stories suggest that the mother will be mortally wounded by her son's desertion—so both from desire to retain her and from fear of hurting her, these young men find it difficult to renounce her or the past she represents.

Another characteristic of the present selves of our subjects is also apparent from the major themes and style of their stories. These stories deal with every forbidden and socially disapproved theme from matricide to incest, from parricide to homosexuality. They abound with insanity, fantasies of world destruction, with obsessed heroes, suicides, deaths, and violent aggressions. And, as is not apparent merely from the excerpts quoted here, many of these stories are stylistically disjunctive, sometimes incoherent, especially when their content deals with the most forbidden themes. Plots lose coherence; mutually incompatible events are said to occur; occasionally, all semblance of narrative organization breaks down in a series of loose free associations. The stories of some of the subjects show many signs of what psychologists call "primary process" thinking—thinking that ignores the rules of logic and reality, that deals with the world in a hallucinatory rather than an imaginative or descriptive way, and in which the conventional rules of intelligibility, sequence, and causality are ignored. Such primary process thinking is usually taken as evidence of uncontrolled breakthroughs of unconscious materials, and it suggests psychological disturbance. Even when we make full allowance for a testing situation that encouraged very free fantasy, we cannot totally dismiss signs in several of these subjects of an inability to assimilate and master powerful fantasies that sometimes threaten to overwhelm them.

This same tenuous ability to cope with inner life is seen in the personalities of many of the central characters of these stories. Heroes are sometimes portrayed as insane, possessed, demented, and murderous. In other stories, the hero's inner division is stressed: one hero has two parts, one sane and the other insane; another hero is literally hollow, molded in plastic, stuffed with straw, and controlled by strings like a puppet. At times, the narrator stresses the contrast between his hero's outward appearance (usually strong) and his inner reality (usually weak and fearful). And almost without exception, our subjects' heroes are irresolute, ultimately acted upon rather than acting upon their worlds. These are clearly not young men who feel themselves masters of their fates or captains of their souls; both fate and soul continually threaten to overwhelm them. Rightly or wrongly, most of them are afraid—though their fears do not always reach consciousness—afraid of madness, afraid of being submerged in the waters of the past, afraid of their inner divisions, afraid of their indecisiveness.

The inner divisions of these young men are often most pronounced in the area of sexuality. We have earlier seen indirect evidence of discomfort in this area, in their portrayals of the problems and frustrations inherent in all encounters of men and women. But sometimes these subjects express a more direct unwillingness to accept their sex roles. One puts this in the mouth of a girl:

> Actually her name is Julianne, but she likes to call herself Julian; she feels it fits her more. . . . When her mother dies, she . . . says to her: "Well, Julianne, . . . nature made you a woman . . . so you can't be like a man." . . . She didn't like the idea ever. . . .

Here the heroine speaks in part for the narrator's own ambivalences. Sometimes, too, the narrator identifies with a woman in a sexual relationship with a man, as in this account of a prim schoolteacher's response to a man she meets in a cave:

> He had a melodious voice which, somehow again, stirred something inside her that she didn't want to recognize . . . she felt his strong arm on her. . . . And suddenly she had the desire to run and yet also a terrible desire to stay because he was pressing her tighter and tighter. . . . And things she had been holding inside of her for a terribly long time—the feel of his body against hers. . . .

In other stories, the heroes are set upon by men in a way that suggests implicit homosexual fears:

> He gets this feeling of fear that everyone around him is one of these people, that he's nowhere safe from these people who are after him, and it begins to affect him mentally. . . . He begins to recover . . . get rid of his fear. . . . The intern begins to give him a sedative and the man looks away. . . . The needle is empty except for air, and he puts it into his blood vessel and kills him, being this member of the Party. . . .

Of course, these young men do not "really" wish they were women, nor are they homosexuals, but they *are* ambivalent and fearful about all that maleness entails. One root of this ambivalence has to do with a fear of women, a fear related to over-generalized prohibitions against incest, and even more to their image of women as potentially possessive, limiting, and destructive. The other root has to do with their dominant image of men—weak, easily manipulated, and basically phony or foolish when they attempt to show strength or decency. Given these unconscious conceptions of women and men, it is not surprising to feel ambivalent about one's maleness.

And finally, the fantasies of these young men illustrate aptly their presently depressed and alienated condition. Just as in ideology they emphasize their pessimism, so in their fantasies things rarely turn out well—and when they do, one subject later commented that he had felt compelled to make up a cheerful story to relieve the gloom of those that went before it. The central characters in most stories are unhappy, full of conflict, depressed, and gloomy—as well they might be given the disasters that so continually befall them. One young hero, a college student, goes home for Christmas to find it "dull and dead," returning to school early only to have a "miserable dull time." Others renounce society for isolation, as in a story where a popular singer is so shaken by being jilted by his girl friend that he renounces success for a remote sheep farm, where he lives totally alone the rest of his life.

One similar story suggests the depression and alienation of the hero and summarizes many of the other themes we have encountered: it can stand as an epilogue to the fantasies we have examined in this chapter:

> He was a student . . . and like so many people who are students of the present generation, he became tired of school . . . couldn't find any goals for which to strive. . . . He set out to find something interesting that he liked. He hitchhiked around the country a good deal . . . shipped out on a tanker for about a year . . . then that began to bore him after a while, because life was monotonous . . . he found himself ill . . . he began to think that there was something wrong with his mind. He was profoundly depressed by this. . . . He knew no one in the entire country he could talk to. So he began to drink heavily . . . his life had no longer become a

quest for adventure. The challenge now was just a matter of survival.

. . . He went out with [a cheap woman]. . . . And then when
the sex act was over, he was disgusted with himself and the whole
world. One thing of particular interest here: the woman was different from most whores he had seen. She appeared to be elegant and
obviously knew a great deal more than a woman of her position
usually would. . . . She told him . . . she enjoyed what she was
doing. He knew this wasn't the reason at all, but she insisted it was.
He begged her to . . . start life anew, both of them. She says no,
all she wanted to do was . . . have more fun. And in amazement
and disgust, he turned away from her, finally, convinced that there
truly was no one in the world with whom he was going to be able
to communicate again. And in his knowledge he could take comfort
and refuge from the world.

# 7    Major themes of alienation

In the last four chapters, I have been concerned with the lives of a group of alienated students, with the similarities in their beliefs, their everyday lives, their pasts, and their fantasies. I have tried to let them speak for themselves, and I have taken them largely at their word. And I have presented the ideology, life style, past history, and fantasy life of these young men without asking how these separate areas of life affect and are affected by each other. This area-by-area approach has obvious disadvantages, some of which can be remedied by attempting to summarize the major themes that run through all areas of the development and current life of the alienated, so as to give a more unitary picture of alienation as it develops and as it appears in early adulthood.

A less obvious problem arises from having so far accepted without question our subjects' accounts of their lives. Every autobiography (and every fantasy) contains not only a reflection of the truth but an interpretation of it, an effort consciously to unify, to find meaning and direction in, and ultimately to justify one's past. Autobiographies often include myths about the self which are themselves interesting psychological data, but which should not be confused with actual events. Fantasies contain expressions of yearning and attempts at self-justification which may reflect actual events only in indirect and devious ways, if at all. Even more sus-

pect are an individual's subjective evaluations of those he was closest to in his formative years: while we must attempt to understand
how and why he arrived at these judgments, we cannot simply accept them uncritically. And every autobiography and fantasy contains omissions which must be filled in. Some of these are obvious:
I have already noted, for example, the frequent omission of the
father from many fantasies. But others are more difficult to recognize, as, for example, the inclination of these young men to view
themselves as largely ahistorical, non-social individuals. Only when
a young man makes an extravagantly ahistorical statement about
atomic warfare like "Whatever happens will not effect my thinking" are we pulled up short by his blithe denial of the power of
history.

In re-examining what the alienated have said about themselves,
we must seek to rectify these distortions and fill in these omissions.
Those fantasies that, because of consonance with other material,
appear to symbolize fairly directly important patterns of behavior
and interaction must be distinguished from fantasies that bear a
more complex relationship to facts. Our subjects' often harsh judgments about their parents must be reassessed, and we must inquire
into the dilemmas and problems of the parents' lives and how they
attempted to cope with them. Furthermore, we can use our greater
distance to ask, as these young men cannot, what effects their past
lives have had on their readiness to become alienated, on their special sensitivity to the faults of their society, on their repudiation of
so many of the central tenets of their culture. And we can try to
correct their blindness to the social, cultural, and historical pressures that have shaped them and their alienation just as surely as
did the private dramas of which they speak so readily.

## Themes of alienated development

A man's personal history begins long before he was born—it ante-
dates him in his parents' lives, and in the lives of those who nurtured and cared for them in turn. Our subjects, like most young

Americans, knew their distant ancestors but little; apart from an occasional grandparent, their forebears are present to them only as reflected and distilled through their parents' eyes. And in our subjects' limited accounts of their grandparents we can surely detect glimmers of the universal human inclination to perceive one's ancestry as heroic—and if not heroically good, then better heroically bad than non-heroic. It is hard to believe that any group of men and women could have really possessed virtues and vices so extreme as these grandparents are said to have had. Yet these students also say enough that is specific and concrete about their grandparents so that we can surmise what they may have been like; and from what we know of our subjects' mothers and fathers we can infer something more of what *their* parents must have been like in order to produce them. And equally relevant, simply from the epoch in which these grandparents grew up and lived their mature years, we can infer other qualities of their lives.

The subjects we have studied were born just before the Second World War; their parents were typically born during the first decade of this century; and their grandparents, in turn, were born during the 1870's and 1880's. These progenitors, whom our subjects knew, if at all, when the former were in their sixties and seventies, were Victorians, and their grandsons' accounts suggest that they possessed many of the strengths and weaknesses we have come to associate with their generation. What must their lives have been like? And how must they have affected their children, our subjects' parents?

The typical grandparent of our subjects was born in this country, in a small town from which his own children eventually moved. Even those who lived physically in what is now an urban center lived psychologically in a small community—be it the little world of recent ethnic immigrants or the equally narrow universe of upper-class Philadelphia or Brahmin Boston. These small worlds had much in common, whatever their dominant creeds and ethnicities. By today's standards, they were provincial and complacent; though in their own day they were merely like almost everyone else in being relatively satisfied with their homogeneous world, sure of its standards, convinced that God moved in His heavens and watched over their special group. Not that these people did not have their doubts and their neuroses—their grandsons sometimes remind us of what we would now term grossly bizarre behavior on their grandparents' part. Yet they did not consider them doubts or neuroses, but rather unhappinesses or peculiarities which were merely part of life. Then, too, their horizons were as limited by their modes of communication and transportation as by their world views; and if we now think of them as narrow in their complacency, it is partly because history had arranged their lives so they could have little contact with anything alien, foreign, or challenging to their outlooks. We should recall that the 1880's and 1890's were days of the White Man's Burden, of American Imperialism and Gunboat Diplomacy, an epoch of Progress, of rapid industrial expansion despite frequent "Panics," a time when anthropology was the complacent study by the idle rich of the curious customs of "savages," and when it was easier than now to believe that God smiled in a special way on Americans, and slightly averted His gaze from various other races and nations.

For most Victorians the world was relatively ordered, structured, and "rational," where things and people had fixed places and where troubles came from violating the preordained scheme of things. The organization of our subjects' grandparents' families no doubt reflected this ordered universe. The classic portrait of the Victorian family table, with the bearded and autocratic father at one end, the wife at the other, and the silent children lined along either side is probably an exaggeration of the ordered roles allocated to each family member; but by and large it reflected the ideal of a Victorian family in which Father truly presided, in which Mother's place was truly the home, and in which children really "knew their place" as children and were obeisant to the adult world.

Our subjects' parents were born into this ordered and orderly world, and yet, in their lifetimes, they moved out of it—out of the

small towns and urban villages of the turn of the century to cosmopolitan cities of the twenties; out of a stable and unquestioned family system into the "New Family" where men and women challenged their assigned "places" in family and social life; and out of
the complacent and secure philosophies of the Victorian world into
the changing and insecure ideologies of the twentieth century.
These children of the turn of the century were reared and prepared
for the kind of world in which their parents had so commodiously
and complacently lived—but when they reached adulthood they
found this world no longer existed. Our subjects' parents came to
maturity in the late 1920's and early 1930's—a time in which
prosperity was ended by a shattering depression, an era in which
"flaming youth" increasingly questioned the moralities of their parents, an era in which older family ways were challenged and collapsed, in which women began to smoke, men were radical, and
revolt against parental restrictions was ubiquitous.

This revolt took both ideological and personal forms. From our
subjects' accounts, we know that many of their mothers were, in
their day, "emancipated women"—women who aspired to a career
in the arts or on the stage, women who outperformed men in academic work, women who were ambitious, intellectual, driving,
often radical in politics, usually in vigorous revolt against the world
that had shaped them. Such revolts usually have origins not only in
a rejection of the explicit values expressed by the previous generation, but also in a more personal rejection of the kind of life one's
parents have led. Our subjects tell us that their mothers moved
away from the homebound lives of their own mothers, went to college, moved up in the social world and forward into another generation where women were no longer satisfied with a life that had fulfilled their mothers. They wanted something different, greater scope
for their talents than kitchen and nursery could allow, the right to
move more freely in a "man's world" and to do many of the kinds
of things that their fathers had done but that their mothers had
been prevented by convention from even imagining.

From this, we can surmise that our subjects' mothers, like many women of their generation, must have identified strongly with their own fathers. Their special feeling for their fathers is indirectly reflected in our subjects' accounts of their maternal grandfathers, almost invariably described as men of outstanding qualities, usually for better though sometimes for worse. And when the alienated mention their mothers' mothers, it is often disparagingly, as if to reflect their mothers' own rejection of them. Our subjects' mothers seem to have been most impressed by the strength of their fathers —whether it was a cruel strength, as with Inburn, or intellectual or humane strength, as with others.

Our subjects' fathers had different battles to fight. Like their wives, they found the constraints and roles of the Victorian families in which they grew up unlivable and, also like their wives, they made early commitments strongly at odds with those of their fathers—they were to become inventors and artists where their fathers had been businessmen and shopkeepers, crusading New Dealers where their fathers were conservatives, international correspondents where their fathers had been homebound tailors. In some of this they merely reflected the historical expansion of the available world in the twentieth century, which has increasingly meant that no one could hope simply to relive the life of his parents. But in other ways they seemed to have been in especially active rebellion against parents whom they felt were domineering, manipulating, and limiting: their revolt against the constrictions of the Victorian world was, like that of their wives, also a revolt against their fathers and mothers who epitomized that world.

Yet our subjects often portray their fathers as men dominated in their childhoods as they were later to be controlled by their wives. Many of these fathers must have worried lest, in abandoning the restrictive values of the previous generation, they were also abandoning the virtues and certainties that made men admirable. So, too, in rejecting the careers and outlooks of their fathers for other life patterns more "cultural" and "idealistic," they must have been secretly concerned that they might have rejected any claim to strength, to masculinity as they had known it in their own families.

In American society, men who choose a vocation that is in some sense "cultural"—that is, concerned with idealism, feelings, self-expression, teaching the young, and the intangible achievements that go to make up "culture"—are choosing a role Americans have traditionally ascribed to women, and are often led to wonder whether such choices are fully consistent with being a "real man."

Our subjects of course know little of the conscious and unconscious hopes and fears with which their parents entered marriage; but from what they tell us about their parents in later years, we can infer much of the earlier situation. Like all couples entering marriage, these must have been looking for qualities in their partners that would strengthen what they thought best in themselves, that would allay their sensed or feared weaknesses and support them in their commitments. For a man in rather shaky revolt against his own Victorian family, a woman who was also emancipated from her parents promised to support his own identity where it was most precarious. And for a woman who rejected her own mother's definition of herself as "merely" wife-mother-and-homebody, a man with "modern" and unconventional ideas, who valued her for her rebelliousness and her artistic or intellectual interests, might have seemed a perfect match. Both wife and husband must have sought a partner who would provide a way out of the past—a man who seemed committed to a relatively individualistic and creative life as teacher, writer, journalist, reforming lawyer; a woman who was vigorous, active, impulsive, "artistic," emotional, talented, and perhaps even charmingly moody and erratic at times.

But subsequent events suggest that both parents, like all those who reject their pasts, retained a real ambivalence about it. Underneath their manifest opposition to their parents and the Victorian world, each must have felt a lingering admiration for and attachment to what they repudiated. To our subjects' mothers, in particular, their own fathers represented not only complacent and moralistic smugness, but strength, solidity, and security. And though our subjects' fathers clearly chafed under the restrictive tyranny of their parents, they must have secretly wondered whether they, who often chose less "masculine" careers, were the men their fathers were. Furthermore, they may have had covertly mixed feelings about women who were ambitious, talented, and energetic, who wanted careers and achievements in the world of men—and perhaps equally mixed feelings about themselves as the men who married such women.

Marriage can sometimes live up to the unconscious hopes of each partner; but often it does not, and it is especially likely not to when these hopes are self-contradictory. The "unconventional" men who sired our subjects were seldom able to support or encourage their wives to develop their talents after marriage—perhaps because their own somewhat tenuous feelings of adequacy were intolerably threatened by a wife who worked, perhaps because after marriage their wives turned out to have less real talent and less determination to pursue it than they had seemed to have during courtship. Nor were they able to sustain their own youthful dreams; discouraged by low salaries, the depression, the pressures of supporting a family, and their desires for material success, or undermined by their wives' lack of encouragement, most of them abandoned their "cultural" vocations and eventually ended in jobs quite comparable to those of their own fathers. Moreover, the wives who married these originally "emancipated" men seem rarely to have supported them in their "youthful dreams," but encouraged them to take the path that ensured success and security even when they simultaneously disparaged this path. Perhaps because they felt their husbands had frustrated their own hopes for self-development, these women turned against their husbands, though they may also have been unconsciously disappointed that these men did not have the "strength" to resist the very pressures they themselves exerted.

Both partners to the marriage must have been disappointed. The wife secretly sought a man who would combine her father's strength with a less rigid attitude towards women's "place"; she found instead a man who succumbed both to the pressures of success and, even more unforgivable, to her own pressures—a man

who unconsciously may have accepted as all too true her implication that he was not the man her father (or his father) was. The
husband found that the charming moodiness of his fiancée turned
into the neurotic instability of his wife, that the bright talents of the
girl he married turned into "sacrifices" she had made for her marriage, and that, far from supporting his revolt against his parents,
she turned against him. In all of this, it is hard to assign blame.
Though our subjects find it easy to condemn their fathers, we must
recall what must have been their disappointment that their marriage did not yield what it promised. And though our subjects
sometimes portray their mothers as "Moms" of the worst sort,
the mothers, too, had their genuine frustrations and disappointments.

Given such frustrations and disappointments in both parents, the
birth of a child—and especially of a first or favored son—provides
a new arena for the expression of the conflicts of marriage. One
way of preserving a marriage (and all but two of these were, after
their fashion, preserved) is to shift the conflict between husband
and wife to a less direct conflict with and over children; one way to
try to compensate for what is missing in a marriage is to seek it in a
relationship with a son. For the mothers of our subjects, the birth
of a son must have reawakened their hopes for a relationship with a
male that would resolve their own conflicts: they would seek from
their son a special understanding of their own felt sensitivity and
talentedness; they would confide in him, directly or indirectly, the
frustrations of their own marriage; they would encourage in him
some of the sensitivity and non-conformity which had collapsed so
rapidly in their husbands. But at the same time their investment in
this son was so great that they would unwittingly try to prevent him
from growing away, binding him by ties of both love and guilt; they
would communicate their own unfulfilled needs to him; and they
would discourage in him any sign of initiative and independence
which might presage the eventual day he would leave them. Moreover, probably without really meaning to, they would transmit to
their son their own image of their husband as a man who had not

lived up to his promise, who had abandoned his early dreams and hopes, a man less than adequate as a husband. But most important would be their own excessive devotion or emotional investment in their son, their fantasy and hope—destined to be forever frustrated—that he would somehow make up their disappointments and sacrifices to them.

For our subjects' fathers, the birth of a son soon came to mean the birth of a rival. American life makes it virtually impossible for most middle-class fathers to take an active part in the day-to-day upbringing of their children, and only a sound marriage and a strong determination to be an effective father can enable even the best father to be "there" for his sons. Here, however, the conventions of American life were exacerbated by the problems of the marriage. The mutual disappointment of each partner with the other, the mother's growing investment in her son and her often active fear that the son would become like the father—these factors conspired to push the father away from the mother-son alliance. This implicit or explicit exclusion must have intensified the father's own doubts about his adequacy as a family man, and thus made his decision to abdicate from the family almost inevitable. Paternal abdication, too, is common enough in American families: the exigencies of work, suburban living, and commuting make it hard to avoid altogether. But for these men, it was more than a problem to be overcome. Rather it was probably with considerable relief that they devoted themselves "monomaniacally" to the pursuit of success, that they accepted jobs that involved leaving their families for extended periods; that they found it impossible to take their families with them to new jobs during the war; and that, when they were at home, they buried themselves in their studies, their perennials, or the newspaper. Our subjects picture their fathers as distant, uninvolved with the family, perhaps somewhat embittered by life, disappointed in their own youthful dreams, and as "absent" from their sons' lives. It is easy to see why.

Ironically, this "acting out" of marital conflict and dissatisfaction on the mother-son and father-son relationship may have been

what saved these marriages: despite the potential and actual
conflicts, only two sets of parents were divorced. Yet divorce is a
real and open option to relatively emancipated middle-class families; and the transmutation of potentially disruptive conflict into the
parent-child relationship in many cases must have represented an
unconscious decision to keep the marriage going at all costs. It is
hard to judge whether this decision was wise; we have no way of
knowing whether open dissension and "broken" homes are easier
for a child to bear than the covert dissension and internally divided
families in which most of these subjects grew up. In either case, the
parents clearly tried to make the best of a bad situation—the
mother by seeking from her son the satisfactions she did not find
with her husband, the husband by withdrawing from the household.

This, in Inburn's words, was "the situation (one might say predicament)" these young men were born into, and like all children,
they were profoundly affected by their parents' frustrations and by
their parents' efforts to cope with these frustrations. Psychological
development is of course more than a simple reflection of parental
influence. It involves innate potentials and constitutional readi-
nesses which partly determine both the child's response to his parents and their response to him. It includes not only what the
parents do for and to their child, but what he makes of it in his imagination and his behavior. And it is influenced not only by parents,
but by an ever-widening circle of family, school, region, nation,
and world which may support, encourage, confirm, push, channel,
pull, undermine, or even destroy any pre-established path of development. Yet in setting the stage for adulthood, parents are central,
especially in our society where exclusive charge of the child is
vested in his mother and father (and in no one else) for the first
years of life. We must therefore ask what our subjects made of
their world and what it made of them, how they responded to and
were influenced by their parents, what residues, strengths, and
weaknesses their childhoods left in them.

As college students, the alienated place enormous emphasis not
only on conscious memories of their earliest years, but even more

on fantasies we have dated to that period. Their early memories are often centered on problems about eating and digesting, and their fantasies abound with themes concerning the loss of supplies and the yearning to recapture a lost past. What are we to make of these themes? Do they betoken some special deprivation of infancy, so intense that it left these youths forever convinced that the world was a cold and heartless place? Or perhaps some overwhelming gratification that they were never able to forget or to stop yearning for?

Our subjects of course can tell us nothing directly about their first year and a half of life. But we have no grounds for believing that they underwent any grossly unusual treatment during this period. To be sure, what we have surmised about their mothers suggests that they probably welcomed the birth of a son, and may have devoted themselves to the care of their newborn with an intensity that grew from eagerness to escape the dissatisfactions of their marriage. But at the same time, the later complaints of these women about all that they "gave up" for their marriages suggests that, like many mothers, they may also have resented the demands made upon them by a helpless infant. None of this is very unusual; some combination of devotion and occasional resentment of the infant's demands is typical of middle-class American mothers, and probably of mothers the world over. Short of a somewhat greater "investment" in their sons, and perhaps a rather heightened ambivalence about motherhood and about the abandonment of imagined or real talents, there is nothing to suggest that these themes of deprivation, loss, and yearning to return reflect gross deprivations or overindulgences in the first years of life.

The best explanation for the continuing importance of these "oral" themes lies not in any hypothetical events of early life, but rather in the effects of later family rivalries. I have already suggested that a, and perhaps *the,* primary issue in competition between fathers and their young sons is the father's desire to retain and the son's desire to gain the total love, loyalty, and attention of the mother. In the normal course of development, the son eventually accepts his father's superior position, and partly because of this superiority, seeks to become like his more powerful father. Most mothers continue to care for and nurture their children with gradually decreasing intensity throughout their later childhoods, which gives the son a chance to give up his mother slowly, to become more independent gradually. In their rivalry with their fathers, the alienated must have hoped above all to displace them so as to be able to command their mothers' primary attention and love; they made their revolutions for the sake of motherly love, to be able to command the exclusive care, nurturance, and warmth of their mothers. In both autobiographical and fantasy materials, we have seen reflections of the special mother-son alliance that developed, the son bound to his mother even in adolescence by special feelings of sympathy and identification, guilty at any effort to break away from her, tied to her both by his awareness of her neediness and frustration and by his own dependency, both mother and son united in their view of the father as distant, weak, and removed from the center of the family. The "victories" of these boys thus entailed a double loss—of a father they could admire and emulate, and of a mother who could love them without making overwhelming demands with which they, as small children, could ill comply.

Furthermore, these children thereby lost any opportunity to "work through" their dependency and neediness in a slow and gradual way which would permit earlier feelings and needs to become incorporated in new modes of behavior. Paradoxically, it is by being loved by our mothers throughout our childhood that we best learn not to need their love too desperately; the continuing willingness of a woman to mother her child, even as she encourages his independence, is probably the best way for an American mother to help him to outgrow her. The mothers of our subjects, however, needed their son's love too much; as a result, these young men as children were plunged suddenly into an uncomfortable alliance in which love was more demanded than freely given.

The intensity with which fantasies of loss of love and supplies persist and the strength of the longing to return to a fusion with a maternal presence can be seen as a reflection of these later events. The subjects' autobiographical accounts of their mothers' "magnetism" and "sensuality" suggest what projective tests confirm—that these women used all of their charms to assure their sons' continuing devotion to them, no doubt implicitly holding out the promise of total and unconditional love. But at the same time that our subjects' mothers must have continually stimulated their sons with unspoken or spoken promises of love, they were unable to provide it adequately, for in the last analysis they needed not filial but conjugal love from their sons. The son thus got something very different from what he had wanted, and found himself bound by guilt and his own needs to a woman who forever promised but never fulfilled her promises. Thereafter, he would dream of a distant and lost past in which he was reunited with his mother not as her equal but as her totally dependent infant. The sharp contrast between these dreams and the realities of family life in later childhood would lead to a romanticization, an idealization, of what these youths dreamed of; and the lack of any opportunity gradually to work through these distant dreams would make them the more persistent in fantasy.

The relationship between these events and relationships and the later alienation of these young men is complex and far from invariant. Yet certain themes laid down early in life are indirectly expressed in their later repudiation of their society and culture. For one, the disastrous victory of these subjects instilled in them thereafter a deep dislike of all rivalry and competition. Their too-successful competition at an early age resulted both in the loss of the kind of mother they wanted and in the abdication of their fathers from their lives. So the son lost thereafter the possibility of having a father who would be close to him and, by virtue of his own more favored position, of a father whom he could admire and desire to emulate. The resulting fear and dislike of competition persists into adulthood, leading to an almost complete repudiation of the competitive business ethos of American society, to a dislike of and avoidance of social situations with a competitive quality, and to the continuing view that competition and rivalry, though ubiquitous, are destructive to all concerned.

But more important—indeed central to alienation—is the conception of adult maleness that resulted from "victory." The family experiences of these youths instilled in them a deep and usually unconscious conviction of the undesirability of adult maleness, and therefore of adulthood in general. At the most personal and unconscious level, this conviction stems partly from the image of their own fathers as weak, easily defeated and controlled, damaged by and unable to defend themselves against women. And another part of this conviction arises from the subjects' own childhood experiences with "masculine assertiveness" and the unintended consequences of their competition with their fathers: aggressiveness, competitiveness, initiative, and rivalry—all qualities usually considered desirable among men in our society—had here led to disastrous results. Furthermore, the struggle for a woman's exclusive love resulted merely in being limited and bound by her. This "lesson" persists into early adulthood, when the alienated still find themselves afraid of reciprocated intimacy with a woman. All of these largely unconscious themes of childhood—the view of men as weak, damaged, and controlled, the fears of aggression and competition, the image of women as controlling and destructive to men— co-operated to produce a highly negative view of adulthood.

The import of these childhood experiences was often underlined and brought home by the repetitive events of later childhood and adolescence. These youths' intricate and ambivalent bond to their mothers clearly consumed much of their subsequent time and attention: they report little of the concern with school activities, with boyhood pals and chums, with sports and "activities" that abounds in the autobiographies of other college students. They were relatively homebound; and they reflect this fact in their continuing disproportionate emphasis on their families throughout childhood. Such an attachment to home effectively deprives a boy or girl of a major chance to "unlearn" the malign lessons of family life, to compare and correct idiosyncratic views of self and others by exposing them to school chums, to form new ties outside the home that make the complications of family life and parental bonds less oppressive. Instead, these subjects merely found the lessons of early life repeated in more nearly adult terms. Their mothers continued to limit and control them, keeping them tied to home and discouraging any activities and interests which might lay the basis for later rebellion and eventual separation of mother and son. So, too, these mothers subtly or directly derided their husbands, conveying by deed if not by open admission that they found their marriages and their spouses less than adequate. This message must have been confirmed in the son's eyes by the father himself, who, as we have seen, usually found ways of absenting himself from the family circle or else of not being "there" psychologically even when present physically.

Nonetheless, many of these young men retain a special kind of compassion for their fathers. In some ways they are deeply attached to their fantasies of what their fathers might have been had they followed through their youthful aspirations and retained their early dreams. But this persisting identification ironically took the form of a determination *not* to let what happened to their fathers happen to them. In order to be like the lost part of their fathers which they value, they must be radically different from their fathers as they knew them. Their fathers often directly supported this view: some, like Inburn's father, explicitly considered themselves failures in their own eyes; and many of the rest accepted a similar implicit judgment.

These judgments of the father, though they were sometimes shared by all of the members of the family, were probably less than fair. Their wives must have been extremely difficult to live with, and withdrawal from the family may have seemed the only course open. Furthermore, these men were often conspicuous public successes—in some cases men with national reputations, and in all but one case men who had done well in their work, attained positions of responsibility and prominence, won respect from those they worked with. Like most middle-class sons and wives, our subjects and their mothers saw only the domestic side of their fathers and husbands; the other side—the side to which these men had often devoted themselves partly in an effort to escape their families—was hidden miles away in an office, a classroom, a laboratory, or a newspaper office which mother and son had rarely visited. That these fathers often accepted the judgment of their families does not prove it correct; it may merely prove the power of one's intimates to affect one's view of oneself. But correct or incorrect, and for better or worse, a central legacy of childhood for most of these alienated young men was the deep conviction that adult men—as epitomized by their own fathers—were not to be emulated, and the further belief that adulthood in general was disastrous insofar as it meant becoming like their fathers.

## Themes of later alienation

The setting of the stage in childhood is of course not sufficient to explain the dramas of adulthood. No invariant relationship exists between the psychic residues of early life and the working out of these residues in adolescence and later life. What happens in childhood provides the unconscious underpinning for adult psychic life, but the ways in which themes of childhood are displayed in adult behavior and belief—or indeed, whether they are directly displayed at all—is in large part determined by the social shaping of childhood dispositions during adolescence. In any society, a generalized disinclination to accept adulthood can take Protean forms, depending in part on individual circumstance, in part on social support and recognition, and in part on the culturally and historically available channels for expressing discontent.

In considering the later fate of the residues of childhood, then, we must especially consider the way in which these were formed by outward circumstances and historical conditions. Each of the later themes of alienation found in the lives of the subjects studied was given concrete form by the social circumstances in which these young men lived—circumstances which include, among other things, being talented and relatively privileged Americans attending an elite college, being members of a highly technological society, living in a world changing at an enormously rapid rate, participating in a long tradition of intellectual skepticism, being the products of a special kind of family system. These circumstances help determine what becomes of the legacy of childhood and what does not become of it—the options that are open, in this case, for the expression of discontent with adulthood and the options that are closed.

Each of the major themes of alienation I will discuss is also a universal human potential whose import goes beyond alienation. Thus, for example, the yearning for fusion which is central to the unconscious lives of these young men is a motif that runs throughout history, a theme restated in every tradition, the core of any mystical religious sect, a psychological concern that anthropologists and psychoanalysts disinter in the most varied cultures and individuals. So, too, the cult of experience is always a potential of those who feel stranded in the present; the possibility of self-fragmentation is a risk inherent in the very search for selfhood; the problem of finding positive values recurs to all those who question the traditionally given; and the repudiation of adulthood is an option open to all young men and women who find the demands of their societies less than attractive. No one of these themes is by itself necessarily a mark of alienation, nor does it presuppose the special past history we have found among the alienated. On the contrary, each motif can be found in one form or another among countless other Americans, young and old; and the widespread prevalence of these themes in our society is itself a major reason why a vague discontent with adulthood has become crystallized into these particular patterns among the alienated.

## The cult of the present

Some outlooks make the past their psychological center and look back nostalgically to the pleasures of lost times. Others, like the traditional American ethos, look primarily to the future, considering both present and past mere preparations for what is to come. Still others consciously focus on the present, which is seen as the central aspect of time and history, the rationale of behavior and the raison d'être of life. Each of these temporal orientations accentuates its characteristic mode of experience: a focus on the past emphasizes memory, history, conservation, and nostalgia; one on the future stresses anticipation, planning, saving, and preparation; and concern with the present almost invariably involves a focus on experience, consumption, sentience, activity, and adventure in the here and now.

Of these three orientations, it is abundantly clear that the alienated focus consciously on the present. Their philosophies emphasize the irrelevance of the past and their pessimism about the future. They reject long-range idealism in favor of the personal and situational needs of the moment; they tell us of their lack of future plans; they experience time as decline or stagnation rather than progress or growth. So, too, in their daily lives they are addicted to passionate intellectual inquiry in the service of present needs rather than to efforts to acquire skills for the future. They are detached observers of their worlds, searching for ways to intensify and heighten the present, not for the wisdom of the past or for lessons for the future. Though the present is often dull, boring, or depressing to them, they can seldom escape it by pleasant fantasies about what was or what is to come. The future is closed by their pessimism; and even their fantasies of past infantile bliss are unconscious and would be unacceptable to their conscious selves. Whatever conscious meaning their lives may have is given by immediacy, experience, the here and now.

The cult of the present can take many forms, ranging from the quest for Nirvana to drug addiction, from aesthetic appreciation to violent delinquency. But we can distinguish two possible directions in any effort to intensify the present. One is a search for adventure, active, outgoing, and vigorous, which emphasizes the role of the actor in *creating* experience, in making new and heightened experiences for himself. An adventurous approach to experience leads to an equation of self and activity, in which the individual seeks to become what he does, in which emphasis is on the process rather than on the product, in which the actor tries to find and reveal himself through his activity. In our own time, such an emphasis can be seen in forms as different as action painting and juvenile delinquency; in both cases, meaning derives from action.

The more passive form of the cult of the present is the *search for sentience,* and it is this search that characterizes the alienated. Here the self is defined not by action, but by perception; and meaning is created by heightened receptivity and openness. Experience is defined as subtlety, sensitivity, and awareness: the purpose of existence is not to alter the world so as to create new experiences, but to alter the self so as to receive new perceptions from what is already there. Whereas the adventurous seeks to change the world so that it stimulates him in new ways, the sentient seeks to change himself so that he is more open to stimulation. The experiencer thus seeks above all to refine himself as perceiver, cultivating "awareness," "openness," and "sensitivity." Along with a search for heightened perceptiveness goes a desire for heightened responsiveness—"genuine" feeling, direct passion, pure impulse, and uncensored fantasy. Some seek sentience through aesthetic sensitivity, others through continual self-examination, others by vicarious experience of the lives of others. The essential quest is the effort to perceive and feel deeply, clearly, intensely, truly.

A major component of this quest is the *search for a breakthrough.* The alienated value most those moments when the barriers to perception crumble, when the walls between themselves and the world fall away and they are "in contact" with nature, other people, or themselves. These times of breakthrough are relatively rare, for much of their lives seem to them dull, depressed, and ordinary. But when such moments come, the alienated describe them in mystical terms, emphasizing the loss of distinction between self and object, the revelation of the meaning of Everything in an apparently insignificant detail, the ineffability of the experience, the inherent difficulty in describing a moment which transcends ordinary categories of language. At other times, a breakthrough may be achieved with a person in a "moment of truth," when the two understand each other in what seems a miraculously total way. Or a breakthrough may be to the inner self, involving a feeling of inner communication and psychic wholeness which—though ephemeral —can profoundly affect the individual later.

Implicit in the search for a breakthrough is the conviction of alienated subjects that they are *constricted by conventional categories,* imprisoned by the usual ways of seeing the world, of coping with their own feelings and fantasies, of dealing with other people, even of channeling inner impulse into activity. One subject described human relations in terms of people attempting to communicate through airtight space suits; others feel that they are bound and hampered in their search for experience by the conventional categories of our culture. Their laboriously acquired educations often seem to them to have built a dark screen between themselves and the world, a distorting filter which blocks clear perception. Despite their occasional breakthroughs, alienated subjects feel that they are unduly constricted in expressing their feelings; that they have lost the capacity for spontaneous appreciation of the world which they once had in childhood; that they are unduly shut off from their own fantasies and feelings. Though most observers would question these self-appraisals, they are a major motive in the continual effort of the alienated to attain more immediate contact with objects, and a further expression of their inability to tolerate any restraint or self-limitation.

For many alienated youths, the search for sentience entails still another corollary, the *desire for self-expression.* As we have seen in Inburn, this is rarely a desire to remedy wrongs or to reform society. Instead, it grows out of their conviction that they have, for brief moments, achieved some truer and more total perception of the world than have most of their fellows. For some, the desire to express this perception has led to an interest in writing, the theater, or painting. We usually see artistic efforts as attempts to communicate and, in this measure, assume they require an audience; but for the alienated, the external audience is relatively unimportant. Their crucial audience is internal: they write or act or paint for themselves, to structure, order, and confirm their own experience, more as subjective catharsis, perceptual therapy, or self-justification than as an effort to reveal to an outer audience. The desire for self-expression thus becomes a facet of their effort to enhance experience, to structure and organize it in new ways that will not obscure its meaning, to order the chaos of sensation with personal form.

The meanings of the cult of the present for these young men are complex. In part, it is a response to a conscious desire to escape their pasts and avoid their futures, but it is more than this. The alienated feel hemmed in and constrained by their worlds (and, unconsciously, by their unruly fantasies and feelings); they reject the culture which shaped them; they chafe under even the ordinary categories through which most men filter experience and feeling. To some extent, they are incapable of employing these categories, for their experience has disposed them to see the world differently; but in part, their ideology dictates that they should *choose* to reject these categories. They are extrao  inarily aware of the blinders of selective awareness and inattention which many men use to hide the seamier sides of their lives from themselves; and though the alienated have, in fact, blinders of their own, they are at least different and unconventional blinders.

The notion of a breakthrough also has multiple meanings. A breakthrough means an ability to slough off the restrictive categories through which most men interpret their lives to themselves; it involves a kind of experience which is above all characteristic of early childhood, when perception was in fact less structured by adult categories and blindnesses, when wisdom comes from the mouths of babes because they have yet to learn what can be noticed and said without fear of adult reprisal. Even in their intense conscious orientation to the present, these youths therefore manifest an *un*conscious desire to recapture the qualities of experience that, they vaguely recall, characterized their early lives. Ultimately they seek to regain the relatively undifferentiated and uncategorized view of the world they had as small children, and to achieve the same total understanding and fusion with another that they had with their mothers.

The cult of the present is, however, not only a theme of alienation, but is found in other forms among many young people. Indeed, among the defining characteristics of American youth culture —the special world of American adolescents and young adults— are a concentration on the present, a focus on immediate experience, an effort to achieve "genuineness," "directness," "sincerity," in perception and human relations. We see this cult in both forms —as a search for external stimulation and for internal transformation—in many of the deviant behaviors of our society: in the search for adventure among delinquent gangs, in the use of drugs to break through the gates of perception, in the "beat" quest for "kicks." And in less extreme form, a similar emphasis on the present exists in the increasing American stress on consumption rather than saving, on the "rich, full life" in the present rather than the deferred goals and future satisfactions of an earlier society. All of this suggests that the alienated are reacting to a problem which transcends the peculiarities of their individual lives, and that the cult of the present is a response to historical pressures which affect alienated and unalienated alike.

## The fragmentation of identity

No clear positive principle or program unifies and gives coherence to the lives of the alienated. The core of their ideology is negative, a repudiation of the central values of their culture, with few clear positive values or goals. Their search for sentience is a search rather than an accomplishment; and their desire to break through the ordinary categories of perception and feeling springs negatively from opposition to the constraints of culture. Lacking positive values, the alienated experience themselves as diffused, fragmented, torn in different directions by inner and outer pulls. They find little self-definition or coherence in their intellectual interests or their social relationships, for these rarely persist beyond the impulses that inspired them. So, too, in their combination of (covert) admiration and (overt) repudiation of those who might become models for them, they reveal both a sense of inner emptiness which leads to excessive admiration and a sense of inner fragility which makes them fear submersion in an admired person. Nor do their pasts provide any clear continuities in behavior and outlook which might unify their conceptions of themselves. Once homebound children, they have now become overt rebels against the kind of world they grew up in; inwardly and unconsciously preoccupied with their lost pasts, outwardly and consciously they live in the present alone.

Any sense of personal identity achieves much of its coherence from commitment. The object of commitment can vary—a life work, a central value, some personal talent, loyalty to a person or a group, a wife or a family, a corporation or a revolution—all can give identity to an individual; but without some positive commitment, a sense of personal wholeness is difficult to achieve. Thus, a primary obstacle to the formation of a unitary sense of self among the alienated is their judgment that *commitment is submission*. Commitment to other people entails loss of individuality, acceptance of restrictions or responsibility, accountability to others who will (deliberately or unintentionally) limit their freedom. Commitment to groups is seen as conformity, as "selling out" to group pressures. Commitment to work means accepting the unhappy requirements of the work role, the burdened life of the worker who cannot call his soul his own. Every commitment means allowing others to have a claim on one; and all claims are destructive.

The problem of identity is also a problem in the exercise of freedom; and these young men experience *freedom as a burden*. They
are an amply talented group, imaginative, intelligent, skilled in language, capable, when they choose, of fulfilling the complex demands of an exacting college. Their past lives have been, if anything, overprivileged when judged in terms of the kinds of schools
they attended, the physical and educational advantages they enjoyed. In principle, our society allows such youths many options,
many "objective" opportunities in the form of possible values, potential life styles, available jobs, girls who might become their
wives, work they might make their own. But paradoxically, it is
precisely for such young men as these that the problem of freedom
is greatest. With a virtually limitless number of options open to
them, with no self-evidently valid criterion to choose among these
options, convinced that commitments are destructive, they vacil-
late, envying those whose choices are fewer and whose lives seem
simpler. Faced with a multitude of opportunities, they eschew
them all, and dimly resent the freedom that makes them responsible for their own fates.

The result is a diffusion and fragmentation of the sense of identity, an experience of themselves as amorphous, indistinct, and disorganized, a repudiation of all commitments coupled with an overwhelming desire to emulate those who are committed, a secret
yearning to give up all responsibility. Insofar as they have any clear
sense of self it is almost entirely defined by what they are against,
what they despise, by groups they do not want to belong to and
values they consider tawdry. Such *negative self-definition* creates
an enormous psychological problem, for it means that the self is
defined by exclusions, estrangements, repudiations, and rejections
—forces that can rarely provide unity, coherence, or a sense of
direction. Only when rejection has a single narrowly defined target
can it provide the basis for the identity of a rebel or the purpose of
a revolutionary. But the alienated, unlike true revolutionaries, have
no single target as they oppose the whole of their culture; and even

a commitment to reform seems, like all commitments, dangerous. As a result, these youths know what they are not, but not what they are; and often knowing what they are not is equivalent to feeling they are nothing.

This sense of inner fragmentation has complex origins. In part it reflects conflicts between the pulls and pushes of their past lives, especially between the pull of unconscious nostalgia for the past and the push of a conscious search for experience in the present. But their systematic effort to remain receptive to experience of the world and themselves itself further undermines a sense of identity. In any society, men must have conventions about what is real and what is significant, partly in order to protect themselves from an excess of stimulation. Such conventions, to be sure, prevent total openness to experience, but at the same time they serve to ward off chaos, to make the world more comprehensible and therefore more livable, to bring order into the sense of self, daily life, and human relations. To reject these conventions without having discovered others to take their place is to invite not merely experience but inundation, deliberately to deprive oneself of the filters and screens by which the self and universe are made manageable. For most men and women, self-definition requires repudiation or neglect of much potential experience; paradoxically, the alienated, who repudiate so much else, cannot and will not repudiate the experiences that most upset their precarious sense of selfhood.

In one obvious sense, then, these students are "maladjusted." Any young man who rejects the chief values of his fellows and of his culture, who dislikes the adulthood that most of his countrymen live, is by definition and by intent not "adjusted" to his society; and he would usually be quick to admit and take pride in this fact. Furthermore, alienated students make a point of their unrelenting honesty with themselves and often revel in their own deficiencies and problems. Their intense and sometimes morbid introspectiveness gives them a relatively extensive acquaintance with their own psychic problems, and their defiant scorn for social proprieties inclines them, if anything, to exaggerate their disabilities. Thus, in some cases, the alienated may look more disturbed than unalienated subjects with equally serious problems but less awareness of them and less inclination to discuss them.

Yet it is difficult to live without some relatively clear sense of self. For all that the alienated proclaim that their discontents are but a reflection of the human condition, this insistence often has a hollow ring, even to themselves. Beneath their repudiation of happiness as a goal, behind their insistence that the world causes their pessimism and unhappiness, under their belief that all modern men are the victims of anxiety, these young men usually harbor doubts about their own ability to cope with life, fearing or suspecting that their unhappiness is partly of their own making. They frequently avoid the very relationships and commitments which might be of greatest benefit to them; they often lose effectiveness as social critics because of the lack of selectivity of their criticisms; they take on the whole world at once and can sometimes cope with none of it effectively. Furthermore, their fantasies show not only the power of their pasts, but a more ominous inability to structure, organize, or give coherence to the present. In all these respects, they pay a heavy price for their repudiation of conventional pathways to adulthood. In part, their neuroses are determined by the often unfortunate family situations in which they grew up; in part, however, they are a direct result of their alienation, which sets them more difficult and at times impossible tasks. But whichever factor is most salient in any particular individual, these young men as college students were rarely happy or psychologically integrated.

Yet though their problems are often especially acute, the inability to achieve a clear, unified, and coherent sense of identity is not a problem of the alienated alone. On the contrary, exacerbated problems of self-definition and identity are extremely common among college students as among other young people, and men and women of all generations increasingly experience identity as a problem. This suggests that we again must explain the fragmentation of identity among these students not only in terms of individual psychology, but in terms of the social and historical pressures on young people as a group in our country.

## The fantasy of fusion

In examining the lives and fantasies of these young men we have repeatedly seen the continuing force of the distant personal past on their adult lives. As a theme of fantasy, it leads to story after story in which the hero's chief aim is to recover the dead, to disinter the past, to recover the lost and buried, to find oblivion in some enveloping medium, even at the price of self-destruction. And as a theme of conscious daily life, the unconscious search for the past dictates that these young men continually yearn for more direct and immediate contact with reality, for more immediate and genuine expressions of feeling, for human relationships in which all separateness is blurred—and that, when they cannot find such experience, the world seems dull and drab beside their unconscious desires. Even in the ideologies of these students, their overwhelming regret at the loss of the past is indirectly reflected in their bitterness about life, their repudiation of those who cannot give them the kind of oblivion they yearn for, and their pessimism about finding future felicity. Paradoxically, it is precisely because unconsciously they so regret the loss of the past that they now consciously devote themselves so intensely to the present, as if they could not bear to recall the bliss they have lost.

When, as with these young men, such a lust for bygone days is strong, it regularly has several consequences. For one, the *past is idealized*. Recall here Inburn's idyllic account of his early relationship with his mother, where he describes a kind of total unity between mother and son which could not really have existed when he recalls it. In the fantasies of others we find a similarly exaggerated dream of the blissfulness of early mother-son relationships, of the capacity of truly maternal women to provide *totally* for men, of the complete absence of distinctions between self and object. Similarly,

the implicit image of ideal experience in alienated youths emphasizes a unity between the perceiver and the perceived which is virtually impossible for adults and possible only in childhood *before* a
differentiated conception of self emerges.

At root, probably the most powerful unconscious motive in
many of these young men is their desire to merge, to fuse with, to
lose themselves in some embracing person, experience, or group.
This *fantasy of mystical fusion* involves the unconscious desire to
lose all selfhood in some undifferentiated state with another or with
nature, to be totally embraced and to embrace totally. But this unconscious desire has its opposite in the conscious effort of these
young men to retain and develop their individuality and to avoid
submersion. In understanding their distrust of commitment and
their inability to achieve a sense of identity, both poles of this ambivalence must be kept in mind: first, their *conscious* desire to be
highly differentiated individuals and, second, their opposite *unconscious* fantasy of achieving a total fusion with people and experience that would lead to obliteration of all individuality.

Contrasted with their idealized fantasies about the past, the present inevitably seems *hollow and empty,* meaningful only insofar as
it can be made to yield a breakthrough to a mode of experiencing
characteristic of the past. When the alienated are depressed, as they
often are, it is because most of their lives seem lacking in the excitement, vitality, and immediacy they can find only in the peak
experiences and breakthroughs which come close to their dreams
of their early lives. Thus, *personal time is seen as decline,* as loss
and as stagnation, as a steady and ever-more-irrevocable movement away from the unconscious dream of perfect union, perfect
fusion, and perfect selflessness.

And finally, the romanticized dream of the lost past in which
mystical fusion was possible entails unconscious *impatience with
selfhood.* A clearly delineated self is, among other things, a barrier
to fusion; what most men experience as the protective boundaries
of personality, the alienated unconsciously feel to be walls that impede merging with experience, nature, or other people. And indeed

it is true that the capacity to merge with another presupposes in the infant an absence of self-definition, just as in adult mystical experience, merging with the universe has always been said to involve a disappearance of mundane selfhood. The inability to achieve a sense of personal identity is in part the result of the unconscious wish for fusion.

I have already traced the personal origins of the search for the lost past, locating the crucial events in the apparent victory of these youths over their fathers and their consequent inability to outgrow gradually their needs for an embracing relationship with their mothers. But we should also recall that the loss of infantile embeddedness is a universal estrangement in human development, with which every individual and every culture must somehow come to terms. As with many other themes of alienation, this is but a heightening of a fundamental problem in all human life, a universal loss made more traumatic in these young men because of its abruptness.

Nor can this theme be separated from the broader social scene. As I will argue in a later chapter, the family constellation which underlies this search for the past, like the sharp contrast between childhood experience and the demands of adult life, are built into our society, producing in most Americans—alienated or not—a special problem about renouncing childhood and accepting adulthood. The fantasy of fusion involves a desire to find in adulthood the qualities of warmth, communion, acceptedness, dependence, and intimacy which existed in childhood; and one reason why this desire leads to alienation from adulthood is because adult life in America offers so few of these qualities. The alienated, to be sure, experience this problem especially intensely, and have been prepared to do so by a personal past that deviates from the norm of American family life. But even among those whose pasts are more typical, the same contrasts between an idealized childhood and a vaguely resented adulthood often exist in more muted form.

## The quest for positive values

It has been hard to locate any unifying positive principles or values in the lives of these young men: their preferred and characteristic stance is oppositional and detached. And in the past lives and fantasies of these students, some of the motives behind this inability to find positive values have emerged: an unwillingness to make commitments that might seem to limit the capacity for experience, an underlying yearning for a state without selfhood in which values are no problem.

Countering this actual absence of positive values, however, we have also seen some evidence for a search for such values. In what I have called the aesthetic quest, alienated subjects seem to be attempting to arrive at a view of the world in which experience, feeling, sentience, passion, and appreciation are central values (though few of them can clearly articulate these values). Furthermore, the preferred stance of the alienated as detached observers, their efforts to expose themselves to stimulating experience, their passionate intellectual interests, and even their desire for some breakthrough can be interpreted as revealing an active (if inarticulate) search for some principle upon which to stand, some "rock-bottom" of experience and perception from which they might build. Yet from the point of view of the alienated themselves, this search has been unsuccessful: as a group, they consider themselves without clear positive values, and their alienated ideology is more developed as a protest and a rejection than as a positive stance.

At the most conscious level, the inability to find positive values and goals is closely related to the distrust of commitment. Stated in terms of values, alienation takes the form of an *ideological distrust of ideology*. The alienated consider ideologies (other than alienation, which they do not see as an ideology) as rationalizations for more sinister personal or class interests, attempts to put a good front on selfish motives. Thus they are especially responsive to the "reductive" sides of many current philosophies—to positivism and its assertion that value statements are "emotive" and impossible to verify; to "psychoanalytic" arguments that conscious values are often rationalizations of libidinal desires; to sociological discussions that point out the relationship of social interests to professed values; to existentialist reasoning that emphasizes the role of religious faith in masking existential anxieties. The alienated associate the worth of any belief with the motives that underlie it, and, with a characteristic search for purity, insist that no philosophy or outlook is valid unless its supporting motives are totally pure.

Another restriction under which the alienated consciously suffer is what they sense as the *impossibility of certainty*. As we have seen, their philosophies are solipsistic, emphasizing the subjective nature of truth and concluding in many cases that any philosophical commitment is quintessentially arbitrary. Given the enormous gulf that they feel separates men, even human consensus about values seems impossible: when apparent consensus occurs, it is probably based on misunderstanding. Traditionally, men confronted with the impossibility of objective certainty on matters of value have often been able to make an existential commitment, a "leap of faith," to values about which they have felt *subjectively* certain. But for the alienated, even such an existential stand appears self-limiting and narrowing. Any commitment would be a major step toward self-definition, and they unconsciously resist anything that, by defining the boundaries of their selves, might stand between them and openness to experience.

Beneath the alienated emphasis on the impossibility of certainty, however, lies a less conscious and contrasting feeling, a *yearning for absolutes*. Just as a conscious distress at self-fragmentation conceals an unconscious wish to renounce selfhood altogether, and just as a conscious emphasis on the present masks an unconscious desire to regain the past, so here lack of commitment to any positive value overlays an unconscious search for absolute, embracing values, causes, and goals. In part the latent desire of these youths for a totally comprehensive ideology results from their conscious confusion: total commitment to a positive philosophy of life would indeed give coherence, structure, and meaning to an existence that is now perplexed, confused, and dull. But the lust for absolutes also corresponds with the search for total embracing, self-annihilating experience. A revolutionary cause, a religious conversion, a total immersion in a unitary group would come close to the loss of self and erasure of boundaries which one part of them wants. Here, as in so many other areas, the alienated struggle most intensely against what they covertly desire. Young men with a heightened potential for self-loss, they fight it by repudiating all values and causes in which they might lose themselves.

If we define ideology as any implicit or explicit belief system, then the alienated, despite their rejection of ideologies not their own, make a series of overt and covert assumptions which are clearly ideological. I have already discussed the defining outlooks of alienation as an ideology, and here need only consider those principles less well articulated by the subjects themselves. One basic, though usually hidden, premise of much of their thinking is the *principle of implicit conservatism.* In alienated fantasies, we have seen repeatedly their presuppositions that revolution ends in disaster for all concerned. The ideological corollary of this fantasy is that one should seek to change the world as little as possible, for no matter how numerous its present evils, they will be succeeded by other evils just as devastating if not more so. The alienated of course vehemently distrust dogmatic political conservatism: insofar as they have any sympathy at all for social and political programs they instinctively incline towards anarchism and iconoclasm, not conservatism. Yet their temperaments push them toward an apprehension about change, toward a contempt for politics and politicians, and toward a conviction that deliberate efforts to improve things usually make them worse. Since they unconsciously view their own personal histories as a steady movement away from imagined past bliss, they find it hard actively to support any program that seeks to accelerate or alter the course of social history.

When actually confronted with a social or political issue about which they feel compelled to take a stand, the alienated often implicitly base their decision on the *doctrine of the lesser evil.* If no change is clearly for the good and if revolutionary change is the most potentially dangerous of all, then when change seems inevitable one can hope only to minimize losses, searching for the course which does the least harm. Despite their dislike of their society and their pessimism about its future, these students seldom support social reform or political action. On the contrary, their pessimism tells them that oppression, exploitation, and misery are the rules of the world, and that no amount of apparent good will can improve the human condition. These students are, therefore, profoundly *anti-Utopian,* seeing most efforts at human betterment in the model of the French or Russian revolutions, which led to terror and oppression even worse than that which they sought to eliminate. This is not to deny that many of the alienated fervently wish there *were* a way to transform society and the world for the better; but when confronted with a question about how this might be done, they most often lapse into facetiousness ("I guess I'd have us all go back to the womb"), pessimism ("The race is doomed to die anyway"), or detachment ("Whatever happens will not affect my thinking").

Beneath this inability to find positive values lie layers of ambivalence similar to those we have found in most other areas of these subjects' lives—a real desire *not* to commit themselves to values and creeds that might close them off from experience—and below this, an opposite yearning for values and commitments so embracing that they would eliminate the self and all the myriad ordeals of selfhood.

But even more obviously than with other themes of alienation, we are here dealing not only with a problem in individual psychology, but with the impact on individual lives of problems created by our social and intellectual history. The outlooks of the alienated are clearly related to the intellectual currents of our time, and are but a slight exaggeration of intellectual trends in which we all take part. An inability to find viable and enduring positive values is common to many, and perhaps most, Americans; distrust of ide-

ology and of Utopian thinking is found among most of the leading
thinkers of our day; the tendency to emphasize the arbitrary subjectivity of values and their role in masking self-interest, class position, libidinal drive, or existential anxiety is shared by most of the
prevalent philosophies of the twentieth century. The alienated
problem of finding positive values both reflects and points to comparable problems in our culture as a whole.


## The refusal of adulthood

When taken together, the themes so far discussed—the cult of experience, the fragmentation of identity, the yearning for fusion, and
the futile quest for positive values—amount to a refusal of conventional adulthood which is the defining psychological characteristic
of these young men. When they were studied, these alienated students were, as a group, "stuck" in late adolescence; and in the very
few years that have elapsed since their graduation or withdrawal
from college, most of them have remained fundamentally alienated,
eschewing conventional commitments, continuing their preferred
role of searchers, observers, and wanderers. For only a few was
alienation in college a passing phase, a transient maneuver in their
personal development, a temporary moratorium on commitment
rather than a permanent refusal of it. For the rest, dislike of their
society was too pervasive and too deep-rooted to be so easily outgrown, and their alienation has continued. Perhaps such unwillingness to accept the premises and demands of one's society is a prerequisite for originality: historically many of the greatest innovators
have been "perpetual adolescents," forever concerned with the
questions of identity, self-definition, philosophical position, and
values which most "normal" adults leave behind in adolescence.
But at the same time, the refusal of conventional adulthood presents the alienated with major problems which promise to persist
and to characterize their lives thereafter.

Most young men and women in any society are more or less "acculturated"—that is, they have already accepted the basic shared values of their culture and, beyond these explicit values, they take for granted the culture's implicit ways of viewing the world, of interpreting reality, of defending oneself against excessive and disruptive stimulation from without or within. Acculturation, though never total, normally involves a fundamental acceptance of the value systems and personality styles blessed by one's tradition and one's fellows, and a basic willingness to reject alternatives that might be personally and culturally disruptive. A complex and heterogeneous culture like our own of course offers many different paths to acculturation; but insofar as ours is a culture, these paths share common, socially learned assumptions about what is important, meaningful, and right. When this learning is incomplete, as with alienated subjects, we can speak of a *failure of acculturation*. On the most conscious level this failure of course involves the explicit rejection of most of the fundamental tenets of the "American way of life." But at less conscious levels, it extends, as we have seen, to the very linguistic categories by which experience is normally interpreted, to conventional definitions of self in our society, to accepted rules about personal relationships. The alienated chafe against their culture in almost every area.

Fundamental to the implicit "rules of the game" in any culture are more or less standard ways of coping with potentially disruptive psychic or external experiences—culturally learned and preferred adaptive techniques by which men and women preserve their psychic balance against anxiety, stress, and fear. An especially crucial aspect of the failure of acculturation among the alienated is, therefore, their systematic *undermining of repression and denial,* two of the most common adaptive techniques in our society (and probably in all societies). Repression simply involves an automatic blocking from awareness of potentially disruptive internal stimuli (fantasies, impulses, wishes, feelings); denial is the blocking from emotional awareness of potentially upsetting external stimuli or experiences (bad news, losses, insults, personal disabilities); and both of these adaptive techniques are deliberately opposed by the alienated. Since awareness and "genuine" confrontation with both inner and outer realities are prime principles for these young men, a great deal of energy is expended during adolescence in breaking down old repressions and in systematically undercutting previous denials. For most alienated young men, the search within the self involves an effort to break through repression of the socially unacceptable and the personally painful; just as they distrust the apparently altruistic motives of others, even more do they undercut their own. And, confronted with external misfortune, they feel honorbound to confront it in its most disastrous implications, denying only that any good could come from evil.

The alienated of course have their psychological defenses, and their systematic effort to strip themselves of illusions and blinders is far from successful. Though they are unusually honest about their failings, they are less aware of their strengths and talents, less open to possible good fortune. As a group, they *accentuate the negative,* in contrast to most of the rest of their culture, which has traditionally accentuated the positive. This selective response to the unacceptable, the unfortunate, and the unhappy itself has a partly defensive function, for it enables an alienated student to insist that even if he is unacceptable and "despicable," he is at least aware of it and his equally contemptible fellows are not. But his "awareness" is far from complete: like most men, he remains unconscious of many of the central themes of his life; he employs other defenses to cope, for example, with his unconscious desires for fusion. But compared with most students his age, he nonetheless remains relatively *un*protected against inundation by internal and external stimuli; and at least some part of this psychic defenselessness is related to his inability to make full use of the defenses most common among adults in our culture.

It is worth underlining that for many alienated students, the refusal of adulthood extends to a *rejection of adult sexuality.* Partly because they carry over from childhood unusually strong unresolved needs for passivity and dependency, but perhaps even more because most adult males in their experience have been inadequate and dominated, these youths find what our society defines as a "normal" sexual relationship between man and woman frightening and difficult. Some of their problems are common to late adolescents and young adults (for example, their difficulties in combining tender and erotic feelings for women), but these are heightened by their fundamental aversion for "aggressiveness," for "initiative," for "activity"—all qualities culturally defined as part of the male sex role—and by their fear of any commitment to another person who might make a destructive claim on them. It would be wrong to give causal primacy to this sexual problem; it is one aspect of a more general attitude towards cultural requirements and adulthood. But to the alienated themselves, faced with the imperative sexual needs of early adulthood and denied the stronger repressions of others of their age group, sexual problems are often consciously troubling and upsetting.

In sum, the alienated consciously and unconsciously see adulthood in our society as asking a price that they are unable and unwilling to pay. Unconsciously, adulthood involves relinquishing for good the fantasy of infantile fusion; consciously, it involves "selling out," abandoning their dreams and visions, committing themselves to people, institutions, and causes which they see as making destructive claims on them. Adulthood means accepting an adult self-definition which entails limitation of awareness, openness, and genuineness; it involves materialism, boring work, being controlled by the demands of others.

Although the rejection of adulthood among the alienated is especially pervasive and far-reaching, a less extreme dislike of many aspects of adult life can be seen among other less alienated young men and women. Often this dislike is phrased in terms of adult work, seen as a "rat race," as a "selling out" of youthful aspirations and hopes. Sometimes, too, the prospects of "settling down" seem frankly unappealing because adulthood involves too great a loss of freedom and too great an increase in constraint. Others see in marriage and family not only fulfillments of their needs for love and intimacy, but commitments that will deprive them of spontaneity, responsibilities incompatible with self-fulfillment. Most young men and women of course are not alienated in the same way as the students we have studied in these last chapters; and most, despite some reluctance, eventually make the commitments that are expected and "normal" for adults in our society. But the very existence of reluctance, sometimes heightened and sometimes suppressed, among many of the young and even some of the old, should make us ask whether the rejection of adulthood may not be related to the demands of adulthood itself. We must entertain once again the possibility that the alienated are responding not only to their own psychic predispositions but to the facts of adult life in America.

## Alienation as a social problem

The psychological patterns and themes that have emerged from this study can be summarized by saying that the alienated have a conscious and unconscious view of adult life which disinclines them to accept adulthood. Specifically, they view adult men as broken, damaged, and hypocritical, adult women as possessive, controlling, and destructive to men, and adult competition and rivalry as damaging to the competitor. Their own abruptly discontinuous development has allowed them little opportunity to abandon gradually their longings for dependency, total union, and fusion, and these longings make the impersonal and cold world of adulthood seem more forbidding in contrast. They bring from childhood a deep reservoir of potential anger at both parents, which in later life is easily displacable onto the "conventional adult world." All of these factors predispose these young men to repudiate adulthood by rejecting what they see as the dominant values, roles and institutions of their society.

Yet, I have earlier suggested, it would be a mistake to assume that these often unconscious psychological factors provide full and adequate explanation of alienation. Psychological explanations by their nature often tend to be interpreted as reductive—that is, as debasing whatever is explained by seeing it as "nothing but" an irrational unconscious reflection of infantile patterns. Such a "nothing but" approach is not only insulting to those concerned, but incorrect. Even as an unconscious reflection of the past lives of most of the alienated subjects studied, alienation is not altogether irrational. Whatever the virtues and strengths of these young men's parents, they were in fact poor parents to their sons. The mothers sought from them satisfactions that they should have found with their husbands or not at all; they bound their children to them with heavy ties of guilt and dependency. The fathers were seldom adequate fathers; they were largely absent from their son's psychological development, and they suggested through deed and word that their sons should *not* become like them. Furthermore, both parents were disappointed and frustrated in their marriages and their lives. Thus, insofar as alienation is an unconscious commentary on the lives of the two adults known best by these young men, it has its validity.

But this is still an oversimplification, for alienation is not *intended* by these youths as a reflection on their parents' lives, or even as a way of criticizing their parents. Occasionally, to be sure, these young men criticize their parents, but more often, as we have seen, they retain considerable sympathy with them, identifying with the frustrations of their mothers and seeing their fathers—for all of their blame of them—as men who were broken by the "system," men who once had dreams and a potential that they have thrown away. Instead of a criticism of their parents, alienation might be more accurately seen as an attempt to excuse them, to absolve them from blame by finding their plight universal. The blame that may originally have been attached to parents is shifted to the whole of American culture: thus, it is not so much their fathers who failed, but society, to which they succumbed, that made them fail. So interpreted, the ideological rejection of American culture is an attempt to explain their parents' failings in terms that make them the inconscient victims of a destructive culture. It would again be hard to term this explanation totally irrational, for our subjects provide considerable evidence that their fathers did, in fact, succumb to the pressures of success in our society by abandoning their best dreams, and that their mothers may in truth have been prevented from fulfilling their aspirations by the conventions of American family life. Insofar as alienation is an unconscious effort to explain and excuse the parents of the alienated, it is also far from irrational.

Yet this is still not an adequate account of alienation, which is intended as a commentary *upon American society*. Alienation thus has two terms—the alienated individual, and the society from which he is alienated—and is by definition a social as well as a psychological problem. Paradoxically, the alienated themselves often throw us off the scent of the social factors which are involved in their alienation. Despite their sweeping criticisms of American society, they see themselves as largely ahistorical figures, and consequently make it all too tempting to interpret their alienation as a private, individual, idiosyncratic response to their society. Other youths in other nations would be more likely to emphasize the social, cultural, generational, and historical factors to which they are responding. But not these students: their intense privatism, their rejection of social concerns, their focus on the immediate, aesthetic, and experimental, their dislike of what Inburn calls "sentimental Uncle Tom's Cabin business"—these outlooks incline them to ignore the possibility that they are responding to stresses in our society which also affect most of their age-mates and, in many cases, all Americans. When one alienated young man meets another, he is seldom able to believe that the other is "genuine" or "sincere" in his alienation; it rarely occurs to these youths that the problems they face, much less their response to these problems, might be common to many others.

Extra-psychological factors impinge upon the development of alienation in a variety of ways. The alienated would be the first to argue that alienation is in part a response to concrete perceptions and interpretations of American society and its values. If ours were a different society, these perceptions and judgments would be different, though they might be equally adverse. Alienation in underdeveloped countries, for example, often takes the form of a rejection of traditional society in favor of modernization: its positive rationale is the development of precisely the kind of technological society which these alienated American students reject. And whatever the factors that make the alienated especially sensitive to the seamy side of our national life, this side is really there, and they are not alone in finding it repugnant. To be sure, alienated students are rarely original social critics: their views of their society reflect in part their extensive reading and the commonplaces of social criticism. But their views also reflect their concrete perceptions of our society, perceptions phrased in familiar terms but ultimately related to their own experience of our society. No understanding of alienation is possible without considering its object, American life and culture.

Furthermore, social factors help determine the particular form that a vague disposition to find adulthood unattractive has taken. In Chapter I, I argued that there are a great variety of ways of rejecting one's culture, ranging from revolution to delinquency, from withdrawal to crime. The emergence of vague discontent into cultural alienation is of course conditioned by such psychological factors as the enduring inclination of these young men both as children and young adults to approach the world with their intellects. But it is also shaped by the ways society defined the options that were open and closed to them. For example, a few subjects in early adolescence began a series of minor delinquencies which could have culminated in a criminal career; but the middle-class worlds in which they lived provided little encouragement for a delinquent identity, but continually pushed them to continue their intellectual strivings. Or again, discontent with adulthood could not develop into a revolutionary ideology largely because of the complete absence of support for revolutionary ideologies in this country. In

other nations with a revolutionary ethos, young men with the same
inclinations might have become the leaders of movements for social reform; that these youths did not is directly attributable to the
intellectual and social climate of the 1950's and early 1960's. The
ideological alienation they chose is, in contrast, a more socially
supported option; many of the chief figures of our intellectual tradition were alienated from their societies, and they are today revered
for that fact.

But there is still another, more fundamental way in which alienation reflects the social, cultural, generational, and historical problems of our place and era. In reviewing the development of alienation, we have seen the countless points at which social history
impinged upon the development of the alienated: in shaping their
relationships with their parents, in defining their parents' work, in
determining their parents' views of how they should bring up their
children, in limiting the options open to them as parents, in the
form of the Flaming Twenties, the Depression, the Second World
War, and the national prosperity and international insecurity that
followed. These forces and events have profoundly affected young
and old alike, all of whom have had to make some adaptation to
the changes in our society in the last generation. Furthermore, I
have pointed out that each of the central motifs of alienation is but
an exaggeration of a pattern of adaptation widespread in our society
at large: the search for positive values is a problem for many who
are not alienated; the problem of identity, the longing for fusion,
the cult of experience, and the rejection of adulthood can be found
in other forms among countless other men and women.

These communalities suggest that *alienation is a response to major collective estrangements, social strains, and historical losses in
our society,* which first predispose certain individuals to reject their
society, and later shape the particular ways they do so. Though we
may find the specific complaints of the alienated somewhat less
than original, the very fact of their alienation often points to problems in our society more profound than the alienated themselves

can articulate. The lives of the alienated can be a more trenchant commentary on their society than are their views. By re-examining the social and historical setting of their lives, we may come to a better understanding of the roots of alienation and, more particularly, of why the rejection of American society is an increasingly prevalent response to it among young adults like these.

The second part of this book will deal with these questions. I will argue that alienation is a response by selectively predisposed individuals to dilemmas and problems that confront our entire society. I will maintain that American society makes extraordinary demands on its members—that they adapt to chronic social change, that they achieve a sense of personal wholeness in a complex and fragmented society, that they resolve major discontinuities between childhood and adulthood, and that they locate positive values in an intellectual climate which consistently undermines such values. Together, these areas of stress make adulthood demanding in ways which we have only begun to appreciate. These demands are subtle; we often lack a vocabulary to define them, much less adequate theories to explain them; but our inability to define and explain them does not make them disappear; on the contrary, it merely prevents us from comprehending our social situation and thus from being able to change it. Taken together, the stresses and demands of our society "explain" alienation as much as do the predispositions of individual personalities. We too often forget that all men are also social animals, cultural creatures, and historical figures, and that to neglect this fact merely makes us more susceptible to social, cultural, and historical forces we do not perceive. Between the individual and the human condition stand the complex structures of society, the traditional currents of culture, and the legacies of history; and *these* determine which of the many human potentials are to be realized, which will be neglected, and what form they will take.

In the chapters that follow, we will therefore have to make a difficult and unfamiliar leap from a small group of individuals to the main trends and problems in our society, asking in each case how the broad social and historical scene affects individuals and, by searching for the social sources of alienation in a small group of "overprivileged" undergraduates, attempting to arrive at a better understanding of pressures that affect us all.

# II  ALIENATING SOCIETY

# 8 Chronic change and the cult of the present

Like individuals, societies often ignore their own most troublesome traits. Usually these remain unfathomed precisely because they are taken for granted, because life would be inconceivable without them. And most often they are taken for granted because their recognition would be painful to those concerned or disruptive to the society. As members of society, we all inevitably suffer from a lack of perspective which prevents us from noting how peculiar, idiosyncratic, and even unreasonable are the suppositions and demands of our own culture: this is one reason why the most astute observers of American life have often been foreigners like De Tocqueville or Bryce. But beyond this simple lack of perspective, we often more actively defend ourselves against awareness of central facts of our collective existence, in much the same way that we defend ourselves against the inconsistencies of our own individual lives. Active awareness of certain social facts would at times involve confronting a painful gap between social creed and social reality, just as most Americans have refused to comprehend the enormous disparity between our ideals of equality and our treatment of Negroes. At other times, we choose to ignore those facts of our shared life which subject us to the greatest strains because we believe that nothing can be done about them anyway. In these days of the Bomb, for example, it is a rare American who does not devote some energy to *not* thinking about the possibility of atomic attack, partly because imagining such an attack is so frightening, but partly because we believe that there is so little we could do to avert it.

Any discussion of American society must thus confront two obstacles to understanding. The first, lack of perspective, is the easiest to overcome, for in the study of other cultures we have a powerful instrument to offset out privileged proximity to our own. But the other, motivated resistance to potentially painful awareness about social life, is more recalcitrant. Truly to recognize a problem in society means to become aware of a problem in one's own life as a member of society; and for most Americans, it entails a felt responsibility to do something about it. Most men resist awareness of problems in their own lives, and they dislike obligations to improve their societies—it is easier to cultivate one's garden behind a wall of blindness. These shared resistances are often supported by a kind of *rhetoric of pseudoawareness,* which, by appearing to talk about society, understanding and praising its virtues, seeks to reassure us that we can rest tranquilly at night.

Such is often the case with discussions of social change in America. From hundreds of platforms on Commencement Day, young men and women are told that they go out into a rapidly changing world, that they live amidst unprecedented new opportunities, that they must continue the innovations which will produce an ever-improving society in an ever-improving world. Not only is social change here portrayed as inevitable and good, but—the acoustics of the audience being what they are—no one really hears, and all leave with the illusory conviction that they have understood something about their society. It occurs to few of the graduating class that their deepest anxieties and most confused moments might be a consequence of this "rapidly changing world."

Academic discussions of social change often fail similarly to clarify its meaning to our society. Most scholarly discussions of innovation concentrate either on the primitive world or on some relatively small segment of modern society. No conference is complete without panels and papers on "New Trends in X," "Recent Developments in Y," and "The New American Z." But commentators on American societies are usually so preoccupied with specific changes —in markets, population patterns, styles of life—that they rarely if ever consider the over-all impact of the very fact that our entire society is in continual, chronic flux. However important it may be to understand these specific changes in society, their chief importance for the individual is that they are merely part of the broader picture of chronic social change in all areas.

And even when we do reflect on the meaning of change in our own society, we are often led to minimize its effects by the myth that familiarity breeds disappearance—that is, by the belief that because as individuals and as a society we have made an accommodation to social change, its effects have therefore vanished. It is of course true that the vast majority of Americans have made a kind of accommodation to social change. Most of us would feel lost without the technological innovations with which industrial managers and advertising men annually supply us: late-model cars, TV sets, refrigerators, women's fashions, and home furnishings. And, more important, we have made a kind of peace with far more profound non-technological changes; new conceptions of the family, of sex roles, of work and play cease to shock or even to surprise us. But such an adaptation, even when it involves the expectation of and the need for continuing innovation, does not mean that change has ceased to affect us. It would be as true to say that because the American Indian has found in defeat, resentment, and apathy an adaptation to the social changes which destroyed his tribal life, he has therefore ceased to be affected by these changes. Indeed, the acceptance and anticipation of an unprecedented rate of continual social change by most Americans is itself one of the best indications of how profoundly it has altered our outlooks.

Each of these approaches obscures the real problem: the view that it is merely a matter of "unprecedented new opportunities" conceals the fact that chronic social change is a deep source of stress to Americans; the concentration on specific changes hides the importance of the fact that virtually everything in our lives is continually changing; the myth that familiarity breeds disappearance obscures the importance of the adaptations we must make to social change. In fact, the rapid changes which are occurring in all areas of our shared lives mean that little can be counted on to endure from generation to generation, that all technologies, all institutions, all values, and even all types of personality are exposed to early obsolescence. Continual innovation profoundly affects our conceptions of time, our visions of the future, our attachment to the present, the myths we construct of the past. The continually changing scenery of our social environment constitutes one of the deepest sources of strain in American life; and we must try to understand it if we are to fathom why our society remains unappealing to the alienated.

## The nature of chronic change

Merely to point out that society is changing is of course to state a truth so universal as to be almost tautological. Social change is the rule in history: past ages which at first glance appear to have been static usually turn out merely to be those in which conflicting pressures for change are temporarily cancelled out. Indeed, the very concept of a completely static society is usually a mistake of the shortsighted, a hypothetical construct to facilitate the analysis of change, or a false image created by those who dislike innovation. All new generations must accommodate themselves to social change. And even if we add the qualifier "rapid" to "social change," the problems of American society are not unique. Though in the past most historical changes have been slow and have involved little marked generational discontinuity, in our own century most of the world is in the midst of rapid, massive, and often disruptive changes, and these may create even greater problems for the youth of underdeveloped countries than they do for Americans. What are the special characteristics of social change in America?

Social change in America has much in common with innovation

in other industrialized countries. In all industrially advanced nations, the primary motor of social change is technological innovation: changes in non-technological areas of society usually follow the needs and effects of technological and scientific advances. But though our own county is not unique in the role technology plays, it is distinguished by the intensity of and the relative absence of restraint of technological change. Probably more than any other society, we revere technological innovation, we seldom seek to limit its effects on other areas of society, and we have developed complex institutions to assure its persistence and acceleration. And, most important, because of the unchallenged role of technology in our society, our attitudes toward it spread into other areas of life, coloring our views on change in whatever area it occurs. This country closely approximates an extreme type of unrestrained and undirected technological change which pervades all areas of life; and insofar as other nations wish to or are in fact becoming more like us, the adaptations of American youth may augur similar trends elsewhere.

Our almost unqualified acceptance of technological and social innovation is historically unusual, if not unique. To be sure, given a broad definition of technology, most major social and cultural changes have been accompanied, if not produced, by technological advances. The control of fire, the domestication of animals, the development of irrigation, the discovery of the compass—each innovation has been followed by profound changes in the constitution of society. But until recently technological innovation was largely accidental and was usually bitterly resisted by the order it threatened to supplant. Indeed, if there has been any dominant historical attitude toward change, it has been to deplore it. Most cultures have assumed that change was for the worst; most individuals have felt that the old ways were the best ways. And there is a certain wisdom in this assumption, for technological change and its inevitable social and psychological repercussions produce strains, conflicts, and imbalances among societies as among individuals. Were it not for our own and other modern societies, we might ascribe to human nature and social organization a deep conservatism which dictates that changes shall be made only when absolutely necessary, and then after a last-ditch stand by what is being replaced.

But in our technological society this attitude no longer holds. We value scientific innovation and technological change almost without conscious reservation. Even when scientific discoveries make possible the total destruction of the world, we do not seriously question the value of such discoveries. Those rare voices who may ask whether a new bomb, a new tail fin, a new shampoo, or a new superhighway might not be better left on the drawing board are almost invariably suppressed before the overwhelming conviction that "you can't stop the clock." Moreover, these attitudes extend beyond science and technology, affecting our opinions of every kind of change—as indeed they must if unwillingness to bear the nontechnological side effects of technological change is not to impede the technological process. Whether in social institutions, in ideology, or even in individual character, change is more often than not considered self-justifying. Our words of highest praise stress transformation—dynamic, expanding, new, modern, recent, growing, current, youthful, and so on. And our words of condemnation equally deplore the static and unchanging—old-fashioned, outmoded, antiquated, obsolete, stagnating, standstill. We desire change not only when we have clear evidence that the status quo is inadequate, but often regardless of whether the past still serves us well. The assumption that the new will be better than the old goes very deep in our culture; and even when we explicitly reject the ideology of Progress, we often retain the implicit assumption that change per se is desirable.

Given this assumption that change is good, it is almost inevitable that institutions should have developed that would guarantee change and seek to accelerate it. Here as elsewhere, technology leads the way. Probably the most potent institution promoting change in our society is pure science, which indirectly provides an ever-increasing repertoire of techniques for altering the environment. Even greater investments of time and money go into applied science and technology, into converting abstract scientific principles into concrete innovations relevant to our industrialized society. The elevation of technological innovation into a profession, "research and development," is the high point of institutionalized technological change in this country and probably in the world. And along with the institutionalized change increasingly goes planned obsolescence, to assure that even if the motivation to discard the outmoded should flag, the consumer will have no choice but to buy the newest and the latest, since the old will have broken down.

The most drastic strains on the individual in such a society occur at the peripheries of purely technological innovation, because of changes in social institutions and individual lives that follow from new commodities and technologies. Consider, for example, the effects of the automobile, which has changed patterns of work and residence, transformed the countryside with turnpikes and freeways, all but destroyed public transportation, produced urban blight and the flight to the suburbs, and even changed techniques of courtship. Further examples could be adduced, but the general point is clear: continual technological change guarantees the steady transformation of other sectors of society to accommodate the effects and requirements of technology. Although our society abounds with planning groups, special legislative committees, citizens' movements, research organizations and community workers and consultants of every variety, their chief task is to "clean up" after technologically induced changes, and rarely if ever to plan or co-ordinate major social innovations in the first place. Citizens' committees worry about how to relocate the families dispossessed by new roadways, but not about whether the new road is worthwhile.

As a consequence of our high regard for change and of the institutionalization of innovation, we have guaranteed that change will not only continue but accelerate in pace. Since scientific knowledge grows at a logarithmic rate, each decade sees more, and ever more revolutionary, scientific discoveries made available to industry for translation into new commodities and techniques of production. And while social change undoubtedly lags behind technological change, the pace of social innovation has also increased. An American born at the turn of the century has witnessed in his lifetime technological transformations unequaled in any other comparable period in history; the introduction of electricity, radio, television, the automobile, the airplane, atomic bombs and power, rocketry, the automation of industry. But even more important psychologically, he has witnessed equally unprecedented changes in society and ideology: new conceptions of the family, of the relations between the sexes, of work, residence, leisure, of the role of government, of the place of America in world affairs. We correctly characterize the rate of change in terms of self-stimulating chain reactions —the "exploding" metropolis, the "upward spiral" of living standards, the "rocketing" demands for goods and services. And unlike drastic social changes in the past (which have usually resulted from pestilence, war, military conquest, or contact with a superior culture), these have taken place "in the natural course of events." In our society at present, "the natural course of events" is precisely that the rate of change should continue to accelerate up to the as-yet-unreached limit of human and institutional adaptability.

So far the characteristics of social change in America could be matched, though perhaps to a lesser degree, by those of change in most other advanced technological societies. Indeed, to achieve and maintain a society with an advanced and flourishing technological basis, it is probably essential that change be viewed as good, that technological innovation not be drastically limited because of its repercussions on other sectors of society, that it be guaranteed by scientific research and the systematic application of science in applied technology, and that, as a consequence, the pace of change should be accelerating. This is true of most countries with advanced economies, like Great Britain, Germany, Russia, and Japan, But in America, the effects of chronic, valued, institutionalized, and accelerating social change are augmented by two historical factors—the relative absence in American life of established forces interested in preserving the status quo, and our traditional American bias against "ideological thinking" and its concomitant, coherent social planning.

Many commentators on American history have noted that America had no feudal past to overcome. If we define "feudal" broadly, so that it includes not only established aristocracies, but land- and mine-owning oligarchies and colonial rulers, America's fresh start as a nation has been matched by only a few former British colonies—none of them with the natural resources of this nation. Concretely this has meant that America, with tremendous unexploited natural riches, has had no pre-technological order to oppose or restrain innovation. In most other societies, the impact of technology on the society at large has been limited by pre-existing social forces—aristocratic interests and values, class cleavages, religious outlooks hostile to technology. In some countries like Japan and Germany technological changes were encouraged and controlled by semi-feudal groups determined to use industrial strength to maintain the social and political status quo; in other nations clerical or aristocratic interests have opposed and diluted the effects of technological innovation, preserving older values and class lines even when they conflicted with the demands of industry. To be sure, the coexistence of a technological economy and pre-technological forces opposed to continual social change can be a major source of conflict in any society—conflict we see daily in nations where rapid industrialization threatens older social forms and power groups. A nation without a vested opposition to change avoids such conflicts—or deals with them early, as in our case in the Civil War, whose outcome left little doubt that the needs of Northern industrialism would prevail over those of Southern land- and slave-owning traditionalism.

The absence of a feudal past has meant that America has from the start been relatively free of entrenched social groups, traditions, and values opposed to technological innovation and distrustful of its social consequences. The relatively weak forces of tradition in this country were first staggered by the decline of the Federalists and the extension of democratic rights in the early nineteenth century, and dealt a death blow with the defeat of the South in the Civil War. The industrial and technological expansion of the nation has been virtually unopposed since the 1870's—and these past ninety years have seen this nation develop into the world's most advanced technological nation. Indeed, one of the reasons we lack a true center of conservative social criticism in this country is because we lack viable traditions or historical institutions to which such criticism might attach itself. Those conservatives who opposed a technological society have been easily dealt with as unrealistic romantics; and even the critics of the Left, who wanted more and faster change, have usually found themselves overtaken by the pace of "natural" social change. Indeed, if the revolutionary goals of a generation ago are often the realities of today, it is not because these goals were accepted as the basis for social planning, but because they usually corresponded with the directions taken by society in the "natural" course of events.

The second factor which uniquely colors social change in this country is the anti-ideological bias of most Americans. Even De Tocqueville commented in the 1830's that Americans' passion for grand ideas was not matched by any parallel passion for putting these ideas into practice. It has since remained true that ideological speculations in this country have usually been a kind of game played by intellectuals who themselves doubted their practicality on a large scale. For example, even though the founders of the Utopian communities which dotted our countryside in the 1800's were discontented with the status quo, they did not attempt to change the whole society through political action or revolution, as they might have done in a more ideological nation. Rather, they withdrew from the wider society to set up their own private Utopias, which were doomed from the start if only because they were surrounded by an opposing and hostile society.

Throughout our history, disaffected Americans have rarely attempted to change their whole society through social and political action, but, like the alienated, have preferred withdrawal, emigration, or exemplary self-reform. As a nation we have always been hostile to efforts to translate grand schemes into political reality; indeed, it seldom occurs to most of us that ideological considerations (or even intellectual ones) have much to do with the way society changes. This distrust of coherent ideology in political and social life has meant an unusual willingness to control, limit, or guide the directions of social change. Any program of social reform invariably requires an ideology—a coherent set of beliefs about the good life that can be translated into concrete social programs. But we have systematically mistrusted those few Americans who proposed channeling or directing the "natural" development of our society along socially desirable lines.

In contrast, most technologically induced changes in other nations have been or are accompanied by far greater foreknowledge of goals and willingness to plan than we have allowed in America. At one extreme are countries like China and Russia, which attempt the total planning of all technological, industrial, and social change. While unplanned changes inevitably occur, central planning means that the major directions of change are outlined in advance and that unplanned changes can frequently be redirected according to central objectives. Furthermore, most underdeveloped nations are aiming at developing a highly technological society; insofar as they succeed, the direction of their changes is given by the model they seek to emulate. Given three abstract types of change— planned, imitative, and unguided—our own society most closely approximates the unguided type. We do little to limit the effects of change in one area of life on other aspects of society, and prefer to let social transformations occur without guidance. As a result, we virtually guarantee our inability to anticipate the social future with any certainty. The Russian knows at least that his society is committed to increasing production and expansion; the Nigerian knows that his nation aims at increasing "Westernization"; but partly by our refusal to guide the course of our society, we have no way of knowing where we are headed.

As a consequence, then, of our fresh start as a nation and our distrust of social planning, the pace of change in this country has been almost uniquely unrestrained. Our society has developed in what we consider a "free," or "natural" way, which in effect has meant that the needs of technological change, and of those who stood to profit by it, have been heeded even at the expense of the clear public good. The burden of proof has always been upon those who sought to "interfere," and they have rarely had the political support or ideological equipment to carry that burden. In other countries with Establishments, whether of title, education, race, or conquest, it has seemed quite natural that the original Establishment or its latter-day successor should co-ordinate and control the paths of social innovation; and in those countries whose leaders possessed and were willing to implement an over-all ideology of social improvement and change, this program has furnished the broad directions of innovation. To our American unwillingness to restrain or guide our burgeoning technology, we undoubtedly owe a good part of our high productivity and standard of living, which could not have been accomplished without a people who were on the side of change and who considered it their obligation to make whatever accommodations were necessary to Progress. But to it we also owe many of our deepest shared anxieties.

## The psychology of chronic social change

Man's individual life has always been uncertain, no matter how stable the society in which he lived. Men can never predict the precise events that will befall them or their children—the mishaps and good fortunes that will come their way. These existential uncertainties are a relative constant in human life, and they persist even in a society like ours, which has greatly reduced the likelihood of premature death and natural disaster. Such uncertainties constitute the existential basis for that irreducible minimum of fearfulness of dreadful happenings and hope of beneficent events with which all men in all societies must somehow come to terms.

But overlaid on and intermixed with these existential anxieties and hopes are others whose origin lies not in the nature of life, but in the constitution of society; and these are, as a result, far more variable. Some societies instill in all of their members a deep and superstitious dread of divine disfavor; others teach abhorrence of all that is bodily and physical; still others implant early in life the unshakable conviction that only continual vigilance and precaution will protect against witchcraft. Such anxieties are shared by all "normal" members of the society; and many of the society's practices, its character, style, and ways of life are related to them.

Such social anxieties lie at the root of the social defenses I have discussed earlier. When a society works relatively well, its members successfully ward off their shared anxieties through shared defenses —common beliefs, rituals, or character traits; and their collective anxieties are seldom experienced as such. Just as compulsive hand-washing may keep the sufferer busy enough that he remains un-aware of his fears of inner dirtiness, so the many individuals who make up a society devise techniques of protecting themselves from shared anxieties—techniques that, if effective, often ward the anx-iety off altogether. Among the most effective of these techniques is encouraging the development of a type of personality which is rela-tively well armored against these anxieties. For example, in a so-ciety with a deep latent fear of chaos and disorder, the men and women best adapted to calm survival are those who allow them-selves no departure from order, neatness, and regularity; or in a society that feels itself surrounded by hostile and vengeful gods and supernatural forces, the ritualistic and propitiating live with great-est inner ease.

Social anxieties always have some basis in the realities of com-munal life. Magic, the anthropologist Malinowski argues of the Trobriand Islanders, begins outside the reef—that is, it applies to the areas of life that are most realistically fraught with danger and uncertainty. Though this view now seems oversimplified, it suggests that shared defenses operate most powerfully in areas where there are realistic grounds for uncertainty and concern. In a primitive

society where survival depends on an uncertain supply of yams, it
is not surprising to find magical rituals to assure their continuing
abundance; in desert regions, primitives dance for rain; and even in
our own supposedly unsuperstitious country, the magic of water
witching prevails in areas where dry wells are commonplace.

The "realities" of a society include more than the physical conditions of its existence. More important are the psychological,
social, and historical realities of which individuals are seldom explicitly aware but affect them the more powerfully for their ignorance. It is, for example, a commonplace anthropological observation that societies in contact with a more advanced culture, and in
a process of breakdown or decline, tend to produce messianic cults
—an observation which can be verified by the ghost dances of
American Indians, by the cargo cults of modern Polynesia, or even,
perhaps, by the development of Christianity in Israel at the precise
moment of Roman conquest and the decline of a territorial Hebrew
power. Or, on a more psychological level, a belief in a historical
Golden Age tends to prevail in those societies where a blissful period of early childhood is suddenly and cruelly interrupted by adult
responsibilities: the myth of the collective Golden Past here parallels the theme of lost bliss in every individual's personal history.

Among the most potent if unexamined of these "realities" of
social existence is the stability, decline, growth, change or stagnation of a society. Around such historical themes as these, men construct their most powerful myths, as if compelled to explain and
universalize the historical drift of their community. Partly because
of that need for relatedness to the personal and collective past
which we have seen at work in alienated students, men have always
concerned themselves with collective time, with their relationship
to their forebears, with their course into the future. In an unchanging society, interpretations of history often have common features:
the world, it is said, was created in its present form in the distant
past—sometimes as a result of a Fall from a higher state, sometimes as a result of the creation of a new and higher form of life—
and it will continue on in much the same way into the indefinable

future. At times in such societies men view history as a process of steady decline from the first creation, and then their first duty is to preserve as much as they can of the ancient truth and glory. At other times history is seen as eternal repetition, and men's ritual efforts are bent toward celebrating the recurrence of the seasons and cycle of human life. In either case, the task of a society is to preserve or celebrate the ancient truths and traditional ways transmitted at the Creation; change is unwelcome and undesirable. Given such a world view, sudden changes will often find the society unprepared: they cannot be assimilated without destroying the historically given; and unless they can be resisted, the older society flounders and often destroys itself in its effort to resist transformation.

Clearly, our own views of change and history differ. Traditionally, I have argued, Americans have seen change as for the good, history as progressive, and time as above all oriented to the future. This view of history and time is well adapted to a time of rapid— but not *too* rapid—social change that results in visibly improving conditions for the great mass of men. The average man's own daily perceptions continually confirm the view that things are changing for the better; by simple extension, the future will be better still. Once instilled, this view tends to be self-confirming, producing men who will work actively to transform their society into an ever "better" place—in American terms, into an even more productive, more prosperous place. There is a direct influence between a shared view of social history and the average individual's view of his own life: in our society, one reason why the progressive view of history has been continually reconfirmed is that individuals have unconsciously felt themselves (as they invariably do) caught up in history, its agents and actors.

The viability of a progressive view of time depends on the ability to maintain a sense of connection with the past and the future. Society must change, but not so fast as to make it impossible to perceive where one comes from and where one is going. To persist, such a view also requires that men feel some sense of control over their own fate—some conviction that they determine their own history and indirectly social history, but not vice versa. And finally, a sense of generational continuity must persist: young men and women must feel that they stand on the shoulders of their parents, or—if not of their parents—of other, preferable exemplars of the older generation. What the parental generation says must remain *relevant* to the young, even if only as something to improve upon or to rebel against. Without some such sense of personal relatedness to the personal past, both individual and social history will be experienced as chaotic and disjointed, and not progressive. (Paradoxically, revolutionaries often have the greatest sense of historical relatedness, in that they continually refer to the historical order they have overthrown.)

But when the rate of social change accelerates beyond a given point, or when historical changes are too drastic and discontinuous, the ability to maintain a sense of connection with the past and future disappears, and with it, a progressive view of history. An analogy may make the point clearer. A man sitting in his garden on a summer day tends to subsist in the present, in contemplation of his immediate situation or in reveries of distant and remote events. The same man walking briskly down a road toward a known destination usually has a clear sense of moving forward, knowing the place he started from and the direction he is headed. But the same man sitting on a jet plane and traveling across a continent at five hundred miles per hour once again lives in the immediate present despite his rapid motion. The landscape moves by so quickly he can no longer comprehend his motion. The place from which he began his trip and the place where he ends it are connected not by a comprehensible trajectory, but by a long moment of immediacy in which he is only aware of the interior of the plane and his own musings. Yet despite his concentration on the immediate present, his psychological situation is very different from that in the garden. On the jet, he lacks knowledge of his more distant surroundings; his mood is set by his rapid and uncomprehended motion; he has a feeling of unreality, of unconnectedness, absent in pastoral contemplation. The present, the immediacy of his surroundings, take on a special protective quality. He deliberately does not think of the fragility of the plane or of the possibility of crashing; to look at the passing scene is to risk vertigo. And unlike his earlier self in the garden or on his walk, he is now a passive agent being acted upon by the forces that rush him to his destination.

Stated more generally, the faster the motion, the more difficult it is to maintain a sense of relationship to one's surroundings, be they temporal and historical or physical and geographical. Extremely rapid and accelerating social change as we know it today in America increasingly entails a psychological distancing of the past, a sense of the unknowability of the future, and a new emphasis on the present.

## The foreshortening of time span

The central psychological effect of accelerating rates of continual change in America is a gradual alteration in the sense of time. Each decade in our lives brings more, and more drastic, changes in our society and our life situation than that which preceded it. A man born in the beginning of this century has seen in his lifetime changes in the quality of life which no one in his youth could have anticipated or prepared him for. Changes that once took centuries —in outlook, in technology, in living conditions, in communications—now take less than a generation. Technological changes that were the science fiction of our parents are the commonplaces of our children—trips to the moon, television, speeds greater than sound, digital computers. And more important psychologically are less noticed but even more profound changes in the constitution of society —in the family, in sex roles, work, and leisure.

The human capacity to assimilate such innovation is limited. Men can of course adjust to rapid change—that is, make an accommodation to it and go on living—but truly to assimilate it involves retaining some sense of connection with the past, understanding the relationship of one's position to one's origins and one's destinations, maintaining a sense of control over one's own life in a comprehensible universe undergoing intelligible transformations. This assimilation becomes increasingly difficult in a time like our own. Whatever is radically different from the present inevitably tends to lose its relevance. As individuals, we often forget our former selves and are reminded of them only with a shock of unfamiliarity and strangeness. So, as members of a society, we increasingly feel a similar sense of unfamiliarity about the not-so-distant past: the Flaming Twenties, the depression, even the Second World War now seem slightly unreal and certainly old-fashioned—as when we comment on how "out-of-date" the films of those recent years now seem. This "out-of-dateness" of even the very recent social past signals the psychological loss of a sense of connection with it, the birth of a new sense of being stranded in the present.

Concurrently, and for similar reasons, the future grows more distant. We cannot anticipate that the years ahead will be basically like the present. On the contrary, our best prediction is that the future will be unpredictably different—that technologies will change and with them the external conditions of our lives, that social institutions will change, that the basic structures of our society will continue to change as they have in the past. A majority of today's college graduates will be entering jobs that *did not exist* when they were born; extrapolating, it is easy to conclude that even more of the new jobs that will be available in another twenty years do not now exist and are in good part unimaginable. Partly because of the characteristic American unwillingness to attempt to shape the future, but partly because the process of unguided technological change is *inherently* open and unpredictable, we cannot envisage the future in which we will live. "Tomorrow" tends to disappear as a center of relevance in our lives, for building toward the future means building toward the unknown.

What is left, of course, is the present, and all that can be enjoyed therein: "today" becomes the one rock of constancy in a shifting sea of change. Yesterday's solutions are often irrelevant to today's problems and no one can know what part of today's wisdom will remain valid tomorrow: an intensification of today results. Savings accounts go out of fashion (inflation, a symptom of social change, eats them up); and in similar fashion the traditional American postponing of present enjoyment for the sake of greater future reward is disappearing as well. The resulting cult of the present takes many forms—sometimes the raw hedonism of the spiritually demoralized; sometimes the quest for "kicks," speed, sex, and stimulants of the beats; often some variant on what I have called, in discussing the alienated, an aesthetic outlook.

We have already seen some of the varieties of this outlook among alienated students—the emphasis on sensation, sentience, and experience; the reluctance to make future commitments; the sense of temporal confusion; the extreme emphasis on the present; the choice of "realistic" and present-oriented values. But there are other manifestations of the cult of the present even among the unalienated. Consider, for example, the question of families. Most unalienated young people want large families; they marry early and are prepared to work hard to make their marriages a success; they usually value family life far more than meaningful work. Families play a special role in American life today—and among the reasons for our increasing emphasis on them is that they provide a place where a man can be himself and enjoy himself *in the present*. A wife and children can be enjoyed in the here and now, and are dependent neither on traditional wisdom nor on future success. Furthermore, children constitute a link with the future that, unlike vocational commitment, will endure regardless of how society changes. Naturally, parents are affected, and radically affected, by social change in *how* they rear their young; but the mere fact of children and family constitutes a point of present stability and a link with history in a changing and apparently unmanageable world.

## The generational gap

Whatever the existential uncertainties of his life, a father in a more or less unchanging society could be relatively certain that his children would confront basically the same society—live in basically the same *life situation*—that he himself confronted. Just as he grew up in a society not importantly different from that of his father and grandfathers, he trusted (and usually correctly) that his children would live in the same kind of world. To be sure, even the most "unchanging" social order changes; but its changes are so gradual as to affect the relationship between the generations little if at all. In such societies, what was good enough for a man's parents is good enough for him, and will be good enough for his children.

Such generational continuity does not, paradoxically, preclude the possibility of filial rebellion. Indeed, in the classic tales of sons who revolt against their fathers, what the father represents is *too* relevant to the son, who rejects it because he desperately fears that he will be forced to become *like* his father. Instead, he chooses some other option through which he can oppose what his father stands for. And in real life, of course, the ending of such tales is usually tragi-comic: the son, after a period of rebellion, ironically ends up by being like his own father after all. Several generations of young Germans, for example, after a period of romanticism and rebellion against their authoritarian fathers, have themselves become heads of authoritarian families from which their sons have in turn rebelled. Far from a sign of generational discontinuity, filial rebellion is here part of a pattern in which the generations repeat themselves almost identically.

The real token of generational discontinuity then, is not overt and visible rebellion against the previous generation, but a vision of parents and those of their generation as irrelevant, as merely old-fashioned or as "square." Rebellion is in most ways psychologically easier than this vision, for the rebel is clearly defined as a person by that which he opposes and by that in whose name he rebels; but the youth who finds his parents simply irrelevant is often merely lost and confused. It is probably easiest to locate positive precepts in the past; it is some help to find negative precepts in it; it is hardest not to know whether the past offers *any* precepts at all.

Nor does generational continuity require an emulation of biological fathers by their biological sons; all that is needed is the discovery of parental exemplars in the previous generation. Here the tales of Horatio Alger are instructive. Recall his basic plots: his heroes were poor but honest lads, usually fatherless but befriended by a wealthy older man, a man highly successful in his society and implicitly more "modern" than the lad's own father would have been. The young hero, partly by dint of his own efforts, but with large amounts of additional assistance from the obliging older man, eventually takes over his mentor's bank or business, marries the boss' lovely rich daughter, and becomes a roaring success. Read as social documents, these tales suggest that the time of their greatest popularity, the end of the last century, was a time when biological parents often failed as models for the changing new society—a failure exacerbated by immigrant origins. But the crucial presence of the helpful older man suggests that models *are* to be found among the more successful and "acculturated"; if one's own parents will not do, there are others of their generation who will. In the face of less rapid forms of social change, one may have to abandon one's parents, but their surrogates are of the same generation.

Or consider the family sagas popular in the same period, with the characteristic portrait of the vagaries of three or four generations. The novels of Trollope, Thackeray, and Galsworthy depend in part on the changes between the generations for theme (without a changing society, each generation would merely repeat its predecessor) and thus they reflect the earlier stages of our present rapid rates of change. But at the same time, their central underlying theme is that of the *relatedness* of the generations, the way each incorporates or reacts against the vices and virtues of the one before it. Though they take generational *dis*continuity as topic, they suggest that generational continuity still exists, albeit in a different and less perceptible form. Like Horatio Alger, these sagas point to the first beginnings of generational discontinuity even at the moment when they argue that such discontinuity is more apparent than real.

The contrast with modern heroes is extreme: our heroes of stage and novel almost completely lack admired paternal figures, or for that matter, paternal figures relevant enough to rebel against. Often they are portrayed, like Augie March, as being fatherless and virtually ancestorless; others, like Holden Caulfield or the heroes played by James Dean have fathers in name only. The fathers of others are so broken by defeat or the tides of time that they inspire sorrow and pity rather than admiration or hatred. (Consider here the heroes of the plays of Arthur Miller or Tennessee Williams.) Indeed, the basic plot of most modern American fiction revolves not around the hero's relationship to his past, but about his lack of connection with it. Parents and their world are left far behind, not because they have been transcended, superseded or replaced, but because they are simply irrelevant to the hero's search for himself in the present. Only Mom is sometimes recalled, and then it is usually because she represents a warm, secure, and innocent state which the hero dimly regrets leaving, and/or because she is seen as manipulative and smothering and he is glad to have escaped her clutches. But in either case he has left her behind. The hero is therefore lost, confused, and searching, a picaresque figure who lusts unfulfilled for commitment. And if he finds any object worthy of his devotion, it is usually a child, or the fact of children—something immediate, concrete, present, and as yet unaffected by historical dislocations.

In the span from Horatio Alger and the *Forsyte Saga* to Augie March and Holden Caulfield, generational continuity, already a problem in the society of two generations ago, has become a dim recollection. Increasing numbers of young Americans find themselves so distant from their parents that they can neither emulate nor rebel against them. Instead, they "understand" them better than previous generations (whose fates were more interwoven with their parents) could afford to. Many young Americans feel toward their parents a sympathy, a compassion, and a pity that most of us can feel only toward that from which we feel ultimately detached; and with this sympathy goes a strong sense—an implicit realization —on the part of *both* parents *and* children that the two generations face such different life situations that the way parents conducted their lives may be neither good nor bad for their children, but simply irrelevant.

## The end of identification

Generational discontinuity is a double problem. For one, the closest link between social history and individual history is the individual's sense of relationship to his own personal history as embodied in his parents, his ancestors, and all they come to represent to him. This sense of relationship defines an individual's sense of self as surely as does his work or his children; when it is missing, men and women tend as surely to feel confused, to lack a sense of identity, as they would without work, love, or offspring. Much of the aimless wandering through experience we see in the heroes of modern novels or in alienated young men, statements like Inburn's "and the place not being there from which he set off any more," and the cult of the present are all related to chronic social change and its consequence, generational discontinuity. But the tie between parents and children has a second and more immediately personal meaning: from his parents a child has traditionally learned the meaning of adulthood, of maleness and femaleness, of work, play, and social membership. By identifying with his parents, by internalizing their ways of doing things, by imitating their behavior, he has known how to become an adult. When, as now, generational discontinuity is extreme, the identification of the generations is vastly complicated and sometimes interrupted altogether.

In the lives of alienated students, I have underlined the central

importance of their inability to identify with their fathers. Part of
this inability has to do with the special family constellation we have
found among these young men; but another part is an increasing
problem for all young American men and women. In more static
and less complex societies, parents rightly bring up their children to
be like themselves in central ways. Young men do what their fathers did; young women copy their mothers; even in societies sufficiently complex to offer several options (e.g., to be a tiller of the
soil, a warrior, or a priest) these options are clearly epitomized by
the members of the older generation. To be sure, parents and children can often disagree, and the transition to adulthood is not always smooth. But relatively static societies usually permit something approaching a total identification of the younger generation
with the one before it. From his father or others of his generation a
man learns not only the personal qualities expected of an adult, but
the religious outlooks and practices, the ways of working, the ways
of dealing with relatives and non-relatives in the community. Relatively total identification means that a young man or woman can
choose an exemplar present in the community and emulate him or
her in full confidence that what proved adequate for one generation
will prove adequate for the next.

The problem of identification is inevitably more complicated for
young Americans. Partly because of the pace of social change,
identifications must be cautious, selective, partial, and incomplete.
Work changes; the skills essential to our parents no longer suffice
for us: it is a rare (and usually unsuccessful) farmer or carpenter
who does exactly what his father did. Women, too, know in their
bones that the ways they were raised as children may not suffice for
their own children, and anticipate that the fashions of child-rearing
will continue to swing as they have in the past. To choose to be
exactly like one's father or mother is to choose obsolescence; indeed it is literally impossible, if only because a pattern of life considered normal forty years ago would evoke such a different (and
incredulous) response from one's contemporaries today.

Replacing the more total identifications of the past are ever more partial, selective, and incomplete identifications. To be able to identify with her mother at all, a modern woman must winnow what remains enduringly relevant about her mother from those qualities that are "old-fashioned"—a product of her mother's particular historical situation. In place of a few deeply admired and influential older people who determine the shape of the self, young Americans must increasingly have either none—as is the case with the alienated—or else many, with each of whom they identify partially and selectively. Both alternatives are difficult. With no exemplars, no objects of identification, and an obdurate refusal to accept them, the result is often that perplexity, self-fragmentation and confusion we see in many alienated young men. With an effort to select the most admirable and enduring qualities from *many* older men and women, great demands are made on the individual's abilities to choose, select, synthesize, and differentiate. These demands are by no means impossible; and many young Americans undoubtedly achieve a workable synthesis of selective identifications. Nor, of course, is this a deliberate and conscious task; it is simply a requirement of our society which few youths stop to consider. But this task is more difficult than in those societies where more total identification is possible—it demands more discrimination, wiser selectivity, and greater powers of synthesis; and these demands constitute still another source of stress in American life.

The pitfalls in selective identification are several. For one, given the historically determined requirement that in our society a young man or woman *must* repudiate his parents in at least some major ways, many young men and women conclude that they can emulate their fathers and mothers in *no* ways at all, that, on the contrary, they must bend every effort *not* to be like them in *any* way. (This outcome is most likely when the parent of the same sex expresses, in his or her life, his or her own failure as a human being to be able to deal with the facts and tensions of family life.) The consequence, as we have seen in alienated youths, is a major problem concerning adult sexuality and adulthood in general. Another mishap may come from selecting the wrong qualities to emulate. A young man who attempts to emulate, for example, that solidity and even rigidity of outlook which we all openly or secretly admire in our grandparents risks finding himself considered "old before his time," and will often be unable to adapt to the changing requirements of his society because of his rigid adherence to principles whose relevance is no longer clear. And most likely and common, an adolescent may admire a great many qualities in others that are extremely difficult to synthesize into a workable identity. The result is likely to be a diffusion of identity, a simultaneous admiration of incompatibles, and a resulting period of confusion, lack of sense of self, and wandering in search of some way of combining irreconcilable psychic possibilities.

## Choose to be changed

Just as social change in the past accentuates generational discontinuity and raises special problems in the identification of the generations, so continual social change in the present and the future raises a related problem for the young. To stay abreast with the transformations of our society requires a special kind of personality, special ways of dealing with the world—heightened responsiveness to events and trends, greater flexibility, increased ability to shift course in midstream—which make new demands on individuals. Not only is there a problem in learning what one is and deciding what to become—a universal problem exacerbated by rapid social change—but the chronic transformation of our society gives all present commitments a tentative quality, and fosters types of personality that have built-in insurance against premature obsolescence. (One reason ours is a culture of youth is that the aged lose the capacity to make these rapid adaptations to changing circumstances.)

We all understand the need for flexibility on the job. Our technological folklore abounds in cautionary tales of those who did not "keep abreast of new developments" in their work, and who consequently were "left behind." We admire men and women who have the ingenuity to learn new skills when their old jobs cease to exist; we have nationwide programs to retrain those whose skills are no longer needed because of changing technology. Even our emphasis on higher education contains an implicit assumption that the most highly educated will be most able to shift with the occupational wind when it changes. In studying alienated youths we have seen the frequent job changes of their fathers; and similar changes are as common among the parents of all students. Indeed, in the responses of the fathers of alienated students we see one of the common tragedies of changing technology: men who shift jobs radically in mid-career, as some of these men did, often feel misplaced and displaced in their new jobs, attributing the change to some failure of their own or allowing others to view it thus. Rapid changes in the vocational and professional needs of our economy mean that most young men must approach vocational commitment tentatively and cautiously, realizing that the skills they acquire today may be obsolete tomorrow.

The shifting job marketplace is, however, only the most visible symptom of other psychologically more important changes, all of which require for successful survival a great increase in sensitivity to the demands of the social environment, an ability to bend with the wind, to accept uprooting graciously. Our phrase "keeping up with the Joneses" implies that the Joneses are themselves changing —otherwise we would say "catching up with the Joneses." Many of our phrases to denote those we emulate have the same ring—the "pace-setters" are themselves moving; the "style-leaders" are setting new and *different* styles. To be a "good mother," an educated modern woman considers it her responsibility to "keep up" with the best opinion about child-rearing; nor must men be "old-fashioned" in their views about women, children, and the family's role in life. Equally anathema is the man who clings so tenaciously to early-acquired values and outlooks that he is unable to "respond" to the needs of others around him or, worse still, remains simply unaware of them. The patterns of life and the values to which we commit ourselves today may soon become outmoded; and those who sense this—as most young men and women do—accordingly must make their commitments tentative, and often are forced to prefer "role-playing" to deep devotion.

There are, of course, some values that endure; and many youths manage eventually to find them and in some way to devote themselves to them. But as the rate of change increases, in each generation there are fewer and fewer such values, fewer practices that have a feeling of solidity, fewer ways of life that have a ring of endurance. As a result, many young men and women choose, as they must, to commit themselves to change itself, usually expressed in terms like "openness," "flexibility," "responsiveness," "sensitivity," and the absence of "rigidity," "intransigeance," and "narrowness." This "other direction," so well described by David Riesman in *The Lonely Crowd*, springs not so much from the population changes to which he first attributed it, but to rate of social change in America and the ensuing need for the utmost in responsivity, sensitivity, awareness of one's human and social environment, and tolerance of today's innovations, which may be tomorrow's established conventions. It is carefully learned in the ways Riesman describes—indeed, the "faddism" of young adolescents, their hyper-responsiveness to almost daily changes in fashion and style, can be seen as a training ground for later responsiveness to more important "fashions" in values, skills, and ways of life.

Though few of us consciously experience it as such, the pressure to respond to changes in every aspect of our lives places us under a great strain, and especially presses hard on adolescents, who are searching for commitments that will last a lifetime. "Choose to be changed" is, as Rilke knew, a once-in-a-lifetime imperative, and is difficult if it merely means a perpetually vigilant responsiveness to the environment. A young man who makes such a conscious or unconscious commitment to continual self-transformation is committing himself to an unknown whose shape he can do little to determine. To satisfy psychologically, such a commitment presupposes a deep faith in the goodness of the social process by which one lets oneself be bent; yet such a radical faith is almost completely lacking among young Americans. When, as now, society is viewed more neutrally, the result is a loss of an active sense of self, an increased feeling of being acted *upon,* of being a victim of a social process one can no longer control or even fathom. The virtues of flexibility, openness, and tolerance are noble; but unless they are supported by a firm sense of self, of identity, and of individual direction, it is hard for most men and women to distinguish these virtues from senseless and passive conformity. And above all, this combination of a universal human need for enduring ground on which to build one's life plus a shifting social order in which to live it places an added burden on young Americans attempting to chart the course of the rest of their lives.

## Alienation and historical dislocation

Man's relationship to time and to history is of central importance to him. The basic events of human life occur within a context of subjective time that helps determine and sets limits on his feelings about all specific events in the past, the present, and the future. Behind this sense of time lies the universal need for historical relatedness, manifest partly as a desire to understand where one comes from and where one is going, partly as a more concrete need to define one's relationship to one's own individual and familial past and future, partly as a need to feel oneself part of a group and a universe with an intelligible past related to a comprehensible future. A man's sense of his own place in time, and of his place in a society and world located in history, is central to his definition of himself, just as a society's definition of its place in history is one of the most distinguishing features of that society.

In this chapter, I have argued that our changing society has produced a sense of historical dislocation, a loss of older American modes of temporal relatedness, an "alienation" from all sense of historical position. This sense of historical dislocation is manifest in an accentuation of the knowable present at the expense of the irrelevant past and the unanticipatable future, in a break in the sense of generational continuity, in an increasing need for ever more selective identifications in personal development, and in the appearance of new types of personality whose major commitment is to flexibility and change itself. Each of these developments makes growing up more difficult, places new demands on the young, adds to the strain of accepting adulthood in our society.

Our changing sense of our place in time and history also brings, of course, notable advantages. The rhetoric of discussions of social change makes amply clear that social change brings new opportunities for those who are flexible enough to seize them. And coupled with these is a new capacity to appreciate the present and all those things that can be enjoyed only in the present: the pleasures of the senses and of the body, the contemplation of nature, the appreciation of art and beauty. The vestigial Puritanism which made all present pleasures sinful and sanctioned only activities aimed at the future—be it the Hereafter or the Bank Balance—is fast disappearing. Further, for those who can tolerate it, historical dislocation can bring an enormous sense of freedom, of not being bound by the past, of creating oneself at each moment of one's existence. Yet characteristically a philosophy of absolute freedom, based on a denial of any necessary relationship with the past, is usually a philosophy of the absurd; the signs of this freedom are not joy and triumph, but nausea and dread; and its possessors are not the creators but the Strangers and Outsiders of the universe. Few men, young or old, ordinary or extraordinary, can live contentedly, must less joyously, without some relationship to time other than total freedom. Paradoxically, it is comforting and perhaps necessary to feel one's freedom limited, if only voluntarily, by one's links with the past and one's projects for the future. When the "times are out of joint" because unprecedented things occur without comprehensible links to the past, most men feel, with Hamlet, not exultation but distress.

Like any broad social development, our increasing loss of historical relatedness is experienced by each individual in the terms of his own idiosyncratic life—indeed in analyzing individual lives we too often see only these idiosyncratic instances and fail to note their relationship to broader historical events. And since, as I have argued, we are now in the midst of these changes, their impact on individuals is extremely uneven. They affect least the very old and the very young, for the very old have another past than ours to come to terms with, and the young have too little past to have any need as yet to come to terms with it at all. They impinge most heavily on the young adults of our society, for these are in the process of realigning their pasts so as to make a commitment to a future life in this society, and questions of historical relatedness are therefore central to them. So, too, those in the byways of our society are less affected than those in the forefront; those in small towns less than those in cosmopolitan cities; those in stable professions less than those in rapidly changing occupations. But to some extent the loss of historical relatedness affects us all, and we all must deal with it.

One response is that alienation from adulthood in American society which we have seen in the students I have earlier described. These students are extreme in their lack of any conscious sense of relatedness to their personal pasts, in their inability to make commitments for the future, in their cult of the present. In their lives we have seen writ small all of the large problems we have considered here: inability to find connections with the past and future, abrupt discontinuity between themselves and those of the previous generation, whom they resolutely refuse to admire; a failure of identification with their parents; a fruitless search for enduring and solid values. Each of these problems contributes to their unwillingness to accept the adult life offered by their society; for a readiness to be a member of a community presupposes either a sense of past relationship with it or a future hand in shaping it, and these young men have little of either.

Other adaptations are of course more common. Despite its psychological difficulties, a commitment to change and flexibility mitigates many of the individual's anxieties about his own obsolescence, and is therefore an increasingly widespread solution. And in our current emphasis on home and family life, on do-it-yourself, home swimming pools, and recreation rooms, on art, music, and sports, many Americans find ways of accenting the present to such an extent that their increasing lack of relatedness to past and future seldom consciously troubles them. Even the characteristic American phenomenon of "youth culture"—that is, the special ways and manners of young men and women who are too old to be considered children and too young to be considered full adults in our society—can be partly understood as a reaction away from parents (who because of their different generational position cannot fully prepare their children for modern life) toward peers who are more sensitive to the demands of the present.

The full list of such adaptations would be long, for there are few aspects of our lives which are not directly or indirectly touched by chronic social change. Such a catalogue would be out of place, for my point is that whatever these adaptations, they involve a heavy demand on the individual, that they are psychically taxing and strenuous, that they make adult life in America more trying and less rewarding. And when such adaptations fail—as they inevitably do at times—the individual is confronted with central anxieties about his own role in personal and social history. Sometimes these anxieties have to do with the feeling of unrelatedness, of being adrift, of not being able to "catch hold" of anything or anyone in our rapidly shifting society—this is the anxiety of historical dislocation. At other times they have to do with a feeling of being left behind, of being out of date, no longer needed, inadequate to the modern world, of not being able to "catch up"—this is the anxiety of human obsolescence. In most of us these anxieties remain at the periphery of psychic vision (our adaptations work), but keeping them there makes our lives more difficult and our society less inviting.

# 9    The division of life

The way our society is changing is as important as the fact of chronic change alone. It is one thing to live in a primitive society that is changing because "Western" technology has undermined its established ways; it is another to live, like Alexander's Macedonians, in a society changing by virtue of unprecedented conquests; it is another to live amidst the changes that followed the Black Plague in the Middle Ages; and it is still another to live in a society like our own, where change results from a self-stimulating technological process. The unprecedentedness of this kind of technological change makes our situation the more difficult to understand, for history teaches us only distant lessons. In this respect, we suffer from being a vanguard society: our example constitutes a model and a caution to other societies, but we ourselves have no models.

Though commentators often disagree in whether they emphasize continuity or change in our national life, there is still considerable consensus on the major directions of social change in America. Most observers agree that we are moving from an "industrial" to an increasingly "technological" society. Two generations ago, American society was characterized by a thoroughgoing exploitation of natural resources by existing techniques of production in order to produce as much as possible. Now, increasingly, our main efforts are directed to the systematic cultivation, exploitation, and application of scientific knowledge—not so much to increase sheer output, but to create new objects for consumption. Put oversimply, the goal of the older industrial society was maximum output; increasingly the goal of our newer technological society is maximum innovation and consumption.

A number of related trends follow from this. Psychologically, Americans today are more concerned with living the "rich full life" (through consumption) and less concerned with saving, hard work, and "character-building" than their grandparents. And the old "inner directed" effort to master the physical environment, to build railroads, mills, and oil empires is giving way to a more "other directed" concern with sensitivity to and control of the human environment. The "robber baron" mentality of the captains of industry in the industrial era is receding before the more group-minded "social ethic" of the technological age. Instead of new canals and railroads, we build new dishwashers with built-in obsolescence; instead of unskilled factory workers and railroad builders, we need skilled engineers, technicians and professionals; instead of a strong back, modern industry increasingly requires long training and expertise; instead of a relatively poor society, ours is increasingly a society of affluence. Our grandparents sometimes worried about how to have enough to survive; we more often worry about how to live well with what we already have.

Anyone with a long memory can personally document countless other changes in our national life: in family life, in politics, in leisure, in education, in morality and values. Indeed, the chief problem in understanding the central drift of technological society is that virtually everything in our social world is changing rapidly. To separate what is fundamental from what is peripheral, to distinguish the main drift of change from the reactions to this main drift —these assignments are impossible if we look only at the details of specific changes. Instead, we must step back a pace and seek the common, underlying patterns involved in all of the disparate changes in our lives. In this chapter, I will emphasize three central tendencies in our society—the fragmentation of tasks, the shatter-

ing of community, and the ascendency of technological values—
asking above all how these social trends affect the lives of individual Americans.

## The fragmentation of tasks

Consider the building of a house. Among the rural majority of
Americans two or three generations ago, this was a job for a farmer
and his friends. Little skill was expected—a minimal knowledge of
carpentry or bricklaying, and little more. Most of the supplies came
from near at hand: the wood from the local sawmill, bricks from
the nearest kiln; only nails and mortar came from afar. Almost
everything could be assembled on the spot, if need be by one man
with a few helping hands to raise the walls. House-building was
rarely a specialized job: most houses were built by men who were
also farmers or who also ran small stores.

Compare the situation today. Houses are now built by the co-
ordinated efforts of a series of specialists, each with his own special
competence and exclusive prerogatives, each operating according
to the special standards and skills of his field. Furthermore, their
individual efforts are co-ordinated by a contractor who builds nothing with his own hands. The task is broken into parts, and each
part of the building has its corresponding role: architect, foundation digger, plumber, electrician, carpenter, heating specialist,
house painter, decorator, glazier, and landscape gardener. The supplies are complex; they come from many parts of the world; and
many of them are themselves the end result of a long process of
manufacture. Who could think of building his furnace on the building site? Or his garbage-disposal unit? Or of making the plumbing?
And what rare jack-of-all-trades today builds his own house?

Or consider the change from the first Ford to the latest Galaxie
equipped with automatic transmission, radio, and heater (white-
walls optional) that emerges from River Rouge. Ford designed and
built his first car himself, made many of the parts himself, put them

together himself, tested the car and drove it away himself. He was, to be sure, already a "specialist" in car-building, but his role embraced every aspect of construction, planning, and repairing. Now, as we all know, the same task is performed by a vast industrial complex, in which no single individual contributes more than a small fraction of the total product. Thousands of people, from specialized assembly-line workers to middle-level management, from foremen in sub-contractors' factories to assistant vice-presidents in charge of sales, have replaced the legendary Henry Ford. The product differs, too: not one model of a relatively simple machine, but a series of "lines," ranging from relative austerity to flamboyant ostentation, each available in hundreds of combinations of colors, motors, accessories, transmissions, and gadgets.

Or take one very different example, the healing of the sick. Even at the turn of the century, the typical physician was still a general practitioner, and within his broad field a jack-of-all-trades, simultaneously internist, dermatologist, surgeon, cardiologist, pediatrician, obstetrician, gynecologist, gastroenterologist, and practical psychiatrist. He was expected to be able to cope with whatever arose in his practice: he rarely sent patients to specialists, for there *were* few specialists. He dealt directly with his patients, many of whom he had known a long time; and for better or worse they were rarely hospitalized, rarely treated with new drugs, and rarely expected to come to his office when they were sick. Today, increasingly, medicine is dominated by specialists; general practice is a rarity; clinics, hospitals, health plans, new drugs, and group practice flourish; patients are often treated in pieces by men who specialize in parts of the body or the mind. Moreover, the individual doctor, whatever his specialty, is usually enmeshed in a series of complex organizations—local hospitals, the A.M.A., other groups representing his specialty. And today a man who does not keep abreast of "new developments" in his field often finds his patients disappearing to those who do.

What has been happening in these two generations? For one, the tasks these men once performed have been broken into component parts: building houses, constructing cars, and healing the sick are no longer unspecialized jobs. Today, we have a series of co-ordinated and organized roles, each assumed by different individuals, who *together* accomplish a similar task. An entire institution is now involved; and although a similar job gets done, no one man is responsible for it.

These older jobs, then, and most others like them, have been fragmented, divided, specialized, and differentiated to the point where they no longer exist. The fragmentation of tasks has several related results. For one, the scope of the task is narrowed; the area within which the individual is expected to be competent has shrunk enormously. No one today would expect a cardiologist to be able to treat his patients' eczema; plumbers are forbidden to drive nails; vice-presidents in charge of sales never dirty their hands on the assembly line (and would not see it at all except for Guided Tours for Management). Most tasks are now accomplished collectively, and the relationship of any one man's work to the finished product or final goal of his organization is increasingly tenuous. Fragmentation thus involves a second process: the individual's specific work bears an ever more partial, more distant, more fractional connection with the total task performed by the organization in which he works.

As the scope of each job narrows and the relationship of any given job to the total task becomes more distant, the number of distinct roles held by any one individual usually increases, and the connection between these distinct roles often becomes more and more tenuous. In a relatively simple society, man is likely to hold only a few basic and embracing roles: he will be a shepherd, a father, and a member of his society—and that is all. What is expected of him in any one of these roles is usually closely connected with what is expected of him in the others. Sharp divisions between work, recreation, and family life are unthinkable; all these aspects of life are part of the same unitary matrix. But in our society, the

fragmentation and multiplication of roles means that any single individual is likely to hold a great variety of distinct roles, each one
of which makes different and unrelated demands on him.

The narrowed scope of most roles in American society does not
mean that these roles have become less demanding. On the contrary, within each small area, much greater competence and skill
are expected. The demands on today's cardiologist are not fewer
than those on yesterday's general practitioner merely because he
now treats only a part of the body: to become a cardiologist today
requires longer, more intensive, more arduous training. Relative to
his grandfather, today's master plumber is a skilled expert in a job
that requires high technical skill and training despite its narrowed
scope. In most specialized areas, it now takes more time, more
education, and higher levels of basic competence to acquire the
necessary skills: as roles become fragmented and narrowed, the
demands of each role increase. Furthermore, the distribution of
jobs in American society is changing, so that the least demanding
jobs are disappearing altogether. Jobs that formerly required only a
strong back and a willingness to work are increasingly being done
by machines. Fewer jobs are open to the illiterate, the untrained,
the inexpert: increasingly, a high school degree is a minimal prerequisite for a good job.

The heightening of demands in our society is most easily seen on
the job but it also pervades other areas of life. Take, for example,
the role of "wife and mother." The scope of a woman's work within her home has undoubtedly narrowed in the last few generations:
no longer must she can the food, care for domestic animals, tend
the vegetable garden, weave, sew, spin, and draw water. Instead,
she is expected to "specialize" in home management and child
care. But within her new specialty, greater demands are made. She
is encouraged to sort her washing into nine piles so as to take advantage of her new washing machine, to become a gourmet cook,
to study the latest psychological advice about child development, to
learn how to operate efficiently her home appliances. To be sure, it
is hard to "fragment" being a mother beyond a certain point; yet

even being a mother is no longer considered merely a matter of innate instinct, but rather a "job" that requires specialized training. In grade school and secondary school, girls take courses on "home and family living" and "home economics," and on how to repair household appliances; in many colleges, women tend to major in fields like child psychology that will give them specialized training for their future motherhood. Despite the much vaunted labor-saving devices that fill our homes and the "easy-to-care-for" homes they fill, the role of "wife and mother" is in many ways more demanding than it was.

As a result of these changes, the complexity of our social world has also increased. Instead of a relatively small number of broadly defined tasks, most of which were understandable to the average man, we now have a multiplicity of highly specialized, complex technical roles, most of which are beyond the capacities of the average man to understand, much less perform. Yesterday's farmer could usually repair his Model T with baling wire; today's must consult a factory-trained mechanic when his truck breaks down. Two generations ago, children had relatively little difficulty in understanding their father's work; today, most Americans' jobs are far beyond the comprehension of most other adults, much less their children. To the average man, ever wider areas of the social environment are an obscure, dark, and incomprehensible terrain. The older view of the world as an open, understandable place, and the older view of the self as a jack-of-all-trades are hard to maintain in the 1960's.

The fragmentation of tasks would lead to total chaos unless some kind of organization were imposed upon the fragmented parts. The division of labor works only when "divided labor" is co-ordinated as in an assembly line; breaking a job into small and specialized components is only feasible when someone is concerned with their reunification. One of the most notable trends of our social landscape is, therefore, the burgeoning of specialized roles that have to do with co-ordination, organization, planning, and overseeing. The contractor's role is typical: he devotes his entire efforts to co-ordinating and planning the work of others who do the actual work of building the house. Like those he oversees, he is a specialist, but his specialty is organization itself. The list of "organizational" roles is endless; managers, executives, foremen, planners, co-ordinators, government officials—all are concerned with organization rather than with primary production. The proportion of Americans involved in the actual production of goods is steadily declining, the proportion working in organizational, sales, and service positions is growing even more rapidly. Today most Americans manage, record, schedule, plan, buy, repair, sell, or advertise. Only a small percentage is immediately involved with production. Management, organization, and service are not new (kings, judges, and priests do these things in any society); but it is unprecedented to have *most* of the population so employed.

The trends I have outlined are of course not completed facts. But as trends, they affect us all, from industrial workers to top executives, from farmers to college professors. Under slogans like automation, division of labor, specialization, rising standards, "upgrading," higher educational levels, human engineering, and industrial psychology, these trends affect even the hold-outs of the unitary life. Even artists and teachers today often find themselves involved in complex organizations, assigned to highly specialized tasks, and pushed to high levels of performance within their specialties. Most important, these trends mean that the quality of life has changed in America over the past two generations, and it has changed in a way which makes greater demands on the individual.

## The shattering of community

In some traditional societies, men live out their lives as members of a community which tells them who they are. In it, the tasks of work, the responsibilities of the family, the worship of the gods, and the pursuit of virtue are fused. In peasant societies throughout history, men's obligation to their work, their children, their fellows, and the Divine has been seen as a part of an indissoluble whole; and in most primitive societies even today, an intimate nexus exists between family, social obligation, work, ritual, magic, and religion. A peasant tills the soil because it is his job, because he must support his family, because industry is virtuous, and because the gods have so ordained it. And all these reasons, which we would consider different, are experienced by him as one and the same.

In such communities, the demands of the mind, the hands, and the heart are fused. The peasant does not merely work his land, he cares for it. The fisherman not only exploits the sea, but stands in awe of its ferocity and prays for its calm. The hunter not only kills the animals he hunts, he also often worships them as his highest gods. And toward his broader community, toward the other members of his village and tribe, he feels a kinship based not on rational awareness of common purpose and custom, but on instinctive loyalty derived from a sense of special humanity. Many primitive communities refer to themselves merely as "the people," thus distinguishing their own special humanity from that of all other barbarians, all "not people." Within such primary communities, what men do and what they think is a part of what they feel and what they worship: cognition, action, feeling, morality, and reverence are fused.

In America such intact communities have long been hard to find. The elements of community are sundered; we live as members of organizations and not of a community. And the same processes we have examined in the fragmentation of tasks are also apparent in the disappearance of traditional community. The shattering of the structures of traditional community began many centuries ago; indeed, today the transition from community to organizations is so far advanced that we must look to primitive societies for examples of intact community. And the stages of this transition are well known to any student of the history of the Western world. First, increasing specialization breaks up aspects of community life that once were fused. For example, law, government, and religion, which are often combined in a single institution in primitive communities, are split into separate specialties in modern society. And within each specialty, further fragmentation has taken place: in government, constitutional offices acquire added agencies and special staffs, and these in turn set up further executive and consultative functions; law becomes more and more specialized as dozens of sub-fields appear; even education is subdivided into myriad compartments and specialties. And with the break-up of traditional institutions come the related processes of narrowing scope and increasing demands. We expect a great deal more of today's specialized schools than our grandparents did of theirs. The demands for governmental performance have grown: today government is expected to take an increasingly active role in guaranteeing full employment, in caring for the indigent, the sick, and the aged. Just as we demand a higher level of performance from today's specialist than from yesterday's jack-of-all-trades, so we constantly expect more from the organizations and institutions that have replaced traditional community.

One of the main consequences of the shattering of community has been the growing division of society into two non-overlapping spheres—a public sphere whose demands are primarily cognitive, and a private sphere which remains the proper arena for feeling, devotion, faith, and reverence. Public institutions like law, government, science, and the economy demand increasingly high levels of "rational" and cognitive competence—a capacity for achievement, objectivity, fairness, and detachment, an ability to deal with high-level abstractions and complex situations, to wait, postpone, and delay, to cope with changing social needs, to resist emotion, partiality, preference, or personal whim, to work with and "get along" with others. In contrast, the family, the arts, recreation, entertainment, and religion have increasingly become the province of the rest of life—passion, feeling, idealism, impulse, love, hatred, and whim.

The fragmentation of community requires a basic change in the way men define themselves. Where individual life is embedded in an undifferentiated community, society merely demands that men continue to be what they are, which is what they were born to be. Self-definition is largely a function of social definition: only the rare madman or rebel defies what his society tells him he is. Merely to grow up in the community is to have most of the central questions of selfhood answered automatically; and child-rearing is often so neatly geared to specific adult roles that the question of "who am I?" can hardly arise as a conscious question. The only problem is how to raise the young so that they will "fit." But when community in this sense no longer exists, the psychology of self-definition changes drastically.

Put in oversimplified form, if the main problem of traditional community is "socialization" or "fitting in," then the chief problem of our technological society is the achievement of individual identity. In a technological society, every youth is confronted with a series of distinct roles, organizations, and institutions, each of which makes different and often conflicting demands. A medieval lad might choose between priesthood and peasantry, and this single choice almost entirely defined the rest of his life: his residence, his work, his marriage, his religion, his friends, and his values. But our society offers no such "package deals," no prefabricated and pre-assembled adulthoods which can be donned like a suit of clothes.

Nor do the organizations and institutions that have replaced intact community really provide an adequate substitution for it. For a very few, religion can still provide a special sense of embracing belonging and selfhood; but for most, religion is but a Sunday meeting house and nursery school, and a recreation center, which cannot adequately define the entire person. And some Americans, especially those whose "Americanism" is of most recent origin, still seek in nationality an object of devotion, loyalty, awe, and service, and try to gain from their national identity a sense of special virtue. But nationality, probably even for the "one-hundred-per-cent American," cannot really replace lost community: to be an American is but the beginning of self-definition.

Other searches and substitutions are more common. Some seek community within their own families, looking to their spouses and their children for a definition of who they truly are. Yet this seldom suffices, for the systematic separation of the "private" family from "public" life means that for men, as increasingly for women, family life is but half a life. Others, the organization men, seek—or are made to simulate—community in the corporations for which they work. But this too usually fails, for the fragmented organizations of our society are designed to produce, innovate, and sell, and not to inspire devotion or reverence. And still others search for community in a thousand voluntary associations, lodges, fraternities, and country clubs which with elaborate ritual and initiation promise to tell them who they are and where they stand. But mostly the promise remains unfulfilled: Rotary, Delta Kappa Epsilon, and the "top" country club—even taken together—can rarely do more than add new external labels to a man's self-concept; and at times they may even create a new set of conflicts between the self that is lodge member and the self that is family man or organization man.

Since these attempts to re-create intact community in religion, nation, family, corporation, or voluntary association usually fail, most Americans are forced to live without community, and must seek in inner integration a substitute for traditional social definition of themselves. Though we are a nation of joiners, we are not a nation of men and women who feel they belong: and themes of homelessness, uprootedness, and a search for a unitary defining context are common in American life and literature. Uprootedness and wandering dominate American literature from Melville to Kerouac, and the loneliness and isolation that both Americans and foreigners see below the surface of American gregariousness suggest our vague sense of truly belonging nowhere. Increasingly, we must achieve—not discover—our identities, and create—not find—our homes.

## *The ascendancy of technological values*

The two trends I have so far discussed are closely related. The fragmentation of traditional tasks and the shattering of traditional community both involve differentiation, specialization, narrowing of scope, and increased demands for performance within a narrowed field. And behind both trends is a set of basic technological values about life, virtue, and efficacy. Did we not tacitly consent to these values, we would bridle at the social changes that increasingly implement them; in societies where men utterly reject these values, a technological society does not and cannot develop.

We usually think of technology, like science, as "objective," uninterested in ultimate values, and uninvolved with basic philosophical assumptions. Thus, to speak of the "values" of technology may seem a contradiction, for among the chief characteristics of technology is that it *has* no final values, that it is little concerned with the ultimate ends of life, and deals hardly at all with the whys, whats, and wherefores of human existence. But though technology lacks final values, it does specify instrumental values, values about the procedures, techniques, processes and modes which should be followed, values about "how to do it."

The question "How to do it?" of course admits many possible answers. Some societies have given highest priority to those techniques we term intuition, sensibility, revelation, and insight. In such societies, inner vision, fantasy, and communication with the Divine are the most cherished aspects of human experience. "Realism," whether in art, literature, domestic life, or personal experience is almost unknown: superstititon, magic, myth, and collective fantasies abound. The favored instruments of knowledge in these societies are those we consider "non-rational": prayer, mysticism, intuition, revelation, dreams, inspiration, "possession." But in a technological society, these human potentials take second place: we distrust intuition and consider revelation a token of mental illness; and in everyday language "sensitivity" connotes the quality of being too easily offended rather than the capacity to experience deeply.

The preferred techniques of technology involve two related principles: that we *give priority to cognition,* and that we *subordinate feeling.* By "cognition," I mean men's capacities for achieving accurate, objective, practically useful, and consensually verifiable knowledge and understanding of their world; and by "priority" I mean to suggest that these capacities have increasingly become superordinate to other human potentials. Thus, feeling as a force of independent value—all of the passions, impulses, needs, drives, and idealisms which in some societies are the central rationales of existence—are increasingly minimized, suppressed, harnessed, controlled and dominated by the more cognitive parts of the psyche. Feeling does not, of course, cease to exist; but insofar as possible, it is subordinated to the cognitive demands of our society.

The priority of cognition involves a series of other instrumental values and stratagems, which we consider applicable to the solution of all problems. Indeed, the very notion that most difficulties in life are "problems" is one of the central assumptions of the technological outlook. We normally assume that the pitfalls along life's path can best be dealt with by treating them as cognitive difficulties whose solution involves the application of "know-how." Ours is a how-to-do-it society, and not a what-to-do society. For every discussion of the ethics of love, we have a dozen manuals in every drugstore on the "techniques" of love. For every discussion of the purposes of life, industry, and society, a thousand hours are spent in discovering how to sell soap, how to peddle the image of a politician, how to propagate the "American way of life." We approach even the question of national survival as a cognitive problem of how to ready ourselves to destroy the Russians efficiently should the need arise, and how to limit their effective capacity to destroy us. Our human troubles and tragedies are largely defined as "unsolved problems"; and our chief attention goes toward attempting to discover the proper cognitive techniques for solving them.

Thus our society characteristically dismisses "final questions" as either philosophically "meaningless" or—more commonly—as "irrelevant" to the pressing problems at hand. The man who insists on asking such questions is usually considered an obstructionist. Discussions of "why" and "what" are relegated to Sunday churchgoing, to neurotic adolescents, and to a few artists and dissidents whose views are occasionally reported, well behind the business news, in our national weeklies. Even the harassed middle-aged executives in modern novels, who question "the meaning of it all," are allowed only a brief regression to adolescent philosophizing and a short sexual fling before being made to realize that selling codfish balls really can make sense after all. The relegation of ministers to their pulpits and intellectuals to their ivory towers effectively insulates the public from any potential gadfly who might raise embarrassing—and to many Americans, unanswerable—questions about ultimate purposes.

What, then, are the cognitive techniques prescribed by our society for solving problems? First among these is to *analyze* the problem into manageable components. Life, tasks, problems, roles, and industrial goals are all said to consist of analytically distinct and separable components. Approaches to a problem that emphasize the continuity or irreducible wholeness of any phenomenon are deemed "merely" aesthetic. Even human life is not seen as an organic whole but as a series of discreet, temporally contiguous events. American psychological theories stress isolated behavior patterns at the expense of continuous human processes; most industrial managers overlook the fact that men can often accomplish more working together than working separately on an assembly line. Despite the daily evidence of our senses that most functioning wholes are a great deal more than the sum of their parts, we often treat even society as a mere collection of individuals bound together by common laws, neglecting the obvious patterns of mutual interdependence that connect us all. To most Americans the term "synthetic" merely suggests bogus flowers or man-made fibers, and not the integrating potential of personality. We most value the "analytic," the "incisive," and the "sharp"—the qualities of intelligence which dissect, analyze, and break apart.

Analysis almost inevitably involves *reduction,* in that it attempts to reduce the large to the small, to divide unities into fractions, to locate the indivisible particles from which all else can be shown to be built. In practice, the impulse to reduce problems into smaller component parts often results in an implicit devaluation of what is analyzed. We attribute greater reality to the separate building blocks than to the finished edifice, perhaps because we assume that every whole is "merely" the sum of these building blocks. In psychology, this devaluation is seen in our countless daily assertions that apparently noble aspirations are "nothing but" rationalizations of other less admirable but more basic drives, that reason is a "mere" slave of powerful passions, that vision, idealism, and wisdom are "only" compensations for underlying blindness, corruption, and folly. Theories of learning frequently proclaim that human learning is essentially no different from animal learning—that Michelangelo in his studio is to the cheese-seeking rat merely as the large computer is to the small. Synthetic principles which might help explain wholeness, intactness, integration, and unity are rarely articulated.

Cognitive "problem-solving" also involves *measurement and comparison.* With the effort to reduce reality to basic building blocks goes the desire to find quantitative standards of comparison for apparently dissimilar entities. Money is one such standard: otherwise incomparable corporations or men share the fact that they make (or lose) money. But beyond this most visible yardstick of worth, our society abounds in other numerical comparisons: miles, horsepower, feet, IQ points, kilowatts, per cents, pounds, reams, grade averages, quires, and quartiles. On the scale of income, human worth can be measured (a $10,000-a-year man); on the scale of IQ points, intelligence can be measured (an IQ of 106); and in percentages, we measure the heart of the nation (48 per cent approved of peace). And though measurement and comparison require overlooking differences in quality and individuality, this is a price we are willing to pay.

All of these characteristics of our technological values presuppose *empiricism*, a special view of reality that most Americans accept without question. In this metaphysic, what is "real" is external, sensory, and consensually validatable: "seeing is believing." Other cultures would of course have disagreed; for most men of the Middle Ages, Truth sprang not from the objective eye but from the divinely inspired soul. But for us, what is real and true is the visible, external, and scientifically verifiable; and the rest is "speculation," "mythical," "unverifiable," "merely a matter of opinion." Empiricism thus relegates the invisible world of poetry, art, feeling, and religion to a limbo of lesser reality, sometimes termed "fantasy gratifications" to permit men to repair the wounds incurred by their daily struggle in the "real world." American psychology sometimes reflects this empiricism by a discomfort at the invisible workings of the mind so extreme that it refers to thinking as "subverbal talking," or defines "reality factors" as those impinging on us from outside—as if fantasy, dream, and idealism were not "realities" as well. "Experience," a term which in principle includes everything that crosses consciousness, has come to mean "sensory experience"—"experience" of the "real world"—and we can suggest that human beings have other potentialities only by adding the awkward qualifier "inner." Those who have overwhelming self-evident inner experiences are relegated to our mental hospitals, though other societies would have honored them as saints, seers, and prophets. Our gods are accuracy, realism, verifiability, and objectivity; while intuition, fantasy, and private illumination are considered useful only insofar as they lead to "objective" achievements or help dissipate the tensions created by the "real" world.

The triumph of cognition in a technological society thus involves a subordination of feeling. The techniques of cognitive problem-solving—analysis, reduction, measurement, comparison, and empiricism—are all non-emotional: they stress objectivity, they demand dispassionateness, they purport to be universally applicable to all situations. Emotion must be "kept in its place"—and this place is ideally somewhere away from public life, work, politics, or the economy. From an early age we are taught that strong feelings on the job cause trouble—unless they are about doing an efficient job, in which case they are desirable. Ideally, the "good worker" is cool, impersonal, always friendly and ready to listen to others but never "personally involved." He does not panic, he is not jealous, he neither loves nor hates his fellow workers, he does not day-dream at work. When all goes well, his work goes "by the book": it lives up to or exceeds the standards established in his field. Even the desire for personal advancement—one feeling our society does admit—must be controlled if it threatens to interfere with the worker's performance: one does not wreck General Motors in order to become its president.

Men and women of course inevitably continue to have strong feelings about their livelihoods, and the people involved in them. But we early learn that these feelings are usually a "problem" to be "dealt with" in other ways—in our families, in recreation—and not "acted out" on the job. The vocabulary of deprecation is filled with terms to describe those who disobey the imperative against emo-tion: "prima donnas," "unstable" or "impulsive" types, "day dreamers," people who "act out." Whatever we really feel, we must *behave* as if we only felt a reasonable eagerness to do a good job, and in reward are called "dispassionate," "objective," "self-controlled," "level-headed," "rational," and "stable."

The subordination of feeling has several regular corollaries. One is the demand for *fairness and impartiality*. In all areas of public life we learn to "treat everyone the same." The highest principle of our legal code involves "equality before the law," and in work as in most other areas of public life men should be treated equally no matter who they are. There are still embarrassing lapses to this principle, especially in the case of dark-skinned Americans, but even here the growing pressure toward greater fairness is clear. In principle, equality means that we judge, punish, and reward people according to what they have done and not according to their birth, sex, age, race, or appearance. Only the family is exempt from the principles of fairness and impartiality, and then only because families cannot exist without a recognition of the inherent differences of gender and generation. Otherwise, the trend toward greater fairness, equality, and impartiality is unmistakable. Preferential treatment, nepotism, and favoritism are universally frowned upon, and expertise, competence, and proven achievements are the chief values of public life.

These requirements of our public world—that feeling be subordinated to the objective task at hand, that everyone be treated according to the same rules, and that a person's accomplishments should determine his rewards—run through much of American life. They are visible in the fragmented roles that determine our public behavior, they are implemented in the myriad organizations that have replaced traditional community, and they are closely related to the real needs of technology. To accomplish its primary goals—the systematic exploitation and cultivation of scientific knowledge to produce new objects of consumption—a technological society requires a highly cognitive outlook and a subordination of feeling to technological tasks. Technology and cognitive outlook have the same justification: if one wants to get things done, this is the way to do them—"facing facts gets results." The dreamer, the visionary and the poet are thought to be of little use in the day-to-day working of technological society; personal expressiveness and "style" are of secondary value except as entertainment.

Even the areas where these cognitive and anti-emotional rules do not apply support the view that they take priority. For these other areas of life, family and leisure, are almost invariably relegated to a secondary role, termed outlets, recreation, havens, or exceptions to the basic rules of our social order. Implicitly or explicitly we view them as compensatory to the "real world"—they are the froth, frills, safety valves, and status-symbols a technological society must allow itself. We pay reluctant obeisance to the need to "work off steam" built up by the emotional suppressions required in work; we allow "unproductive" people like young married women with small children to occupy themselves with arts and antiques; we study emotions scientifically to learn how better to subordinate them; and we even approve if our pianists beat the Russians on the concerto front of the Cold War. A rich society can afford its clowns and dreamers; and a cognitive society may need them as "outlets." But let a young man announce his intention of becoming a poet, a visionary, or a dreamer, and the reactions of his family and friends will unmistakably illustrate the values most Americans consider central.

Merely to deprecate these values would be to overlook their role in creating the many advantages of our technological society. Few of us would want to live in a society where partiality, unfairness, inequality, preferential treatment based on birth, arbitrarily applied whims, and uncontrolled passion ruled. But similarly, merely to praise the technological values of our society is to overlook the psychological demands these values entail, and thus to overlook their role in producing alienation.

## Social fragmentation and psychological wholeness

The trends I have discussed in this chapter are familiar to anyone conversant with the mainstream of social criticism and analysis of technological societies. For almost a century sociologists have pointed to differentiation, fragmentation, specialization, "upgrading," the decline of intact community, and empiricism as important characteristics of societies like our own. But these analyses often stop short of considering the human impact of these social trends, and here we must continue beyond them, asking at what points the fragmentation of tasks, the shattering of community, and the ascendency of technological values subject individual Americans to the greatest psychological pressures.

*The burden of choice*—Our intellectual tradition has always held freedom of choice to be a positive value. If there has been any traditional "problem of freedom," it has been the problem of attaining the greatest possible freedom from social restraint. For centuries, our most vital political slogans have emphasized freedom from political, social, ideological, and, of late, psychological constraints on freedom. Some of the success of these political and ideological slogans has been accidental—increasing social fragmentation alone has meant an ever greater availability of life options. Whatever the reasons, the actual extent of choice in American society—and in democratic technological societies everywhere—has increased enormously in the past centuries. But though our political slogans continue to demand greater freedom, many Americans have come to experience this freedom as at best a mixed blessing and at worst an acute problem; the demand that one choose and make commitments in the face of an enormous variety of socially available options is increasingly felt as a heavy demand.

Consider the commitments that the average high school student must make in our fragmented society. For one, he must choose a *career*. From among literally tens of thousands of job posibilities, he must select *the one* which seems best suited to his talents, motives, needs, feelings, values, and background. And he must inevitably make this choice in relative ignorance of what most of these careers involve, yet fully aware that what they involve today may be quite different from what they will involve tomorrow. Whether he will be a plumber, a car-dealer, an engineer, a carpenter, a grocery man, an insurance man, a factory worker; whether he will go to college (and which college and to major in what), whether to seek fame or wealth or public service, whether he is talented enough for job A or too talented for job B, whether he has the motivation for job X or job Y—none of these questions admits an easy answer. Furthermore, at the same time or soon after, he must choose a *wife*. And this decision too can be difficult. When to marry? Now? Later? What kind of girl to marry? A beautiful girl? A practical girl? Wealthy? Intelligent? A good mother? And what kind of marriage to try to achieve? How many children to have? How much do you have to love someone to marry her? Many societies solve these problems with arranged marriages and ignorance of contraception; ours leaves them up to the individual.

But there is more: an American youth must also decide what he believes, where he will live, what style of life he will lead, how he will vote, what role he will play in which organizations, how he will spend his free time. Our society offers no "package deals" in which one choice takes care of most of the rest, no clear "blueprints for life" that an individual can take or leave as a whole. Each choice involves other choices; each commitment requires others; each decision is a preface to another new point of no return.

But of all the choices our society asks of us, the hardest is the "choice" of who to *be,* for this decision underlies the rest. To call it a "choice" is of course to make it sound more conscious and deliberate than it is; for most youths, "who to be" is hardly a matter of conscious reflection, but of unconscious selection and synthesis. Yet from outside, and over a long period, we can often see the slow development of an unspoken determination not to be like one's father but to be like some admired teacher; the gradual commitment to and cultivation of one set of capacities at the expense of other potentials; the evolution and strengthening of some psychological defenses and the wasting away of others. Most often, the battle of "who am I?" is consciously fought out on the battlegrounds of vocation, marriage, friendships, family size, home ownership, group membership, style of life, and a multitude of other specific choices. But to the individual, these specific commitments are important not only in themselves, but in their bearing on the deeper questions of personal identity.

"Freedom of choice" can be a problem only when there are real alternatives but no criterion for choosing among them. Were there a clear "rational" way to choose *the* one best career, it would solve the problem of choice. But of course no such standard exists: there are dozens of considerations; and so many careers exist, each changing so rapidly that no one can hope to know about more than a small fraction of them. Or if there were some simple way of choosing the *one* best spouse from among the millions available, "choosing a mate" would be little problem. Lacking such certainty, we must try to commit ourselves to vocations, people, and futures about which we cannot be sure.

Some young Americans can do just this: they can live without a guarantee that they have made the best or the only choice: and this capacity to make commitments *without* guarantees is a prime symptom of strength of character. But others—perhaps most young Americans—undergo a period of confusion beforehand, and often seek escapes from their freedom. We seldom recognize, for example, that "falling in love" is among other things a way of avoiding a reflective choice of a mate. In a situation where "rational" calculation is almost impossible, romantic love defines the choice of mate as an area where rational calculation is simply irrelevant: romantic love overwhelms the doubt, hesitation, and vacillation which must beset any man or woman who tries to decide "rationally" what he and his spouse will be like in forty years of marriage. So, too, "following in Dad's footsteps" can be a way of avoiding the difficult freedom that would follow from choosing *not* to be like Dad.

But the most common adaptation is to slide, not to decide—to limit one's choices by seizing only the opportunities that fall into one's lap, to choose the employer and the career which promises the most money, or to marry the first available girl with a nice personality and good figure. Sliding rather than deciding works best for those who have few inner obstacles to commitment, and for those at whose door opportunity knocks once, loudly, in the form of a renumerative employer or a nice pretty girl. It works less well for the underprivileged, the overprivileged, and for those who find commitment difficult. Opportunity knocks but lightly or not at all at the doors of the underprivileged, and it appears in threadbare clothes. And for the privileged, the talented and versatile, opportunities may knock too often and too loudly, appearing in guises so glittering and Protean that to choose between their beckonings is impossible. Furthermore, for those who distrust all commitments, no opportunity seems sufficiently attractive to overcome their distrust. The youths who live most easily with their freedom are the *moderately* talented, the moderately good-looking, the moderately ambitious, and the moderately capable. The stars, beauty queens, and the geniuses are often overwhelmed with offers; the paupers, the ugly, and the dull receive none; and the alienated, whatever their talents, find all offers counterfeit.

For all these youths, as for the simply indecisive, the "freedom of choice" in our society constitutes a major human problem, which is ultimately the problem of identity. Ideally in America, commitment and self-definition go hand in hand during adolescence, so that each new commitment further clarifies identity and each clarification of identity permits new commitments. But the ideal seldom occurs: for most youths indecision, vacillation, and doubt precede commitment and sometimes replace it. Having to choose, having to make commitments, is then experienced not as a joyous freedom but as a heavy burden.

*The meaning of work*—In most traditional societies, young men and women have had little choice as to their work: they worked *because* they were men and women; their work was their life; and work, play, and social life flowed over into each other. Under such circumstances, men rarely think or speak in terms of "work" (which implies something else which is "not work"); they merely speak of the tasks to be done, the catching of fish, the tilling of crops, the saying of Mass. All things run together; distinctions between sectors of life are meaningless: "I work because I am a man."

For most Americans, in contrast, "work" has vaguely unpleasant connotations. It is most frequently paired with words like "hard," or used in phrases like "all work and no play." Work is implicitly felt as something to be gotten out of the way. If we ask the average American why he works, he will answer, "To earn a living"; and this expression says much about the relationship of work and life. The goal of work is to earn the money necessary for "living" when one is not working. The purpose of work is to make possible *other* things (a "living") which are only possible after work. Implicitly, work is seen as a necessary instrumental evil without inherent meaning. Just as for the Puritan, good work and good works were the way a man demonstrated his salvation—the pain of this life which guaranteed bliss in the next—so for most Americans, work remains a mildly painful ordeal.

The reasons for our implicitly negative attitudes toward work can be inferred from the characteristics of most jobs. The fragmentation of tasks means that the individual's relationship to the total product or the total task is highly attenuated. As specialization proceeds, each worker finds himself assigned a smaller and smaller corner of a task; the whole job, the finished product, the whole person as client or patient recedes into the far distance. A sense of connection with a tangible accomplishment and a sense of personal responsibility for what one does are inevitably vitiated in our highly organized society where the Ford Motor Company, the Community Hospital, or DeVitale Homes, Inc., is responsible for the task. Even at upper levels of management, it takes considerable imagination for the executive to feel a personal relationship with, and to derive a sense of value from, his part in the production of iceboxes, soft drinks, insurance policies, or compact cars. Indeed, the reason high-level executives usually say they are relatively "satisfied" with their jobs may not be because these jobs are in fact more "meaningful," but merely because the executive's education, training, and conceptual ability gives him greater capacity to understand his tenuous relationship to his work.

The rising demands for performance on the job further affect a man's feeling about his job. In some highly skilled jobs, growing demands for training and skill may permit a feeling of personal competence which compensates for a tenuous relationship to the total task. The skilled surgeon, the senior machinist, the executive trained in organizational theory, industrial management, and human relations—all may be able to enjoy the use of their highly developed skills. But for many men, more demanding job requirements simply mean more taxing and exacting work, greater demands to "keep up" in order to succeed. Too few jobs challenge

the heart, imagination, or spirit. On the contrary, most work enjoins a rigorous subordination of these feelings to the cognitive requirements of the job itself. It takes a very special kind of person to
derive deep fulfillment from meeting the same exact specifications
day after day, no matter how much skill these specifications require. The growing demands for precise and high-level skill, for a
capacity to follow exact routines in an orderly way, to mesh without friction in large and highly organized firms, assembly lines, or
sales offices often make work less rewarding to the individual despite his higher level of skill.

Nor do the cognitive demands of most jobs add to the meaningfulness of work. Most men and women cannot suppress emotion
easily; they *do* have strong feelings about the work they do and the
people they do it with, and the pressure to be cool, objective, and
unemotional is a pressure to subordinate their deepest feelings. Inevitably, we find it hard to treat all our fellow workers the same
way, since our feelings about them are never identical; and it is not
easy to judge others only according to their "job-relevant" accomplishments, when in ordinary human relationships these are usually
among the *least* determining factors in our feelings about them.
Businessmen, like industrial workers, therefore traditionally arrive
home tired from their work, full of pent-up feelings which their
wives are exhorted to help them "release."

As a result, Americans mention "working for a living" a hundred times more often than they mention "living for their work."
Even work that really does contribute to a socially useful product is
often so organized that it yields little personal satisfaction. Most
important of all, we have long since given up on work, long since
stopped even expecting that work be "meaningful"; and if we enjoy
our work, it is usually because of good working conditions, friends
on the job, benevolent supervision, and above all because the
"good living" we earn by working enables us to do other, really
enjoyable things in our "spare" time. The phrases "meaningful
work," "joy in work," "fulfillment through work" have an increasingly old-fashioned and quaint sound. Even our labor unions have

given up any pressure for more meaningful work in favor of demands for less work and more fringe benefits and income to make "living" better instead. The loss of meaning in work goes far beyond the problems discussed by the youthful Marx, namely, the loss of worker's control over the means of production. It extends to the fragmentation of work roles, to the heavily cognitive demands made within work. Even when workers themselves own or control their factories, work often remains meaningless.

The spirit of work and the human qualities demanded by work inevitably colors the worker's conception of himself. In every society, men tend to identity themselves with what they exploit to earn their living: in our society, we often become identified with the machines we exploit to do our most onerous work. This identification is magnified by the parallel between the characteristics of a good worker and a good machine. Whether at high levels of management or on the most menial assembly-line tasks, the good worker is highly specialized, is expected to show few feelings, to operate "by the book," to be consistent, systematic, and precise, to treat all individuals impartially and unemotionally. A man operating under such a regime finds the most important parts of himself—his hopes, feelings, aspirations and dreams—systematically ignored. Like a brilliant child with less brilliant contemporaries, he is forced to suppress the major portion of himself on the job—to have it ignored by others and, most dangerous of all, to ignore it himself. To be treated as if one were only part of a man—and to have to act as if it were true—is perhaps the heaviest demand of all.

Work therefore assumes a new significance in technological society. It requires a dissociation of feeling, a subordination of passion, impulse, fantasy, and idealism before cognitive problems and tasks. As breadwinners, most Americans neither find nor even seek "fulfillment" in their jobs. Work, split away from "living" by convention and tradition, becomes instrumental, a dissociated part of life that makes possible, yet often vitiates, the rest of a "living." Yet to spend one's days at tasks whose only rationale is income and whose chief requirements are cognitive is another demand in our lives

which makes our technological society less likely to inspire enthusiasm.

*The problem of integration*—We all marvel at the complexity of
our society's organization and at the high levels of technological
productivity it has achieved. But society which "works" well, as
ours does in many ways, may nonetheless create great stresses on
individuals by virtue of *how* it works. And no psychological adaptations are more burdensome than the maneuvers required to integrate individual life in a fragmented society. Men and women need
a sense of coherence, integration, and wholeness; but to attain such
personal wholeness in our technological society is not an easy task.

Consider once again the problem of identity. I have earlier emphasized two ways technological society intensifies this problem:
first by requiring a multitude of choices for which "rational" criteria are not available; second by dissociating work from the rest of
life and by destroying even the expectation that work might in itself
be meaningful. But even if a young man has somehow made all of
the necessary choices and accepted the fact that his work is merely
a way of "earning a living," he still faces a third problem—how to
integrate the pieces of his life so that he has some sense of being
"of a piece."

The days are long past when a youth could choose to be a
farmer, peasant, merchant, soldier, or seaman, and by this single
decision resolve a variety of other questions: the kind of woman he
must marry, the place he must live, the things he must believe, the
style and shape of his adult life. Moreover, those who seek to ele-
vate one sector of life into the central principle of their existence
have difficulty in doing so, for such an "integration" is in continual
danger of collapsing by virtue of its incompleteness. Work in our
society is not intended to satisfy most of our deeper feelings and
needs. Those who seek a unifying principle in family and recreation
—and this is the most common solution for middle-class Americans—also run the risk of one-sidedness, for our families are so
arranged as to exclude any satisfaction of what Thorstein Veblen

called "the instinct of workmanship." No matter how desperately we may seek an organizing principle for our lives in any single activity, belief, or affiliation, we are likely to be disappointed.

Thus, the only workable solution for most Americans is to attempt a unique integration of their own lives, an idiosyncratic synthesis of their disparate and divided activities, convictions, and commitments into a pattern that yields a sense of personal unity. This assignment is of course supported by the deep human need for psychic wholeness, which pushes all men in all societies toward integration and consistency. But it is continually frustrated by the dissociation of work and family, of cognition and feeling, of thinking and affect. Social fragmentation pushes toward psychic fragmentation: without institutions or ideals to support psychic wholeness, inner division is a continual danger.

Indeed, if an American persists in seeking a life where inner wholeness is reflected in the outer consistency of his daily activities, he is almost inevitably led to repudiate the life led by most Americans, with its careful dissociation of work, cognition, and public life from family, feeling, and fun. Those who insist upon or need outer consistency must instead usually choose—or create—a deviant role. The life of an alienated painter or writer promises, at least, that one's lifework and one's "living" will be united; some teachers manage to work at what they love and to love their work. At best such "deviant" vocations can join the spheres of family and fun with those of work and skill. These are, of course, the vocations most favored by the alienated—who as second choice also choose other integrated and old-fashioned lives where work and life are of a piece, like the "dairy farmer" mentioned by one student.

Most Americans are not, of course, ideologically alienated; but the problems that lead to alienation in a few are there for the many. Only a rare man or woman genuinely "solves" the problem of psychic integration short of choosing a deviant role. Furthermore, few men and women have the tenacity of purpose and strength of character to tolerate the dissociation of their outer lives without some feeling of inner fragmentation. When these few are with their families they are able to "shut off" the cognitive values and outlooks required in work; on the job they can dismiss the feelings they have at home; when having fun they can enjoy themselves without "working at it" or collapsing into self-indulgence. But to manage such a compartmentalization of self and life—and not to feel inwardly torn and confused—requires unusually great strength of character. And to feel that one truly "belongs" in our society takes a remarkable capacity to unify one's piecemeal "belongings" into a coherent inner sense of community.

Most of us lack these capacities. When asked the terrifying question "Who are you?" we can reply with a list of our social memberships, our roles, and even our personal characteristics. "Businessman, father of three, Rotarian, Methodist, Republican, homeowner, and decent man"—the list often contains only the unity of outer correlation, and leaves the speaker with a vague sense of being harried and harassed, of having no vital center, of being only what he does and of doing things which have no relationship to each other or to the central self. And when asked where we really "belong," we usually avoid the question or respond with another list that itself testifies to not really belonging anywhere: "At home, with my family, in my office, with my friends." Even "home" is not the natal home you can't go home again to; and few of us really feel we "belong" in the apartment houses or suburbs where we live. We manage to live with all this—mostly because we must but partly because everyone else lives the same way. But in the dark hours of the night, how many men and women secretly feel a vague sense of inner disunity? How many wonder what ties their lives together? How many feel that at root they belong nowhere? For those who ask these questions, as for those who would but do not dare, our society has made wholeness hard. And though men can survive without a sense of inner wholeness or social community—and in our society they often must—a society that requires them to do so may fail to capture their deepest commitments.

## Alienation and technological society

The growing fragmentation of our technological society makes
three heavy demands on individuals: that they choose without adequate criteria between the many social roles, "opportunities," and
organizations that have been fractioned out of traditional society;
that they work not because their work makes sense but merely to
earn a "living" somewhere else with its proceeds; and that they
somehow integrate—or live without being able to integrate—the
fractured roles and organizations which fail to define and unify
them. These demands are heavy ones; and among the common responses to them are to experience choice as a burden and seek an
escape from freedom, to expect and therefore find no fulfillment
and satisfaction in work, to feel psychologically divided and socially homeless. Moreover, like all heavy social demands, these are
potentially alienating forces. In alienated youths like those we have
studied, the demand to choose without criteria, to work only for a
"living," and to integrate one's life unaided—these demands cannot or will not be met: they help inspire a rejection of American
society and a determination to find another way of life. And even
for those who are not alienated, these demands can cause vacillation and indecision, a feeling of emptiness and lack of meaning, a
sense of being inwardly divided and outwardly homeless.

In every society, new means of production, new inventions, and
new technologies have always meant personal dislocation and uprootedness. In America, where technological refinement and development has become the dominating purpose of society, alienation
follows from the qualities of technological society itself. Thus, the
totalness with which the alienated reject the assumptions and practices of their society may be at least partly justified. Yet the alienated are both products of and rebels against this society. They are
its products in their refusal of freedom, in their rejection of commitment, and above all in their sense of psychic fragmentation.
And they are rebels—albeit without a cause—in their negative

definition of themselves as those who are *against,* in their rejection of the basic values of American society, and in their search for values based on feeling, passion, and sentience. And they are probably right in thinking that—for them at least—the only adequate life would be a life where external unity supports and encourages inner wholeness—and that such a life is hard to live in the mainstreams of American society.

# 10      Family, feeling, and fun

The family always mediates between the individual and society, transmitting the traditional ways of the culture to each new generation, fulfilling human needs that cannot be satisfied elsewhere, and sometimes defining a man's entire position in the world. Children are inevitably raised in families, and here, the world over, men and women satisfy many of their needs for sex, love, and security, and their need for a tangible link with the future through their children. The family provides a special bond of mutuality with a manageable number of people; and in many societies, family position— as father, eldest male, younger sister, brother, mother—alone determines most of an individual's daily dealings with others, his work, his religious life, his political role and his economic position. Every society, however, elaborates its own variations on these universal themes, and the middle-class American family is extreme in its smallness, its isolation from the mainstreams of public life, and its intense specialization.

## The reduced family

Traditionally, families have consisted not merely of mother, father and offspring, but of an extended group that embraces distant relatives of several generations. An individual was defined by his ties not only to his parents and siblings, but to grandparents, cousins, aunts, uncles, great-aunts, great-uncles, and numberless other relatives. The English language reflects the smallness of our families: unlike many "primitive" tongues, ours provides no easy way of even designating kinsmen who are elsewhere central to family life. In societies with extended families, children grow up in what appears to us a confusing wilderness of complex family relationships, usually involving strictly prescribed behavior toward men and women whom we would think very "distant" relatives. A child's mother's brother may be his disciplinarian; or the eldest male kinsman on the father's side may govern all the members of his clan; or custom may rigidly limit marriage to a small group of first cousins on the side of the parent of the opposite sex.

A child in such a community is often "related" to all of the people he sees daily; and from infancy onward, he learns that his behavior toward each of these relatives must be governed by their family relationship to him: deference to his mother's brother; avoidance of his father's mother; a joking relationship with his father's brother's children. How a man fares in life—whom he marries, whom he defends with his life, whose debts he pays, whose children he cares for, what he does, and where he works—all may depend on his position in his family. Men and women who have grown up in such a world of course take it completely for granted, automatically accept their defined position amongst their kinfolk, and think it barbaric that anyone else could live in a society without the same complex family rules and definitions.

In such communities, every man, woman, and child is expected to be economically useful to his family. As in traditional farm families in this country, children start with family "chores" very young; and the doing of these chores often constitutes their only schooling. The games of children emulate the continually visible activities of grownups—fishing, hunting, cooking, cultivating, herding—and soon shade over into adult work. Women are expected not only to raise children and "care for the home," but to cultivate the crops, clean and dry the game, or salt the fish; and a good wife is above all a good worker. Children, too, soon become economic assets who can make the family richer in whatever the society deems riches—yams, fish, game, wheat, or cattle. The family, not the breadwinner, produces.

Within such a society, any one couple and their offspring (what anthropologists call a "nuclear family") are embedded, absorbed, or lost within a larger family group. What we would consider "family life" is inevitably a public affair: the physical arrangements of living alone prevent privacy; no couple can ever separate itself from some wider kinship group. After infancy, a child may be reared by his father's sisters, be disciplined by his mother's brother, or form part of a gang of children whose upbringing is shared by all the women in the community, all of whom he calls "mother." And even when responsibility for the child's upbringing falls primarily on his biological parents, their activities are always open to public scrutiny. "The public," often largely relatives by blood or marriage, feels few qualms about commenting loudly on child-rearing techniques of which it disapproves. Neighbors and relatives soon learn who lives amicably, who fights, who has affairs with whom, who is well, and who is sick. Marriage, children, the family—all are open and exposed to public scrutiny, comment, influence, and control. Moreover, the individual's emotional ties are likely to be diffused over his entire extended family, expressed partly through rituals of communal solidarity, partly through attachment to his own or his adopted children, partly in his work. The rigorous distinction between "family life" and "other life" possible in Western society is thus inconceivable: life flows together as an undifferentiated whole. Passions still exist, jealousies and affections still flourish, men and women still love each other and their children—but these feelings are rarely separated from the rest of life or "saved" for the hours after work.

The contrast between such societies and our own is extreme. Our own families are small and isolated from extended kin. Grandparents and other "distant relatives" are *not* expected to live with a couple and their children; when they do, they are usually relegated to second-class citizenship in a family that has no place or use for them. Upon marriage, each couple is expected to set up a household of its own apart from both sets of parents; living with parents after marriage is normally the result of financial hardship. Most middle-class children therefore see their grandparents rarely when they are children (recall the vagueness with which the alienated remembered their own parents' parents). Nor are other relatives—aunts, uncles, cousins—present except on ritual occasions—birthdays, Christmas, Thanksgiving. Isolated from the previous generation and from the wider family, parents and their children have greater freedom to work out their own ways of life, to move from place to place and job to job without breaking continuing family ties, to move up or down in the world, change status, occupation, and ideology without daily reminders of what they have abandoned. And because of their isolation, American families are exquisitely responsive to our rapid rates of social change, and can change residence, outlook, child-rearing techniques, status, or occupation without having to live with what they are trying to live down.

Nor does an individual's position in his family determine his position in the wider society. Adults are equal before the law regardless of whether they are the oldest surviving male in the family, a single daughter, or a married uncle with children. We studiously ignore family position in public life, and concentrate instead on the individual's abilities and deeds. Only in a few vestigial cases (e.g., a wife's right not to have to testify against her husband in court) do we formally recognize any special privilege for the marriage relationship. In work, too, a man's family status makes little difference in his ability to get and hold a job, and even sex is slowly becoming less of a formal obstacle to occupation. Only when a worker's family role threatens to interfere with performance (as with recently married women likely to become pregnant) is it clearly relevant.

At the same time, the family in American society has ceased to be a productive unit. Only among a dwindling number of farm and shopkeeping families do wives and children still work at a family

job. When women "work" in this country, they work outside the
family and often only so as to be able to buy luxuries they could
not otherwise afford. Men, though they *are* expected to work, again
work outside the family; and the family's position in the community depends largely on the husband's status in his work. Thus a
division of labor unthinkable in most simple societies occurs within
American families: the husband is usually the only family member
who is "productive" in the wider community; the wife is generally
expected to devote herself to her role as "wife and mother"; children are not expected to "pay their way" until they are in their late
teens or early twenties.

And finally, American middle-class families are assured extraordinary privacy and freedom from outside interference. The sanctity
of the home continues to be a respected principle despite picture
windows and togetherness. Once the door is shut, only the invited
can enter; the telephone can be left off the hook; and the tog333ther-
ness, sociability, and group living of the suburbs is limited—and
made possible by—a recognition of the ultimate right to privacy.
This privacy means that women (with their husband's support) are
unusually free to raise their children as they please: no one else
lives in the household to comment, criticize, help or—most important—dissipate their impact on their children. No one really knows
what happens within the marriage, sheltered by custom from unwanted intrusions of extended family and by thick walls from the
observations of neighbors. Each family is an island, insulated from
public scrutiny, control, and interference, and because of its protected isolation able to function as a haven against the demands of
the rest of society.

## The family as emotional center

Americans increasingly think of the family as the center of a man's
or woman's deepest feelings and allegiances. We justify this fact as
"normal" by appealing to the universal tendency of mothers to care

for their young and of fathers to provide for their families; and it therefore seldom occurs to us how idiosyncratic our own family arrangements are. More is involved here than universal needs to care and provide for the young: these needs also exist in other societies where the "nuclear" family is submerged in wider kinship ties and where men and women's primary allegiance is not to their spouse and children but to the community as a whole, to their mother's lineage, or to the gods. But in America, the family is the primary area where feelings can be fully expressed; and the emotional, tender, passionate sides of life have become concentrated within our small family circles. Increasingly, the heart is where the home is.

Several factors make this concentration of emotion possible. The virtual disappearance of traditional extended families means that there simply *are* no other available relatives with whom these feelings can appropriately be played out. Also, the small number of children born to American families contributes to the concentration of family feeling. In societies with high infant mortality rates and no knowledge of contraception, women bear children until the menopause or death ends their fertility. But modern medical care has doubled and tripled the life span in two centuries, so fewer children must now be born to maintain the population: most children now survive to adulthood. This increased rate of survival permits parents to make a greater psychological investment in each of their children. A woman who knows that her offspring will almost certainly survive to adulthood can allow herself to love them more deeply than can a woman certain that most of her children will die before maturity. And finally, the decline of the family as a productive unit helps free it to "specialize" on its members' feelings. A family that has work to do as a family—as in farm, peasant, or hunting families—can attend to its members' feelings only when they interfere with the jobs to be done. Where life is hard and economic survival depends on the productivity of the family as a whole, maintaining a "pleasant atmosphere," having a "relaxed and attractive home," or developing a "deep interpersonal understanding" must necessarily be subordinated to economic survival.

All of these factors make family "specialization" possible, but what makes specialization *necessary* is more than anything else the nature of work and public life in our society. Work, I have argued, increasingly requires the subordination of feeling, passion, and "non-job-relevant" fantasy; furthermore, the fragmentation of work makes it hard to feel emotional involvement, loyalty, or attachment to a job. As work becomes merely a way of "earning a living," the "living" one earns is increasingly centered on the family. Men and women need some center for their lives, and most of us have feelings that refuse to be permanently subordinated. When work and public life offer little visible meaning, attractiveness, interests, or challenge, then the family is what remains.

The "reduced" American family is admirably suited for the role of contrast and compensation to work. On the job, everyone is judged according to the same rules, but within the family, individuals *must* be treated differently according to their sex and generation. In their work, men are judged by their visible achievements, but the family *must* accept them as they are born—birth order, age, generation and sex being the primary determinants of family behavior. Work demands a highly cognitive, unemotional, and analytic outlook, but our small families *inevitably* concentrate powerful emotions on a few people considered wholistically, seldom analyzed, responded to with love, pride, embarrassment, and jealousy rather than with the intellect. At almost every point, then, the demands of the family are diametrically opposed to those of work: the feeling, support, sensitivity, expressiveness, tenderness, and exclusive love of the family contrast with impersonality, neutrality, cognition, achievement and accomplishment of work.

In practice, the family often becomes not only a contrast but an escape from work. To many an American, moving from job to home means shifting gears radically, becoming a different person, expressing a side of personality that must be rigorously suppressed during working hours. Many men heave a sigh of relief upon returning home: they only feel "really human" when they take off their office clothes, put on their slippers, play with the children, and "putter." If one examines critically the advertisements in women's magazines, the escape valve function of family is apparent. Among the implied functions of the family—and of the wife as its manager —are to send the husband off to work in a "good mood" and have a cheerful and relaxing reception awaiting him when he returns exhausted and full of pent-up feelings after a "hard day's work." Implicitly, then, work leads to the accumulation of "bad" feelings which can only be "released" at home; rarely is work seen as satisfying, creative, or leading to a joyous overflow of happy feelings accumulated on the job. The wife is the "mood manager" of her family: she must sense the husband's moods, encourage him to talk about his problems with her, follow his work enough so that she can understand these problems, keep the house, the children, and above all herself relaxed and attractive, be warm, open, responsive, attentive, and never tired or bored. That part of a woman's life that is not taken up with her children should be, according to exhortations of the mass media, devoted to anticipating and dealing with the feelings of her husband.

To be sure, a husband has his obligations, too. But most of these have to do with his role as breadwinner outside the home: he must earn a decent "living" for his family and achieve a respectable position in the community. And within the family he must be a good father to his children and a considerate, attentive husband to his wife, remembering her feelings with flowers on anniversaries, surprise "dinners on the town," and willing attendance at the cultural events to which she takes him. Furthermore, he must be a genial host at the social amenities his wife initiates. Unlike his grandfather, he is expected to confine sociability largely to family affairs, eschewing "stag dinners" for "family gatherings." Wives, too, are expected to join their social lives with their family lives: when women get together with other women, it is usually because their men are away at work; only "bad wives" go out with the girls when their husbands are home.

The "fun" a family has together also contrasts sharply with its breadwinner's work life. The new American affluence has brought organized fun on an unprecedented scale: fun at the barbecue pit, fun with the outboard, fun in the summer cottage, home pool, garden, or in the ubiquitous "family room," which far outshines the "living room" in size, comfort, coziness, convenience, and fireplaces. Many such recreations can best be understood as escape valves from the pressures of work. Consider the satisfactions of the "do-it-yourself" home workshop: a man works by himself, sees the job through from start to finish, and has a tangible product at the end. But on the job, the same man usually does *nothing* by himself, *never* sees a product through from beginning to end, and *never* has a tangible product to crown his labors. Given the conditions of work life, the simplest leisure tasks—mowing the lawn or cooking a steak over pre-prepared charcoal lit with an aerosol-type charcoal lighter—can become soul-satisfying human accomplishments. Family and fun, by providing the compensatory "living" for which most Americans work, help make it psychologically possible for them to continue fulfilling the cognitive demands of their jobs. When the family becomes the emotional center of life, the non-emotional demands of public life seem less oppressive.

## Bringing up the young

Children do not just grow up, they must be *brought* up to perform the tasks which society will later demand of them. From the vast range of human potentials, child-training must selectively support those that will enable the child to do the later work required by his society. With proper upbringing, any healthy newborn could become an adequate member of any society in the world; the distinctive character of the members of each society is in large part the result of their similar childhood training. By manipulating and controlling the child's environment during his first years, his parents teach him the skills, outlooks, and motivations he will need as an adult, who must be *able* and *willing* to perform his socially allocated tasks.

Children must be taught the skills, virtues, and outlooks of their society and its favored motivations: their training must teach them to *want* to be adults, to accept the renunciations and embrace the consolations available to grownups.

The first responsibility for bringing up the young obviously falls upon the family, although in a very few societies like our own, schools also share this responsibility. But even in America, the family's responsibility is primary: only if his parents have laid the groundwork for later schooling will a child be able and willing to learn what he is taught in school. Though the functions of the American family are few in number and reduced in scope, they are highly specialized around the problem of bringing up children; and in the family, as elsewhere, specialization has brought an increase in demands for performance.

In bringing up children, our middle-class families must work within the limits set by the family's "isolation" from kinship and work. This isolation entails the psychological isolation of the mother, who is "protected" from the pressures of an extended family. Separated from her own mother, she need not follow the child-rearing practices of an earlier generation; and given her typical lack of experience in child-rearing, many a young mother becomes extraordinarily responsive to the "expert advice" offered in countless women's magazines about how to raise her children. Such responsiveness to the "best and latest" in child-training fashions, whatever its problems, is fully consistent with a rapidly changing society in which emulation of previous generations can mean a commitment to obsolescence.

Women are obviously those who must bear children and care for them in the first years of life. But American society has chosen to underline this biological necessity by minimizing men's responsibility for both emotional life and child-training. The physical facts of modern American life alone make any other arrangement impossible. With the father away at work (or commuting to and from it) during the greater part of the day (and sometimes the night) and with the extended family living elsewhere, there is no one but the mother who *can* rear pre-school children. Blame and praise for their character and success thus fall upon her; responsibility for their misdeeds is hers. It is she who must visit school, wipe children's noses, "civilize" them, toilet-train them, and form the early bases of their later character. Within the family, she occupies a central position toward her children.

Although the father's job determines where the family lives and where it "stands" in the community, his role with his children is circumscribed. He is expected to support his wife in her major activities as home manager and child-rearer, but not to interfere. He should appreciate her efforts, back up her discipline, cherish her as a person, and let her know he likes her cooking—but not tell her how to run the house. His wife is the executive manager of the home, and he is the chairman of the board—who occasionally discusses over-all child-rearing policy with his wife and is the ultimate recourse when her discipline fails: in an emergency, he may administer a spanking. But he is not expected to take over the daily management of his children, and indeed he could not do so because his work keeps him away from home. Similarly, he may decide to do the evening dishes to help his wife out, or occasionally care for the children and change their diapers; but if he cleans, cooks, and cares for the children as a matter of course, we still consider it "unmanly."

A mother's job is therefore difficult: almost unaided, she must prepare her children for a society changing at an unprecedented rate toward ever greater social fragmentation, specialization, and impersonality at work. Our society probably demands more of some sides of human personality than any other in history—cognitive skill, education, ability to suppress emotion, to dissociate feelings, to accept responsibility, and to be self-sufficient, initiating, and independent. American mothers must therefore often rear their young with a purposiveness and consistency that could not be greater were it based on an explicit plan. In fact, of course, such plans are rarely conscious, but society provides a "plan" in the form of child-rearing techniques which seem "natural" and "right" to most women. What are these techniques?

The keystone of bringing up middle-class American children is their intense dependence on their mothers. In other societies, the initial dependence of an infant on his mother is often soon dissipated in a wide network of extended family, clan, or village relationships. But the American pre-school child has no one else to turn to but his mother or his security blanket. For ten or twelve hours a day, she is the only adult present; all bounty, favor, approval, kindness, and punishment come from her. American children seldom "run with the pack" in their pre-school days; even nursery school, our closest equivalent to the gangs of small children in some primitive societies, is a deliberate effort on the part of parents to move their children *away* from their mothers and thus points to the primary importance of the mother-child tie.

Closely related to the intense dependence of child on mother is the permissiveness of American parents. American families of course vary enormously in their strictness, but contrasted with families in other societies, ours allow children great freedom. From an early age, children are allowed to explore their own environments, to feel out the natural limits of any situation. The pre-school child is given vast areas within which to experiment: his mother usually intervenes only when he clearly transgresses the bounds of physical safety. He is early allowed much autonomy and independence; though never too far from his mother's watchful eye, he is encouraged to "learn from his own mistakes."

By setting few precise limits on the mother-child relationship, permissiveness intensifies that relationship. Clearly structured and narrowly defined ties between parent and child give both *limited* and specific rights and obligations. In a permissive family, in contrast, the relationship between mother and child is diffuse, non-specific, based on feeling rather than on clear-cut rules. No socially-given boundaries define the dealings of a mother and her children; all the rules must be worked out between them on the basis of their own personalities and needs. A child is guaranteed few areas of privilege or privacy from his mother's supervision and intervention. Furthermore, a small boy who is permissively allowed to "make his own mistakes" and "learn from experience" actually needs his mother around far more urgently than one who is confined so as to prevent mistakes or unsupervised experience. Paradoxically, then, granting a small child greater freedom simultaneously serves to heighten his dependence on his mother.

The intense dependency of a child upon his mother makes it possible for her to invoke the most powerful of all disciplinary sanctions—the withdrawal of love, variously expressed as "disappointment" in him, or loving him when he is "good" and disapproving of him when he is "bad." We take these techniques so much for granted that we seldom reflect on the variety of other methods available for inducing children to "behave": physical punishments, isolation, punitive work, and—very important in primitive societies—ostracism and social shaming. Though all of these other techniques are available to and used by American mothers, what most American middle-class children fear from their parents is moral disapproval, "disappointment," being judged "bad." Furthermore, when applied in the context of a small, dependency-encouraging and permissive family, the main psychological meaning of physical punishment or shaming is still a withdrawal of love. Most middle-class spankings hurt the feelings more than the bottom; and shaming by the mother may suggest she does not care for her child.

These characteristic child-rearing techniques, involving an intense dependency, permissiveness, and withdrawal of love are especially well suited to producing early autonomy and independence, early development of the capacity for self-control, and early acquisition of cognitive skills. Since all of a small child's needs are focused on his mother, his desire to please her inevitably leads him to try to behave as she wishes and to be what she wants. From a very early age—often before he can talk—he begins to learn to postpone and delay instinctual behavior, to assess the consequences of his acts, to acquire conceptual skills, to subordinate feelings to the "realistic" needs of the situation. Without a strong mother-child bond and without the mother's willingness to "exploit" that bond to bring up her child, our culture's difficult first lessons cannot be learned.

Learning these lessons is a subtle process: between the ages of one and four a child gradually comes, as it were, to carry his parents within him even in their physical absence. His judgment of his own acts and consequently his self-esteem increasingly comes to depend on doing what pleases his mother and avoiding whatever leads to the loss of her love. The more intense the dependency of the child on his mother, the more deeply he internalizes her approving and disapproving presence; the more permissive and diffuse the ties between the two, the more subtly attuned he becomes to the slightest expression of her approval or disapproval. Dependency and permissiveness are the vehicles of early learning of our culture's lessons; as a result of their use, American children are early able to move outside the family while carrying within them its internalized representatives.

Most discussions of the "internalization of culture" emphasize the development of the superego—of internalized parental prohibitions that enjoin the child to desist from pleasurable but anti-social activity. But in our culture, an even more important "internalization" involves the child's capacity to regulate and control his own behavior. More is involved than learning a sense of right and wrong: much behavior does not involve moral questions at all, but is concerned with the efficacy, appropriateness, and "adaptativeness" of one's actions: How can I get what I want and need? How can I fulfill the demands made on me? How can I choose the course of action that will best lead to satisfaction? How can I avoid inner conflict? How can I avoid conflict with those I love?

In these terms, our child-rearing techniques promote not only early and strong superego development, but even more, an early development of the capacity for *self*-control, *self*-guidance, and psychological *self*-government. Most mothers spend far more time teaching Johnny to "stand on his own two feet," to "make up his own mind," and to "do things for himself," than they devote to teaching him the difference between "right and wrong." Superego demands of course exist: direct expressions of aggression are particularly frowned upon in American middle-class families; children are systematically taught to displace and sublimate their aggressive feelings, to hammer on the Playskool Cobbler Bench but not on their brothers and sisters. But even more important is the teaching of other qualities like "realism," independence, autonomy, "reasonableness," and an early cognitive outlook.

The capacity for high-level cognition and for special appreciation of "facts" is of course only one of many human capacities parents can encourage in their children. Other societies encourage private experience, fantasy, dreams, revelations, superstitions and magic. But Americans disapprove ever more strongly of these orientations, seeing them as "childish," "irresponsible," and "selfish." From an early age, our children are pushed to harness their play to more cognitive activities. The sandbox soon becomes a chemistry set; the elaboration of private fantasy is, with the beginning of school, displaced onto reading and shared fantasy. "Creative playthings" patterned on IQ tests start the child early along the path to conceptual skills. The free and fantastic drawings of children are soon replaced by more "realistic" representations of the objective world. Things are "explained" to American children; and quite apart from the particular explanation, the very process of explaining communicates that the world is conceptually organized and cognitively comprehensible. We adduce "reasons" for our commands; and the very fact of "reasoning" conveys our expectation that children will eventually "understand" and be guided not by our commands but by their own understanding of the reasons behind them. "It was only a dream," we tell our children; and the "only" expresses more effectively than any argument our high valuation of cognition.

Along with an objective, rational, and cognitive outlook goes a strong pressure for early "achievement"—for efficient and competent mastery of the external environment (including other people).

Parent's pressures in this area are easiest to see when their children are in school: school accomplishments are lavishly praised, bad report cards bring scorn and disapproval. A boy's academic, social, and athletic achievements are greeted with overwhelming approval by his father, and a girl's "social conquests" rarely go unnoticed and unpraised by her mother. But even before the child goes to school, the same pressures exist: tying shoes, building with blocks, and staying dry at night are enthusiastically approved by parents; while failure to achieve, to develop quickly, and to construct real things in the real world bring subtle disapproval. From an early age the child learns that his parents' love is at least to some extent conditional upon his accomplishments. The very frequency with which American parents need to reassure their children that they love them "no matter what" implies that this love cannot always be taken for granted.

These two pressures—toward cognition and toward achievement —are both necessary if the child is to be capable of early independence. In some cultures, custom decrees the behavior appropriate in all routine situations, and life is so arranged that the non-routine rarely if ever happens. Moreover, men and women are seldom out of earshot of their lifelong familiars, who guarantee conformity to custom. Americans, in contrast, must prepare children to make autonomous decisions, to set their own goals, to cope with the unexpected, and to work far from the supervision of those who know them. Our children must be taught early to "size up" a situation accurately and to regulate their own behavior; American mothers therefore encourage their children to "take initiative." Children who need continual help, supervision, and support are thought "clinging" and "overprotected"; and if the mother does not use the child's dependence on her to push him to independence, father usually steps in to make sure that he learns to "stand on his own two feet." Paradoxically, it is the child's devotion to, dependence on, and need for his mother that motivates him to become independent because she wishes it. And if the mother's wishes are genuine and

her pressure consistent, independence eventually becomes a goal in
its own right.

Long before he enters school, then, a middle-class American
child has already begun to develop the basic skills and qualities
required of adults in our society. His intense dependency on his
mother makes him extraordinarily responsive to her stated and implied wishes, and she uses this responsiveness to foster cognition
and reason, to encourage a desire to achieve, and to push him to
independence. These strategies of bringing up the young are not
conscious or thought-out techniques, but as often happens in a society, the ways of raising children that appear most "natural" and
"right" are those that best inculcate the basic qualities demanded of
adults.


## Goodness of fit and built-in conflicts

In many ways, our families fit in well with the needs of our society.
Indeed, if families fail completely to "fit," something must give
—families must change to prepare their children better for the demands of society, or the demands of society must change to cope
with the needs of individuals ill-prepared by their families to live in
it. The isolation of the "reduced" American family gives it unusual
flexibility to change with the times, to modify itself, its definitions
of its member' roles, and its techniques of child-training to accommodate the changing needs of a changing society. Furthermore,
American families fit in nicely with the needs of work and the "job
market." Small and isolated, they are geographically, psychologically, and socially mobile. Families can move to follow the opportunities of changing job openings, and they can readily make the
psychological and social adaptations that are required by new
jobs, new "opportunities," and new styles of life. And our families
provide middle-class men with a haven from work, a place to lead
an emotional life even when their work is basically anti-emotional.

Perhaps most important, American middle-class families are well organized to teach small children the basic lessons of cognition, achievement, and independence which they will have to know by heart as adults.

But for all of their "goodness of fit" with other sectors of American society, our families do not always fit the needs of their members. As the price for family-society congruity, individuals must often confront built-in conflicts in their family life—inherent conflicts in the socially given requirements of their family roles. Some of these conflicts arise from contradictory demands made on men and women within the family; come from contrasts between family and public life; and others, even weightier, stem from discontinuities between childhood and adulthood. Taken together, these conflicts add to the stresses of adulthood in America.

*Kindergarten and kitchen*—The strains in a woman's role are especially acute, for the sociological isolation of the family entails the psychological isolation of the woman in charge of the family. This isolation is especially telling when it comes to raising children. Many American women have little prior knowledge of children other than what they can recall from their own childhoods; and even if memory were accurate, it is a fallible guide, given the determination of many women to do things differently from the way their parents did them. Most middle-class women therefore feel great uncertainty about how to raise their own children and even about how to "be" with them. Even the search for guidance in Dr. Spock can sometimes arouse as much anxiety as it allays: no matter how reassuring it tries to be, reading-matter is not an adequate substitute for the experience of living with children and being helped by those who know them. The easy passage of lore about children from one generation to the next, in a community where children are always underfoot and are everyone's responsibility, has completely disappeared from middle-class American life; and the substitutes do not fill the emotional gap.

As a result, most young middle-class mothers feel a great deal of normal anxiety about their newborn children. And as a consequence of this anxiety, they establish lasting patterns of relationship with their children just when they are most nervous and therefore most prone to act from inner idiosyncrasy rather than from calm wisdom. In this era when mothers are the villains of psychological dramas, we all know the "Mom" who "works out her problem with her children" or who "uses them to gratify her own needs." But we seldom note that our society indirectly encourages this villainy by its systematic isolation of women and their children. When it is easy for a woman to get started on the wrong foot, it is hard to get back in step later on.

The privileged privacy of American families adds to a woman's problems: she gets little support or help from those most able to give it. The neighbor who observes that a mother is doing "the wrong thing" with a child will hesitate to "meddle." There is no one who can legitimately help her, tell her how to proceed, point out the interference of her own needs with the child's development. Even her husband is in a poor position to help: he is not supposed to interfere except in emergencies; he usually knows even less about children than she does; and in any case he is away from home so much that he can rarely observe, much less follow through on his observations. In primitive societies, idiosyncrasies in child-rearing can sometimes be detected and corrected early by other members of the community. But we catch the products of aberrant child-rearing techniques and distorted family relationships only when we see their indirect results in mental illnesses of later childhood or adulthood. And by that time, pathogenic family patterns are often so long-standing that they can be changed only with immense difficulty, if at all. Mothers sense all of this in their bones, and it adds to their worries, making it the more difficult for them to sort out unaided their sound "maternal instincts" from "harmful" expressions of personal needs. Child-rearing is seldom the unmitigated fulfillment portrayed in the toilet-paper ads.

An equally fundamental problem inheres in the disparity between a woman's needs for personal development and the demands of her family role. In keeping with our disposition to treat everyone the same, we do not segregate the sexes in school, and we encourage in both sexes the development of the same cognitive abilities and skills. Within our families, we treat boys and girls in very similar ways, according them similar privileges at the same age, expecting similar responsibilities, disciplining both in similar ways—in short, developing much the same kinds of basic motivation and character in both sexes. Psychologically, this means that women are often equipped and motivated to use highly developed cognitive skills in work. With the virtual disappearance of physical strength and endurance as job prerequisites, few jobs remain that women cannot fill adequately; and with the development of higher education for women, increasing numbers of women have the training, skill, and motivation for these jobs.

At the same time, however, our definitions of women's family role discourage work. Women are usually taught that when they marry, their only job should be their family: our popular magazines abound in cautionary tales about career women, women who are dissatisfied with their families, and women who fail to find "fulfillment" in their homes and children. As a consequence, women with young children work—even part-time—only under unusual circumstances: either extreme financial want, or an unusually unambivalent determination to have a life outside the home. Most women of course enjoy their homes and children, and some—a decreasing few—want nothing else in any corner of themselves. Were it possible, as it is in many societies, for a woman to make a permanent commitment to the role of wife and mother, her lot would be easier. But in our long-lived society, women who try to make a total commitment to motherhood inevitably wake up in their forties or fifties to find that the objects of their commitment have grown up and left home, leaving their devoted mothers with thirty empty years ahead. Conflict is virtually inevitable—even those who initially demand no life outside the home find that eventually the home does not demand them. For most women, possessed of some latent desire for more "fulfillment" than family alone allows, fully aware that their time as mothers is limited, the problem is acute, though its sources usually remain unconscious.

Every American woman must somehow deal with this potential conflict. Very few risk the disapproval of husband and neighbors by working when they have small children; and it is still too rare for a woman to re-enter a job she left or train herself for a new one after her children are in school. More common are attempts to "solve" the problem by seeking some satisfaction of non-maternal needs *in* family life, community life, and related activities—in the volunteer organizations that organize, plan, and embellish every suburban area in the country, in the book societies, garden clubs, bridge clubs, classes and lessons, pottery and ceramics with which middle-class women so often occupy themselves. Other women take up golf, "write a little," develop hobbies; still others concentrate on preserving their youthfulness as if to deny the day and age when their unique role will be ended.

But perhaps the most dangerous "solution" is for a woman to transfer her own frustrated ambitions, needs for achievement and independence onto her husband and children, pushing them to the accomplishments from which her role blocks her. We see this solution among the mothers of our alienated subjects, who view their mothers as pushing men to accomplishment, as the real centers of initiative in the family, as driving, ambitious, frustrated, and capable. This "solution" often places unbearable burdens on children, who are now required to achieve both for themselves *and* for their mothers. Children soon sense, even when they cannot articulate it, that their primary meaning to their mother is as someone who will achieve *for her;* and while this awareness can sometimes lead to the development of a powerful drive to excel, it also means that much of the child's worth, even within the family, becomes dependent on the same standards of accomplishment used to judge men in the "public" world. The family, which in our society can be a shelter against the demands of public life, becomes instead the place where these demands are most keenly felt.

Another difficulty in vicarious living is that mothers come to need their children so desperately that they cannot let them go. All mothers of course need their children psychologically, and derive many of their deepest satisfactions from them. But in our society, a mother should need *most* for her children to grow up into independent men and women so that they can leave her: we demand an especially altruistic form of motherhood. This is a difficult psychological task at the best of times, and it becomes almost impossible when a mother unconsciously finds in her children her only avenue to vicarious accomplishment. The sense of loss that every mother feels when her children leave her—be it for nursery school, for college, or for marriage—is heightened to the point where it becomes unbearable. Such mothers try to hold their children, and especially their sons, from whom the most visible accomplishments can be expected. For these sons, growing up comes to mean abandoning a woman who will suffer as a result. This is of course a major theme in the fantasies of alienated students.

The conflicts in women's role thus stem in large part from the isolation of the family. No longer integrally embedded in the community, the family has become specialized in the related tasks of managing feelings and bringing up children. As "guardians" of the home, women are still expected to specialize in kitchen and kindergarten, homemaking and child-rearing, tasks which contrast sharply with the cognitive, achievement-oriented, and independent world of work and public life. Trained and often motivated for working life as well, they are forced to suppress, sublimate, and displace their desires for "fulfillment." One common result is seen in the mothers of alienated students: women displace their own frustrated ambitions for achievement on their sons, expect their sons to make up to them "the things they gave up for marriage," "overinvest" in their sons, and thus bind them in a special intimacy. The characteristics of the mothers of alienated subjects thus turn out to be not merely personal idiosyncrasies, but efforts to solve problems inherent in women's role in our society.

*Being a good father*—Women most often suffer because they continue to be excluded from the more cognitive public world. For middle-class husbands and fathers, however, the problems created by our American family system are different: they arise from the demand for a radical split between public cognition and family feeling, and from the human difficulty in complying with this demand.

The "normal" solution is for an American man to compartmentalize his life. He expresses his feelings in family and fun, and satisfies his needs for achievement and cognitive performance in his job. Ideally, this compartmentalization remains solid and unshakable: he does not daydream, weep, or have fits of rage and love on the job; nor does he approach his wife and children in the same cool and impersonal way he must approach his work. On the contrary, he is warm, responsive, and loving with his wife and children, playful and "fun" at home; at work he is competent, practical, "cool," and quietly effective. When it works, this compartmentalization almost literally permits psychic survival; a man can tolerate the cold unemotionality of his work because he can "live for the weekends," and—though it is less obvious—he can put up with the sometimes vacuous round of family feeling and fun because his work—however meaningless in ultimate terms—permits him to use his highly developed cognitive skills. Just as his psyche is compartmentalized, so his energies are divided in a *split commitment* to both family and work. His family permits him to answer, after a fashion, the question of work's meaning: work at least permits him to "support" his family. But psychic compartmentalization is hard to maintain, and continually threatens to break down. I earlier discussed one form of "breakdown," the feeling of inner fragmentation. But two other forms of "breakdown" are equally common, especially among mature men who have already embarked upon family and career. I will call these *familism* and *careerism*.

Especially when work is monotonous, uninteresting, routine, and empty, the split commitment which our society expects of men becomes difficult. The result can be withdrawal of any interest in work and a total investment in the family. Familism is the consequence. It has many virtues. In a chaotic and increasingly incomprehensible world, the family provides a small, relatively stable universe where "things make sense." Given work which demands emotional restraint and control, the family provides a haven for the "release" of feelings, an arena where achievements are visible and efforts can be tangibly useful. Given the tenuous relationship to the future engendered by chronic social change, children in the family provide a concrete link to the future. Given the shattering of community, the family provides a pseudo-community which partly tells a man who he is and where he stands. Given the fragmentations of social roles on the wider scene, the family provides a narrow stage within which life promises to be of a piece—a stage where to be "husband and father" can be a way of life.

But the problems of familism—for men, their wives, and their children—are equally impressive. A total psychic investment in the family puts enormous strains on family life. A man who hopes for *all* satisfactions from his family asks something American families can rarely give. Veblen was, I think, right when he postulated an "instinct of workmanship" in human nature. Men and women need to feel—and be—genuinely productive. To some extent (though it is often inadequate even for them) women can be productive in bearing and raising children. Men cannot, and need something more. If it were still possible, as on a few farms, for the whole family to work together, then the fantasy of total family fulfillment might be within reach. But old-style farm families are rare, and familism usually most prevails among middle-class families that have been most separated from any joint economic task. The search for productivity within the family thus leads men to a forever-frustrated hope that somehow washing dishes, polishing the car, or working in the home workshop will substitute for useful, challenging, and meaningful work. Whence springs the endless amount of unproductive "puttering" of many American males: the lawn mowed too often, the hours spent in building teetering tables better purchased at a furniture store, the endless polishing of cars, the continual casting about for "home projects," the chronic search for something that needs "fixing." And hence, too, comes the continual feeling of vague dissatisfaction that—even after the lawn has beeen mowed, the car shined, and the locks all oiled—somehow the unconscious search for productive work has not been fulfilled.

The displacement of the instinct of workmanship onto "family projects" also serves to vitiate real work. Men (or a society of men) who did not permit themselves this displacement would be better able to demand workmanly work—work that was worthy of psychic investment, that challenged rather than bored them, that made sense in itself and not only as a way of making a living. But familism drains attention and potential indignation from work and public life in general. Politics, international affairs, civic problems —all of public life—are psychically "disinvested." Those whose work is least tolerable—industrial workers—are usually those who ask least that their work be made more meaningful and workmanlike. A vicious circle ensues: the worse work gets, the less is expected of it, and the less we expect of it, the worse it gets.

Furthermore, the demand that family be all-satisfying creates an enormous strain on the family itself. American families are highly specialized institutions, intended to manage their member's feelings and to bring up children to be the right kinds of adults. To ask more than this is to ask something middle-class families are not set up to provide, and to risk enormous disappointment. A man who has only one source of satisfaction, who expects his wife and children to provide the entire meaning for his life, will be filled with inordinate disappointment when they fall short. One reason for our high divorce rate is that we ask so much of our families that they cannot provide us.

And finally, a familistic man conveys an unfortunate lesson to his children—especially to his sons. By word or deed, he communicates that his work does not matter, that he spends his days doing something he must come home to escape. Since children invariably take their parents as typical of adults, they "learn" that work is something one does with reluctance and abandons with relief. Since one-half of children's waking life as adults must be spent at work, the familism of fathers inevitably colors the outlooks of their sons toward adulthood in general. One common consequence is a precocious familism in youths who as yet have no families: they will follow in their fathers' footsteps, avoiding psychological investment in adult work altogether.

The other common response of men to the split of family and work is careerism, which usually springs from frustrated familism. Careerism is a compulsive flight into work, an inability to leave work at the office, a driven concentration on career to the exclusion of all else, an investment in work so total that the rest of life becomes totally subordinate to it. This "solution" is most tempting to those who possess in high degree the cognitive skills required by "high-level" jobs: these men are most likely to become "wrapped up" in their work, to work the longest hours, to take their work home with them at night. In many ways, they are among the most "acculturated" Americans—as shown by their success in their careers and by their insistence upon carrying out the American imperative for the subordination of feeling even at the expense of their families. But they are also driven men, men likely to develop ulcers or a coronary in their mid-fifties, men for whom retirement is equivalent to death.

Careerism should not be confused with a genuine involvement in meaningful work. On the contrary, careerism is compulsive and driven, and, like all compulsions, ambivalently motivated. The work to which the careerist is devoted is typically not especially significant, meaningful, socially useful or relevant; it is usually specialized, technical, and cognitively demanding. It thus requires cognitive skills that take many years of renunciation and training to acquire; and using one's hard-earned skills can be satisfying, even if it be in promoting an inferior product or in fixing prices. But behind this genuine satisfaction there usually lurk other motives closely related to the frustrations of family life. Many men bring to their family lives enormous and excessive hopes, which are related to the fantasy that their wife and children will somehow be *totally* satisfying, much as their mother once was. When these unconscious hopes are not fulfilled, the careerist attempts to deny them altogether and withdraws all commitment from the family. His solution is thus "compulsive" in the full psychological sense; the frustration of unconscious fantasies about family leads to a total repudiation of family and a compensatory over-investment in career.

Men can of course be driven by unconscious frustrations to great achievements, and an *un*compulsive commitment to vocation is highly desirable. But compulsive careerism is not this happy solution: it asks more of work than work can provide. Few jobs in America are arranged to satisfy most emotional needs—and when these needs are displaced onto a job, they are almost inevitably frustrated. When these frustrated feelings cannot be integrated into a career, they go underground, causing symptoms, vague anxiety, discontent, or a driven inability to "slow down."

Furthermore, careerism obviously damages family life. Though a man's family responsibilities are limited, they are none the less crucial to his wife and children. Like the mothers of our alienated subjects, many middle-class wives have "given up a lot" to be wives and mothers; when their husbands "desert" them for a career, these women have sacrificed for nothing and the temptation to turn for consolation to their sons often becomes overwhelming. Moreover, sons need fathers who—though they may be away from home during the working day—are nonetheless responsive to their sons when they *are* at home. A father who, though physically present, is psychologically absent is not merely a poor model, he is unavailable as a model at all. The only model left is the mother, and to identify with her creates major problems for her son.

Under the best of circumstances, it is hard enough for a middle-class American male to be a "good father" to his son. Of the two types we have considered, the familist probably has the best chance of succeeding, though he too, indirectly, teaches his son unfortunate lessons about adult work and life. The careerist, on the other hand, has almost no chance at all: emotionally detached from his family and children, secretly disappointed and embittered, he is simply "not there" for his children. This careerist pattern most nearly characterizes the fathers of alienated students. On the whole, these fathers were highly successful in their careers but not in their families, and their sons sometimes sensed their fathers' hidden disappointments and frustrations. A few of these alienating fathers choose still another solution akin to careerism—withdrawal from family into hobbies and fun, as with the father who preferred his perennials to his family. But in all cases, the underlying dynamics are similar; the father brought to his family overwhelming hopes for total fulfillment, but when these hopes were dashed, withdrew into some other area of endeavor.

The family constellations of the alienated thus result in part from efforts to "solve" problems inherent in the organization of American families and in their relations to the wider society. The detached father who is "not there" to his sons is as much a product of the inherent stresses in the middle-class family as he is of his own psychology or the unique dynamics of the marriage relationship. It is easy for an American father to slide, run, or to be pushed away from the center of family life; and when he is psychologically absent, his children paradoxically feel his absence more keenly than they would have felt his presence. The controlling, seductive, and frustrating women who mothered alienated young men are partly attempting to deal with the limitations of their family role. Each of these reactions makes the other more probable: a woman who pours her own frustrated ambitions onto her son encourages her husband to withdraw; the husband who "disinvests" himself of his family encourages his wife to concentrate her entire attention on her children. We cannot know where this vicious circle began— whether in the wife's excessive devotion to her son, in the father's readiness to withdraw when disappointed, or in some subtle chemistry of the feelings of both that led them to seek each other out in the first place.

## The paradoxes of growing up

Childhood training can be more or less continuous with adulthood experience. Some societies approach complete continuity: for example, sex play among children may be freely permitted and even encouraged, and the physical arrangements of community life may make the facts of life a matter of daily observation for children. Adolescence here requires no drastic unlearning of sex taboos instilled in childhood, no enlightenment to fill in areas of childhood ignorance, but merely a further extension of behavior and knowledge fully sanctioned in childhood. In peasant societies, children from an early age begin to assume the same responsibilities for the family economy that they must fully shoulder as adults. Or the inevitable dependency of a small child may be continued in adult life by a social organization where an adult, too, is locked in a web of mutual dependencies on kin and community.

Individual development in any society can be judged in terms of its continuity or discontinuity. Continuous development, involving a fundamental consistency between childhood and adult experience, leaves the adult with relatively little nostalgia for childhood: the gradualness with which new responsibilities, demands, and requirements are imposed reduces developmental discontinuity. Abrupt developmental discontinuities, on the other hand, are likely to leave adults with a greater backlog of unsatisfied childhood needs. The typical development of middle-class American children is drastically *dis*continuous, and these discontinuities are most pronounced in the related areas of dependency and sexual identification. In both areas, childhood and adulthood differ markedly, and adult symptoms of nostalgia and unreadiness are commonplace.

*Dependency and the "cold adult world"*—The central paradox in the upbringing of American children is the inconsistency between our systematic cultivation, intensification, and exploitation of the dependency during childhood and the adult demand for a high degree of self-sufficiency, especially among men. I have earlier argued that the intense, diffuse, and permissive mother-child relationship eventually provides a crucial instrument for teaching and encouraging cognitive skills, the desire to achieve, and the autonomy required of adults. Ultimately, the child's dependence upon his parents can become the most powerful incentive for him to learn to "stand on his own two feet" in order to please them. Furthermore, under ideal circumstances, the shift from dependency to independence does not occur suddenly or drastically: rather, the pre-school and school child is weaned gradually from his attachment to his mother. Nevertheless, the mother-child bond encouraged in middle-class households is so intense that few children can avoid carrying a residue of regret at its disappearance; and the problem of "unfulfilled dependency needs" is among the central problems of adult Americans. Like any human potential that is exploited in one stage of life and later neglected, these dependency needs neither die nor fade away, but go underground, whence they continue to affect behavior indirectly.

The adult manifestations of denied dependency needs are therefore ubiquitous in American society, and only the fact that most of us share these needs and have a vested interest in not noticing them keeps us unaware of them. Parents, for example, are often puzzled when children whom they have encouraged to become independent become suddenly sullen and hostile during adolescence. Such anger makes little surface sense when directed at permissive and loving parents who are prepared to grant their children freedom without a fight. Adolescent hostility is more understandable, however, if it is interpreted as an effort by the adolescent to destroy his own *internal* ties of dependency on his parents. By repudiating his parents, a youth can repudiate his own unconscious desire to continue to be their child, a desire which usually "interferes" with his independence far more than the parents whom he consciously blames.

Even so common an American phenomenon as "falling in love" is partly motivated by the same needs to be loved, cared for, cherished as a unique and irreplaceable person, fused with another person whom one trusts absolutely. Such needs are powerfully reinforced in early childhood, and when adolescent pride compels their disappearance from consciousness, they lurk just below the surface, ready to attach themselves to the first person who shows any sign of reciprocating affection. The suddenness, overwhelming intensity, and irresistibility of romantic love all attest to its origin in powerful motives ultimately based on the intense mother-child bond. Relatedly, the intense hopes for *total* fulfillment which many Americans bring to marriage—and the readiness with which Americans become disappointed in marriage—are often founded on an unconscious desire to recapture a relationship that, like Mother's early love, needs no supplement.

Frustrated dependency needs also play a major role in many common psychiatric conditions. They are often central in the development of depressions. And the finding of "repressed dependency needs" in psychosomatic disease is so universal that it attests more to the universality of the problem of dependency in our society than to its specific role in "causing" any one set of psychosomatic symptoms. Indeed, illness in general in our culture permits the sick person to be dependent on others and is therefore especially attractive to those whose needs to be cared for are strongest and least gratified in everyday life. The "sickness-prone" are usually those whose dependency needs play a major role in increasing their vulnerability to sickness.

These same themes of dependency are indirectly manifest in our idealization of childhood. Though we may recall the misery of our own personal childhoods, as a society we still view childhood as a time of carefree, happy, and irresponsible pleasure. Children do not bear the heavy responsibilities of adulthood, do not need to be self-sufficient and independent: they are still "cared for," in every sense of this rich phrase. By implication, adulthood is different—a time when "no one really cares" and when men and women must "make their own way," "stick up for their own rights," and "stand on their own two feet." Though our views of childhood often exaggerate the contrast of adulthood, they again point to the loss of childhood dependency.

Another common reaction to the problem of enduring needs for dependency is a compensatory assertion of total independence. This stance is striking in the alienated, who deny their deep needs for fusion by an ideology of total self-sufficiency and absolute autonomy. But a comparable if less extreme ideology is found in every stratum of American society. Sometimes it is expressed in international affairs as a determination to rely on no foreign allies, or a virtually psychotic belief that national self-sufficiency is possible in a world of 100-megaton bombs. Or sometimes it is manifested, especially by men, in a firm and "manly" denial of any need for love, help, care, or support. And sometimes it is expressed in a vicious intolerance of those whose neediness is all too clear: in rejection of the poor, in repudiation of the sickly, in scorn for the indigent.

This contrast between the vaguely recalled and often romanticized dependency of childhood and the cognitive, demanding society in which we live out our adult lives predisposes many adult Americans to a vague feeling that their lives lack something essential. "Public" life in America *is* impersonal, cold, highly fragmented, and cognitive; and men and women might find it hard to accept this kind of life joyously under the best of circumstances. But the contrast with the pleasures of childhood makes adulthood the more unattractive. This contrast is sometimes felt as a wistful envy of children (or even as avoidance of them because they make us envious), sometimes as a vague dissatisfaction with adult life, sometimes as mild lack of enthusiasm for what one does, sometimes as boredom, sometimes as a feeling that something is missing, sometimes as a tendency to flee into fun and recreation, and sometimes in efforts to find a substitute mother in one's wife. Among the alienated, of course, this contrast between childhood and adulthood is fundamental and extreme; the most basic theme of their lives is the loss of their maternal paradise, their enduring desire to regain it, and their rejection of conventional adulthood because it offers so little of the warmth, caring, intimacy, and fusion they desire.

How much of a problem dependency is in adulthood depends in large part on whether the mother is sincere in her efforts to push her children to independence and on whether she is supported by her husband in this effort. Least likely to succeed are mothers like those of alienated youths, women whose own conflicts lead them to pull their sons toward them at the same time that they push them away. And if the father's own life and marriage suggest that an adult can be happy and emotionally fulfilled, his children will be more likely to enter adulthood eagerly. And finally, the problem of dependency is more intense for men than it is for women, who are permitted to remain more "emotional," dependent, and "clinging" than are their husbands. But for many Americans, unconscious problems of dependency, intimacy, being cared for, solaced, nurtured and cherished remain sore spots throughout life. A developmental estrangement that the alienated experience close to consciousness is a conflict few Americans can hope to avoid altogether.

*Becoming a man*—A second major discontinuity in American middle-class development concerns sexual identification. For boys, the source of this discontinuity can be stated simply: American boys are increasingly brought up by women—mothers and school teachers—who have the greatest power and authority over them. This "matriarchal" situation tends to encourage identification with women, their functions and their activities. Yet as adults, the same boys must have a relatively firm sense of their own maleness.

The structure of the typical American family complicates masculine sexual identification for a boy. His close bond with his mother, combined with his father's absence at work during most of the day, conspire to push him toward a deep early involvement with his mother. It is she who controls most of the things he wants: love, approval, security, material benefits, and privileges. In recognition of her position, a boy is likely to imitate her gestures, her expressions, and her activities, and to model himself on her in his earliest years. All this is "normal" in American middle-class families: young children belong to their mothers. For girls, early identification with their mothers poses fewer problems; but for boys continuing identification with and dependency on their mothers is frowned upon, and most of all by their fathers, who actively push their sons away from "sissiness" toward a more masculine identification and greater independence.

If all goes well, sons eventually accept their fathers' role, attempt to emulate them (shifting identification from mother to father) and ultimately "forget" about the whole problem. But a variety of circumstances not uncommon in American families can prevent this "normal" outcome. The son may, for example, perceive that his mother is the real center of power and initiative in the family and/ or that she prefers her son to her husband. When this happens, his incentive to emulate his father is greatly diminished: Dad has few desirable qualities and controls little of what the boy wants. Or the father may have absented himself from family involvement so completely that he is simply unavailable as an exemplar: the son must either search elsewhere or continue to identify with his mother. Or the mother's fears of masculinity, her ambivalence about her husband, or her need to retain "possession" of her son may make it hard for her to let him become a man. By undermining her husband and other men, such a "Mom" can make the normal shift to masculine identification very difficult.

Sexual identification is not, of course, an all-or-nothing matter: everyone, no matter how "genuinely" masculine or feminine, retains some identification with the opposite sex. But our society, by intensifying the family dramas of early childhood, by providing no early models other than parents, by encouraging an especially intense mother-child tie, and by keeping men away from their children for most of the day, makes the attainment of a genuine and untroubled masculinity especially difficult. Most American men experience considerable adolescent anxiety about their adequacy as males, and for some this anxiety persists throughout life.

The extreme consequence of a failure in sexual identification is homosexuality, which involves a refusal of the male sex role. But for the vast majority of Americans, the problem of identification is less severe, and its symptoms are not homosexuality but a fear of it, combined with a compensatory emphasis on masculinity, a pose of "toughness," and an extreme repudiation of softness and passivity. Among adolescents, these postures are especially striking. The prolongation of adolescence in our society requires American youths to live for many years without that social confirmation of maleness that marriage and fatherhood inevitably entail, and the stylized dress and mannerisms of American adolescent boys are readily identifiable as protesting masculinity too much. Less obvious are other adult symptoms of similar anxieties: American men's fear of bodily contact with each other, the pose of hardness and toughness, the excessive fear of passivity. In foreign films, American men are often portrayed with a special quality of sexual immaturity and nervousness, of bravado and bluster covering insecurity: this portrait touches a particularly vulnerable point in our self-image, apparent even in the American vocabulary of international discourse. Those who emphasize "carrying a big stick" in dealing with foreign nations, who fear "being caught with our pants down" if we "let down our guard" or "make overtures" to "potential aggressors," can sometimes allay their personal insecurities by identifying with social and international aggressiveness. Even the phallic image of a rocket assaulting the (traditionally feminine) moon may help a little.

I am not arguing that middle-class American families make most boys into dependent or effeminate adults: on the contrary, most American males are relatively independent and their sexual identification is primarily masculine. My point is that the developmental discontinuities in our ways of raising children produce, to greater or lesser degree, inner conflicts between the dependency needs exploited in childhood and the independence required in adulthood, and between the strong identification with the mother in childhood and the need for a masculine identification in adulthood. These conflicts are only rarely incapacitating. And when they are visible in adults, they usually show themselves in behavior we consider socially acceptable: in a reactive emphasis on independence and toughness, in compensatory masculinity and bluster, in a dislike of things soft, flabby, receptive, or weak.

Were the demands of adulthood less acute, these same childhood needs and identifications would cause less adult conflict. Developmental discontinuities are contrasts between childhood and *adult* experience; and there are other societies more indulgent of adult dependency and less insistent that men be "manly" by rigorously denying in themselves the special virtues of women. Japanese society assumes that adults will continue to be dependent upon each other and will admit their emotional neediness; and in India masculinity is socially defined to include gentleness, sensitivity, and a capacity for a "softness" and passivity. American definitions of adulthood and manliness, however, make little allowance for the neediness, dependency, passivity, and feminine identification which is an inevitable part of all human nature, male or female.

## Alienation and the family

Families and parents are too often made the sole causes and culprits for the problems of their children: to do so neglects the role of later influences in human development and it gives parents a role of prime movers which they do not possess. Parents are themselves caught in social pressures, cultural conflicts, and definitions of family role which they did not create but with which they must cope. How they raise their children is determined not only by their personal needs and histories, but also by their society's definitions of what good parents should do and how good children should behave. Decent, loving, and devoted parents can through no fault of their own have "problem" children. Most parents do the best they can by their offspring; and when their best is not enough to enable their children to cope—or to want to cope—with all life's pressures

and demands, it will not do—either for children or observers—
merely to heap blame upon the parents.

But it would be an equal mistake to overlook the family's critical
role as the mediator between society and each new generation. No
other social institution plays a comparable part in shaping the motivations, the adaptations, the inhibitions, and the values of the
young. When the same conflicts are prevalent among most adults in
a society, the roots of these conflicts will often be found in their
family life. And when most of the members of a society possess the
same defects of character, the social patterning of these defects will
usually have first begun in their families.

Our middle-class families, despite their "goodness of fit" with
many aspects of American society, involve inherent conflicts in the
roles of mother and father, and produce deep discontinuities between childhood and adulthood. The parents of alienated subjects
are, in part, trying to "solve" problems posed by the social definitions of "mother" and "father." And two of the major themes in
the lives of alienated students—their longing for fusion and their
discomfort with masculine sexuality—are extreme forms of collective estrangements fostered by the discontinuities in middle-class
development. The "solutions" of these alienating families are of
course not typical. But the reactions of these parents and their sons
point to stresses that *do* impinge on typical Americans, and to demands with which typical Americans must somehow cope.

In brief, these demands are the requirement that women, though
skilled and motivated for work, abandon these skills and motivations for much or all of their lives, gaining full satisfaction from
their families without "needing" their children too much; that men
maintain a precarious split commitment to both cognitive public
life and family, feeling, and fun without falling into either careerism or familism; that children gradually "outgrow" their early dependency on their mothers and become independent adults without
excessive regret, nostalgia, or backsliding; and that boys, despite
their deep involvement with women throughout their childhood,
form a positive masculine identification which will remain solid

and unthreatened in their adult years. These demands are not impossible to meet; and most young Americans and their parents more or less succeed. But our society makes parenthood difficult, and we prepare our young for adulthood by accentuating needs that adulthood will deny. It is no wonder that many Americans—whether alienated or not—feel a certain ambivalence toward the adulthood our society offers.

# 11    The decline of Utopia

The most obvious way to account for any human or social problem is to locate the pressures, conflicts, and stresses that help produce it. In explaining the psychological problems of an individual, we usually look for deformations of development in early life that predispose to later illness, and for conflicts, pressures, and stresses in the present that precipitate breakdown, regression, or maladaption. Similarly, in trying to understand social problems we normally search for historical and social conflicts that lead to social malfunction and misery. In other words, we conventionally see individual and collective problems in terms of *active forces that push toward pathology;* and we feel we have "explained" the problem once we have discovered these forces.

But this approach, useful as far as it goes, has major limitations. "Normal" individuals are sometimes under as much or more external pressure than their more neurotic fellows, but manage to cope with it better. In the past lives of "normal" individuals, too, we often find the same striking deprivations and psychological hardships as in the more neurotic, yet somehow the "normal" individual has managed to survive and even prosper from these apparent handicaps. Some men and women thrive on or even need internal tension and psychic conflict that would and does incapacitate others. In all these instances, the presence of pressures, hardships,

and conflicts in an individual's past and present life is not enough
to account for the level of living he achieves. There is something
else—some missing factor—which explains why some individuals
thrive, others survive, and others succumb to very similar stresses.

Similarly, "objective" deprivations alone cannot account for
many social problems. Historians have noted that revolutions usually occur not when the conditions of life are at their worst, but
when they are beginning to improve. Men revolt not so much from
sheer objective misery, but when they have an overpowering vision
of their just deserts that cannot be attained within the existing social order. Social deprivation, like individual suffering, is always
*relative* to socially shared views of what one is entitled to, what one
can legitimately demand, and how much one should endure without
protest. Cruelties and hardships considered unbearable in our society were (and still are) endured without thought of protest in societies where no alternatives are conceivable. And on the other side
of the coin, men will willingly endure enormous deprivations if they
suffer in the service of some ideal or goal they deem worthy, exciting, or noble. Recall the nostalgia with which Englishmen remember the glorious days of the Blitz (when the objective conditions of
life were worse than ever since) or the regret with which many
Frenchmen confront the passing of the Resistance (a time of terror, torture, and constant struggle). In both cases, what made
suffering worthwhile was the shared vision of a future worth suffering for.

Thus any account, like this one so far, that focuses merely on the
actual pressures that push *toward* alienation is bound to be incomplete. For in addition to these active, present factors, we must consider as well the forces which might have prevented alienation but
are absent in our society. In individual life, we frequently find that
the crucial difference between the healthy individual and the neurotic lies not in the intensity of outward stress, but in the resiliency
and strength of character of the "normal" and the inflexibility of
the neurotic. And in searching for the origins of this resiliency, we
sometimes find it in apparently insignificant events: in the presence

of a single teacher who imbued the individual with an early sense of dedication, in a kindly aunt whose love laid the basis for enduring self-esteem, in a tenaciously held vision of aspiration and purpose that armored the individual against subsequent adversity. One way of understanding neurosis and mental illness, then, is by trying to account for the absence of such intangible but potentially strengthening factors as these. Similarly, no account of alienation can be complete unless it also looks to the absence of values and ideals which, if present, might have encouraged and supported commitment to our society despite its many real demands, stresses, and pressures.

Men are unique among all creatures in that their visions of the ideal, their myths of the good and bad life, their conscious and unconscious expectations about their just deserts and their merited sufferings—all profoundly affect not only their interpretations of their experience, but the subjective "feel" of experience itself. Thus, among the central factors underlying contemporary alienation is the absence of any shared conscious myth, vision, or conception of the good life that would make the demands of our society worth accepting.

## The uses of myth

"Myth" has become a bad word, quickly applied to the false, the superstitious and the manipulative, but seldom to the valid, the ennobling, and the challenging. The term "myth" is usually preceded by "merely a" or "only a," as if to suggest that to label a belief a "myth" is to destroy its validity. Myths, we have come to believe, are cognate to "mythologies," to the Olympuses of gods and goddesses we study as children, observe among more "primitive" peoples, and examine in those we dislike. So, too, myths are often seen as devices for manipulating others while concealing one's own selfish purposes: we speak pejoratively of the "myth of the classless society," "the myth of free enterprise," "the myth of one world";

the very prefixing of the term "myth" suggests that what follows is merely a fairy tale whose underlying purpose is exploitation.

It will take some pages to explore the reasons for the modern denigration of myth; for now, let me only question whether this denigration is justified. The pejorative usage of the term assumes that it is possible for men to live without myth—without a non-empirical, non-scientific, unprovable, symbolic interpretation of existence, without a set of animating though unconfirmable convictions about the deepest meanings of life, history, and society, without a set of symbols, themes, and conscious and unconscious visions of the desirable and the undesirable, the holy and the profane. Yet this assumption is clearly wrong: all men have and need conscious and unconscious premises that shape their experience, their interpretations of life and their behavior; and in every individual or society these premises are organized into a more or less coherent mythic whole. We have earlier seen the intellectual superstructures of two such myths in the contrasting alienated and "typically American" world views. And in the assumptions and principles that govern our responses to social change, to our social organization, and to the typical patterns of our family life, other mythic elements are clearly visible—unrational, unprovable assumptions about reality and the ideal, symbolic interpretations of experience which significantly shape its meaning and impact.

All men need, then, some more or less coherent set of implicit assumptions, symbolic meanings, characteristic configurations, and explicit beliefs that help them to organize and guide their lives; and we can call this need a need for myth. The alienated demonstrate the power of this need, for though they reject the prevalent myths of American life, they go on to formulate another opposing ideology, and still actively struggle to find some further sense of positive vocation and value. In most men and women, the mythic interpretation of reality is largely implicit and unconscious: the average American, for example, seldom stops to reflect on his conviction that changes are for the good; indeed he may deny it if confronted with it so baldly stated (though we can often see the behavioral corollaries of this conviction in the patterns of his commitment to the future). Nor can we always articulate our implicit conceptions of science, of society, of the relations between men and women, of the deepest meanings of life. For most men and women these myths remain unconscious.

Thus, in defining either an individual's private myth or the animating shared myths of a society, to stop with conscious beliefs and articulate assumptions is to notice but the top of the iceberg. Beyond and below these conscious assumptions are layer upon layer of preconscious and unconscious fantasy and belief. In seeking the personal roots of alienation we have seen such unconscious personal myths: in Inburn, for example, the unconscious fantasy of expulsion from an early paradise; in him and in other alienated youths, the unconscious assumption of a disastrous victory over an early rival. These personal fantasies are truly mythical and, like all myths, they have a double reference: on the one hand to idiosyncratic themes of personal history, and on the other to archetypal collective motifs of outcastness and revolt.

In any society, one of the basic binding forces between men is their collective myth—the points at which each individual's personal myth overlaps with that of his fellows and is influenced and confirmed by it. Several facts make such overlap probable: as members of the same society we all early acquire from each other a set of common categories, of similarly tinted spectacles through which we interpret our experience. Many of our most basic myths about life's meaning and purposes are subtly learned from parents, teachers, siblings, and friends. And, perhaps most important, one of the most fundamental ties that bind the members of any enduring society is their more or less common pattern of psychological development in a more or less similar environment, which—given the communalities of human nature—produces in most analogous fantasies and imagination. In our society, these common patterns of upbringing produce a collective estrangement from early childhood, intensified by the discontinuity between childhood and adulthood; this collective sense of estrangement finds symbolic expression; and most members of society respond to the mythic symbols of shared estrangement with similar unconscious recognition and feeling. Thus there develops a set of shared meanings, conscious and unconscious symbols, common themes of imagination and explicit doctrines of philosophy and religion which constitute the myth of a society.

The official pronouncements of our society show but the top and most rationalized layer of our social myth. Just as in personal life, fantasy and imagination constitute the deepest, most vital levels of myth and mythmaking, so in collective life we must search for deeper strands of myth among collective fantasies, in folklore, in entertainment, fiction, films, and television. Often the myth of an age can be found in the issues it takes for granted—in the question it never asks, in the assumptions so universally shared they remain tacit. Indeed it is often only in contrast with other societies, with other myths, that we become aware of our own. Moreover, at least a part of our collective myth has a defensive, self-protective role as well as an interpretive one, in that it serves as a social defense against shared social anxieties and unwelcomed recognition of unpleasant social realities; and this defensive role makes it even harder to recognize the existence of core components in our collective myth. And finally, it is only as an abstraction and an oversimplification that we can speak of social myth at all: in actuality, we are dealing with as many private myths as there are individuals, private myths that touch and converge at some points but differ and depart from one another in countless other ways.

The functions of social myth are many. Men are united by their common responsiveness to their shared myth; members of the society usually feel a kinship for their compatriots (especially when far from them) which originates in part from this implicit sense of unconscious sharing. One reason many foreigners, though externally acclimated to our society, continue to feel outsiders in it, is because their own childhoods in another land prepare them to respond to other themes than those of our own dominant myths. The

social myth helps members of a society think and feel in inner concert, and thus relieves the sense of isolation inevitable in anyone
whose interpretations of experience are merely idiosyncratic. To
the extent that they interpret the world through the prisms of a
common myth, men and women will respond to reality in similar
ways, will act in harmony, will support and help one another. And
not least of all, no individual, however creative, is capable of developing alone an adequate set of categories by which to understand
his existence, or an adequate set of purposes to guide his actions.
The collective myth provides each individual a set of lenses polished by the experience of generations; and though the implications
of myth are sometimes wise and sometimes foolish, no man can
attempt to do without them unless he is willing to condemn himself
to the stumbling incoherence of the caveman. Social myths, like
their conscious epiphenomena, explicit cultural traditions, indirectly express what men have learned (or mislearned) in the long
course of human history; and men cannot totally repudiate these
residues of history and remain men. Even in our own era, when it
has become fashionable to deprecate myth, we are still conditioned
by our myths, as all men must be; and this conditioning is nowhere
more obvious than in those whose modern myth is to live without
myths.

Thus, the myth of a society helps determine the commitment or
lack thereof of its members. Those who possess a vision of their
community as noble, challenging, exciting, assisting the greater fulfillment of its members, will usually give their enthusiasm to their
society no matter what "objective" deprivations it imposes. Leaders have always known that if their followers believe they are
engaged in an active struggle for a noble cause, they will make
enormous sacrifices to achieve this cause. Among individuals, those
who seek wisdom above happiness and see suffering as the path to
wisdom will countenance and even deliberately seek suffering as
the means to this noble end. But even the most open and affluent
society cannot guarantee the commitment of its citizens if they dis-

trust its purposes, are bewildered by its future, question the nobility of its values, or are bored by its persuasions. So too, a society that advances no positive myth of itself as a valued, challenging, stimulating, and ennobling human association, a society in which each individual is forced to define his private aims in isolation, can hardly evoke the enthusiasm of its members. Alienation can result from the absence of any positive myth in society.

The converse may be true as well: commitment may flag when individuals possess aspirations that society cannot fulfill, when men cannot translate their individual dreams into public reality. Many obstacles can intervene between the private vision of the good life and the concretization of this vision in social reality—a disadvantaged social position that bars access to all but the most menial statuses; a tyrannical political system which thwarts the needs and visions of individuals; or the fact that private hopes for public good are unconscious, implicit, repressed, and expressed—if at all—in terms of oppositions rather than propositions that could stimulate improvement. Alienation can spring not only from the lack of a shared positive myth, but from individual aspirations that outrun social realities. Both of these phenomena occur in modern American society, and to understand them, and with them the absent forces that might reconstruct commitment, we must explore the fate of myth in our time.

## The submersion of positive myth

Every age has its characteristic balance between *positive,* eductive, hortatory, constructive, imperative, visionary, Utopian myths, and *negative,* deterent, cautionary, warning, direful, destructive, and counter-Utopian myths. In some periods of Western society, images of violence, demonism, destructiveness, sorcery and witchcraft have prevailed; in others, myths of blessedness, justice, cooperation, and universal concordance with divine order have dominated. Other times, perhaps the happiest, have been able to include visions of both light and darkness in one mythic embrace: only in such times do we find a clear public articulation of the existence of and the links between the divine and the demonic.

But despite the great differences between the predominant positive myths of one age and the predominantly negative myths of another, a more subtle equilibrium also prevails. The sweet reasonableness of the Enlightenment is the backdrop for De Sade's most demonic of all envisioned republics. When the devil is denied he manifests himself nonetheless—the more so because his existence is no longer recognized and thus cannot be combated. Similarly, the divine reasserts itself most powerfully in individuals when collective myths ignore the Good: saints live in times of the devil. Though there are real contrasts between different ages in their ratio of positive to negative myths, the impulse to both types of myth is always present, sometimes on the surface, sometimes submerged deep below the dominant consciousness of the time.

There is also another equilibrium, between those aspects of the myth of any age that are open, public, and consciously accepted by the members of society, and those that are covert, private, and consciously rejected by most men and women. Societies also have their secret and "dirty" thoughts, their pornographies and their secretly fascinating perversions whose existence is publicly admitted only in cautions and warnings. In an atheistic society the existence of God may be publicly admitted only in warnings against religion, and His worshipers can be forced to behave as criminals and outcasts. In Nazi Germany, the myth of universal peace (though most cogently stated by a German, Kant) found only perverted expression in the myth of a Pax Germanica. Some of what men express in their collective myth always ashames and repels them, and they surround its expression with warnings, repudiations and rejections, or—as often—they expressed shared fantasies in disguised and transmuted symbolic form. The German fear of dirt and inner pollution found public expression during the Nazi period only in projections onto

Jews; our deep American potential for violence is now chiefly expressed in nominally cautionary tales of criminals whose violent transgressions are, in the last act, finally punished.

Few would deny that ours is a time whose most visible public myths are negative, deterrent, even satanic. To be sure, social fantasies of violence, cruelty, discord, and crime are ostensibly presented as warnings against vice; but what dominates the screens of television, the pages of popular novels, or the sheets of our tabloids are images of brutality, sadism, and empty sex. And more fundamentally, the central images of our highest artistic and intellectual achievements are rarely visions of concord, communion, and consonance, but of dissidence, discord, and disintegration. Here, as always, the artist in part reflects the deepest myths of his age, phrasing shared unconscious images in symbolic language to which others can respond. Symbols of analysis replace those of synthesis; fission, fusion; asymmetry, symmetry; regression, growth. Even in world politics, the myth of The Bomb and of Inevitable War has greater cogency than any belief in peace or concord.

Though we see it most clearly in the last fifty years, this shift to predominately negative myths has been long in the making. The specific disillusionments and the tragic experiences of recent history only partly account for it; indeed, the very willingness to be disillusioned and to consider history's lessons tragic is itself a part of the more general submersion of positive myth. Historically, the change in our dominant myth has involved two related stages: one, the *intellectualization of positive myth;* the other, *the debunking of intellectual ideology*. To chronicle these stages adequately requires nothing less than a cultural and intellectual history of the past six centuries; here I can only suggest in general terms the main processes involved.

The public philosophy of the Middle Ages, as expressed in Thomist Catholicism, was an eminently synthetic world view, an outlook that attempted to include and order all modes of experience in one embracing system of thought, subordinating them only to God's purposes and will. Both reason and revelation were sanctioned, though neither to the exclusion of the other. Heresy was defined as a too exclusive concentration on partial truth: rationalism and mystic quietism were both deemed wrong because each attempted to make a whole from a part. So, too, both the divine and the demonic in man were recognized, and sin might result from too great a self-identification with either the one or the other— from pride or from demonic possession. Medieval Catholicism, which embodied and expressed the dominant myth of the age, was a theology of "ands," not "ors": freedom *and* determinism, the divine *and* the demonic, the cognitive *and* the passionate, the angelic *and* the satanic, the rational *and* the revealed, were all included in a hierarchical order of Being which extended from God to his most insignificant creature, and which seemed to embrace and reconcile every possible dichotomy, opposition, and polarity.

Yet there proved to be one flaw in this colossally synthetic *Weltanschauung:* and this flaw proved fatal. The very success of medieval Catholicism led to its demise: men and their experience were so inextricably "placed" in an ordered chain of Being and in a hierarchical society that mirrored this chain, that they rebelled against the smothering embraces of their myth, their theology, and their society. The Renaissance brought a renewed sense of man's autonomy, his personal creativity, his capacity not merely to *find* his place but to *create* a place in the world; and this spirit of individual autonomy and creativity inevitably clashed with, and eventually destroyed, the medieval order with its constant mythical and social reminders of man's inextricable embeddedness in God's hierarchy. Individualism always chafes against a myth of moderation, hierarchy, and order, for if an individual is to be free to realize himself, he must be allowed the option of total self-immersion in the divine, the demonic, the passionate, the rational, or the spiritual—even if it means his self-destruction. Moreover, he must believe in his own strength and capacity to create a world for himself, to interpret his life in his own manner, to violate or change the order of his society. All of these possibilities were denied him by the medieval myth—synthetic in all respects except with regard to

man's self-creating individuality, which was denied as a fact and
forbidden as the sin of pride.

With the rediscovery of classical knowledge, the achievements of
Italian city-states, and the great economic expansion of the late
Middle Ages, the doctrines of the free and creative individual became more powerful; and as they strengthened, they began to undermine the medieval myth. "Reason" became the most powerful
symbol of the new myth, for reason seemed the greatest of man's
gifts, which enabled him to discover and even create truth and
beauty; and reason now appeared to inhere in the individual perceiving self-evident truth, rather than in the divine order. Thus rationalism, as it emerged during and after the Renaissance, attempted to dissociate reason and faith, extirpating superstition and
basing belief on the sounder tenets of "self-evident reason." The
Cartesian critique of religion, although it finally arrived at religious
truths almost identical with those from which it had started, nonetheless founded these truths on a primarily cognitive and intellectual basis. Faith was not really necessary; reason alone could arrive
at truth in matters of value just as in matters of science. Ironically,
each new effort to restore the older myth ended by undermining it
more completely. Descartes was attempting to give a more rational
formulation to the traditional beliefs of his Church; but by elevat-
ing reason over revelation, he paved the way for later generations
whose "self-evident reason" would give other, less traditional, answers to the central problems of life. And by challenging the epis-
temological underpinnings of Catholicism in an effort to support its
doctrines, he opened the door for others who would later challenge
even Cartesian rationalism.

The steady effort to "demythologize" religion did not, of course,
result in the disappearance of myth as I here use the term, but
merely in a new kind of myth, which we can call an intellectual
ideology to indicate its primarily intellectual content and to distinguish it from other myths more directly rooted in passion, faith,
imagination, and poetic experience. This new faith in reason
merely separated the emotional and cognitive sources of myth,

abetting the rationalistic critique of the affective, imaginal components of the medieval myth, and producing a new myth which, on
the surface at least, was far more rooted in reason and less attached
to fantasy and the non-rational. This ideology, carrying a vision of
a new society made to serve the individual, was expressed above all
by the French *philosophes* of the eighteenth century, and its Utopian aspects culminated in the French Revolution.

But the non-rational and demonic side of myth, excluded from
the public domain of established doctrine, merely went underground. We seldom connect the excesses, brutalities, and insanities
that followed the French Revolution with the rationalism of the
*philosophes;* we usually attribute the eruption of the satanic during
an epoch of reason to the fact that men were not reasonable
*enough.* But there is another possibility—that the effort to suppress
unreason from social myth, to dissociate the demonic from public consciousness, merely forced these to expression in other areas
of community life—in the practice (as opposed to the theory) of
politics, in art, in private life, and in entertainment. The choice of a
prostitute to incarnate Reason in the pageantry of the French Revolution illustrates more effectively than any abstract argument the
tendency of the non-rational to reassert itself in an age of Pure
Reason. Indeed, the excesses of the French Revolution might well
have taught that the optimistic rationalism of the Enlightenment
had ignored important aspects of human experience, for it was unable to anticipate or even to comprehend the eagerness with which
men rejected Reason and in its name chose first Terror and then
Napoleon.

But in fact, of course, this lesson was not learned. Instead of
deepening what had become a primarily intellectual myth, this myth
persisted in the same form and merely proved itself more open to
attack. Purely cerebral values are usually the most vulnerable; those
that are rooted in personal experience are more passionately held.
Without a sanctioned basis in feeling, tradition, and fantasy, the
intellectual values of the Enlightenment were difficult to defend.
Just as it was easy to show that the rationalists' natural laws had no

basis in physical fact but were themselves rooted in faith (now disreputable), so it proved simple to demonstrate that intellect alone was impotent to arrive at valid conclusions about ultimate questions. Concepts like "progress," "reason," and "perfectability" could readily be shown to be principles of interpretation, not facts: bereft of their non-intellectual foundations, they too have collapsed. Since history continually refuted the claims of the rationalists, and since they had voluntarily deprived themselves of any appeals but those to the intellect, they could do little to defend their causes.

In place of these causes, two manifestly opposed though secretly related ideologies have emerged. I will call these scientism—the ideology of devitalized reason—and irrationalism—the ideology of degraded passion. Scientistic ideologies seek the foundations of truth in empirical knowledge; irrational ideologies make passion, blood, self-interest, and instinct their criteria of validity. Much of the intellectual history of the West since the French Revolution can be interpreted as the interplay between these two opposing ideologies, and the destruction in the modern era of positive yet vital public myth owes much to their battles. For each ideology has proved highly vulnerable, though well equipped to point out the vulnerability in the other. Irrationalism as expressed in romanticism, vitalism, and racism (and even in some interpretations of psychoanalysis) was rightly open to the charge that it underestimated man's capacities for thought, self-direction, and mastery through intelligence of his environment; moreover, its proponents, despising reason, were easily found guilty of illogic, incoherence, and mere appeals to emotion and superstition. But, similarly, openness to debunking is a necessary characteristic of any scientistic ideology that attempts to separate itself from the non-rational, unverifiable, and negative. At each step, opponents have pointed out that the assumptions of scientific empiricism or positivism are themselves unverifiable; that the decision to be rational is nonrational; that the scientific method cannot demonstrate its own desirability by scientific methods; that the choice of cognitive outlook is not a cognitive choice.

Partly because of this continuing ideological struggle, modern ideologies are often more powerfully developed as weapons than as assertions. With a fury born partly from frustration, modern thought has systematized the techniques of intellectual subversion. Whatever their positive content, psychoanalysis, positivism, vitalism, empiricism, existentialism, Marxism, and even modern "philosophical analysis," all start from a systematic discrediting of established belief. Psychoanalysis attacks those who challenge its assumptions by challenging their motivation, imputing motivated "resistance" to recognizing psychoanalytic truths. Existentialism criticizes the fundamental errors in an "essentialist" view of the world and suggests determined blindness as the obstacle to seeing existential truths. Even so academic a school as philosophical analysis attributes previous philosophical errors to "misunderstanding" about the use and usage of ordinary language. Though the techniques of debunking vary, all agree in finding most previous belief in error; and most devote more brilliant efforts to the criticism of past error than to the reconstruction of current truth. The result is usually the same: conviction is undermined by associating established belief with undesirable partiality, prejudice, fear, misunderstanding, resistance, or self-interest.

Through this intellectualization of positive myth and the continual debunking of the scientistic and the irrational ideologies which followed, little remains of our former faiths. What started as an attack on specific beliefs and superstitions has ended as a general onslaught on positive conviction. Attempts to find new, more solid and unassailable foundations for basic beliefs have again and again succeeded in destroying older foundations only to crumble themselves before the next attack. The frontiers of certainty have vastly shrunk in the last four centuries, leaving few if any modern equivalents of the Cartesian axioms of "self-evident" reason. Our positive myths have been shorn of their strengths and justifications, separated more and more from the non-rational, deprived of emotional underpinnings which could give them coherence, fascination, and excitement.

This submersion of positive myth is nowhere more apparent than in the transvaluation of Utopia, and in the resulting decline of cultural commitment and morale—of co-operation based on a common vision of a shared future. There was a time when "Utopian" was, for at least some men, a term of praise; and when Utopias were defined as tangible and desired possibilities that men might write about and actually set out to realize. From Plato's *Republic* onward, men have concretized their values in visions of a society more noble than any in existence; and though most Utopian thinkers have realized full well that no real society could ever *completely* match their vision, the imaginative construction of a Utopia implied a constant faith in the possibility of human betterment. This faith was an essential part of earlier forms of rationalism, which believed not only in man's rational capacity to discover the truth, but in the capacity of his reason to guide him toward the actualization of the ideal. In the last century, the Brook Farms and Nauvoos of America, the Proudhons, Saint-Simons, Owens, and Fouriers of Europe—all expressed the conviction that there *were* rational values which should be implemented concretely through new forms of social organization, and that such implementation was within the practical, immediate possibilities of ordinary rational beings. And, most important, America as a whole was often in the last century felt to be a Utopian experiment, especially by those who saw their scientific, egalitarian, and democratic ideals partly realized in this country. In the past, many Americans have believed that our nation had a special role in creating a new kind of good society, in producing a new kind of rational man—and these are surely Utopian visions. Those who preached otherwise—those who, like Melville and Hawthorne, were more impressed by the continuing power of the demonic than by the triumphs of reason— were misunderstood or unheeded until our own day.

Perhaps it is symbolic that Brook Farm, initially the most American of our Utopian communities, perished in a holocaust and was never fully rebuilt. A parallel destiny has pursued not only the other attempts to implement Utopian vision in this country, but the Utopian spirit in American life as a whole. As thinkers, Americans rarely if ever now attempt to construct an imaginary society better than that in which they live; and at the same time, the faith that our society *is* in some sense a Utopia has as surely disappeared. Utopian thinking has always proceeded from a faith in man's capacity as a rational being to shape both his environment and his ultimate purposes; the decline of Utopian thinking is thus part of the deeper loss of faith in reason. The rediscovery of the irrational, the demonic, and the destructive in our own time, our new appreciation for the "possessed" in our own tradition—these have not brought any new synthesis of reason and passion, but a reduction of both.

But if we define Utopia as any attempt to make imaginatively concrete the possibilities of the future, Utopias have not in our own day ceased to exist, but have merely been transvalued. The contrast between nineteenth- and twentieth-century Utopias is drastic. Our visions of the future have shifted from images of hope to vistas of despair; Utopias have become warnings, not beacons. Huxley's *Brave New World,* Orwell's *1984* and *Animal Farm,* Young's *The Rise of the Meritocracy,* and ironically even Skinner's *Walden Two* —the vast majority of our serious visions of the future are negative visions, extensions of the most pernicious trends of the present. They are deterrents, cautionary tales: Utopia has become counter-Utopia. And the connotations of "Utopian" have similarly changed: the term is now unequivocally associated with the unrealistic and self-defeating and, for some, with man's deepest and most prideful sins. Characteristically, our modern counter-Utopias point to the uses of the instruments of reason—science and technology— in the service of demonically twisted ends: the typical counter-Utopia is a technological wonderland and a human nightmare. Thus, it underlines the latent modern fear that reason is powerless before the irrational, that the highest creations of intelligence—science and technology—are mere tools of destructiveness, that what was once considered the most determining of man's faculties is but a secondary and ancillary servant of his emotions.

The reasons for this shift to counter-Utopian thinking are complex. Certainly one factor is our unhappy experience with attempts to make real the Utopian visions of the last century—above all the vision of Marx. Whatever the reasons for the failure of Marxism in Russia to achieve its high moral and spiritual aims, the repercussions of this failure have been disastrous. Not only has the world been divided into two hostile camps, each with the power to destroy the other at an instant's notice, but—if possible even more important—the failure of this one Utopia has further crushed hope in attaining a better world. Communism in Russia involved far more than a parochial national revolution that failed. It was an attempt, like that of the French Revolution, to create a world in which men would be free not only from the tyrannies of want and power, but from the oppressions of their social and economic order —an attempt to make concrete the spiritual promises of Christianity. Its failure has been a tragedy for the entire West, one which has materially undermined our declining faith in our capacity to improve our world.

But I doubt that the failure of Marxism is really adequate ground for the far-reaching conclusions that many have drawn from it. The collapse of one enterprise, however mammoth, does not necessarily show that all such enterprises are doomed. Perhaps the most general lesson that can validly be drawn from such a collapse is that means and ends are inextricably related. It is difficult to attain peace through violence, or mass happiness through genocide: it is impossible radically to change an entire society in a single stroke. But the inferences we have drawn go far beyond this obvious lesson: they involve the conviction that *all* attempts to alter the shape of the future are doomed; that rational planning by men of good will inevitably succumbs before the forces of greed, power, lust, and hatred. And the willingness to draw such inference springs not only from the actual events of the Russian Revolution, but from the decline of positive myth I earlier discussed.

Another symptom of the submersion of positive myth has been the sundering of reason and passion, and the degradation of both. Under attack from the irrationalists, the advocates of reason have reduced their claims: reason, once the sovereign ability of man to determine the "what" and the "why" of his existence, has now become merely an ascertainer of the "how"—a matter of technical expertise, scientific verifiability, and instrumental effectiveness. Spengler speaks of "technicism"—an exclusive concentration on the techniques, instruments, and means for attaining desired ends —as the mark of a declining civilization. Other writers have commented on the replacement of "substantive" reason, which can judge the validity of ends and goals, by "instrumental" reason, which can only determine the efficacy of techniques in attaining preordained ends. This technicism is more and more pervasive: in every area, methodology replaces substance; technical proficiency is valued over final excellence; the analysis of philosophical questions substitutes for their resolution; "know-how" supplants wisdom; "whither?" has become archaic, but "how?" is on every man's lips. It is small wonder that men should feel powerless before a social order in whose day-to-day workings they are technically enmeshed but whose directions they feel unable to judge.

If reason is seen as powerless to discover men's purposes, then what is left is of course instinct, passion, and feeling. Yet, separated from reason, these potentially benign and liberating forces have been more and more reduced to blind animal drives. In an individual, when the basic instincts are separated from controlling intelligence, they tend to become crude and bestial; and so, in intellectual history, the cleavage between the apostles of passion and the advocates of mind has brought an abasement of our conception of passion to an equation with the forces of destructiveness, self-seeking, the call of the blood, and the imperatives of lust. When the idealisms of reason disappear, the claims of unreason can scarcely inspire the enthusiasm of a whole man, though they are there to fall back on when there seems to be nothing else.

The effects of this polarization are nowhere more obvious than in discussions of ethics, the field most concerned with the proper purposes and ends of life and society. Here, technicism reigns almost unchallenged. Academic ethics has concentrated more and more on what was once only a prelude to substantive ethics: the logical and linguistic analysis of ethical propositions and their characteristic justifications. Philosophers now seldom try to define the Good Life, but rather consider the several senses in which the term "good" can be used. Popular philosophy is of even less help. Our most characteristic tracts on popular ethics have a certain "how to do it" quality; how to think positively (about doing in your neighbor?); how to get along with people (what if they are not worth getting along with?); how to cope with guilts and anxieties (but suppose you *have* sinned?).

Even non-academic philosophers offer few non-instrumental suggestions. Perhaps the most appealing moral terms of our time are words like "spontaneity," "individuality," "authenticity," "identity," "autonomy," terms usually most fully developed by psychoanalytic or existential writers. Yet one can spontaneously commit murder, and authentically—God forbid—press a guided-missile button. These terms give us criteria for judging *how* a thing is done, but only indirectly if at all for evaluating *what* is done. To recur to an old philosophical distinction, the manner in which an act is performed may be a necessary condition but is not a sufficient condition for its virtuousness. To suffice, a virtuous act or goal is also needed.

Yet we lack clear and compelling concepts of virtue. Reason and the good have been firmly associated since Plato, and the reduction of reason to scientism has undermined the attractions of virtue as well. Our positive myths have been shorn of their imaginative vitality, separated from their roots in fantasy and feeling, desiccated from substantive to instrumental reason. The vitalities the positive myth once possessed have passed, by default, to the negative myths of unreason. Lacking vital concepts of virtue, our imaginations are secretly captured by the negative images of chaos, destructiveness, and perversion. To be sure, we rationalize our fascination with these images by appealing to their deterrent effects. An evening of violence and brutality on the television screen is deemed a morality play because the culprits are punished in the last moments of the last act. But Satan dominates the play; and the demonic secretly triumphs, as it is wont to do in our day. To determine the purposes of our conduct, we are forced back on these negative visions, on self-interest, on power, on seeking for status, even on mutual exploitation and cruelty. And not without cause, for by accepting the emotional desiccation of positive myth, we almost guarantee that emotion should be on the side of the negative, whatever intelligence may dictate. Evil always has its seductiveness; but when good has been deprived of adventure, poetry, and excitement, the fascination of the demonic becomes almost overwhelming, even when we believe we observe it merely to learn its negative lessons.

## The dissociation of fantasy

Imagination and fantasy are at their best when they are related but not tied to the problems that confront the imaginer in his everyday life. When this is not the case we can speak of the *dissociation of fantasy:* fantasy then not only has a life of its own, but this life bears little relationship and has little relevance to everyday life except as an escape. It is perhaps unreasonable to expect that every act of an individual be garlanded with rich and symbolic meaning; yet acts that are so enriched assume significance far beyond their immediate consequences. When fantasy and life are separated, imagination continues to operate but becomes sterile and escapist, no longer deepening life but impoverishing it at the expense of another dream world that contains all that "real life" lacks.

Thus, when fantasy and imagination are kept apart from everyday life they tend to become compensatory, even reactionary, to daily reality. A student of dreams found the most vivid dream world among all his subjects in a solitary elevator man who eagerly returned from his monotonous daily work to a lonely apartment where he conjured up vivid technicolor dreams. We all know, too, the stereotype of a secret sadist whose mild and kindly daily life contrasts with the cruelty of his fantasies. A similar relationship obtains between the technological values of our public lives and the dissociated fantasies we most enjoy. Never before have such quantities of "packaged fantasy" been so widely available and so eagerly consumed. In *Raw* magazine the IBM operator reads of cannibalism on the Amazon while the computer relentlessly writes checks; the benign image of Arthur Godfrey lulls the housewife through her routine housework; the fearless exploits of Batman counter the dull afternoon monotony of P.S. No. 117; and the tired and friendly businessman relaxes in the evening to the sadism of Mickey Spillane. These packaged forms of imagination are not in themselves new, but their prevalence, availability, and acceptance are new.

To be sure, insofar as private fantasies are projected upon a television screen or into a comic book where they can be shared with others, they may, under the right circumstances, tie society together more cohesively. But the price of cohesion is high. For one thing, our shared fantasies are contrasts to our daily life: thus they seldom serve to enrich life but rather to vitiate its imaginative vitalities. The "self-alienation" of which Erich Fromm and others have written is the alienation of man from the creative potentialities imbedded in his fantasy life. When a man's primary contact with his own imagination is through these negative visions of the comic book or the television screen, these potentialities remain unexpressed. Social cohesion, if it is thus gained, is not the cohesion of shared goals but shared escapes and dreads. Fantasy that deepens the meaning of work, love, or play becomes less and less potent.

Most of our dissociated fantasy ultimately deals with the socially unacceptable: with crime, violence, passion, prejudice, mental illness, murder, perversion, and unsanctioned desire. In any single day, the average American is enticed by a thousand seductions of the forbidden—so many that he fortunately cannot notice most of them. Walk into any drugstore and consider the blurbs and pictures on the paperback novels that line the cases, look at the covers of the flood of popular magazines on the racks near the door. Or turn to the movie advertisements in any daily newspaper and analyze the emotions appealed to therein. Or in the evening, when most Americans cluster around their television screens, listen at random to the "dramas." The dominant themes are much the same: greed, crime, sex without love, distortion, cruelty, and power-seeking. That these fantasies are "out there" on the television screen or in the pages of a book makes them easier for the average decent man to countenance; were they "his own" they would make him anxious, perhaps even suggest that he shared the forbidden passions depicted. The punishment of the vice in the last moments of the drama also helps block awareness of one's own involvement with the vicious. After all, the explicit message is that crime does not pay. But the implicit message, repeated a thousand times over, is that excitement, glamour, passion, and fascination all inhere in the negative and the forbidden; and when these virtues are absent in our daily lives, our unconscious response will inevitably be to identify with and envy the possessors of these exciting qualities.

Of course, some of the packaged and dissociated fantasy of our culture does not fit this description. But much of the rest, though less vicious, is still best understood as a contrast and escape from daily life. The dedicated idealism of Dr. Dooley contrasts with the absence of idealism in our daily round; the valor of American soldiers in warfare underlines the absence of any opportunity for valor in everyday life; the glamour and romance portrayed in women's magazines highlight the lack of novelty in the life of the average housewife. These fantasies of course need not be repudiated or disguised; they are personally acceptable to all of us. But nonetheless they remain dissociated, "out there," alien to and opposite to everyday life, so that instead of enriching the round of our daily activities, they impoverish it.

Even in American society, with its ready availability of dissociated fantasy in public entertainment, not all fantasy is shared with others or expressed through social symbols and mass media. Private fantasy, at some points dissonant with social myth, remains. But even here, similar dissociations usually operate. Most Ameri-

cans have been conditioned by their technological values to consider fantasy—public or private—less valuable and "real" than
tangible activities in the outside world. We connect our private fantasies not with inspiration, but with self-indulgence, sordidness,
and self-abusing shame. This connection is often self-confirming;
and the habit of dissociation is reinforced by the availability of so
much alien fantasy in the mass media. A man or woman conditioned from childhood to "having" fantasies only via the television
screen will find it hard—no matter what his feelings about his private fantasies—to reintegrate imagination into his daily life.

The fate of fantasy in our society summarizes as well the fate of
all the habitual objects and characteristics of fantasy. In dissociating fantasy from our social myth and even from our daily lives, we
also dissociate the most powerful forces of passion, idealism, aspiration, and yearning. By removing imagination from contact with
everyday reality we deprive our daily existence of any conscious
link with the non-cognitive, affective, and symbolic stratum which
might otherwise support and enrich it. Whatever links persist between fantasy and life are too often merely links of opposition, of
satisfaction in alien fantasy *instead* of life, of impoverished everyday reality from which we *escape* into imagination.

## Some latent purposes

The dissociation of fantasy in our culture involves a separation of
everyday life from its deepest sources of potential vitality. The continual bombardment of images from the mass media vitiates the
imaginative potential of everyday life, and even private fantasy is
often separated from contact with the conscious and self-accepted
part of the personality. The deepest roots of idealism, of animating
value and positive myth, are largely kept from contact with conscious life.

But lack of consciousness does not mean disappearance. The

most potent determinants of behavior are often unconscious needs
and fantasies, and we are usually their most helpless victims when
we are least aware of them. Similarly, a man who cannot articulate
the purposes of his life does not cease, because of his muteness, to
have such purposes. Even if he is mute, we must still search for his
*latent purposes*—for the *implicit* themes and unconscious values,
for the unavowed goals and hidden forces that determine his behavior. Such latent purposes, because they are hidden from consciousness, will often be different from his conscious values: what is hidden is often debased, and what is debased is often kept hidden. The
same basic motives that, if exposed to consciousness, intelligence,
and the demands of daily living, could become dignified and even
noble, become degraded and debased when assiduously blocked
from consciousness. Unconscious lust is one source for conscious
adult sexuality; unconscious scorn and condescension, when made
conscious, can sometimes be transformed into a desire to serve the
less fortunate; the latent will to power can become the conscious
will to lead others to good ends. Consciousness makes a difference,
not merely in "rationalizing" ultimately base motives, but in truly
transforming them, in alchemistically transmuting base to noble
metal. And conversely, lack of consciousness, separation from intelligence and the co-ordinating ego, can make an otherwise noble
motive base.

Partly because of the lack of any powerful collective myth about
ultimate goals in our society, no coherent set of purposes animates
us as a people. We too often suppress the still small voice that asks
"why," "whither," and "wherefore," and therefore we unconsciously serve not one, but a variety of sometimes contradictory
and opposed purposes. What are these latent purposes?

*The apotheosis of means*—Technological values are concerned,
I have argued, with means rather than ends, telling us how to proceed rather than where to go. Yet in the absence of other positive
values the instrumental values of our society are often uncon-

sciously elevated to ends, apotheosized to final purposes. This deification of instrumentality has two chief aspects—pursuit of sheer quantity and the quest for expertise.

The instrumental values of our society place great emphasis on measurement, numbers, quantities, and metrical comparisons. I have earlier noted the indispensability of measurement and comparison in science and technology. But these instrumental values are also given the status of final purposes: among the most common assumptions of our culture is the questionable axiom, "the more the better." The more money the better; the more IQ points the better; the greater the national rate of growth the better; the more cars, dishwashers, television sets, and magazines produced the better; megatons are better than kilotons. "Extensions" and "expansions" are tacitly assumed to be good: extensions of power, expansions of industry, new wings on homes and factories, more allies in international conflicts. This assumption can at times be correct: other things equal, increased production *can* mean fewer unemployed and improvement in the quality of life; more money *can* sometimes lead to an increase in security and peace. But we seldom stop to ask the rationale of "more" in terms of other values: e.g., the quality of individual life or the pursuit of peace. Rather we take it for granted that quantity is desirable, to the extreme of urging consumer purchases not because they are useful but to increase the gross national product.

We are, in consequence, a prodigal, spendthrift, extravagant, and wasteful nation. Frugality, poverty, small scale, and understatement are neglected qualities in America. Even saving and economy are justified primarily by their merit in amassing still more. We assume that the more people in college the better, regardless of the quality of the college or the talents of those in them; we boast of how much things cost regardless of their function or beauty; we even attempt to sell commodities by proudly advertising their greater expense. To escape such quantitative extravagance Americans must look abroad to countries like Japan where traditional respect for reduced scale, neatness, frugality, and order within contained form have not yet been overwhelmed, or to those (usually non-American) thinkers who have questioned the relationship between prosperity and virtue, wealth and wisdom, the amassing of goods and the good life.

Of course "the more" for the other fellow is not necessarily "the better" for us, especially if we assume that the more he gets the less we have. And Americans often act on this zero-sum assumption in their dealings with others: the more our neighbor earns, the less we ourselves will have in comparison; the higher our classmate is graded, the lower our grade will appear to be; and—almost universally—the more the Russians produce, the worse off Americans will be. There are, no doubt, a few rare situations in life where one man's increment is another man's decrement; but most of life, and even international warfare, is not a game of "winner takes all." An increase in the prosperity and dignity of the American Negro would bring an increment in the quality of life for even white Southerners; and certainly in an atomic war, the loss of Russian cities would not mean our gain but the destruction of ours as well. Yet our striving for sheer quantity is often made more invidious by our implicit view—though we really know better—that life is a game of Monopoly.

The other means most commonly treated as an end in American society is skill. "Competence," "know-how," "efficiency," and "expertise" are prominent national virtues; and though we may consciously acknowledge that these are at best instrumental qualities, we often unconsciously pursue them as independent goals. Thus we sometimes admire efficiency regardless of the purposes it serves, as with those who praised Mussolini because he made the trains run on time. Our nation is increasingly controlled by experts whose high technical competence in a narrow area often makes any question as to their other human and ethical qualities appear irrelevant. Values of competence and efficiency indirectly control much of our economic organization, where automation—because it seems more efficient—has gone virtually unopposed except by those whose jobs were immediately threatened. I do not mean to argue

against efficiency, automation, or competence; my point is rather
that we rarely ask the purpose and rationale of these qualities, but
assume instead that they are self-justifying and good in themselves.
The mere possession of expertise casts a general halo over the pos-
sessor: the "efficient" presidents of successful automobile compa-
nies are considered automatically qualified for high public office;
the views of nuclear physicists on society and human survival are
given special weight; while those men whose only qualifications are
wisdom, understanding, and breadth of human experience go unheard.

These trends are seldom fully conscious, and they would seem
absurd to those whose behavior they most govern if baldly stated as
universal principles. "The more the better," "Life is a Monopoly
game," and "Efficiency is all" are patently inadequate assertions;
and were they openly proposed as universally valid principles their
inadequacy would be obvious. It would be equally absurd to dis-
parage quantity per se, to deny that fixed resources on rare occasions make one man's gain another man's loss, or to deprecate
skill and efficiency in the pursuit of worthy ends. But the merits of
quantity and skill depend entirely on the purposes they serve; they
become independent guides to behavior only because other positive
values are so few in American society.

*From passion to impulse*—Wholesome passion is rare in American life. Passion is usually placed "out there"—in the other fellow,
in the movies, in uncivilized countries, or even "out there" in some
far corner of our psyches for which we feel neither kinship nor responsibility. In an earlier chapter I suggested that the demands of
work in a technological society encourage this suppression, projec-
tion, and disengagement of strong feelings and desires. The dissociation of fantasy further foments this same disavowal of intense
personal needs and wishes. The changed meaning of the word "passion" itself illustrates this disavowal: in colloquial speech, "passion" has become virtually synonymous with sexual excitation, and
rarely means deep or ennobling feeling.

Of all the forces of human life, however, passion—intense feeling, fantasy, need, and desire—is the least amenable to repression and the most prone to reassert itself in some other form. Pushed down, it springs up; denied in one form, it reappears in disguise; refused, it still makes its claim and exacts its price. When denied a central and conscious place alongside of intelligence, it becomes ugly and degenerates into mere instinct. Like rejected Caliban, its claims become animal and repellent to the conscious self. There ensues a vicious circle, familiar to any student of human misfortune: each effort at repression produces a further degradation of the passions and their reappearance in still more unacceptable guise.

Many Americans still allow themselves strong feelings; but the drift of our society is toward ever greater demands for the suppression of passion. We see the consequences in the reappearance of passion as mere "discharge-seeking" impulse or "outlet-seeking" drive. In part, such blind impulse, often turned nasty and destructive, reappears in the dissociated fantasies with which we try to fill our non-working hours, and attains indirect catharsis through our covert identification with the impulse-ridden villains of our entertainments. But full catharsis through alien fantasy is rarely possible, and the passion that remains seeks disguised expression in daily life. The suppression of sexual passion leads to pornography and a secret search for excitement in forbidden places; the suppression of legitimate anger leads to surreptitious backbiting, nastiness, and undercutting. When basic drives for leadership are denied, they degenerate to "hidden persuasion" or covert efforts at dominance, which—because they are covert—injure those they touch. When personal neediness, whether material or psychological, is suppressed, it becomes secret dependency, hidden greed, and envy. The thwarted poet becomes an "image maker" on Madison Avenue. Deprived of legitimacy, men's need to have some tangible effect upon others turns into an effort to manipulate them. The idealist frustrated in his idealism turns to carping criticism of the ideals of others.

Such degraded passions then often guide our actions. Beneath our open, practical, and cheerful American faces, we are often impelled by the frustrated phantoms of our erstwhile legitimate feelings. America is not only a land of opportunity, optimism, and progress, but of leers, dirty jokes, and dirty closets, of manipulative half-truths, of greed and hidden persuaders, of surreptitious affairs, of subway pushers and disregarded men who disregard their fellows, of hostile men who are "only kidding." The evidence is all around us: in the pervasive emphasis on "sexiness" in American life, in the insecurity of men who hide behind "hardness and toughness," in the ostentation and acquisitiveness of those who have no pride of possession.

My point is not that Americans *have* no strong feelings, no deep passions, no intense needs, and no violent loves or hatreds. Every man does, and our American proneness to deny them direct expression does not cancel their existence. Nor do I think that most Americans are especially vicious, mean, or nasty in their daily lives; on the contrary, I suspect there are few other nations where so high a level of everyday decency prevails. And finally, none of these characteristics are exclusively or even especially American. But I am arguing that many of the latent purposes that guide Americans ultimately spring from unnecessarily suppressed passions, and that suppression often degrades passion into sordid and blind impulse that secretly guides life's purposes.

*Comparison and conformity*—Another unstated guide line for action of many Americans is based on comparison or conformity. Merely making a comparison entails no necessary judgment of value; and traditionally in pure science comparative evaluations are devoid of moral implication. Uranium 235 is not "better" than oxygen 16 by virtue of its comparatively greater atomic mass; nor does the comparative price of two washing machines necessarily tell us which cleans better. Only if we believe that costly equipment is always better than inexpensive equipment is the costly washing machine obviously preferable. Only judged in terms of efficacy in producing atomic bombs is uranium better: if we value the capacity to sustain life, we will prefer oxygen. Comparisons only become invidious when we assign independent value to the standard by which we compare. And this is what we do. When we assume that "the more the better," we assign value to quantity, and comparisons between men, objects, or nations in terms of "how much" consequently imply value judgments.

The central dilemma in the pursuit of quantity is the problem of deciding "How much is enough?" and comparative judgments play a major role in this decision. Americans have often answered "as much as or more than the Joneses," and thus transformed quantity first into comparison and then into competition. But note that in this competition the competitors become intimately dependent on each other for their respective goals. Unlike two gladiators fighting to the death, American competition is seldom totally hostile, but involves a secret reliance on one's competitor for one's own standards of achievement. The eager student does not wish the destruction of his fellow students; he merely strives for higher grades. Teachers know that not giving grades often produces marked anxiety among students whose intellectual self-esteem has become dependent upon competitive judgments. Economically, we acknowledge the interdependency of competitors by refusing to allow the logical denouement of destructive competition—the swallowing of all competition into one monopoly. Linguistically, we recognize our dependence on those we compete with by such phrases as "pace-setters," "market leaders," and "sales stars"—all admirable men who are leading the pack.

This benign American form of competition—wherein competitors determine each other's standards of performance, and where all the runners in the race run against each other and not against the clock—has been a constant feature of our society since De Tocqueville's day. Traditionally, all of the players in the game are more or less agreed that *the* central standard of comparison is money. But in recent decades, with the rise of an increasingly affluent technological society, the pursuit of riches has lost much of its former appeal: as I have suggested, the quest for quantity in other forms and for expertise is increasingly supplanting wealth as a social goal. With the de-emphasis on older forms of competition and acquisitiveness has come an even more direct interdependence of men upon each other for their goals, their aspirations, and their feelings.

This new American interdependence has been much discussed of late: we deplore it under the name of "conformity," praise it as the new "togetherness," and describe it sociologically as "other-direction" or as "the social ethic." There is no point in attempting to add to these descriptions; but we should note that the search for purpose in others is but an extension of the interdependence implicit in earlier forms of invidious competition. With the decline of wealth as a purpose, the actions, feelings, and behavior of one's neighbors—rather than their incomes—become guides to purpose. I need not labor the problems inherent in this other-direction: radar is useful when one has a course and a destination of one's own, but the effort to make interpersonal sensitivity the determinant of life's purposes is bound to fail when others are looking to us for exactly the same cues.

Lacking clear conceptions of the whys and whithers of life, men often see little alternative but to attempt to act like their fellows, on the assumption that *they* know where to go. Yet along with this radar-like sensitivity goes an increasing fear of conformity among sophisticated Americans like our alienated students, and a tendency to see *any* group action as "mere conformity to the group." No one argues against conformity with others in a good cause; what we fear is conformity as the sole criterion of purpose: "not standing out," "keeping up with the Joneses." The problem of conformity is thus coextensive with the lack of good causes. Were such causes more apparent, we might be able to consider specific instances of conformity in terms of whether they serve good purposes —and would be both less tempted by and less fearful of conformity per se.

These latent purposes of deified technology, instinct, comparison, and conformity are of course very differently distributed in our society. Their prevalence depends upon sex and age, occupation and religion, region and ethnicity. Women are less likely to revere sheer quantity (except, at times, of children) than are men, who are more prone to deify the instrumental values of technology. So, too, conformity as a criterion of behavior is more prevalent among "bureaucratic" families, while the older standards of comparison and competition still prevail among those less in the forefront of social change. Furthermore, these purposes are truly latent: few of us would admit them as guiding principles of action, though a disinterested observer might readily infer their existence. They do not constitute a coherent or adequate scheme of values: each leaves major questions unanswered, all would fail the test of full consciousness (which is why we prefer not to recognize them), none constitutes an ideal capable of inspiring the devotion of whole men. Most of us alternate between these several purposes in our daily lives, being guided now by the desire for quantity or expertise, now by instinct, now by the behavior and feeling of our fellows. And we come by these inadequate and latent purposes partly by default, because of the deflection and repression of any Utopian spirit.

## The deflection of the Utopian spirit

America is a nation with a strong Utopian tradition. Our intellectual heritage is inherently rationalistic, and rationalism, with its faith in human nature and the efficacy of reason, tends toward Utopianism. Our land was first settled by men and women who came here because this nation promised more than their homelands: many immigrant ancestors arrived with the literal hope of finding streets paved with gold, and most others held equally Utopian hopes that this would be a land of freedom, happiness, and prosperity. In the nineteenth century, this country was dotted with Utopian communities, and many Americans believed our nation as a whole was destined to produce a new kind of man in a new kind of society. Such traditions die hard, and are the more difficult to erase when they express deep and universal human capacities and needs—in this case, men's capacity to envisage ideals more perfect than their realities, and their need to strive toward such ideals. Whether one ascribes the persistence of such traditions to "racial inheritance" or, as seems more likely, to the enduring continuity of culture, a sharp eye can usually perceive the ruins of former traditions even in men and women who have apparently discarded them.

The direct expression of the Utopian spirit in modern American life has been suppressed by the factors I have considered: by the devitalization of reason, by the prevalence of debunking ideologies, by the suppression of passion, by a social system that separates feeling and competence, work and family, by the continual bombardment of dissociated fantasies. Yet if this argument is correct, the Utopian spirit, which is a universal potential specifically encouraged in the American tradition, cannot have totally disappeared, but must have gone underground and been deflected onto other targets. And indeed, these new targets are not hard to find: in our day, Utopianism is indirectly expressed in visions of total technology and private Utopia.

Most Americans, if asked to envisage an "ideal" future, will respond, if at all, with a science-fiction fantasy of a technologically improved society. Transportation will be faster, every man will have his helicopter, housewives' kitchens will be automated further, men will live in radial or garden or otherwise totally technological cities, telephones will become telescreens, food will be completely preprocessed, etc., etc. A brief tour of any exhibition like the 1964–1965 New York World's Fair shows such technological images projected with all the organized prodigality of our large corporations: our visions of a "Utopian" future are akin to, and often derived from, the research and development centers of General Motors, General Electric, and General Foods—more advanced cars, toasters, and frozen dinners. The values implemented therein are speed, convenience, and efficiency; seldom mentioned are happiness, fulfillment, peace, or inner satisfaction.

Yet such visions as these, though they amaze the eye and stagger the imagination, provide little food for the soul. The troubled housewife, the jittery executive, and the bored schoolgirl can find scant comfort in these glittering images of a world of total technology. More speed and more efficiency are more of what we already have in excess, and less sloppiness and less privacy are hardly the answer for a society whose problem is already too little tolerance for natural human disorder and too little time or place for private thoughts. Moreover, such "cities of the future" as these are the outward locales for the most demonic visions of our anti-Utopian writers: 1984, Brave New World, and a host of other hells on earth are housed in just such formats. In some corner of themselves, most Americans know that "total" technology is almost as good a setting as total squalor for total misery. And for most of us, an even more technological society hardly seems an adequate object of human striving: we are taught that it is inevitable—as indeed it may be—and in any case, most of us feel that the course of social change is quite beyond our capacity to control or even to influence.

As a result, the pseudo-Utopia of total technology has little deep appeal for most Americans; although, for lack of anything better, it comes readily to mind when we are asked about an ideal future. Only a few—engineers, planners, research and development experts—are genuinely and deeply enamored of an exclusively technological vision; few others consider an efficient and streamlined world necessarily a better one. For the rest of us, what remains is to invest the Utopian spirit in private hopes and endeavors, and especially in those areas farthest from technological society.

Of these areas the family is the foremost. I have already suggested that family life is increasingly becoming an escape and a haven from the pressures of work, and that the most valued qualities of the family are those most opposite to the requirements of technology. Its accentuated distance from the rest of society makes the family an ideal repository for the Utopian spirit. Often the expectations with which Americans approach marriage are not only Utopian in the positive sense, but in the more everyday sense of "unrealistic." Even the dream of the large family evokes in many American women an idealism, a hope for "total" fulfillment in motherhood, and a willingness to disregard her own needs which we traditionally associate only with the noblest of causes. We expect from our families miracles of compensation for the inadequacies of the rest of our society, and we are prepared to make colossal sacrifices to make these miracles come about.

We should not merely scoff at this displacement: the Utopianization of the family has really improved family life; and many Americans now find in marriage and their children, in the shared fun and genuine togetherness of their families, satisfactions other generations would not have deemed possible. Yet the Utopian hopes displaced onto the family are often so colossal that no conceivable family could fulfill them. Paradoxically, our high national divorce rate is a token of these often impossible hopes: it is because we expect so much of marriage, give so much of ourselves to it, channel so much aspiration and Utopianism onto it, that we are so often later disillusioned.

The privatization of Utopia extends to other areas: to recreation, to leisure time, to art, poetry, and hobbies. The modern equivalent of yesterday's dreams for social improvement are the hopes of today's unalienated youths for a nice house, a little place in the country, a good, warm and loving spouse, and many children. The rising interest in hobbies and crafts, participant sports, music, and the fine arts betokens not only a rise in prosperity but a new Utopia of leisure. Men and women today work at their recreation, at the cultivation of their private talents and interests, with a zest, excitement, and idealism totally lacking in their work itself.

The unifying characteristic of all these "Utopianized" activities is their deliberate distance from public life. Because family and leisure have become the prime repositories and outlets for feelings and fantasies suppressed at work, they are also the best targets for idealism. Most other activities are seen as "business," where the canons of hardheadedness, efficiency, and "realism" apply. Yet much is lost in this channeling of Utopianism away from public life. Private endeavors, however worthy, are rarely capable of satisfying the Utopian impulse: at best, the goals of the "rich full life," of a good family and well-spent leisure time, simply cannot fully satisfy a man's latent idealism. Furthermore, I have argued that excessive hopes pinned on private life often backfire, producing disillusion and ultimately withdrawal into a compulsive and barren careerism. From a social point of view, as well, the withdrawal of idealism from work, politics, or the economy is appropriate only in an era in which men are fulfilled in their work, politics is the expression of the best in national life, the economy operates fairly and justly for all citizens, and peace is guaranteed in the world. None of these conditions obtain in America today; and the deflection of the Utopian spirit therefore leads to a withdrawal of idealism from the areas of our shared lives that most need a Utopian vision.

There are, of course, some men and women to whom these comments do not apply. But they are few in number, and must constantly fight the anti-Utopian, debunking spirit of mid-century America. Among young Americans, genuine Utopianism is most often directed at other societies than our own: the favorable response to the Peace Corps, for example, is partly premised on the distance and "primitiveness" of the societies where volunteers serve. It is difficult for most of these same youths to feel a similar idealism and hope of serving in their own society. Though the Utopian spirit still continues as a deep strand in American life, it has been repressed, displaced onto private endeavors, or transferred to the underdeveloped nations.

It may seem paradoxical to speak of the repression and displacement of the Utopian spirit, for we are accustomed to thinking of repression as applying only to the "bad": according to the model of Freudian repression, only destructive and libidinal fantasies can be repressed. But there is increasing reason to believe that Freud's definition of the contents of the unconscious is a historical one, relevant primarily to the Victorian world in which he lived. Psychoanalysts comment on the increasing rarity of the hysterical and compulsive symptoms upon which Freud based his views of repression: today more patients arrive at the analyst's office aware of their anger and sexuality, but seeking to find some purpose for their lives. Perhaps a more general statement of the determinants of repression is this: whatever would, if it were conscious, cause the individual trouble (discomfort, pain, guilt, ridicule, shame, etc.) tends to remain unconscious. This formulation suggests that good impulses, drives, fantasies, and aspirations may be repressed as well as bad ones. And a number of psychoanalysts have developed terms that permit us to speak of such unconscious "good" fantasies. Erikson's "positive identities," Horney's "real self," Sullivan's "personifications of the good me," Fromm's "creative potentialities"—all of these positive aspects of the self admit of repression, and the analyst sees one of his tasks as making the patient aware of them.

In principle then, there is no reason why the impulse to idealism —the Utopian spirit—should not be repressed, and like any repressed impulse deflected onto substitute targets. We have already seen evidence of this repression and deflection in the Utopianization of technology, the family, leisure, and things abroad—while truly Utopian visions of our own lives and our own society's possibilities are lacking. But perhaps the most cogent evidence of the repression of Utopian thinking is to be had simply by conversing with people about what they desire from life. There is normally a signal incongruity between the superficiality, banality, and remoteness of their expressed aims and purposes and the depth and "feltness" of their implicit goals, which must usually be inferred from what they dislike and seek to avoid. Young men and women today —indeed men and women of all ages—feel great uneasiness and discomfort at expressing any ambition or conception of life that has not long since been sapped of any real vitality for them or their fellows. Were such unease, embarrassment, and incongruity be-

tween overt and covert values evident in a discussion of sex or
hostility, we would know what conclusion to draw: beneath these
expressed views lie less conscious, contrasting, and opposite values
and attitudes.

The repression and deflection of the Utopian spirit are closely
related to the devitalization of reason in our intellectual tradition.
Not only alienated students but intelligent men as a group have
come to bear a deep and ultimately despairing conviction that not
only Utopias, but every rational attempt to translate ideals into
practice, especially in the social and political spheres, is similarly
doomed to defeat—or worse, to that reinstallation of the worst
evils of the old regime which has followed many major revolutions.
Given a widespread conviction that deliberate attempts at reform
lead to greater excesses than those they seek to correct, the easiest
solution for the individual or the culture is never to voice the principles by which reform might be guided. Disillusion of high hopes
has produced cynicism—not the cynicism of the native opportunist,
but the more corrosive cynicism of the man or culture that has seen
its best hopes dashed.

Beneath this cynicism, which usually expresses itself in apathy
toward idealism or in boredom at high aspirations, lie more concrete fears. If one articulates the set of principles, constructs a Utopia or a positive myth—for himself, his society, or both—he automatically becomes in some ways *responsible* to this vision. Most
men consider the cynicism of not acting to promote one's avowed
purposes a worse offense than the cynicism of not having any purposes at all. But to act to promote a positive vision of the future
is—in our current world view—to condemn one's self to certain
frustration and probable failure. The thought that it may even
make matters worse is still more paralyzing for men of good faith.
Thus, a welter of good intentions, desires not to do harm, doubts as
to whether there are *any* means to promote worthy ends, and fears
of failure conspire to make it easiest not to articulate any positive
morality in the first place.

But even if a man overcomes these obstacles himself, he must next overcome the neglect, skepticism, or even hostility of his fellows. I have argued that our dominant ideologies are more systematically developed as instruments of deflating and debunking, and that our most powerful myths are deterrent myths which point out the probable evils that would follow certain (indeed most) courses of action. Any attempt, however tentative, to enunciate a principle of positive action must thus face attack on two fronts. First, the motives of the proponent will be thoroughly and hostilely investigated, with the intent of showing that the proposals conceal "irrational," "ulterior," or other undesirable motives, interests, or errors. And second, the proposals themselves will usually be attacked as merely leading to further evils, usually by extending some already undesirable trend. To take but one example, the World Federalist must answer charges that he himself is uprooted and without sound national ties, and furthermore that his proposed One World would merely lead to further extremes of homogenization, uniformity, legalism, bureaucratization, or whatever the predominant present evils are seen to be.

Many an advocate of a worthy cause, however, would be grateful for criticism, which at least acknowledges the existence of his proposals. His more common fate is neglect. Indifference is perhaps a greater rejection than attack: as Dostoyevsky knew, the ultimate insult to a man is to stare through him without seeing him. Whether neglect and criticism are or are not valid is not an issue here: the point is that the complete predictability of such reactions makes even the most affirmative hesitate before affirming in public. Little subtlety is needed to unearth the reasons for these responses. In some cases they may be justified. Some purportedly good causes and many Utopias are what all are said to be: "crackpot," "harebrained," "naïve," and "unrealistic." But the response to any proposal for reform is so invariant that this explanation will not suffice. He who proposes innovation must face opposition grounded in the universal inertial unwillingness to move from the familiar to the unknown. And even more important, just as a man of virtue is a reproach to those without virtue, so a man with vision shames those who lack vision, implicitly finds them wanting, and calls for them to reform. When proposed change involves making explicit what for good reasons is kept unstated, indifference and (if this fails) angry rejection can surely be foreseen.

But often the most potent deterrent to the enunciation of Utopian vision or even to the search for any more positive myth is the genuine humility of those who are most conscious of our cultural problems. If a fear must be found here to parallel the fear of responsibility and failure or the fear of criticism and neglect, it is the simple fear of being wrong. To those who lack agreed principles for the interpretation of reality, our technological society seems increasingly complex. Experts, each with his own special canons of selection and judgment, dominate their fields. There is so much to be known. And even if we knew it, who would really dare to judge and, more, to propose alternatives? Our real problem is not so much that we lack requisite knowledge, but that the purposes from which we might build have ceased to exist in the public mind. The advocate, reformer, or mythmaker seems to face a superhuman task: he must first of all unearth the very values that he will then attempt to develop, illustrate, enhance, and implement. Faced with this task, humility is the only response; and the most probable—though by no means the only possible—behavior is withdrawal into some manageable private domain where the job to be done has defined and attainable ends.

## Alienation and the decline of Utopia

We all daily live the consequences of these convictions, writ large in the absence of positive myth, in the apotheosis of technology, the dissociation of fantasy, the latent and contradictory purposes we serve, and the deflection of the Utopian spirit. In their futile quest for positive values the alienated youths from whom we began are both reacting against the solutions adopted by most men and yet, at a deeper level, also reflecting the dilemmas and lacks of our mythic tradition. Many of the adaptations chosen by others are closed to the alienated. They reject the technological myths and empirical definitions of reality prevalent in our society; for them truth resides in feeling, passion, and subjectivity. Their private fantasies usually prevail against the dissociated fantasy of our culture: their own childhood-dominated imaginations are too compelling to allow them vicarious satisfaction in the aggression of a TV Western or the sex of a pocketbook. Sheer quantity and pure expertise attract them not at all: they are advocates of quality and intense experience. Nor do the private Utopias of family, children, and recreation draw them: the residues of childhood conflict make marriage seem remote to most, and they are usually incapable of the ordinary pleasures of "fun," devoting themselves instead to the passionate and obsessive search for private knowledge. The image of total technology repels them; and their pessimism inures them against enthusiastic hope for the developing nations. Neither the vestigial positive myths nor the displacements of the Utopian spirit that comfort their fellows can comfort them.

Yet total repudiation of one's cultural tradition is impossible; and even these repudiative young men make selective use of their culture's assumptions in order to repudiate it. They are deeply anti-Utopian, distrusting high social and human ideals; like most Americans, their latent Utopianism is directed toward private goals— sentience, receptivity, and responsiveness to experience. From their cultural heritage the alienated have culled heady draughts of skepticism, a tendency to see all reason as rationalization, a distrust of ideology as manipulation. And in their fear of revolutionary change and their distrust of social planning, they reflect not only their personal histories but the intellectual history of our culture.

Their alienation is thus at once a repudiation of the purposes of most men in our society and at the same time an expression of continuing trends of our intellectual tradition. These two aspects of alienation are closely related: the absence of positive myth in our society, which is itself the result of the recent history of ideas in Western civilization, offers these students little object of positive

commitment; this same absence of positive myth produces the diffused and often contradictory latent purposes the alienated reject;
and finally, the same intellectual tradition provides these students
with the reductive intellectual skills and weapons to demolish any
tentative idealism in themselves or others. Like many intelligent men
in our society, they are wary of all that smacks of "positive thinking," fearful of manipulating or being manipulated, determined to
see the real misery and unhappiness of the world. And like many
others, they are wary of all affirmation and thus continually undermine the possibility of success in their own search for intellectual
ground on which to stand. Even the most alienated are members of
their society; and their alienation is both a reaction against and an
expression of the absence of any positive myth, any Utopian vision
in American life.

# 12    The dictatorship of the ego

Men normally take their society's demands for granted. The adolescent Sioux thought it only natural that he was expected to travel alone and starving across the plains until he was blessed with a vision that would forecast his adult life. The young Spartan took it for granted that he should undergo cruel ordeals to prove his courage. In many primitive societies today, young men and women eagerly anticipate their painful rites of initiation. In the Admiralty Islands, carefree adolescent boys are plunged into lifelong indebtedness when they marry, but for many generations they experienced their indebtedness—and the system which required it —merely as an unchangeable fact of adult existence. Those who experience the demands of their society most intensely usually consider them merely a part of their environment which, like the geography or the weather, they must make the best of.

Social demands are thus part of the social scenery: and as with any feature on the landscape, we soon grow accustomed to them, stop noticing them, make an unconscious adaptation to them, and turn our attention to the more visibly changing features of our environment. Like physical scenery, social scenery is only apparent when it changes; and like our physical surroundings, it often changes so slowly that we fail to notice it at all. New demands arise gradually, over a period of years and generations; and we only become aware of what and how much is asked of us by comparing one society or one epoch with another. Yet, like the geography or the weather, the social scenery profoundly affects our moods, our ways of behaving, and our relations to our fellows. The Eskimo adapts to the snow and ice he takes for granted; the mountain dweller climbs on peaks he no longer truly sees. Yet the lives of both are profoundly affected by their geography: physical setting defines the limits within which one must survive. In a similar way, our unnoticed social scenery profoundly affects our lives and what we make of them.

The dominant demands of every society are closely related to the special human qualities it considers most virtuous. Men usually define as their highest virtues the human qualities their society most needs of them. Where collective survival requires smooth co-operation, the virtues of harmony must be stressed from childhood on; where social survival requires warding off enemy attack, fearless courage will be prized. Child-rearing techniques in any society try to implant the virtues required to be a "successful" adult; often the best way to locate the characteristic virtues of any people is to inquire into the qualities it most stresses in raising the young. Some societies succeed far better than others in teaching the required virtues. At one extreme are communities where most youths already possess in full measure the modest virtues their adulthood will require; at the other are societies like our own whose demands are intense, extreme, and highly specialized, and where many lack the qualities we deem most necessary. And everywhere, too, those who do not comply with their society's demands are made to perceive themselves as lacking in virtue, merit and adequacy.

Americans rarely experience their society as making inordinate demands or asking extraordinary virtues. On the contrary, we accept as "natural" such exceptional requirements as the demand for prolonged education, for a long adolescence, for high levels of expertise and emotional restraint in work. We consciously welcome the continually changing society in which we live. We "naturally" expect of ourselves the independence and developed capacity for self-control which is needed even to survive, much less flourish, in our society. Nor do we normally chafe at the compartmentalizations, fragmentations, and dissociations imposed on our lives by our technological order. Most of us simply accept these features of the social scenery, unconsciously make the necessary accommodations to them, and think ourselves abnormal when we cannot fulfill our society's demands. In American society as elsewhere, most men and women somehow survive no matter how society treats them, but the *quality* of their survival depends in good part on whether they possess the required social virtues, and on their consequent ability to meet their society's demands. Some men barely survive, while others flourish.

These differences in the socially-given quality of human experience are often overlooked because of the theory of infinite human plasticity. By insisting that men *are* what their society makes and demands of them, this theory entails that no matter what a society asks, its members will be able to comply without undue strain. Anthropology sometimes seems to buttress this view by observations of the enormous range of social demands men manage to live with; among psychologists, the theory is sometimes defended by pointing to the centrality of social experience in shaping personality. And if human nature *is* infinitely malleable, then of course no one society can be said to "violate" human nature more than any other, for men can mold themselves into what ever forms the society provides.

The theory of infinite human plasticity, however, errs by confusing the ability of men to adapt *somehow* to overwhelming pressures with their ability to adapt *successfully* to these pressures; it confuses the ability to survive with the ability to flourish. Though "human nature" is indeed shaped differently by every society, and though men and women are indeed flexible in adapting to their society's demands, there are limits beyond which they cannot be safely pushed. Some of these are rooted in physiology: no society can expect of women the physical strength it asks of men; nor can any society expect men to care for infants. There are constitutional limits on human ability to endure protracted shock, stress, fatigue, or starvation. And similar limits exist, though they are harder to define, with regard to psychological adaptability. Systematic terror can reduce men to an animal level of existence; or when a man or a people is deprived of its dignity and integrity, it may lapse into apathy and defeat.

To be sure, the will to live permits men to *survive* under incredible demands, and to *adapt,* somehow or other, to extraordinary social stresses. But when the stresses become excessive, survival and adaptation require a lowered level of life—a brutalization of behavior—and result in fearfulness, terror, apathy, and a curtailment of responsiveness, will, openness, and of all the qualities we consider most highly human. As the intensity of stress, whether physical or social, increases, more and more men and women reach a breaking point—sometimes manifest as insanity, withdrawal, and a desire to escape, or as ritual, or sometimes merely as a reduction in the capacity to do justice to complexity. We all know in ourselves our tendency to fall back on simpler responses in times of crisis: a similar proneness to regression can affect an entire society. The capacity to survive somehow under extreme social demands thus does not prove the infinite malleability of human nature, for when we look more closely, we usually find that adaptation has been bought at the price of regression. Psychosis is after all a form of adaptation, and its occurrence in virtually every society suggests that human nature has limits beyond which men cannot be safely pushed.

To define these limits absolutely is impossible, for they vary with every individual and with every society. Every society, for example, must provide its members some sanctioned expression for both love and hatred; but how much expression, and how, when, and to whom, varies from society to society and from man to man within societies. One man is more able to live without hatred than another; one society cultivates in its children aggression that must be granted "outlet" in adult life, while another imbues in its young deeper needs for love and dependency. Thus the precise areas in which men are strongest or most vulnerable depend in part on their childhood training; where independence is early taught, autonomy can be expected of adults; but a community that overwhelms children with love, support, and praise cannot expect its grownups to live happily without it.

Much of what we consider "social pathology" can be interpreted as a response to the violation of the limits of human plasticity, as a reaction to social demands greater than psychological supplies, as a result of demands for which no conceivable childhood training could prepare an adult, or for which particular individuals have not been prepared by their particular childhoods. Widespread psychosis or neurosis clearly suggests some collective flaw in child-hood preparation and/or adult expectations; criminality, delin-quency, and perversion point to similar inadequacy in early forma-tion and/or environmental demand. Many other types of behavior can also be "maladaptive adaptations" to intense social stresses: ritualistic conformity, curtailment of initiative, withdrawal, apathy, ritualism, addiction, disinterest, disengagement, all can be seen as symptoms of social pathology. And though we may deem them less than pathological, the more articulate forms of alienation (revolu-tion, reform, social criticism, and ideological alienation) indirectly point to social demands which men find unendurable.

## Motive, inhibition, and ego

I have so far spoken only of the limits on *how much* a society may demand, suggesting that each individual has a breaking point, and that this breaking point is defined both by his individual personality and his social setting. But societies differ not only in how much they demand, but in *what* they demand. And to understand the special quality of social demands in our society, we must first con-sider some of the kinds of demand a society can make.

In oversimplified terms, individual personality can be viewed as consisting of three kinds of forces. First, individuals have *motives,* needs, impulses, drives, desires, and wishes which are rooted in biology but are shaped, channeled, encouraged, discouraged or transmuted by social experience. Secondly all men have a set of socially learned *inhibitions,* constraints, restraints, and prohibitions which apply largely to these fundamental motives. And finally, all men have a capacity for self-regulation, for coping, adapting, perceiving, and guiding their behavior in accordance with the possibilities and requirements of their environments. This last is the capacity of the *ego,* of the governing, regulating, organizing, synthesizing, and co-ordinating part of the personality. In a crude analogy, we might compare individual personality to a society consisting of three classes: the masses, composed of a large disorganized group of pleasure-seeking and unruly individuals; the aristocracy, which concerns itself with laws, rules, cultural inheritances, and the judicial system; and the ruling middle-class, which is technologically skilled, adept at governing and absolving conflicts, practical, hardworking, realistic, objective, and impartial.

All societies must demand virtues that correspond to each of these psychological forces: men and women in any society must have the "right" motives, adequate inhibitions, and strong egos. Motivational virtues call for the cultivation and accentuation of some special motive like love, aggression, nurturance, obedience, or courage. Inhibitory virtues, in contrast, are rooted in opposition to other basic motives and drives, and they discourage both their initial cultivation and their subsequent expression. And finally, every society must teach ego virtues, expecting skill, competence, flexibility, and accuracy from its members. Every society, for example, must encourage some form of love, care, or nurture between men and women; no society tolerates the unlimited expression of aggression within the society; and every society requires competence in performing the appointed tasks of the community.

But at the same time, societies differ in the *relative* emphasis they place on each of these areas of virtue. Among the Sioux, a warlike people, the demand for aggressive motivation was central. From an early age Sioux children were encouraged to be aggressive, repeatedly frustrated to provoke rage, and then encouraged to express it freely. Accentuated and cultivated throughout childhood, these basic motivations were then demanded of the aggressive buffalo hunter and warrior. A Sioux youth given to peaceableness, whose childhood left him with a lesser reservoir of anger, lacked the proper motivations for an adult. In other societies that ask tenderness of adults, individuals of bellicose and hostile nature are the misfits; and communities that insist on motives of obedience, respect, and deference make life difficult for those who are driven instead to challenge authority.

The central virtues of other societies concern inhibition rather than motivation, and those who suffer most are those who can inhibit least well. Inhibitory demands can often be extreme, calling for the utmost restraint on self-seeking, aggression, sexuality, acquisitiveness, or dominance. The major thrust in child-rearing in such societies consists in inhibiting, minimizing, denying, suppressing, and "sublimating" these motives; the conventions of adult life further discourage their direct expression. A man whose upbringing or constitution leaves him unable to inhibit the forbidden motives is considered weak or vicious, and in the effort to avoid this judgment he may develop a deviant role or a set of symptoms which further witness his disability. The dependent man whose dependency is neither sanctioned nor satisfied by his society may develop an ulcer; the Victorian lady who tries to deny her sexuality may develop hysterical symptoms; the aggressive man who finds no approved release for his aggression may be given to explosive outbursts of rage.

And finally, ego virtues may predominate. A society may concentrate its major demands on the development and primacy of the ego over both basic motivation and conscientious inhibition, encouraging qualities like adaptability, skill, rationality, efficiency, independence, impartiality, tolerance, autonomy, fairness and neutrality. It may approve of men and women who are controlled, rational, efficient, realistic and unsentimental; and it may censure equally the impulsive and impetuous, and the inhibited, repressed, and conscience-ridden.

## From Victorian inhibition to technological ego

The central demands of any era are usually mirrored in its vocabulary, though it may take a later generation to fully understand this reflection. In our era, the vocabulary of psychoanalysis is particularly sensitive to the dominant demands of society. Because psychoanalysis originates from efforts to understand the sick of society, its most useful terms are likely to be those which most adequately characterize the problems of the average patient, and thus will point to the social demands that cause the greatest toll. The vocabulary of psychoanalysis has changed radically since Freud's early writings. Especially in America, new terms, concepts, and theories have grown off his. Briefly to trace the evolution of psychoanalytic language from Victorian Vienna to technological America may help us pinpoint the dominant demands of our era.

Freud's first studies were of hysteria and dreams, and in each case he sought to explore their *unconscious* meaning. Dreams were "the royal road to the unconscious," a means of penetrating through the "censorships" of the conscious mind to the more "real" and fundamental foundations of unconscious motivation and fantasy. And in hysteria, Freud saw symptomatic evidence of sexual repression; his first view was that sexual inhibition and repression alone was the primary cause of all neuroses. In these early investigations, he set what was to be the lifelong pattern of his research: the effort to penetrate through the disguises and defenses of the conscious mind to the raw, nastier, and more basic drives of the id.

Throughout his life, Freud's central orientation remained to what he called "instincts and their vicissitudes." Reacting against the academic psychology of his day, he deprecated the independent importance and autonomy of the separate "faculties" of the mind:

cognition, perception, conation. He emphasized the ancillary role of "higher" mental processes in disguising, sublimating, and expressing the deeper drives of which his Victorian society remained obdurately unaware. He pointed to the importance of infantile sexuality in an era that was blind to it; he made psychosexual pleasure-seeking the driving force of life in a society where sex was taboo; he thought libido fundamental to art, creativity, and culture. In his division of the psyche into id, ego, and superego, he considered the id first and primary. The superego was the internalization of culture as communicated by parents; its energies derived from the child's erotic attachment to his parents and thus, ultimately, from the libidinal drives of the id. And Freud sometimes referred to the ego, the more conscious and "reality-oriented" part of the personality, as merely the "battleground" for the struggle between id and superego; one of his lasting insights was that in mental illness the ego is fragile and succumbs to the forces between which it mediates. Thus Freud's chief interest in the ego was in its role in *intra*-psychic conflict: the defenses it used to block unacceptable wishes or to rationalize or transform them so that they were acceptable.

Freud was, to be sure, a rationalist exploring the irrational, and part of his rationalism is expressed in his statement of the therapeutic goals of psychoanalysis: "Where id was, there shall ego be." The object of the psychoanalyst's intervention was to strengthen the patient's weak ego so that it could mediate more effectively between id and superego, between blind pleasure-seeking and the moral realities of society. Nevertheless, Freud's primary interest was with the id, with the fate of the repressed, with the disguises of libido, and with the patterns of unconscious psychosexual development. Though he was indeed a rationalist, his most enduring contribution has been to show the power of the irrational, the fragility of the ego, the human importance of the socially unacceptable.

A psychoanalyst's preferred concepts, I have suggested, are related through the symptoms of his patients to the society in which he lives. Freud's first patients were largely middle-class Viennese women in the late Victorian era. In retrospect, we can see that part of his therapeutic success came from the close connection between his theories and the problems of his society. He saw all of civilization, like Austrian society, as an inhibiting and repressive force; and in his later writings he feared that the ego would be ever more overwhelmed in a heightening war of instinct with social conscience. As a description of all civilization, this analysis now seems questionable, but as a comment on Victorian society, it was largely valid: the demands of Victorian society were indeed inhibitory, repressive, and constraining. Thus one reason his message has been so liberating to the inhibited and the repressed was because it was so specifically directed against the human toll of a repressive society: it provided a rationale and a vocabulary for those who would later call for new instinctual freedoms. By stating, restating, underlining, and perhaps even exaggerating the importance of the id, by demonstrating the psychic toll of excessive inhibitory demands, Freud made clear how large a part of psychic life his world ignored.

Especially in America, the major emphasis of psychoanalysis has shifted since Freud's day. As a group, psychoanalysts are no longer as interested in the vicissitudes of instinct, no longer as fascinated by libidinal development, less concerned with repressed wishes and fantasies. For an increasing number of American analysts, these concerns take second place to a new interest in the ego as an autonomous agent. Many analysts now postulate that from the beginning of life, the ego operates as a sovereign power and not merely a vassal, as a central governing agency of personality and not merely as the mediator for conflicts or the creature of id. Furthermore, the origins of psychopathology are increasingly sought not only in libidinal fixation but in ego weakness as well. In discussing mental illness as in explaining mental health, psychoanalysts increasingly point to what is missing and present in the patient's ego; and terms like ego integration, ego identity, ego fragility, ego lacunae, and ego strength are the stock phrases of many American analysts. The basic trend of psychoanalysis in America is away from a study of the harmful effects of repression and toward a study of the ego.

The psychoanalytic concept of the ego should not be confused with the popular notion of the ego as the center of self-interest, vanity, and pride. In ordinary parlance, a wound to the "ego" means damage to self-esteem; a man whose "ego" is involved in his work is a man whose sense of worth depends on his success: "ego" is synonymous with egocentricity and self-esteem. For psychoanalysts, however, the ego is the organizing, governing, co-ordinating center of personality, whose primary tasks are to maintain psychic harmony and to "adapt" to the demands and possibilities of the environment. In performing these tasks, the ego has at its disposal a variety of functions: defense, synthesis, dissociation, assimilation, selection, timing, perception, intention, reality-testing, anticipation, differentiation, automatization and a host of others. Ego "breakdown" occurs when the ego "regresses" to more primitive and less differentiated levels of functioning, relies on more childlike and less adaptive defenses, and becomes incapable of the fine accommodations and subtle compromises which can characterize ego functioning at its best.

Whatever our ultimate judgment about the scientific validity of psychoanalytic ego psychology, the development of this new field reflects the major demands of technological society. A crucial difference between Freud's world and ours is mirrored in the shift from a view of man which traces psychopathology to excessive inhibition and repression to a view which focuses on the problems and potential failures of ego development. Put in oversimplified form, the primary demands of Freud's society were inhibitory, while the dominant demands of our own society are ego demands; the prevalent pathologies of Victorian society reflected an inability to inhibit and constrain the motives society deemed vicious, whereas in a technological society the most visible pathologies arise in those who cannot attain the requisite levels of ego functioning. The vocabulary of psychoanalysis reflects not only universal scientific truth, but the psychic toll of social demands: it is no accident that psychoanalytic ego psychology has been most highly developed in the most technological nation in the world.

## Training the technological ego

The most burdensome demands of our technological society, then, are ego demands, and the most characteristic pathologies and alienations of our society are related to the inability or unwillingness to meet these demands. Before ego virtues, other virtues take a secondary role: for every Sunday sermon in favor of love, a hundred weekdays are spent acquiring skill; for every praise of constraint, there are a dozen paeans to competence. Yet merely to call these demands "ego demands" takes us only part way to defining their special characteristics: for among all of the functions of the ego, our society selects only one set for special emphasis, and neglects the rest.

Central among the neglected potentials of the ego in our society are the capacities sometimes termed "regression in the service of the ego"—that is, the ability of the ego to, as it were, "shut itself off" and thereby to remain open to the childish, the sexual, the creative, and the dreamlike. The highest creativity, be it biological procreativity or artistic innovation, presupposes an ego that can abandon control of instinct and temporarily renounce a cognitive orientation so as to permit fantasy, orgasm, childbirth, or even sleep. In each case, the ego permits and encourages the gratification of instinctual needs, allows expression to the basic biological drives on which much of human behavior is ultimately based. Then, too, the ego has a "synthetic" or integrative role in harmonizing and co-ordinating personal motivations with social demands and objective opportunities so as to produce behavior that serves the individual's basic needs as well as his higher purposes and the needs of society. In all of these ways, the ego at its best serves other interests than its own: it remains responsive to instinct and basic motives, acknowledging at the same time the socially learned dictates of conscience; it can retire to the wings to allow playfulness, openness to fantasy, sexuality, relaxation, and impulse; it serves rather than dominates the other parts of the psyche. One of the prime characteristics of genuine "ego strength" is a flexible lack of "self-interest" on the part of the ego: it shows its strength by self-denial.

In terms of my earlier analogy, a strong ego is to a tyrannical ego as a strong government is to a dictatorship. A strong government is vigorously active when activity is needed to serve the public interest; it governs not for the sake of governing but for the sake of the people and the law. Good government allows itself to "wither away" when it is not needed, though it can intervene decisively and vigorously when intervention is in the interests of those it serves. A dictatorship, in contrast, rules for the sake of ruling, serving neither the people nor the law. However benign a tyranny may be, its primary goal must be to continue governing; and it will never allow itself to wither away or fail to intervene if intervention is possible. A good government subordinates itself to other interests than its own self-maintenance; a dictatorship gives its governmental claims priority over all other interests.

In these terms, the virtues of our technological society require a dictatorship of the ego rather than a good government. The self-denying potential of the ego is minimized: playfulness, fantasy, relaxation, creativity, feeling, and synthesis take second place to problem-solving, cognitive control, work, measurement, rationality, and analysis. The technological ego rarely relaxes its control over the rest of the psyche, rarely subordinates itself to other psychic interests or functions. Though its tyranny is seldom obvious, it is firm and unrelenting. Although apparently benevolent and reasoning, seeking to "understand" the motivations it regulates, ignoring the pangs of conscience when it can (and when it cannot, seeking to undermine their claims), the technological ego still dominates rather than governs well.

The social demand for ego dictatorship is closely related to the major stresses in our society: the specialized ego functions we most prize are those that help us cope with these stresses. Continual social change, for example, requires extraordinary flexibility and adaptability to a changing environment, and further demands the ability to make highly selective and partial identifications. The decline of Utopia and the absence of positive myth in American society asks that men live without high idealism or animating faith, substituting instead empirical goals, short-range aims, and a "realistic" and "practical" outlook. Above all, the fragmentation of traditional roles and the shattering of intact community pushes the individual toward a cognitive outlook, toward the subordination of feeling, toward the dissociation of private and public life. All of these social stresses bear most heavily on a few specialized ego functions: rapid adaptation, selection, discrimination, choice, reality-testing, cognition, and dissociation. In a society where cognition takes priority over feeling, where questions of "how" are given precedence over questions of "why," and where fantasy, idealism, and the Utopian spirit must be subordinated to the "practical" world, the cognitive, instrumental, and practical sides of the ego must dominate.

If we accept our society's values as given, then the greatest human need of American society is to "produce" enough men and women with highly developed technological egos. In virtually all primitive societies, in contrast to our own, the simple fact of social membership enables most men and women to understand and do the jobs their society assigns them. Family life alone suffices to teach children what they need to know of adult skills. These skills are relatively few in number and simple to learn; furthermore, most adult work bears a simple and tangible relationship to the immediate facts of adult survival. The fisherman's family eats the fish he catches; the peasant woman wears clothes she makes herself; the warrior's survival depends upon his prowess in battle. A woman may be more or less excellent as a weaver of cloth; a man may be a better or worse fisherman, dancer, or hunter; but to be at least minimally competent in any of these realms is within the reach of

ALIENATING SOCIETY

almost everyone within the society—the stupid and the intelligent, the unskilled and the skilled.

The situation in our own society is sharply different: even to survive for one day, the average urban American requires a kind of personality organization that in many societies even the most out- standing individual does not possess: a capacity to govern his own behavior, to make his way in a world of strangers, to do a job requiring years of training in the basic skills of literacy, to cope with unexpected situations and unfamiliar people. Even so routine a performance as driving a two-ton automobile at sixty miles an hour requires not only highly automatized skills but extraordinary capacity for concentration, co-ordination, rapid judgment, and adaptation. Increasingly, only the most menial tasks are within the competence of the uneducated; even jobs we consider "unskilled" usually presuppose the relatively high skills of literacy. And most desirable positions in our society require advanced and specialized training and, with it, high levels of dispassionateness, ability to remain cool under stress, capacity to concentrate, to maintain long- range goals yet to adapt rapidly to new conditions, to deal with remote and distant situations, to abstract, to co-ordinate complex operations, to synthesize many recommendations, to plan long- range enterprises, to resist distraction, to persevere despite disap- pointment, to master complex conceptual assignments, to be im- partial, to follow instructions.

Indeed, without a minimal level of such capacities, we do not permit men and women to live within our society at all, but must shut them away in special centers for custody or treatment. Every society has its forms of insanity, but most often the insane are per- mitted to live among the sane, and sometimes they are honored as possessed and prophetic. Even in nineteenth-century America, there was still room for "village characters" and "crazy uncles in the attic," and the possessed and the demented were often farmed out to citizens for whom they might productively work. The rele- gation of the mentally ill to mental hospitals, largely an invention of the last century, is a symptom of the steady rise in demands for minimal ego strength in our society.

Our growing inability to tolerate the insane, like our ever more inclusive definitions of insanity, points to the steady growth of demand for technological ego functioning. More and more men and women are pushed to perform at the peak of their ability. In some societies, men's ambitions are limited primarily by their lack of endurance, their lack of motivation, or their lack of constraint. In ours, their "success" is limited when they reach the peak of their ego capacity. "Peak ego performance" is asked of us all; and our society's greatest human need is to produce more and more men and women with an ever higher peak.

Until recently, the supply has been adequate to the demand: enough young men and women in each generation possessed enough ego skills to meet the growing demands of society. Indeed, America may have earlier possessed an untapped reservoir of "ego talent," of men and women who were functioning at *less* than peak performance, whose potentials were not used by their current lives. The reports of European observers in the last century suggest that even then American children were raised with a combination of permissiveness, love, and early training for independence which we now know is the best background for our major social virtues. Perhaps one reason for the extraordinarily rapid development of this country was that the child-rearing techniques that early evolved in this country produced a surplus of men and women with the needed ego qualities; and these men and women proceeded to create a society where their virtues would be used.

But since the Second World War, there are increasing signs of a growing shortage of people with the "right" kind of personality. Specifically, we find an ever more urgent and deliberate effort to "produce" men and women with technological egos and to prevent the "human failures" who lack the characteristic virtues of our society. A glance at the employment pages of the New York *Times* or the *Scientific American* will confirm the scarcity of those with the most highly developed technological skills. In some of the developing nations, such men and women are a glut on the market: university graduates go unemployed by the thousands; but in our society, though the supply is increasing, the demand is increasing faster.

To appreciate the symptoms of "technological ego scarcity" we must first recall how this specialized ego functioning is learned. The roots of ego development lie in the family, and in the earliest years of life. Unless parents consistently teach and reward such skills as postponing, concentrating, waiting, manipulating, and conceptualizing, these talents develop slowly or not at all. A middle-class mother, by teaching her child that waiting will be rewarded, lays the basis for a later ability to concentrate in school; and parents who reason with and explain things to their children encourage them to deal with the world conceptually and verbally, a lesson that stands them in good stead when it is time to learn to read and write. Parents who combine dependency with demands for achievement, who make their love and approval conditional on the child's accomplishments, are readying their children for school and adult life in America. And families that push children toward independence and autonomous self-control before school begins lay the basis for virtues which will enable the child to "do well" in school and in technological life.

School thus already presupposes the prior development of specialized ego potentials. A child who arrives in kindergarten unable to wait, unresponsive to "reasons" and "explanations," dependent, and unfamiliar with demands for achievement already has two and a half strikes against him, for the primary psychological function of American education is the further expansion, development, and rehearsal of social and cognitive skills whose foundations must have been laid in the home. Social skills involve the capacity to "cooperate," "to follow the rules of the game," to "be a good loser," to "wait one's turn," to subordinate personal needs to the interest of a group or institution—all qualities needed in our tightly organized society. But even more fundamental are other cognitive skills: the ability to concentrate, conceptualize, analyze, abstract, organize, schedule, defer, arrange, measure, and co-ordinate. The successful finished product of such an education is an individual who has the capacity to concentrate for long periods on assigned tasks, to remain cool, dispassionate, accurate, and objective in work, to undertake and carry through unaided complicated and long-range projects, to operate at high levels of abstraction, to work for long periods on tasks with no relevance to his everyday needs and experience.

Obviously, education teaches specific vocational skills as well. But psychologically these are secondary in importance to the "character" training it involves. Even "intelligence," normally considered more innate than learned, is—at least as measured in most schools—a largely acquired talent. Most intelligence tests emphasize the ability to conceptualize, to use numbers, to perceive similarities and express them abstractly—all largely learned talents. Even the ability to *take* an intelligence test presupposes a capacity to sit still for an hour, to persist in a difficult task despite failures, to resist distraction. Similarly, the very fact of "getting an education" for twelve years itself requires the capacity to "wait for life" until the late teens, the willingness to defer marriage and work (and real adulthood) despite physiological maturity, the ability to renounce immediate satisfactions for greater goods in the future.

The symptoms of the growing scarcity of men and women with adequately developed ego skills are most apparent in child-rearing and education. Consider, for example, the increasing emphasis on "love is not enough" by child-rearing experts, the ever louder assertion that permissiveness must be tempered with high standards, "limits," and pressures for independence and achievement. I have earlier suggested that permissiveness tends to intensify the dependency of the child on his mother and that a mother who is *only* permissive without demanding cognition, achievement, and independence is likely to have an overly dependent child who is unable to leave her. Highly dependent children are those most likely to develop "school phobias" and "learning blocks" which prevent doing well in school. Thus, the attack on unalloyed permissiveness and the plea for "parental standards" is also an attack on child-rearing techniques that may imperil autonomy, independence, and the full involvement of the child in school, and a plea for other techniques more adapted to the acquisition of specialized ego virtues.

Or consider our growing national concern over the effects of "deprived" homes on children. These homes usually turn out to be lower-class homes from which children arrive in school already too impulsive, too impatient, and too oriented toward action to be able to take advantage of schooling aimed at teaching technological virtues. These children may make good athletes, good street fighters, good dancers, and good gang members, but they lack the ego qualities to make good pupils. It is these same children, ten years later, about whom we have recently grown so concerned because they "drop out" of high schools. Drop-outs, it is argued, cannot get adequate jobs, their "talents" are wasted, and they become the dregs of a labor market that needs skilled experts. Yet the basic problem behind "dropping out" is not the failure to acquire specific vocational skills: in many cases these can or must be learned on the job. Rather the fact of dropping out indicates a prior inability to postpone, defer, and to use concepts, and thus points to a lack of the ego skills that are needed in almost every position of even moderate prestige or pay. A high school diploma is above all a token of ego proficiency; we assume, quite rightly, that someone who can put up with twelve, sixteen, or twenty-one years of education is likely to be able to put up with the demands of most jobs. If drop-outs were those of an especially *great* ego proficiency, employers would undoubtedly talk less of the virtues of a high school diploma and more of the importance of "on the job training" and "getting an early start."

Another symptom of the demand for peak ego-performance is the "search for talent" in our schools. In practice, this laudable aim has often collapsed into an effort to give preferential treatment to children and adolescents who do especially well on IQ tests. Those who are given "enriched curricula" are thus those who already possess the skills that contribute to high scores on intelligence tests; and the increasingly systematic search for such people and the subsequent efforts to train them for positions of adult leadership witness the growing scarcity of such adults. Indeed, the whole gamut of anxieties triggered by the "post-Sputnik" re-evaluation of American education would almost certainly have come about without Sputnik, for these anxieties originate in the increasing demands of our society. The premonitions of the "post-Sputnik" re-evaluation have been there for decades in the rapid rise in average educational level, in the professionalization of education as a field, and in the entry of social scientists and child experts into the field of educational psychology. Although the supply of the "right" kinds of ego skills increases, the demand increases even faster.

The growing gap between ego supply and ego demand in American society is also clear in the growth in systematic planning for mental health. I have already noted the recent inability of our society to find a place within it for the mentally ill. But in other areas the same pressure for "mental health" is apparent. In "progressive" communities, psychiatrists, psychologists, and social workers increasingly co-operate with teachers to spot early signs of mental illness and treat them at once. Schools do not consider it their business systematically to teach honor, courage, love, or wisdom; but let there be early signs of "ego weakness" and the professional staff moves in. We have no professional staff to encourage thrift, chastity, abstemiousness, or frugality in the young, but we do publicly support those who concern themselves with school phobias, "learning problems," under-achievement, "reading blocks," excessive impulsiveness, distractibility, and the inability to subordinate fantasy to consensual reality. Paradoxically, the watchfulness with which we are beginning to oversee "emotional development" in schools usually aims not at the development of a rich emotional life, but at the subordination of emotion to cognition.

In American society at large, educated men and women increasingly pay "mental health" the highest compliment a virtue can be paid: we no longer recognize it as a virtue at all, but see it merely as an objectively desirable condition. (Only an alienated college student can cry "Help stamp out mental health," and he does it more to shock more than to persuade.) At the same time, our definitions of "mental illness" have grown more inclusive. New and broadened definitions of psychosis and neurosis have come to prevail. Many a man or woman who two generations ago would have been merely termed a "character" is now seen as a "borderline" psychotic; and marked qualities of personality (e.g., extreme parsimony, frugality, or obstinacy) are now interpreted as "character disorders." A recent survey in midtown Manhattan found only one out of five people in "unimpaired mental health."

And finally, as I have suggested, the language of psychoanalytic ego psychology itself reflects and implicitly accepts the technological virtues of our society, at the same time that it provides concepts with which we can diagnose these virtues. Though the ego in principle includes the many self-denying potentials I have discussed, much writing on ego development heeds these potentials but little, stressing instead the organizing, cognitive, and "dictatorial" side of the ego. The term "regression in the service of the ego" is used to characterize creativity in all forms, dreaming, openness to the childish and the archetypal, spontaneity of response, playfulness and capacity for sexual abandon; and this usage implies that whenever the ego relaxes its control the result is somehow "regressive" and thus, implicitly, "bad." Here the phraseology of psychoanalysis clearly reflects the dominant demands of American society.

Our dominant social virtues, then, encourage ego dictatorship at the expense of other human potentials that involve loosening or abandoning ego domination. The main formative influences on personality development, the family and the schools, are ever more specifically geared to "producing" the technological ego; and those who lack these virtues increasingly find no honored place in our midst. So unchallenged is the dictatorship of the ego that we forget that, on the scale of world history, the juvenile delinquent, the dropout, the under-achiever, and the deprived child are far more "typi-

cal" of human development than are the virtuosos of the ego we
acclaim.


## The dangers of ego dictatorship

Whatever the price we pay, we cannot simply dismiss the dominant
ego virtues of our society, calling romantically for a movement to
pure feeling or conservatively for a return to a society dominated
by the virtues of constraint. Without technologically specialized
ego functioning, most of the qualities we most value in our society
would be impossible. Though we may deplore a one-sided emphasis on cognition, neutrality, achievement, dissociation, and "following the rules," we would find unendurable a total emphasis on feeling, judgment by birth, partiality, nepotism, lack of fairness,
subjectivity, and *in*ability to follow the rules. The high over-all
standard of living we enjoy is premised on the availability of a vast
reservoir of men and women with the skills necessary to work together to make our social, economic, and political system work. The
innovations we so eagerly seize and enjoy are made possible by the
dispassionate efforts of science and the technological skills of those
who apply it to consumption. And even those who could do without material well-being and technological innovation would find it
hard to forego other aspects of our society equally premised on ego
virtues: the supremacy of law over individual whim, the possibility
of free choice, the opportunity to speak relatively freely, the insistence on equality and fairness.

Without a sufficient group of men and women with the specialized ego capacities I have described, a society that is both technological and democratic is probably impossible. We see this clearly
in the developing nations, whose most crucial need is usually not
for capital or natural resources, but for skilled, efficient, hard-
headed men and women with the learned capacity for abstraction,
restraint, planning, objectivity, and fairness to implement industrial

and technological goals. And in the past generation, we have seen again and again that without such men and women no set of constitutional checks and balances and no amount of foreign aid is enough to insure a democratic government. Democracy presupposes a citizenry with a minimal capacity for fairness, a certain "rationality" and objectivity, a capacity to recognize and reject demagogues, and, above all, sufficient detachment to allow their political enemies to win and rule. Technology and democracy both require high ego-skills.

But though we should not dismiss the relevance and importance of technological virtues, we can challenge their supremacy over all other virtues in our society. Ego dictatorship, I have said, is not the same as ego strength; and the dangers of ego dictatorship are many. Technological ego skills can only be justified as good in themselves via a fundamental confusion of means and ends, of the instruments of virtue with virtue itself. Means and ends are of course intimately related, and the choice of an inappropriate technique to accomplish a virtuous goal may subvert the goal. But the techniques of action are not the same as the ends of action. We may judge an end good or bad, virtuous or vicious; but of techniques we can properly say only that they are appropriate or inappropriate, facilitating or subverting, effective or ineffectual.

"Adaptability," for example, is virtuous or vicious depending upon what one is adapting to. To adapt to the legitimate needs of those one loves is a virtue, but to adapt to the corrupt practices prevalent in one's profession is not. "Dispassionateness" may be a virtue in a judge or a juror, but is not appropriate in a husband's relation to his wife. The ability to postpone and delay is essential for one who seeks higher education, but it is wrong to postpone and delay when a situation requires action. The cognitive skills taught in our schools can be used to help the needy or to exploit the downtrodden; but six million Jews have been systematically liquidated with a thorough "efficiency" which could only be attained by those with highly developed technological egos. Even planning and executing a "preventive" thermonuclear war would require vast technological ego capacity: span of attention, concentration, ability to remain cool under stress, dispassionateness, capacity for planning, abstraction, foresight, and co-ordination of complex operations. But these same capacities can be as well used to reclaim the desert, help the poor, promote democracy, or support the development of one's fellow men. The ego is bad or good according to the purposes it serves.

Moreover, the qualities we stress in our homes and schools rarely include the highest capacities of a strong and flexible ego— its capacity to withdraw to the wings when it has no role. To repeat: creativity, fantasy, direct feeling, immediacy of experience, openness to the sensual, biological, and animal, capacity for full sexual enjoyment or easy childbirth, ability for play, humor, adult childishness, even the ability to sleep and dream—all require an ego which can leave the stage. When this capacity is lacking the result is tightness, the forced smile, the stifled orgasm, the inability to feel strongly, to experience directly, to be refreshed by sleep, to play spontaneously. The human result is a life that, though often rational, cognitive, adaptive, and stable, lacks zest, exuberance, vitality, immediacy, and the capacity for either joy or despair.

Unconscious fear plays a major role in the self-perpetuation of ego dictatorship. This fear is first transmitted by parents themselves threatened by the vivid impulses and direct feelings of their children. It is sustained in adults by the fact that our dissociated passions degenerate into potentially overwhelming impulses, and our denied idealisms decay into potentially tyrannical consciences. As with any dictatorial regime, a vicious circle ensues: the less expression allowed passion and idealism, the more unruly these forces become and the more energetic must be our efforts to suppress them. Most often these efforts involve psychic "bread and circuses": we try to find "harmless outlets" for our passions that will not interfere with the domination of the ego; we allow ourselves idealistic activities in our leisure time so that questions of ethics need not intrude in our daily round. Yet, as in Rome, "unruly masses" are not long appeased by bread and circuses: deprived of a share in government, they threaten more fiercely. Dictatorship is purchased at the price of continual fear that what is subordinated will try to break loose and rule.

This fear has much basis in fact: The ego, incapable of determining its own ends unaided by passion or conscience, may rationalize an alliance with instinct as necessary to maintain its own domination: a "fling" enables one to concentrate better the next day, and after all, we are only human. Conscience, too, easily degenerates into narrow moralism when denied by the ego. Most often, the secret alliance of ego and moralism is rationalized as "realism." A moralistic dislike for those who are different is transformed into the "realism" of recognizing their inferiority or perversity; a moralistic sense of the superiority of the American way of life is transmuted into "cold war realism" and a policy of national self-interest. When conscience and ego are truly united, ethical sense can develop; when conscience is denied, it can nonetheless dominate as intolerant moralism.

Psychologically, then, the growing social demand for ego dictatorship raises two related problems: ego dictatorship is difficult to sustain; and even when it can be maintained, it is in continual danger of collapsing. Men have a deep need for psychic integration, and this need becomes more salient in a society like ours where pressing economic needs have become less urgent. A life dominated by one set of functions at the expense of others continually frustrates this need. The ideal of personal wholeness, of the harmonious integration of passion, conscience, and ego, is systematically undermined by our social definitions of virtue.

But a vague dissatisfaction results, sometimes felt as a sense of being inwardly divided and fragmented just as one's life is outwardly divided, sometimes experienced as a sense that some crucial quality of vitality, vigor, and contact with life is missing. The "aesthetic" qualities which the alienated seek—immediacy of experience, spontaneity and directness of feeling, the sense of living fully and passionately in the world—are hard to achieve. Furthermore, a tyrannical ego is in continual danger of being overthrown. Unable to retire gracefully or renounce its claims, its brittleness and rigidity subject it to secret subversions, to new and secret tyrannies of instinct or conscience. Yet to be dominated by impulse and instinct is to fail to be truly human; to be tyrannized by conscience is to have little self. Democratic government that serves and mediates without dominating is as hard to attain and maintain within the psyche as within the body politic.

## Alienation and the technological ego

Probably no other society in human history has demanded such high levels of specialized ego functioning as does ours. Our ability to tolerate those who lack minimal ego competence has decreased; our effort to teach and promote technological ego skills in family and school has become more and more systematic; the demand for peak ego performance has grown. Although American society is supplying more and more men and women capable of high levels of ego functioning, the demand is growing faster than the supply, and the stresses created therefore mount.

In practice, of course, what I have here grouped together as "technological ego demands" resolve into a hundred smaller demands and dissolve into the social scenery of American life. In previous chapters I have discussed these component demands in greater detail, attempting to trace them to more specific features of our social scene. And in speaking of the "technological ego" as if it had a will of its own, capable of "dictating," and "being overthrown," I am speaking loosely. Only men and women have wills of their own, and not ids, egos, or superegos. But men and women *can* and often do identify their best selves with their ego functions, seeking to maintain the supremacy of the ego over all psychic life. And then it is very much *as if* the ego had a will of its own and sought to dictate and dominate. The best evidence for psychic wholeness is, in contrast, that no one aspect of the personality becomes identified with the "best self"; and the goal of personal inte-

gration requires that passion, ego, and ethical sense be harmoni-
ously involved in every action. The ego is at its best when it has no
will of its own, but wills the fullfillment of the whole man.

It is hard to weigh the psychic demands of modern society
against that of our own society in the past, or against that of other
societies. I know of no way to measure quantitatively the qualitatively different demands of different societies. But though we cannot make exact assessments, we can try to pinpoint the areas where
the gap between society's demands and men's ability to comply is
greatest, and to underline the dangers to human fulfillment inherent
in these demands. In our technological society, the greatest gap is
between ego demands and our capacity and willingness to meet
them, and the greatest danger is that of ego dictatorship.

The alienated are always those who cannot or will not meet the
dominant demands of their society. In a repressive and constraining society, they will be those who cannot or do not adequately
repress and constrain: they will be the Victorian ladies with hysterical symptoms or the apostles of passion and license in an inhibited community, or perhaps even, in a different way, men like
Freud, who obdurately point to the central role of aggression and
sex in an age that tries to deny their existence. In an age whose
heaviest demands are for "right motivation," the alienated will be
those who lack it: the timorous in an age of courage; the rebellious
in an era of obedience, the aggressive in an epoch of brotherly love.
And in an ego-demanding society like our own, the alienated will
be those who cannot or will not comply with these ego demands.
The refusal of adulthood will spring ultimately from a refusal of the
technological ego, a refusal which may be in turn produced by
simple absence of the demanded virtues or by the presence of other
virtues that are held in higher esteem.

To return, then, to the alienated youths from whom we began,
"ego dictatorship" is a way of characterizing the social demands
they find most oppressive. Their emphasis on the present is an indirect refusal of the *time-binding* capacity of the ego; the "totalness"
of their repudiation is a rejection of the ego's ability to *select and*

*differentiate.* Their refusal of freedom and distrust of commitment is a repudiation of our society's demands that we *will* and *choose* in the face of uncertainty and complex alternatives. Their persistent longing for fusion suggests an unwillingness to *renounce* the past. And most important, the search in these youths for personal wholeness, artistic expressiveness, immediacy of experience, and spontaneity of feeling, their preference for passion over reason and imagination over "realism"—all attest to a refusal of the ego virtues that define technological man.

# 13  Alienation and American society

The search for the sources of alienation in a youth like Inburn has led us far afield. We have had to consider not only the lives and backgrounds of youths like him, but such apparently distant forces as the nature of social change, the process of social fragmentation, the organization of the American family, the intellectual history of the West, and the dominant demands of our society. The "predicament" into which Inburn was born extends far beyond the immediate family of which he so readily speaks: it includes all of the seldom-noticed features of our social scenery, the cultural context in which he grew up, and the history of the society he now rejects. Alienated students, like all of us, are social animals, cultural creatures, and historical figures. Every individual is in this sense his society writ small—though he is more than this, and though there are many scripts for the transliteration of society to personality. A man's life history includes so intimate a factor as his childhood fantasies and so global a force as the intellectual tradition of his culture.

What began as a study of a very small group of college students has therefore ended as an effort to characterize the major stresses and demands of our technological society: the intensive study of individuals has led to an awareness of their continual involvement with society, culture and history. Though individuals may notably influence and change the context in which they live, they do so as participants in this context. To give causal primacy either to individuals or to historical forces is to oversimplify: all men are ultimately historical figures and all history is ultimately a story of individuals. The division of this book into two parts, the first dealing with the psychology of alienation, the second concerned with the alienating society, is therefore an oversimplification justified only by the needs of exposition. In fact, all of these factors are continually interdependent, influencing and being influenced by each other. There are no simple causal chains in individual and social life, but only complexly interrelated processes, like a vast network of simultaneous equations, all of whose terms are dependent on all others.

## The sources of alienation

The stresses and losses and demands of our technological society are, I have tried to show, an *integral part* of the lives of alienated students. "Chronic social change" is not merely an abstract explanatory principle, but a continually present fact in personal development, felt in the value these youths early learned to attribute to words like "new" and "modern," apparent in their unspoken awareness of the differences between themselves, their parents, and their grandparents, exacerbated in the problems of identification so central to their personal development. "Social fragmentation" is not merely a disembodied sociological construct, but a way of describing concrete perceptions of adulthood, specific observations of how parents and adults live, anticipated demands of adulthood. The social conventions and historical changes of American family life *are* the context in which these young men grew up; and the "isolated nuclear family" is the *same* family within which these young men were sheltered, nurtured, and taught. Nor did their first contact with the "intellectual tradition of the West" come when they studied this tradition in college; it was the ideological air they breathed long before they were aware that "intellectual history" existed. And finally, the "specialized ego demands" of our technological society were with these youths from the earliest years of their lives, determining much of how they were raised, schooled, exhorted, warned, and rewarded.

Their alienation is therefore not a function of personal *or* social factors, but of both inextricably intertwined. Their alienation was not produced merely by an *early* personal development that predisposed them to alienation in response to *later* social demands, but of a continual interaction throughout life of social pressures as modified by their individual circumstances. We have had to view their alienation from a variety of perspectives, one at a time; but for a complete portrait we must include all of these perspectives and their relationship to each other. Though we may conceptualize the forces that help produce alienation as psychological, sociological, cultural, and historical, at any given moment all of these forces are fused in the individual's experience; and only with the cumbersome phrase "psycho-socio-cultural-historical" can we adequately indicate this fusion.

To be sure, the relative weight of each of these factors often seems different in different individuals. In some the burden of childhood bitterness seems so heavy that they might well have rejected any conceivable society. Yet even here, the fact that they carry this burden is intimately connected to their families, and through their families to the more general dilemmas of our society that were there reflected. Moreover, the shaping of a diffuse distrust of adulthood into ideological rejection of American culture (and not, for example, into delinquency, revolutionary activity or schizophrenic withdrawal) is related to the immediate social realities of their lives and to the less tangible ideological history of our society. In other alienated youths, the scales of personal and social history seemed more evenly balanced: these were young men whose search for a unifying purpose and vision was most intense, and who may yet find in some deviant sector of our society a home where they can be both adult and not "conventionally American."

And for a few, the realities of American society seem overwhelmingly important in their alienation: the legacy of their childhoods was to lead them to ask *more* of adulthood than our society provides, and their rejection clearly proceeds more from the inability of our society to provide what they seek than from any prior personal disposition to refuse its offerings.

Yet any effort to weigh the relative importance of developmental, social, historical, and cultural forces—to say of some youths that development is primary and of others that history is primary—is pointless and impossible. To repeat: all of these forces are interpenetrated and interdependent at each moment in our lives; that we choose to perceive or emphasize one factor does not cancel the influence and importance of the others. As "atypical" youths, these students were bound to be different from their fellows in a variety of ways; anyone who is "different" is likely to differ not only in his upbringing, but in his personality and in his responses to his society, his culture and his history. To produce the kind of alienation exemplified in an Inburn undoubtedly takes both a special personal history and a society like our own.

In mid-century America, to admit that any belief has psychological sources, even among others, is open to misinterpretation. I have earlier noted the common tendency to add an implicit "nothing but" to all psychological explanations: "alienation is (nothing but) a reflection of deviant personal development." To add this phrase to my account would involve a major distortion of my intention. Finding common themes of individual development among alienated subjects tells us nothing about the validity of their refusal of American culture: the factors that dispose a man to a belief are never conclusive in deciding whether this belief is correct. Knowing the psychodynamics of an ideology helps little in judging its consequences or merit, for unmotivated beliefs do not exist. All creative men are "deviant" if for no other reason than by simple virtue of their highly developed creativity. And any effective innovator is likely to be, by the standards of his time, an "abnormal" man with a "deviant" background. But the atypical psychology of the dissident, the innovator, or the creator need not be viewed as the pathology of innovation: it can be seen as its enabling precondition. We could as well view the personal development of these youths as the fortunate factor that sensitized them to the real stresses in our society which their "typical" age-mates are unable to see.

In assessing the sources of alienation, we must try to strike still another balance: between those who *cannot* meet the demands of their society, and those who *choose not* to do so. There are obviously many Americans whose alienation springs ultimately from an inability to live up to our dominant social demands. Countless men and women simply lack the requisite human qualities for anything approaching success in American society: they go jobless, they cannot "achieve," they do not succeed, they are not wanted, and they become embittered, sour, and rejecting of our society as a whole. Many of the prime symptoms of alienation—distrust, anger, a bleakly existential view of the world, a cult of the present—are undoubtedly most prevalent among those of lowest status and most deprived position in our society, for cynicism, feelings of powerlessness, and a low view of human nature are common among the underprivileged. Juvenile delinquents, for example, commonly lack the ego qualities I have called technological: they are impulsive, they "act out" their feelings rather than talking them out, they cannot wait, delay, postpone, concentrate, be objective, accurate, or efficient. As a result they can find little valued place except in their own delinquent gangs. Similarly, those who "choose" insanity rather than adulthood during their late adolescence indirectly tell us that adulthood—as they perceive it—demands of them more than they can give.

Alienation thus can result from real or felt disability before the demands of our society. Those who are unable to meet a demand have two alternatives: they can accept the legitimacy of the demand and with it their own inadequacy, or they can repudiate the demand so as to retain their self-esteem. Usually they do both. The man who cannot run does not enter the race, and most often despises it altogether. In our society, those who lack the constitution and upbringing upon which technological ego skills are based are "disabled" psychologically; and like the physically disabled they often develop a compensatory repudiation which conceals an underlying sense of inadequacy. The strut of the juvenile delinquent, the bravado of the petty criminal, the ostentatious scorn of the "far-out" for the "square" can all indicate compensations for an underlying feeling (and often fact) of disability. The characteristic virtues of such technological rejects and misfits—physical expressiveness, daring, "heart," stealth, acquiescence, bravado, agility, courage, or passionate group loyalty—win them few prizes.

In any society the rank and file of the alienated is likely to be recruited from among such psychological misfits and rejects, from among those who lack the motives, inhibitions, or ego qualities demanded by their society. Misfits are almost always forced into some kind of alienation, be it emigration, delinquency, or withdrawal. Indeed, if there are enough such "misfits" and they can organize together round a common purpose, they will often be able to change their society so it will fulfill their needs and need their fulfillment.

Thus, the core of any revolution, the rank and file of any protest group, the mass of dissidents, or the bulk of the alienated is probably always comprised of "misfits" and "rejects," of those who would like to be "in" but lack the credentials for entry—be they birth, race, social position, skill, or, most likely, the requisite social virtues. One reason established orders are invariably so scornful of "revolutionary rabble" is because in fact the bulk of the alienated are those who are unable to "make it" in the existing society. Yet when such "rejects," "misfits," "dregs," and "rabble" comprise a significant proportion of a society, their very existence constitutes a criticism of the society. Any social order in which a goodly proportion of its citizens do not fit is in that measure a society whose demands have outpaced its ability to prepare men to meet them.

The mere presence of a body of misfits, revolutionary, criminal, withdrawn, psychotic, or merely ideologically alienated men and women tells us something about the faults of a society.

Yet not fitting can come either from having no shape or from having a clear shape of one's own. A round peg as surely fails to fit a square hole as does a peg with no definable shape at all. And among the alienated students studied, not fitting can hardly be said to spring from any simple disability. These youths were socially "overprivileged": their families had provided them with every material and educational benefit; they were well trained and well schooled. Moreover, they were verbally gifted and intellectually talented; they did excellent work in a demanding college; and if they left, it was because *they* chose to leave and not because they had failed to meet the college's requirements. Whatever their personal problems, they had far more technological ego skills than do most Americans; and given a desire for conventional adulthood, few doors would have been closed to them. Psychologically, to be sure, they had been deprived of a "present" father and a mother who could remain *only* a loving mother; but even this real deprivation was partially canceled by their special place in their family— their privileged intimacy with their mother, their felt psychological victory over their chief childhood competitor. I have stressed the ways this victory was Pyrrhic; but their triumph did give them a position of special intimacy with the woman who was (and still is) the key person in their lives. Whatever the many psychological problems created by this victory, it gave some of these students an underlying sense of their own ability to prevail. Even their real psychological deprivations were partly canceled by their victories.

Among the students we have studied, then, alienation most often arose because they had an incipient shape of their own, and not because they were in any simple sense "misfits" or "rejects." Their personal shape was, as we have seen, far from complete; and no doubt many, and perhaps most, will fail to complete it. Moreover, it is impossible to draw a precise line between misfits from disability and malcontents from conviction. Both are always present together: even the psychotic, whose mental illness obviously attests his inability to meet the demands of a sane life, often has extraordinary awareness of the feelings and motives of others. Even a delinquent who lacks the endurance and cognitive ability required to stay in school may be a good thief, a good friend, or a good fighter. And many a "Westernized" African has, by virtue of his Westernization, acquired technological skills and ego assets not shared by his compatriots; these skills and assets effectively alienate him from his fellows and he is often forced to choose between emigration to a world more receptive to his virtues and revolutionary activity to transform his society into one that needs and values him.

Moreover, we know all too well that external coercion is not the only impediment to free choice, and that psychological freedom is harder to attain or even define. Yet if such freedom has any meaning at all, these youths had a great deal of it in "choosing" their alienation. Recall their achievement of academic and social success in secondary school—and their inner repudiation of their success and those who accorded it to them. Recall, too, that their withdrawals from college were at their own behest, and remember their implicit quest for some "aesthetic" fulfillment, some special quality of experience, feeling, fantasy, and passion, which our society at large deems of little value. While it would be a mistake not to appreciate the role of childhood in determining these "free" choices of alienation, it would be a greater mistake to attribute their alienation to simple disability.

Instead, we should look for the factors in their pasts that disposed them to seek *other* values than technological values, other fulfillments than those of conventional American adulthood, other virtues than those of the technological ego. The first half of this book is an account of these factors, and here I need only recall some of the most salient. These youths were raised by mothers whose self-professed aesthetic talents were frustrated by their marriages: partly for this reason, they encouraged in their sons a special sensitivity to beauty, feeling, passion, and idealism. Any young man so reared is likely to become alienated from major sectors of Ameri-

can life—from all that is ugly, tawdry, blighted, and disproportionate. In their fathers, these youths came to see an incarnation of
"defeat" by the American way of life, a man whose own youthful
idealisms had been frustrated, and who was now as a result cold,
detached, inwardly disappointed, and "a failure in his own eyes."
Any young man who so perceives his father is likely to search for
some other way of life, some means of retaining his youthful
dreams even if it means rejecting the lot of his father and the adulthood his society offers him. And finally, partly because their at-
tachments to their mothers did not allow them to invest their
energies in the more extroverted world of boys, sports and gangs,
these youths developed powerfully the resources of their imaginations, preferring to solve their problems with fantasy rather than
with their fists. And any young man possessed of an unusually vital
imagination will find it hard to "buckle down" to the cognitive demands of American life. He will instead be likely to emphasize, as
do these students, the priority of passion over rationality, and even
at times of fantasy over fact.

Yet again, behind the childhood factors which disposed these
youths to reject conventional adulthood lie other social factors. In
their parents' own coming together to marry we have inferred a desire to escape the values and ways of a Victorian past, made obsolete and constricting by our continually changing society. Or when
our subjects' fathers abandoned their idealistic dreams of youth, it
was partly in compliance with the objective requirements of most
American jobs, which make it hard for a man to find work which
satisfies youthful idealism along with cognitive demands. The "absence" of these fathers from their sons' psychological development
is but an extreme example of the difficulties most American fathers
have in being "present" to their children; the eventual withdrawal
of these particular fathers from the emotional life of their families
was an effort to solve problems inherent in our family structure.
So, too, the possessiveness of our subjects' mothers stems in part
from conventions of family life and definitions of woman's role that
make it hard for an ambitious woman not to overinvest in her

children. And even the extraordinary intensity of the mother-son bond in these families is premised on our "isolated nuclear families," where all a child's loves and dependencies are inevitably concentrated on his mother. Further examples could be adduced, but the point is surely clear: though our subjects' families were not typical, the forms of their deviation from the typical were given by the social scenery.

Throughout these last five chapters, I have tried to show a similar interpenetration of personal and social factors in each of the major themes of alienation. I have argued that the cult of the present is a response to the loss of a sense of historical relatedness produced by chronic social change. Personal fragmentation and a sense of homelessness result from social fragmentation and the shattering of traditional community. The fantasy of fusion is a product of the sharp discontinuity between the warm childhood dependency encouraged in American families and the realities of the "cold" and independent adult world. The quest for positive values is made both urgent and difficult by the absence of positive myth in our society. And the rejection of conventional adulthood is made more likely by the demand for technological ego dictatorship in adult life. Here as elsewhere, it is impossible to separate the personal from the social, the cultural, and the historical.

To summarize the sources of alienation in a long, if still oversimplified phrase: alienation is a response *of* individuals especially sensitized to reject American culture by their early development, a development which in part reflects their families' efforts to solve dilemmas built into American life; and it is in part a response *to* social stresses, historical losses, and collective estrangements in our shared existence. Other Americans respond in other and often less alienated ways, but given the existence of these stresses, losses, and estrangements, it should not surprise us that our society inspires scant enthusiasm.

## *The alienated and the apparently unalienated*

In an earlier chapter, I suggested that the study of alienated students might sharpen our eyes to similar but less visible patterns of behavior and outlook in other Americans. Throughout the intervening pages, I have tried to point out parallels between the major themes in the lives of the alienated and comparable motifs in the lives of others, young and old. I also suggested that a search for the sources of ideological alienation might enable us to define stresses, pressures, and demands that affect many others in our society, and I have subsequently attempted to pinpoint and characterize these demands. Yet surely the question of how far we can generalize from these youths remains, and we must confront it again.

Recall one final time the many ways these youths are not typical. They are "overprivileged" socially, educationally, and economically; they are "overendowed" in intelligence, imagination, health, and strength. They were part of a class of 1100 men chosen from 5000 applicants at a college to which only the most intelligent and aspiring dare bother to apply. This college draws not only the especially gifted, but within this elite group its image as a home of free inquiry selectively attracts young men of especially inquiring mind who are likely to be more alienated from their society than those of comparable talent who apply elsewhere. And once accepted at the college, freshmen are immediately involved in a program of studies deliberately intended to promote the examination of established doctrine, the re-evaluation of ancient truth, and the questioning of traditional knowledge. In such an atmosphere, the students studied were among the *most* alienated: nine out of ten of their fellows were less alienated than they.

Furthermore, their youth itself made them atypical of Americans at large. In part, this is a simple function of their age when they were studied: a vast majority of Americans *are not* between the ages of 17 and 22. Yet youth is not merely a matter of years, but also a social phenomenon; and an extended youth is a privilege accorded some longer than others. Compared with high school graduates of the same age who are married and working, these students had been allowed to prolong their adolescence on the assumption that they would ultimately be better formed as a result. Thus, according to our American definitions of youth, they were as yet not involved in the "real" world, they as yet bore none of the responsibilities of adulthood, they had not yet "settled down," they could still live in the "ivory tower" of personal experimentation.

On both counts, then, this is an extraordinary, atypical, unrepresentative group. This means that a vast majority of young Americans of their background are less disaffected, more committed or conformist. To be sure, I have suggested that among the underprivileged, unfortunate, untalented, rejected, and excluded of our society alienation is more prevalent than among this general group; but the alienation of social rejects and misfits is likely to take inarticulate and unconscious forms, and thus differs from the ideological alienation of these youths.

Further, the privilege of a prolonged youth permits a special kind of alienation impossible to those who have "settled down." Movement to later stages of life alone *forces* commitment of a sort. Ten years out of college one must be doing *something*, no matter whether one enjoys it, believes in it, or finds it interesting; and holding a job is at least a surface commitment. And twenty years from college, an erstwhile youth who has not been able to commit himself to a wife usually finds that whether he meant it or not, he is considered committed to bachelorhood. More important, we often believe that adulthood itself brings more genuine psychological commitment to the existing order of things. To paraphrase an item from a famous questionnaire to measure authoritarianism, "Young people sometimes get alienated ideas, but they get over them when they grow up and settle down." Or, as we commonly say of rebellious adolescents, "They are only going through a phase."

Obviously, then, we cannot generalize to others without many qualifications. But we can, I think, use what we have learned of the themes of one kind of alienation to re-examine the more ordinary outlooks and behavior of other young Americans. And we can apply what we have inferred and proposed about the stresses of life in America to assess the quality of the commitments of those who *are* in the "real world" of adulthood. Specifically, I will suggest that the period of youth in America is a period of socially enforced alienation and that, partly as result, the adult life of the apparently well-adjusted in America is shot through with "little alienations."

## Youth culture as enforced alienation

What we call "youth culture"—the distinctive values, outlooks, manners, roles, activities, and behavior patterns of youth considered as a separate age group—is not a uniquely American phenomenon. In other technological societies, national variants of youth culture are increasingly visible. But in America, the most advanced of the technological nations, youth culture shows its greatest scope and development. Here, youth culture involves not only the privileged and educated, but all sectors of society; it includes not only our "teenagers," but many who are advanced into their twenties. And though we commonly take it for granted that youths should exhibit special and often erratic, bizarre, and deviant behavior simply because of their age, not all societies make this assumption. On the contrary, in many, adolescents are seen primarily as young adults or as old children: they are expected to exhibit no distinctive behavior by simple virtue of their age. Even in our own country two generations ago, youth was largely defined as a time of apprenticeship: adolescence was a matter of "learning the ropes" and memorizing the map and the timetable for the road of success ahead. Gawky, awkward adolescence was a phase to be outgrown as quickly as possible.

Some few Americans still retain this view of youth, but most of us do not. Increasingly we expect that youth will have a special culture of its own, with characteristics that are those of neither childhood or adulthood. Our language reflects this expectation: we seldom speak colloquially of "youths" or "adolescents"—terms that implicitly suggest the transition to adulthood—but rather of "teenagers," "hoods," and "beatniks," all of whom are seen as ensconced in a world of their own with a world view of their own. Increasingly, we expect adolescents and young adults to behave in idiosyncratic ways which are symptomatic of their age.

The growth and dominance of youth culture in America means that most young Americans spend their formative years in a special culture only peripherally related to the adult world. We expect teenagers to be different, and they come to expect it of themselves as well. Most adults view a youth of seventeen with a firmly established adult outlook as someone who is "too old for his years." The values and behaviors of the youth culture are rarely explicitly anti-adult, but they are explicitly non-adult; and the dominant virtues of adolescent society are not those of the adult world. This means that the average young American must undergo two major transitions en route to adulthood: first he must move from childhood to the youth culture, learning its ways and adapting to its requirements; and later, when he "drops out" of the youth culture or is expelled by commencement, he must make a second transition into the "real" world of grownups.

To be precise, we should speak of many "youth sub-cultures" which share common characteristics rather than of one embracing youth culture, for under this rubric we must subsume a great many different groups, variously labeled "typical teenagers," "rock-and-rollers," "Joe College students," "youthful beatniks," and so on. F. Scott Fitzgerald's picture of Princeton before and after the First World War has come to epitomize one of the earliest American youth cultures, that of "flaming youth." In our own day, we have more various and contrasting versions, ranging to the black-jacketed delinquent to the oversensitive Catcher in the Rye, from the misunderstood James Dean to the fun-and-football fraternity man. A few of these sub-cultures are clearly alienated, like the delinquent gang or the youthful beat world; and if we are not to prejudge the issues of the tie of youth cultures with alienation, we must consider the other, more socially acceptable versions. Writing of these more than twenty years ago, Talcott Parsons suggested that they shared an emphasis on physical attractiveness, irresponsibility, lack of interest in adult things, and interest in athletics; but to this list we must now add further characteristics.

Let us take, then, as the most articulate form of the youth culture, the relatively unalienated group from which our alienated students were drawn, and attempt to characterize some of their dominant views and outlooks. And let us concentrate on those of their views which seem especially distinctive to this age group. This composite portrait, then, will be one of "elite youth," of those who have the ability to "fit in," of those whom society has fully embraced, of those from whom tomorrow's leaders will likely be drawn.

Few of these young men and women have any doubt that they will one day be part of our society. They do not actively or enthusiastically *choose* to be part; rather they unreflectively assume that they *will* be part; and problems of "choosing" conventional adulthood, so central to the alienated, rarely even occur to them as such. They wonder about where they will fit, but not about whether. They take it for granted that they will one day "settle down"; and if it troubles them, they push it out of their minds or consider it a problem to be solved by finding a suitable wife and career. By and large they "approve" of American society if asked, though normally they do not think in these terms. Society is simply there.

But at the same time, these young men and women often show a lack of deep commitment to adult values and roles. They are not alienated as are beatniks, delinquents or our group of alienated students. Rather, they view the adult world they expect to enter with a subtle distrust, a lack of high expectations, hopes, or dreams, and an often unstated feeling that they will have to "settle" for less than they would hope for if they let themselves hope. A surprising number, despite their efforts to get good grades so that they can get into good graduate schools and eventually have good careers, despite their manifest desire to do well in the existing social order, nonetheless view it, in Paul Goodman's phrase, as "an

apparently closed room with a rat race going on in the middle."
Whether they call it a rat race or not is immaterial (though many
half-jokingly do); the point is that they expect little in the way of
personal fulfillment, growth, or creativity from their future roles in
the public world. Essentially, they recognize that adulthood is a
relatively cold, demanding, specialized, and abstracted world where
"meaningful" work is so scarce they do not even ask for it. Thus,
the majority stay "cool" when it comes to the "real world"; and
"coolness" means above all detachment, lack of emotion, absence
of deep commitment, not being either enthusiastic *or* rejecting of
adulthood.

Toward their parents, who are psychologically the most crucial
exemplars of adulthood, most students show a similar lack of conscious or articulate involvement. They are neither ardently devoted
nor explicitly rebellious. Indeed, many a youth is so distant from
his parents, in generational terms if not in affection, that he can
afford to "understand" them and show a touching sympathy for
their tentative efforts to guide and advise him. His parents, too, usually sense their distance, fear that they are "dated" or "square,"
and become reluctant to interfere by imposing their own values and
styles of life where they might be inappropriate. The result is
frequently an unstated gentleman's agreement between the generations that neither will interfere with the other. To be sure,
beneath this agreement, most students are deeply and usually unconsciously involved in relinquishing their ties of personal dependency on their parents; and many of the 10 to 20 per cent of students who avail themselves of psychiatric help when it is available
are concerned with this problem. But dependency is not commitment; dependency *on* parents is often the greatest problem where
commitment *to* what they stand for is impossible.

Most youths approach the wider world, social problems, political events, and international affairs with a comparable lack of deep
involvement. There are notable exceptions in the civil rights movement, as among other student activists, but they are very few in
number. The vast majority are well informed and uninvolved. Ulti-

mately, most students feel a strong underlying sense of social powerlessness which dictates this lack of involvement. Few believe that
society could, must less should, be radically transformed; most
consider the world complex far beyond their power to comprehend
or influence it; and almost all see the stage of history and social
change as inhabited by vast impersonal forces which are quite
beyond human control. The more sophisticated are sometimes
drawn to Toynbeean or Spenglerian theories of the rise and fall of
civilizations; the less sophisticated subscribe to theories of "the
market"; and almost no one thinks that he, even in concert with his
fellows, could alter the irrevocable course of events by so much as
an iota.

The adult world, then, as seen from within the youth culture,
inspires neither enthusiasm nor deep commitment. Most youths expect to be of it, but not for it or "with it." In fact, most do not
expect very much at all of adulthood: they think about it rarely and
ask little of it. Instead, their dominant focus is on the present, on the
years of the youth culture itself, on high school or college life and
on the pleasures to be derived therein. To be sure, many take
courses whose goal is ultimately vocational: to become an engineer,
a teacher, or a doctor; but most spend little time (as little as possible) thinking about what a career will involve. Instead they live
within the present, for the present; the future will take care of itself.

Until that happens, the youth culture provides a distinctive and
separate world, many of whose central themes are familiar from
our survey of the motifs of alienation. One such theme is an emphasis on the present, on experience. In its most extreme form, this
is the intense and obsessive alienated search for sentience; beatniks
characteristically define experience as "kicks"—speed, sex, and
stimulation. But most college students seek milder forms of experience: good times, girl friends, fun with the gang, the exploration of
nature, happy days in summer, even art, music, and poetry. The
American myth of "carefree college days" is dominated by an
eternal present where things are done "just for the fun of it." For
some students, the present means a bull session with the gang or a

shopping expedition with the girls; for others, it means an opportunity to experiment, to make tentative commitments, to try on roles or selves with the option of returning them if they do not fit. The disappearance of the Protestant ethic among college students has entailed the demise of the concept of a "life work"; in place of yesterday's Horatio Algers are today's more easy-going, relaxed young men and women who are learning how to enjoy themselves.

Yet this cult of the present has a hidden rationale, the search for identity. Consciously, this search is usually defined as a question about "what to do with my life," that is, about careers and vocations. But less consciously the cult of the present, the freedom of the youth culture to experiment, and its authorization from adult society to postpone binding commitments—all allow young men and women time to confront the difficult freedoms, choices, and selections their society demands of them. Adolescence in America is considered a place for legitimate "role-playing," for testing alternatives, for provisional commitments followed by a loss of interest, for overwhelming enthusiasm followed by total apathy. In a few students, especially at the most demanding colleges, problems of choice and commitment may reach full consciousness; and there, many a graduating senior on the eve of graduation wonders "Who am I?" in a cosmic as well as a vocational sense. And at a few "elite" colleges, "I'm having an identity crisis," becomes the proud self-justification of any self-conscious youth. Though it can be exploited and caricatured, resolving this "identity crisis" is indeed a central function of the youth culture as a whole, which allows what Erik Erikson calls "a psychosocial moratorium" on adult commitments, and gives time and room for role-playing and experimentation.

The very discontinuity of the youth culture with the demands of adult society allows youth a "breathing space" between childhood and adulthood, time to try to resolve the developmental discontinuities between these two stages of life, and, above all, space to try to achieve some sense of inner unity, self-sameness, and continuity that promises to endure despite continual social change, to cohere despite the dissociative demands of our society. By providing a waiting room before adulthood, the youth culture offers a protected space in which to do the psychological work which adulthood presupposes. Most of this work is done unconsciously and quietly, "acted out" on the stage of college activities, summer jobs, going steady, and a continuing reassessment of one's links to the personal past. The youth culture permits experimentation in the service of unconscious choice, exposure to experience for the sake of selection, and trial commitment in the interest of future self-definition. Acute self-fragmentation, the alternative to success in these pursuits, only rarely occurs. But the problem of identity is there for all.

Much of this unconscious work ultimately involves redefining one's relationship to one's parents, to childhood, and to the childhood self. Those who founder often do so because the backward pulls of childhood are too strong. Like the alienated, they unconsciously find the fantasy of childhood embeddedness more compelling than the "cold adult world." Given the pull of childhood dependencies, alienation is but one possibility; others are so normal that we scarcely note them at all—the almost inevitable homesickness of freshmen, a tendency to alternate between nostalgic idealization of one's parents and acute embarrassment at their limitations, a readiness to plunge into some substitute and often premature intimacy with a girl, a reactive assertion of independence, masculinity, toughness, and autonomy from parents. College students are normally prone to become excessively dependent upon advisers, counselors, and even upon psychotherapists, who at best duplicate the role of the "good mother" by exploiting their patients' involvement with them in order to promote their eventual disengagement. The underlying fantasy of fusion often finds partial expression in fusion with some college group—a fraternity, a "crowd," a set of dorm mates, a sorority—all of which can inspire almost mystical feelings of solidarity, self-sacrifice, and devotion despite their actually limited goals and even meretricious values. At some colleges, this adolescent potential for self-

surrender is channeled into "college spirit," which can bring un-
ashamed tears to the eyes of a football player who would die rather
than weep for his mother. The dependency and need for embeddedness fostered by our small intimate families must somehow be
dislocated from mother, family, and childhood until it can be refo-
cused on the second true love of one's life. The youth culture
abets this rechanneling.

Though the youth culture permits narrowly defined forms of solidarity and surrender to a group, it enjoins against overt idealism,
especially in any Utopian cause. It is normal to be loyal to college and fraternity, but not to an ideology. Even those who hanker
after political careers rarely admit ideological commitment. To remain "popular" and "normal," they must avow a healthy cynicism,
professing politics a "job like any other" and disavowing any intent
to "change the world." Whatever one's real purposes (and these
often are idealistic), the youth culture requires that one not admit to
noble motives. Thus, young men and women who devotedly trudge
each week to dismal mental hospitals to work with and sometimes
save "hopeless" chronic patients will more often say that they
"want the experience" or are "testing themselves" than they will
confess to a genuine desire to help or serve. And a youth who joins
the Peace Corps will often find it easier to term his decision a way
of "solving his identity crisis" than to admit his Utopian hopes and
goals. Idealistic motives and Utopian aspirations extend out of the
youth culture into the wider society, and thus fall under the injunc-
tion to "coolness." Furthermore, because their childhoods often
leave them so full of deep and sentimental nostalgias, American
young men are fearful of all that might appear sentimental. Since
once, in the distant and repressed past, it was so good to be cared
for and enfolded, young Americans (and especially young men)
are anxiously fearful of seeming "suckers," of being "taken in," of
being embraced by any embracing cause.

Yet beneath this apparent cynicism there usually lies a deeper
search for commitments of ultimate worth and value. When something like the Peace Corps comes along, a surprising number, disa-

vowing idealism, are willing to join this idealistic cause. Philosophical or religious inquiry offers an avenue to commitment for a few; and others turn to the study of psychology, which seems to promise the "discovery" of positive values within the psyche. The arts, drama, poetry, music—all of which are undergoing a revival on better college campuses—also offer solace, if not purpose. And above all in the civil rights movement an increasing, though still small, number of students (most of whom are not ideologically alienated) can find a creative channel for their idealism. The struggle for equality for Negro Americans, like the Peace Corps, offers a vehicle for the expression of idealism without ideology, a simple moral commitment to work for the welfare of one's fellow men.

But for the great majority, commitment is sought and found in individual private experience—in leisure, in comradeship, in sports, in a girl. All of these commitments, which David Riesman calls "privatism," involve turning away from the wider social and public world toward the more manageable domain of personal life. Whatever dim glimmerings of Utopian spirit are visible in the youth culture can be seen largely as diffused through these privatistic pursuits. The Utopian quest, the search for positive values so clearly seen in the alienated, is here muted into the precursor of the ethic of family and fun in adulthood.

Yet we should recall that permission is granted to remain in the youth culture only so long as academic requirements are met. Those who quit, drop out, or are failed out, either enter adulthood forthwith or must enter upon serious delinquency or the "beat" world. The power of exclusion is a powerful sanction, and it is one reason Americans often prefer education to the "real world" for so many years. By indirectly encouraging prolonged education, this requirement also promotes the high-level ego training of precisely the kind our society requires: higher education is especially designed to inculcate and develop the specialized cognitive skills needed for success in American society. The price of admission and permission to stay in the youth culture is steadily rising academic performance: the most talented and hard-working can therefore stay the longest. The liberal arts colleges usually attended by such eager and able students explicitly disavow any intent at providing vocational training. They explicitly aim at training the mind, at developing powers of analysis, criticism, selection, and organization, at encouraging independent work and study—in short, at developing and defining ego skills that will be useful no matter what the job and even if its requirements change. The freedom of the youth culture is purchased at the price of the continuing acquisition of the ability to meet our society's ego demands.

The elite youth culture I have characterized is thus closely related to the major themes of alienation and to the central demands of American society. This group of talented young Americans, most of whom are not alienated, nonetheless show in their youth culture comparable themes to those found among the alienated: a preoccupation with the present, a concern with the search for identity, many symptoms of continuing problems of dependency, a quest for positive values which aborts in private commitment, and a preoccupation with the ego demands of our technological society. There are enormous differences between a college booster and an Inburn; but they have their underlying similarities as well.

More important, however, than any similarities between the themes of alienation and the motifs of the youth culture is the fact that the youth culture as a whole *requires* a refusal of conventional adulthood for the time one is in it. Its values are discontinuous with those of adulthood: it is not a simple transition or apprenticeship between the child and the man. In one sense, then, we normally *expect* its members to be alienated: not to undertake irrevocable adult commitments, to experiment and experience, to live in the present, to be irresponsible and carefree, to value and create color and excitement, to be physically daring and sexually attractive. All of these qualities are secondary, subordinated, or actively discouraged in adult society. Furthermore, youth culture and adulthood are defined as irreconcilable: any youth who is prepared to make an immediate commitment to adulthood *must* leave the youth culture, *must* stop his education, and *must* enter the world of grownups.

The youth culture therefore permits American youth as a whole to be "institutionally" alienated without having to be personally alienated. It provides a socially supported period when the average young man or woman simply finds it imposible to enter the adult world. It therefore points to the unreadiness, psychological and ideological, of most young Americans to accept adult commitments and to meet the difficult ego demands of our society. By "taking off the pressure" for a period ranging from five to fifteen years, the youth culture permits most youths to remain uninvolved in the adult world without having to take an open stand against it. By sanctioning and even requiring *de facto* alienation, it removes the need in most youths for a more focused and articulated alienation from adulthood. And it takes the pressure off longest for those on whom adult pressures will eventually be greatest: the highly educated, of whom most will be later required.

The relation of youth culture and alienation is therefore paradoxical. Youth is defined in America as a stage of systematic disengagement from conventional adulthood; the values of the youth culture involve a lack of any deep commitment to adult society, parents, and the adult world. But at the same time the socially supported alienation of the youth culture acts to absolve most young men and women of any need for personally repudiating conventional adulthood: their membership in the youth culture does it for them. During this long moratorium on adulthood, young Americans must undertake a series of major psychological transitions: they must attempt to abandon childhood identifications and commitments for the more selective and partial identifications of adulthood and for commitments that promise to weather the ravages of chronic social change. They must make the many choices our society demands and integrate them into one coherent sense of self. Perhaps most difficult psychologically, they must gradually renounce their ties of dependency on their first families and free themselves to form new ties to adult social groups and their own families. Somehow, usually without much conscious thought, they must find where they stand ideologically—*what* if anything they stand for, *how much* they will stand for, and *where* they stand. And simultaneously, they must develop to the limit of their ability and patience their capacity to meet the stringent demands of our society.

All of this means that most American youths have a double orientation to adulthood. On the one hand, they see themselves as free and feckless participants in the youth culture, by virtue of that fact committed (for the time being) to non-adult values and distrustful of the adult world. On the other hand, most take for granted that they will one day enter adulthood and see themselves as preparing themselves for it. Many of the controversies over the real nature of American youth—over whether it is irresponsible and hedonistic or sober and dedicated—stem from this double orientation. Some observers see one face of youth, and other observers the other; and both observers often mistake the part for the whole.

Such oversimplification is especially hard to avoid because young people themselves present now one and now another face, all the while maintaining there is no more than meets the eye. Not that they deliberately deceive older people as to what they are like—on the contrary, when a young man or woman is with representatives of the adult world (teachers, ministers, admissions officers, poll takers) he not only acts like a future citizen of America, he really *feels* that way. And the same youth under other circumstances—when with friends, at Daytona Beach or Newport, in campus coffee houses, fraternities, sororities, or dormitories—really *feels* like a hood, a beatnik, a college Joe or a Deke. But in each of these stances some of the same ambivalence exists, despite the frequent insistence of the young (with a characteristic adolescent combination of ambivalence and intolerance for ambivalence) that there is only one side of the coin.

Compared to the extreme group we have studied, then, their classmates are "alienated" as members of the youth culture but rarely as individuals. Our society evokes scant enthusiasm in them; but

since it need not be actively confronted, it evokes little overt or articulate rejection. In many ways, the alienated are alienated because they have not been able to *use* the youth culture to escape the
pressures of adult society. For them, there *is* no moratorium on the
demands of adulthood; these demands continually push at them,
epitomized by parents, teachers, and images of the "cold adult
world." Paradoxically, though they vociferously reject conventional adulthood, the very act of rejection also makes them more
continually concerned with it than are their less alienated fellows.

## The little alienations of the well-adjusted

But even if youth culture involves a rejection of adult standards,
an enforced refusal of adulthood, is this not only a "phase"? And
will not even the alienated youths to whom we have devoted so
much attention eventually "settle down" to a normal American
life? Enough time has elapsed since these youths left college to
answer the second question negatively. Some of the alienated have
opted for the chancy life of an artist, and are deliberately headed
for an alienated sub-culture which will permit them to retain their
alienated views. Others have chosen to become teachers, and for the
time being have tried to conform to the requirements of a Ph.D.
program. But as graduate students, they, too, retain their alienated
ideology, have often married girls who share (or at least tolerate)
this ideology, and continue to view their subject matters, departments, and universities with the cynicism and distrust characteristic of the alienated. And finally, although one or two appear to
be headed for more "conventional" careers, their deep alienation
continues in an articulate view of their career as a rat race, a consciously calculated attitude toward adult "role-playing," and a profound cynicism about the professed purposes of conventional American life. Though the passage of years has begun to force these
alienated students to play out their alienation on new stages, their
basic stance toward American culture has changed but little.

We obviously cannot simply generalize from these alienated youths, and must consider separately the vast majority from whom they differ. Do *these* not eventually approach their adulthood with greater enthusiasm? And is not the youth culture by definition a transitional phase whose chief function is to prepare the young so that they *can* commit themselves to adulthood? In short, does not our society inspire about as much enthusiasm from its "typical" and "well-adjusted," members as any society could be expected to inspire?

To answer this question fairly, we must obviously exclude from consideration these alienated students and others like them, who are not "well adjusted." And we must also not look at the millions of Americans who are hospitalized and unhospitalized psychotics, nor at our large criminal class, nor at the millions of Americans who live in misanthropic isolation from society. Moreover, we should not count the one-tenth of the population that is Negro, and whose enforced alienation is daily shifting to more revolutionary forms. And we must of course exclude the traditionally alienated artists, the Bohemians, and the intellectuals. We should also not consider various other groups like Puerto Ricans, Mexicans, migrant workers, and others who have little commitment to the miserable adulthood our society offers them. And there are others like the cynical huckster, the role-playing executive and the disaffected accounts manager who are explicitly uncommitted to their lives. And finally we must exclude those whom Michael Harrington calls "the other Americans," the one-fifth of the nation who live in poverty despite surrounding affluence and who hardly have reason for enthusiasm about what their society offers them. None of these can be considered "well-adjusted Americans."

Of course we have now excluded much of the American population; and the "typical American" becomes typical only of those who are not alienated for one reason or another. To be sure, with the growing exception of Negroes, these Americans form no organized group; the bases for their alienation from American life are extremely diverse; they have little political power; and in most cases they lack the human resources, the leadership, and the ideology to make their alienation felt. But let us accept for now that these Americans are not "typical" and turn to the rest—to the more conventional, "well-adjusted," "successful" men and women, largely of white European parentage and middle-class background, who are not impoverished, who are not intellectuals, artists, or social critics, who are not dissidents and malcontents, who are not calculating or cynical about their lives. These are the Americans who, though they may actually be in a minority, exercise the greatest social and political power, dominate the "image" of America, and have traditionally constituted the "pace-setting" sector of the population about whom most books are written. Surely these white middle-class Americans are not alienated.

Most are not. Many conform willingly to the demands of adulthood and a few are genuinely and deeply committed to our society. Millions of Americans are of course fully convinced that they enjoy life: they tell public opinion pollsters that they are happy (indeed most people think they are happier than most other people), that they enjoy their work (on the whole, the more men earn, the greater their satisfaction), and that they love their wives and children. Nor should we complain too much if we decide that their primary relationship to much of American society is one of conformity rather than "commitment," for deep commitment based on profound understanding and loyalty is probably, in all men, reserved for a few people, a few tasks, a few institutions or causes. Even among college students, whose position in the youth culture prevents present commitment, one occasionally meets young men and women who are genuinely and unequivocally eager to make such commitments, who envision lives that challenge and inspire them, and who will as adults be genuinely committed to their adulthoods. If we ask most Americans, and especially these "typical" ones, what they think about American society, those to whom the question has any meaning at all will usually approve. In all these ways, well-adjusted Americans are not alienated.

But still, I think, well-adjusted American life is shot through with "little alienations," secret refusals, unconscious nostalgias, and half-admitted rejections which belie the unalienated percentages of the pollsters. These little alienations rarely add up to the big alienation of an Inburn; they are rarely expressed in an integrated ideology of refusal, much less in social criticism or reform. On the contrary, they are quiet and often concealed even from those in whose lives they reside. For many well-adjusted Americans, the tasks of the youth culture have not been completed, and they leave youth without a sense of historical connection, without a sense of inner wholeness, without having sufficiently renounced childhood, without having achieved an ideology that tells them where they stand, and without the full willingness and ability to satisfy the ego demands of our society.

These little alienations are rarely visible through the inverted telescope of the public opinion poll, which opens on only the most public vistas of American life. But we can see them if we look not only at what men do but at what they fail to do, listen not only to their statements but to their omissions, consider not just what they ask of life but what they fail to ask. In our current American emphasis on consumption and leisure, for example, we see the consequences of a loss of historical relatedness on the mass scale, visible as well in the growing generational gap, in our shared uncertainty about our personal and collective future. So, too, many Americans feel inwardly fragmented and homeless as they live their daily lives, and our society makes personal integration difficult to achieve even for those who outwardly prosper. The deep needs for embeddedness cultivated by American families are hard for most Americans to renounce, and we all, when confronted with the impersonal, specialized, and demanding adult world we inhabit, feel some small desire to go home again to childhood. Moreover, the prevalence of debunking ideologies and counter-Utopian myths in our intellectual ethos makes it hard for anyone to find positive values, and results in a diffusion of purpose in our personal lives and in our society as a whole. And finally, even the most talented in

our society are pushed to what I have called "peak ego performance," are expected to live a public life dominated by ego functions and controls, and thus find it hard to have world enough or
time for play, dreams, fantasy, zest, sadness, or even sometimes
love.

None of this is the same as alienation. This little alienation of
the man who hates his job, or of his work-mate who likes it only
because it earns him a good living, is not the ideological alienation
of Inburn. The bored housewife who must live her entire life
through her children does not reject the adulthood she lives. Nor
does the car-salesman or insurance adjuster who wonders of a
sleepless night what he lives for (but forgets the question unanswered in the morning) reject the dominant roles, values, and institutions of his society. The devoted father and husband who ignores the wider world for his family does so not because he despises
the American way of life but because, as a part of it, he feels helpless to grasp or influence the public world. Most Americans raise
few ultimate questions about our society. Yet beneath apparent
commitment and conformity, public enthusiasm is at best halfhearted.

Americans revere children and childhood for many reasons, not
least because the young are the hope of parents the world over. But
beneath the special American heightening of this universal hope
there lies a deep if seldom voiced belief that children have the best
of it, that childhood has qualities and joys for whose loss adulthood
never really compensates. We love our children so well because in
part we loved our lives as children best. Whatever the miseries of
childhood in individual lives (and they are many), we view it in the
image of happy irresponsibility, carefree play, and a ready shoulder
to cry on. Perhaps we sacrifice so readily for children because by
living on in them we hope we can spare them, our new selves, the
adulthood we ourselves must live.

But of all the ages we most revere, youth is the foremost. We are
a society that adds to its youth culture a cult of youth. No doubt,
the capacities of youth for rapid growth and change again partly

inspire our respect. But elsewhere, and even in our own American past, youth was largely laughable in its awkward imitation of adult things. What makes the modern difference in America is the inevitable incompleteness of our own adolescence. Psychologists have shown that we remember best the tasks we fail to finish. The tasks of youth in our own society are so overwhelming that most of us leave our adolescences with a vague sense of not being ready, of not having done, of having failed to finish some one or all of the crucial tasks of adolescence. As a consequence, we do not merely look back on our own youths fondly, as we would if youth were only a time of a job well done. Instead we weep for our lost youths, fear the gathering years that separate us from them, seek to preserve a "youthfulness" of outlook and visage which will belie these years, and warn our young against wasting their youths. Youth is not only a time of hedonism and irresponsibility which contrasts with adult cares and worries, but a stage we were not (and are still not) ready to abandon. Because we so often could not finish what we had to do, we view our own youths with an implicit "if only"— if only we had known then . . . , if only we had had time . . . , if only this instead of that. . . . The weeping of old grads at football games is both a mourning for what they had then but have lost, and a mourning for what they might have been but never became.

The idealization and mourning of childhood and youth, which is most common among the white, competent, "well-adjusted" middle-class, suggests that the typical quality of commitment to adulthood in America is at best halfhearted, that (at the very least) enthusiasm is scant, and that something more is involved than the simple fact that in no society do most men and women have a commitment to their adulthoods that is both deep and articulate. Our attitudes toward childhood and youth suggest that our commitment to our adulthood is not only shallow and inarticulate, but, at the deepest level, that it often gives way to a sense of historical loss, of developmental estrangement, of existential uprootedness, and of alienation.

A careful reading of much current American fiction yields a similar conclusion. To be sure, the writer in a technological society is likely to be an alienated man; and the artistic ambitions of many alienated students should make us hesitate before deeming the artist a representative of his time. Nevertheless, he has traditionally been a portraitist of the deepest trends of his time; and if this is so, these trends in our time can only be called alienated. Portraits of "typical" Americans are almost without exception pictures of men and women who are historically dislocated, inwardly fragmented, nostalgic, and ideologically confused. Most of the picaresque heroes of modern American fiction, though far from "typical" Americans, are figuratively and often literally "strangers in a foreign city," uprooted, homeless, scorned by and/or scornful of their society, searching for some other truth though seldom finding it. They are "invisible" Negroes, dislocated Southerners in a stagnant culture, uprooted Jews, or just plain Americans whose lives are suddenly revealed to be empty, pointless, and sterile. And though such novels may ultimately try to affirm some faith in man's capacity for self-renewal, they rarely suggest that our society supports this capacity. Our best writers are alienated men writing about alienated heroes in an alienating society.

If all this be true, the myth of the contented, committed, well-adjusted American must be reassessed. First we must recall that such "typical" Americans probably constitute something less than a majority of our nation. And second, we must recall that discontent and lack of human fulfillment is expressed in social protest, programmatic alienation, or rebellion with a cause only under special conditions which do not obtain in modern America. The "little alienations" of the well-adjusted never amount to a rejection of our society: the well-adjusted man makes the best of his life because it does not occur to him to articulate anything better. He resists grand ideologies and would usually deny the social sources of his own discontents. And in some ways he is genuinely happy—perhaps with his wife, his children, on his vacations, or in his spare time.

But his little alienations often add up to a vague sense of dislocation, fragmentation, loss, uprootedness, of simple exhaustion, which witnesses the human toll of our technological society.

## The merits and dangers of alienation

This book has been largely devoted to trying to understand alienation, to tracing its roots in personal life and social history, to studying the connection between youth and alienation, and to assessing the relevance of the ideological alienation of a group of atypical students to the other forms of alienation in our society. I have made many a judgment, implicit and explicit, about American society, suggesting that alienation is one attempted solution to very real problems in our shared existence and arguing, in essence, the alienated have good reasons for being alienated. But I have so far not considered the merits and dangers of alienation itself, considered both as a personality style and as a social phenomenon. Put simply, is alienation good or bad?

The most common answer in American society would be "bad." Those individuals who are alienated, it would usually be said— the revolutionaries, criminals, psychotics, apathetics, and the ideologically alienated—are misfits, rejects, and malcontents, and their presence is to be deplored: they are wrong and society is right; they need punishment or perhaps treatment. I need not repeat in detail why I think this answer is oversimplified. I have already argued that even the alienation of social misfits points to the human cost of our society and to its real problems; and the alienation of outsiders like the youths from whom we began equally points to values and strivings that cannot be realized within American society and thus once again to its real problems. It cannot simply be said that society is right and the alienated wrong; alienation may point more to a society that needs "treatment" than to an individual in need of therapy.

Another negative judgment of alienation involves more complex reasoning. We might indeed recognize the roots of alienation in both personal deviance and social history, stressing the real social, cultural and ideological problems to which alienation is in part a reaction. We might sympathize with and understand alienated individuals, and still argue that alienation was bad because it was a product of an alienating society. A good society, the argument would run, would neither require compulsive conformity nor produce alienation: it would merely inspire commitment. Alienation would thus be bad insofar as it points to remediable defects in society: in a good society, everyone would be genuinely committed. It is important to underline this last assumption: that a society is conceivable and desirable in which no one was excluded and no one was alienated.

If my argument so far is correct, however, this assumption is wrong. I have maintained that all societies make demands on their members, defining social virtues to coincide with these social demands and shaping the young so that as adults they can comply with what society asks. Furthermore, I have maintained that in every functioning social order there is always a "social myth," a set of interpretations of reality, experience, and virtue which may be more or less adequate to social or human needs. Out of the vast range of human potentials, the myth selects certain potentials as primary and others as unimportant, certain aspects of experience as most real, certain human qualities as most virtuous. Every community therefore stresses some demands at the expense of others, making especially heavy demands in some areas, pushing men hardest there. Given the vast variability of inborn constitution, the inevitable vagaries of child-rearing, and the accidents of life, every society will inevitably produce some men and women who are misfits or malcontents. The vision of a totally committed society is therefore an illusion.

In the absence of such a perfect society, the total disappearance of alienation would inevitably entail stagnation. No existing social order and no conceivable one is without its remediable inconsistencies, its needless stresses, its excessive demands. Furthermore, it will presumably continue to be true that every social gain, however major, entails a loss of the virtues of the past and a creation of a new set of problems for the future. Total commitment to any society therefore means a commitment to remediable evil. Without at least some men and women sufficiently alienated to challenge the established order, to decry its assumptions, to suggest remedies for its faults, and to agitate their less alienated fellows into sufficient dissatisfaction, no social innovation is possible. From a social point of view, the cultivation of and tolerance for alienation, at least in some individuals, is a prerequisite for any major social improvement.

But just how much alienation, and what kind, is another question. Some forms of alienation are usually destructive to both the individual and his society. The alienation of the common criminal normally leads to no profound social reforms, but merely to a more repressive attitude toward criminals: it is usually as destructive to the society as it is to its agents and victims. Similarly, the suicide, the psychotic, and the apathetic can rarely lead themselves or their fellows to fundamental improvements in their condition: their alienation is again both personally and socially destructive. In general, the unconscious and inarticulate forms of alienation, wherein rejection of society is indirectly expressed through behavioral deviance or personal maladaptation, usually involve little individual fulfillment and less social improvement.

The more articulate forms of alienation hold a different promise. Among the outspoken, the outsiders rather than the rejects are concentrated: their refusal of their society is more likely based on principled convictions. They are most apt to have a shape of their own rather than no shape, and they are consequently best able to criticize effectively and innovate constructively. But even among outsiders, some are more effective socially and more complete personally than others. Social effectiveness requires that personal alienation be coupled with social impact: that the outsider be able to communicate his discontented vision of his society and—if he is to initiate improvement—to articulate the principles from which he rejects and the changes to which he aspires. For the individual, an explicit alienation can at times lead to a greater involvement with the public world—to an "alienated commitment" to be ultimately *for* one's society even if one is not *with* it.

But in the youths we have studied, and, I think, in most Americans, alienation usually takes private and self-insulating forms. It is coupled with a scorn for politics, a feeling of social powerlessness, with withdrawal in the face of the complexity of the modern world. The quests of most alienated Americans are private quests—for personal sentience, for intensified subjectivity, for kicks and stimulation, for individual artistic expression—and the alienated express themselves more to achieve self-definition than to persuade others. Thus, few "politically active" students are alienated in this sense; and a youth like Inburn is not likely to join, much less lead, any movement for reform in society. For him, as for most young Americans, there are too many obstacles: distrust of explicit political ideology, absence of any vision of the future which might animate commitment. To be sure, there are exceptions to this rule in those youths who are committed to the attainment of civil rights, in an even smaller number dedicated to peace, and in those who can still find commitment in the developing nations. Yet the focus of these "political" activities is very narrow—either abroad or on single issues which lack (at least to those involved) the apparent moral complexity of other equally pressing social and political problems. And the numbers involved are very small.

As for the "private" alienations of the rest, we cannot simply dismiss them as without value. From such alienations as these can spring poetry, painting, art, and the highest achievement of culture. It may be that some, at least, of the privately alienated can find in their alienation a freedom from social pressure which will enable them to follow their own stars and ultimately achieve greater fulfillment than is granted most Americans. But private alienation has its dangers, both personal and social. If the most talented of those who reject our society merely withdraw cursing and devote them-

selves to personal endeavors, the most contructive potential for social improvement is thereby lost. Society is left to the alienated
without talent—to the rejects—and to the committed and the conformists. "Inner emigration" becomes the solution for the potential
social critic. He goes underground to Madison Avenue where his
novel is never written; he emigrates from the main streams to the
backwaters of a dairy farm in Vermont, where he is only an embittered eccentric; his potential for infectious and innovating indignation becomes mere grumbling; and his Utopian spirit is deflected
onto his family or reversed to cynicism. If our society were free of
problems, if it were the best society we could imagine, if we could
envisage no ways in which it could better promote men's fulfillment
—then private alienations would be good. But private alienations
are a luxury that only Utopia can afford.

Moreover, such alienations can rarely lead to personal fulfillment in a grossly imperfect society. To try to ignore the social and
political facts of the day is motivatedly to deny a reality which will
affect one nonetheless. To say of an atomic war, "Whatever happens will not affect my thinking" is to be closed to experience and
the world and to deny even the alienated principles of responsiveness and sentience. To try to escape the fate and fortune of one's
fellows—whether in America or abroad—is possible in the second
half of the twentieth century only via the total withdrawal of the
psychotic. A refusal to recognize one's inevitable involvement with
social and political reality can rarely be considered a mark of the
fullness of human development.

Since they can define no coherent stance on society beyond refusal, the alienated are compelled to fight on every battlefield at
once, and therefore to fight effectively on no front. To be sure, to
expect from college students effective and original social criticism,
much less decisive action to reform their societies, would be unrealistic; and the mere fact that these students' reasons for their rejections are not original proves nothing about their ultimate efficacy in
improving their society. More telling, however, is the alienated style
of life, in which non-commitment and blanket repudiation predom-

inate. These students on the whole wax more indignant at the stuffiness of Boston ladies than at the condition of the poor; confronted with atomic annihilation, they idealize the jellyfish or the tree; they scatter their fire in broadsides so indiscriminate that none of their targets are damaged. Perhaps some may come to a more selective and principled rejection coupled with affirmation of alternatives; but many will be prevented from both selectivity and affirmation by the diffuseness of their inner angers and the anti-Utopian spirit of the times.

And finally, considered not as a social phenomenon but as an individual way of life, their alienation leads these youths to little sense of personal fulfillment. To be sure, we may agree with them that happiness is in itself hardly a noble goal, and we may even agree that any man of integrity, personal wholeness, and principle is likely to find himself at odds with much of American society. But at the same time, some sense of personal fulfillment should ideally be a by-product of a valid way of life; and some men have found deep satisfaction in their principled opposition to the basic trends of their society. Though ultimately it may be American society that creates the unhappiness and self-doubt of its dissidents by giving them no honored place, some individuals have been able to deny their society's judgments of them. And though the unhappiness, inner fragmentation, and self-contempt of the alienated is partly founded on the wider society's adverse judgment, the particular sub-society they inhabited—their college—usually tolerated and even supported their views. Thus, the sources of their personal unhappiness lie partly in characterological necessity: in their distrust of *all* commitments, even those which might be benign and facilitating, in their ambivalent search for *total* freedom and individuality, in their *complete* refusal of the conventional categories of experience, in their view that their *entire* cultural inheritance is a burden. Such total repudiations lead almost inevitably to personal frustration.

I mean none of this to deny these youths the right of private alienation, nor to deny that society can indirectly profit from the cultural achievements to which such alienation can lead. But I am suggesting that there are good reasons why, apart from the wider society's lack of support, these young men feel so fragmented and unfulfilled; and that these reasons are closely tied to the "totalism" of their rejections, to the unselectiveness of their refusals, and to their inability to articulate the bases for their alienation and the shapes of their preferences. And more important, I am arguing that a society that, like ours, systematically pushes its alienated toward private withdrawal thereby deprives itself of its own potential for self-renewal.

The alternative, clearly, is an alienation that is articulate and "public," in which selective refusal of one's existing society goes hand in hand with affirmation of a better one, in which rejection is principled and in the interests of reform and revolution. The virtues of revolution are currently much neglected in America, despite our revolutionary start as a nation. The only revolutions we now condone are the impersonal revolutions of technology—communications, synthetics, weapons—for here the agent is not human will. Where human will and deliberate planning are involved, we invoke the specter of the reactionary ends to which revolutionary slogans have sometimes come, and deny our interest, equating revolution with terror. Yet if by revolutionary alienation we mean merely alienation that might propose fundamental and far-reaching changes in our thinking and social organization—alienation that is radical in that it goes to the root of social problems and tries to correct them at the root when necessary—then it is hard to oppose revolution in principle. We might disagree with this or that revolutionary proposal by considering it unwise or inadequate; we might decry this or that "radical" analysis because it is not radical enough or merely wrong; but the desirability of radical or revolutionary alienation can hardly be opposed in itself.

What is missing in the alienation of the youths we have studied, as in the little or big alienations of most other Americans, is any radical criticism of our society or any revolutionary alternative to the status quo. I have tried to account for this absence by detailing the decline and deflection of the Utopian spirit. But though we may understand it, this absence injures us all. It means that the social sources of our personal discontents remain hidden, that we can only see their reflections in personal pathology. And above all, it means that discontent with our society is rarely transformed into deliberate efforts to imagine a better society and work toward its achievement, but is siphoned off to private grumbling and personal unhappiness.

But finally, neither alienation nor commitment nor conformity can be judged good or bad at all apart from their objects. To be alienated from a tyranny is a high virtue; to be committed to a vicious organization is wrong; to conform to evil is wicked. The merits and dangers of alienation cannot be judged outside the context of our society, our time, and our place. Alienation is chiefly important because it points to its own causes, directs us to what is intolerable, frustrating, and malign in individual life and social process, and suggests what needs to be done. Just as the effort to understand the sources of alienation has led us to the social scenery of our American landscape, so alienation cannot be evaluated apart from American society.

## The human toll of technological society

This book has been directly and indirectly concerned with the human toll of our technological society. I have not stressed its many human and social achievements, partly because they help us little in understanding alienation, partly because we hear all too much about them already, and partly because it seems more useful to try to understand the problems of American society than to celebrate its accomplishments. Another book could be written on the committed and the sources of their commitment. But how we strike a final balance between the human accomplishments and the human toll of our society seems to me to matter little. The historical gains of America—in health, material goods, opportunities for choice, freedom from dogma, in pluralism, political freedom, and in sociability—may well outweigh the problems I have detailed, yet the human toll of our society should still concern us most. In fact, however, I think it concerns us hardly at all: we attend too fully to the technological achievements, values, virtues, and skills of America, and forget the price we pay.

The chief importance of the new alienation in our society is that it suggests this price, though without being able to define it or suggest a remedy. What distinguishes this alienation is its lack of program, purpose or coherent ideology of radical reform and revolution. Though it affects millions of Americans, it remains at the level of grumbling discontent and rarely reaches proposals for needed change. I have tried to go beyond the words of the alienated to the personal and social sources of their rejections, defining the major stresses inherent in our social scenery, characterizing the dominant demands of our collective life, and asking how and why they contribute to alienation. And I have argued that the big alienations of atypical Americans like these alienated students have their counterpart in the little alienations of the appparently well-adjusted.

Through all my comments run several consistent themes, and by way of assessing the human price we pay for our social membership, I will recall these themes. Central to American society is the unquestioned primacy of technology in virtually every area of our collective existence. Technology provides the motor for the continual social change to which we must somehow adapt, and rather than challenge the value of technology we have been willing to lose much of our sense of historical connection. The rationale for the fragmentation of social roles and the shattering of traditional community has been the values of technology: specialization, organization, efficiency, rising role requirements, innovation: by simply accepting these values we risk inner fragmentation and social uprootedness. Our family structure, too, is geared to the needs of a technological society: the roles allocated to men and women within the family, like the techniques we use to bring up children, fit technological requirements, though not necessarily those of full human development. The decline of Utopia and the primacy of instrumental values are both intimately related to the needs of technology for men and women of cognitive and unemotional makeup. And the demand for technological ego dictatorship is a demand for precisely the human qualities that are needed to make a technological society work.

The values, requirements, demands, and virtues of technology are not in themselves bad; but their unquestioned supremacy is a human and social misfortune. Judgments of skill, competence, and effectiveness have replaced usefulness, beauty, and relevance to human needs as criteria of worth; instrumental values have replaced final purposes; and cognitive skills have replaced virtuous character as standards of human value. Nor is the technological process necessarily destructive: it only becomes destructive when men and women serve it, rather than vice versa. The human problems in our society stem not from the fact of technology, but from the supreme place we assign it in our lives. We grant it this place largely because in the recent American past higher productivity *was* a prerequisite to a decent life for our people. But this is no longer true, and. increasingly technology dominates by default—because it is *there,* and countervailing values, goals, and purposes are not. The dominance of technology therefore springs ultimately from the failure of positive values in our society, and from a collective failure of imagination in the West as a whole. To ascribe causal primacy to technology itself—to make economics the motor of society—is a mistake. Equally important is our willingness to *allow* it to be the motor, and this willingness is ultimately a matter of ideology and social myth.

The primacy of technology leads to the dissociation and subordination of all that is not technological, of all that we can call the affective and expressive sides of life. Our society sharply splits the public from the private spheres of life, subordinating the latter. Feeling, family, and fun, leisure and fantasy, idealism and relaxation are split off and relegated to inferior status, deemed necessary only as the price of peak ego performance in public life. We encourage those human potentials in which the technological ego dictates over the rest of personality, and neglect the ego's potential for self-denial and subordination to the whole man.

Put very simply, we allow our society to divide our lives and ourselves into two compartments, one for cognition, work, instrumental values, and ego skills, the other for all the rest of life; and we further insist of ourselves that the first compartment will take consistent precedence over the second. This creates a variety of human problems. The psyche resists compartmentalization: men strive toward integration. To maintain a divided life takes a heavy toll of energy; and even when it succeeds it exhausts us and leads to a sense of inner division. More often the attempt to dissociate fails, and then it conflicts with explicit social demands; the worker is not cool but hotheaded, the parent is not warm but cold. The subordinated, like the repressed, returns; impulse and instinct secretly dominate the ego they are supposed to serve. The dictatorship of the ego can become so tyrannical it allows no respite from its demands: then play, fantasy, refreshing sleep, love, and creativity are stifled beneath control and watchful fearfulness.

Furthermore, the supremacy of technological values means that our society has no honored place for those who do not possess the virtues of its values. Those who fall below the minimal level of ego competence are relegated to the scrap heap of mental hospitals; those who lack cognitive skills fall into the ranks of the unemployed, the indigent, the unwanted, the poverty-stricken. And those who hold in higher esteem other values and virtues become the moralists who thunder or grumble unheard, the "impulsive" who must indulge their impulses beyond the social pale, or the alienated who withdraw from the wider society. All of these men and women are not only alienated from our society, they are actively alienated by it.

What our society lacks, then, is a vision of itself and of man that transcends technology. It exacts a heavy human toll not because technology exists, but because we allow technology to reign. It alienates so many not simply because they do not share its wealth, but because its wealth includes few deeply human purposes. It is a society that too often discourages human wholeness and integrity, too frequently divides men from the best parts of themselves, too rarely provides objects worthy of commitment. In all these ways, it exacts a heavy human toll.

# 14          Beyond technology

History sometimes presents societies with genuine turning points, eras when men are collectively confronted with a real alternative, ages when crucial decisions can be made which will affect the future for many generations to come. At some such forks in the historical road, men take what later generations will judge the wrong turn, or merely stand bewildered before the alternatives which confront them. In other eras, men choose wisely and well, acting from a courage that permits them to move forward, an understanding that enables them to refuse stagnation. Usually, such eras of potential choice are evident in a widespread sense of historical loss, a feeling that existing values and institutions no longer seem adequate, a realization that men live uneasily with values that now seem empty. In such eras, disquiet and uneasiness pervade men's lives, a nameless dissatisfaction and an even more inarticulate sense of hope for change.

Such collective watersheds are often marked by some striking political event—a revolution, a new constitution, a decisive war, a new regime. But just as often, when men can respond to the changed needs of their society before their discontents grow too great, no dramatic event signals the change: only a slow transformation, a quiet change of heart, a subtle alteration of the status quo. For every turning point marked by a violent revolution, there are many others that we perceive only in retrospect as gradual yet decisive transformations. Indeed, violent revolutions are enduring only if they are accompanied by slow and quiet transformations of men's attitudes and aspirations.

In American history there have been turning points of both kinds: some visible and dramatic, like the Civil War, others slow and quiet like the gradual extension of democratic rights in the first half of the nineteenth century. One of the most crucial of these turning points occurred between the Civil War and the First World War, the era when America changed decisively from an agricultural to an industrial nation. Beneath this visible change in the economy, and making it possible, was a deeper transformation of men's aspirations, whose importance we can only now fully appreciate. During this period, for the first time, Americans became convinced that material sufficiency, economic security, a decent living, and even prosperity were within their personal reach. These values, though long embedded in Western society, had heretofore been taken seriously as personal goals only by the wealthy, the extraordinarily ambitious, or the exceptionally lucky. Despite a slowly rising standard of living in the pre-industrial era, and despite the universality of the *dream* of affluence, most men knew it was *only* a dream, and that in reality they were destined to finish their lives as they had begun them—poor. Freedom from material want had been an impractical vision, not a concrete and immediate personal goal. But three or four generations ago, our entire nation began to transform that dream into the practical aspirations of individual Americans. Instead of merely envying the prosperous, the poor began to emulate them. From believing that only a few of any generation were destined for economic security, a whole nation came to believe that prosperity was within the reach of every man who would work and save. Freedom from want, which prior generations believed obtainable only by God's grace in the next world (if then), became a goal to be achieved by human effort in this world.

For the Americans of three generations ago—for Inburn's grandparents—the goals of abundance and prosperity made enormous sense. Poverty was still a daily reality for the vast majority of Americans; and even the prosperous, try as they might, could not completely insulate themselves from the surrounding want. For those who lack it, a decent living, an adequate home, and a good education are high and noble goals to which a whole man can unhesitatingly commit himself. Like many revolutionary visions, the dream of prosperity could be transformed into concrete personal goals only when the times were ready: the growing industrialization of America made possible the fulfillment of these aspirations of affluence, and was in turn spurred on by them. Because of the wealth and energy of this nation, the ideology of plenty proved self-confirming: convinced that history, destiny, and the laws of economics were on their side, Americans proceeded to create a society that confirmed their conviction.

In the past two generations, then, we have moved closer and closer to the millennial goal of prosperity. The vast distance between today's world and the upwardly mobile, striving, competitive, and still impoverished world of Inburn's grandparents has been the theme of much of this book. This distance cannot be quantitatively measured, but it is manifest in the contrast between the poverty of Inburn's grandparents and the relative affluence of his parents today, in the gulf between the bearded patriarch of the Victorian dinner table and the shirt-sleeved father of today's suburban cookout, in the chasm that separates the shopkeeper, milkman, farmer, and immigrant of the turn of the century from his comfortably off, well educated, economically secure (and sometimes alienated) grandson today. Most Americans no longer want for material goods, adequate homes, or educations; starvation is virtually nonexistent; and our most pressing economic problems no longer concern how to produce enough, but rather how to distribute fairly the goods we already have and to live well and nobly with them. The abolition of poverty is within the reach of our society; and for most Americans, the achievement of abundance is a fact and not a distant dream.

With the age-old goal of universal prosperity within sight, we must question whether the methods—the technological values and virtues, the instrumental goals of our affluent society—that helped us approach this goal will serve to take us beyond it. For most of us, the urgency has gone out of the quest for prosperity. The second television set means less than the first, though it may cost more. To struggle to pay a mortgage on a split-level ranch house beyond one's means is somehow less challenging than to struggle to buy a decent home to begin with. The effort to earn enough for one's childrens' ice-skating lessons is somehow less relevant than the struggle to insure them an adequate education. The acquisition of goods, money, gadgets, and commodities becomes increasingly empty; the pursuit of quantity, the cult of competition and comparison, become increasingly empty. The more one possesses, the less meaningful are new possessions.

We are approaching, I believe, a new turning point in American society. Despite our growing affluence, despite the triumphant march of technology, despite the innundation of our society with innovations, something is clearly wrong. All the signs are present: our mid-century malaise, increasingly shrill cries to "rededicate" ourselves to outworn ideologies which can no longer inspire our commitment, a loss in the sense of social power, and all of the attitudes, feelings, and outlooks I have here called the "new alienation." The vision of an affluent society no longer excites us; and so too, we are losing our implicit faith in the ancillary beliefs of technology. In nations where affluence is still a distant dream, the situation is different: in Peru or Nigeria, in Thailand or Samoa, the struggle to attain some small freedom from suffocating poverty is still a compelling struggle. Nor is the achievement of affluence complete even in America: the spate of recent books on the "forgotten fifth" of the nation, on our "invisible poor" eloquently documents the distance we must still travel. Yet these same books, with their appeal for affluence for *all,* indirectly attest to the triumph of technology. Who, a century ago, would have complained that *only* 80 per cent of the people were prosperous? And who would have dared insist that *all* might be well fed, well housed, well educated, and well leisured?

Thus, paradoxically, at the very moment when affluence is within our reach, we have grown discontented, confused, and aimless. The "new alienation" is a symptom and an expression of our current crisis. The individual and social roots of our modern alienation, I have tried to suggest, are complex and interrelated; yet if there is any one crucial factor at the center of this alienation, it is the growing bankruptcy of technological values and visions. If we are to move toward a society that is less alienating, that releases rather than imprisons the energies of the dissident, that is truly worthy of dedication, devotion, idealism, and commitment, we must transcend our outworn visions of technological abundance, seeking new values beyond technology.

## Some deterrents

In the next decades of this century, Americans will be called upon to choose between three fundamentally different options concerning the future course of our society: whether to attempt to turn the clock back so as to "re-create" a bygone society in which our modern alienations did not yet exist, whether to "continue" the present triumphant march of a technological process which has created these same alienations, or whether to begin to define a new vision of a society whose values transcend technology. The first two choices would lead, I believe, to regression or stagnation; only by beginning now to articulate a vision of a society in which technology is used for truly human purposes can we create a nation of individuals, a society, that *merits* the commitment of its citizens. Yet such a redefinition of purpose has not been forthcoming, and social and political thought in America continues to be dominated by those who would have us regress to the past or those who would merely have us continue our present drift. What is it that prevents our imagining a society radically better than and different from our own?

Throughout the preceding pages I have emphasized the inherent hostility of technology to Utopian and visionary thinking. The fundamental assumptions of technology and science are metrical, comparative, analytic, and reductive. Technology concerns itself with instrumental questions and dismisses Utopian visions as impractical or irrelevant. Moreover, the growing pressure for ego dictatorship increasingly subordinates and suppresses the passions and idealisms from which cogent criticisms of our society and radical propositions for its reform might spring. Convinced that all Utopian thinking is impractical and self-defeating, we therefore cling to a technological empiricism that merely perpetuates the status quo. No doubt all established orders and all great ideologies resist fundamental change; but the technological society we live in is unusually well armored against attack, especially well equipped to subvert its critics, peculiarly able to discourage thinking that does not start from technological assumptions.

But beyond this, the very speed with which technology has accomplished its original goals has caught us off guard. The triumph of technology has occurred in an extraordinarily brief span of time: only one century separates our own era from the Civil War, technology triumphant from the beginning of the industrial era. Like a victorious and powerful army whose enemy unexpectedly surrenders, we now find ourselves without clear goals, mobilized for action that is no longer needed, and scarcely aware of the extent of our victory. We have been overtaken by success, surprised by triumph, caught off guard by victory. We have only begun to realize how far we have come, let alone to think of what might lie beyond.

Paradoxically, then, we live in a society in which unprecedented rates of technological change are accompanied by a fundamental unwillingness to look beyond the technological process which spurs this change. Even those who are most concerned over the future course of our society continue to conceive that course in primarily technological terms, emphasizing quantity, comparisons, economic output, and dollars and cents. And the imagination and commitment needed to define a future qualitatively different from the technological present are deflected—even for those most concerned with our social future—by a series of specific fallacies about the social process.

*The fallacy of the psychosocial vise*—A characteristic conviction of many modern men and women is the sense of being trapped in a social, cultural, and historical process they have no power to control. This sense of being inescapably locked in a psychosocial vise is often most paralyzing to precisely those men and women who have the greatest understanding of the complexity of their society, and who therefore might be best able to plan intelligently for its future. And although the sense of being trapped in history is widespread, it often appears to receive particularly cogent justification by social scientists. Recent years have seen a growing understanding of the connections between individual character, social process, cultural configuration, and historical change. Just as psychoanalysis has shown that even the most aberrant behavior "makes psychological sense" and serves definable psychic ends, so sociologists argue that social patterns that seem senseless also make a kind of sociological sense, serving "latent functions" corresponding to the unstated needs of individuals. We now know that the link between how men are raised as children and how they lead their lives as adults is a close one; that small changes in one sector of society can have enormous repercussions in other areas; and that apparently small historical transformations may spread and generalize to transform an entire community.

This awareness that individual, social, cultural, and historical processes are intimately connected is often taken as the basis for social pessimism. Because social institutions have a function, it is assumed this function can never be changed; because individual behavior, even the most irrational, has adaptive value, it is thought that no other behavior could be more adaptive. The fit between individual character and social structure is seen as a perfect fit, and the "gears" which convert historical pressures to psychological responses are seen as having a fixed and invariant ratio.

The result is a deterministic sense of being caught in a psychosocial vise, locked so tightly it cannot be loosened without destroying it altogether. As a consequence, we dare change nothing at all.

In practice, the fallacy of the psychosocial vise can lead either to despair or complacency. Those who despair are usually all too aware of the enormous problems of our age: they despair because they can see no way of changing anything short of changing everything. Those who are complacent take comfort from the fact that (in retrospect) everything that happens in American society in some way "makes sense," can be explained and understood in terms of individual motives and social processes. The most dangerous trends in American society can be explained away as mere "reactions to social strain" which an omniscient sociologist could well have anticipated.

The facts, however, justify neither despair nor complacency. The "fit" between individuals and society, culture and history is never a perfect fit and is not always even a good fit. In this book, for example, I have been chiefly concerned with those who do not fit, who reject what their society demands of them. Moreover I have argued that the closeness of fit between, for example, family structure and social structure does not entail a comparable closeness of fit between family demands and the psychological needs of family members. There is, then, a kind of "slippage in the gears" of psychosocial transmission. Social institutions that now serve one function can later serve another or be replaced altogether; two men with essentially the same potential can end very differently; cultural needs and values that are salient today may become subordinate tomorrow. A "functional view" of social institutions does not require the assumption that comparable functions cannot be assumed by still other and better institutions.

To be sure, all social planning must be undertaken with the greatest possible understanding of its likely consequences. And we are probably in a better position than any previous generation to assess and gauge what these consequences will be. But the obvious fact that changes in one area of society have repercussions in

others need not prevent social action. On the contrary, an understanding of the complexity of society can be an aid to social planning, helping us identify those points and moments of maximum
leverage where small actions can have large consequences. There
is often a kind of social "multiplier effect"; there are virtuous as
well as vicious circles. Far from discouraging social planning and
action, an understanding of psychosocial process can help us guide
and direct it more intelligently.

*The fallacy of romantic regression*—One of the most common
reactions against technological society is to deplore it by invoking
images of a romanticized past as a guidepost for regressive social
change. In future years, as at present, Americans will be increasingly called upon to accept or reject the ideology of romantic regression. This ideology starts from the valid observation that our
post-industrial society has lost intact community, socially given
identity, stable and accepted morality, certainty and a clear collective sense of direction. From this valid observation, the regressive
position attempts to re-establish a simple "organic" community,
longs for Jeffersonian agrarianism, seeks a "new conservatism"
which will "preserve" the values of the nineteenth century, turns to
Fascism with its appeal to blood feeling and the "corporate state,"
or is tempted by the syndicalist vision of re-attaining "genuine" self-
governing communities of workers. All of these outlooks see the
solution to the problems of post-industrial society as some form
of restoration, re-creation, or reconstruction of the simpler, more
intact world that technology has destroyed.

Given a romantic idealization of the past, programs for social
action invariably have regressive aims: to *reduce* the complexity of
the world, be it material or moral; to *limit* the choices and opportunities which now bewilder men; to *inhibit* freedoms to which men
owe their modern anxieties; to *narrow* the alternatives which give
rise to current indecision; to *constrain* those who complicate moral,
social, political, and international life; to *simplify* moral dilemmas
into clear-cut decisions between good and evil. In short, the romantic

seeks to solve the problems of the modern world by regressing to his image of an earlier world where these problems did not exist—be it the New England village, the grit-and-gumption ethic of the nineteenth-century entrepreneur, or even the Polynesian island.

Among social scientists, this ideology often takes the form of an idealization of primitive communities or peasant life. In such static communities, the problems of social change cannot arise; in an undifferentiated society, the problems of a divided life, "not belonging," and being forced to choose do not exist; the family cannot be specialized because it has too much work to do to survive; and ideological crises rarely occur because men and women unthinkingly accept the ideology they were born to.

The image of such a primitive community is, I believe, useful in highlighting the contrasting qualities of our social order. But it is a grave mistake to take primitive society, peasant life, the New England village, medieval life, or the entrepreneurial ethos of the nineteenth century as an adequate model for the future of our own society. On the contrary, few of us would freely choose to inhabit such a world. However romantically appealing the technicolor image of the Polynesian village, the idealized portrait of the "intact" peasant community, or the zest and simplicity of the frontier, harsher realities lie behind these romanticized images: endemic disease, grinding poverty, high infant mortality, lawlessness, and often the absence of the most elementary requirements for subsistence. Nor is the low standard of living in such communities accidental: it results from attitudes to change, to social organization, and to child-rearing that make a prosperous society impossible. And even if we could put up with such material deprivations, few of us could tolerate the oppressive social demands of such communities. Americans today may "conform," but we usually do so from choice; in most primitive societies the issue of conformity cannot arise as such because there *is* no choice. Our society may demand the arduous achievement of individual identity, but peasant communities "solve" this problem simply by allowing the young no options. We may suffer from the pressures of chronic social change, but we would suffer more in a society that persisted in its traditional ways despite evidence that they were destructive. And we may lament the loss of mythic vitality in the twentieth century, but we would lament even more an age where those who challenged the collective myth were outlawed or destroyed.

Moreover, in appealing to the image of the primitive or "intact" community as a guide for social action, we forget the eagerness with which those who dwell in such communities seek to abandon them. The destruction of tribalism, of feudalism, and of "intact community" continues to correspond with the wishes of the vast majority of those who have a choice: in the emerging nations of the world men lust after affluence and technology, not after tribal embeddedness. And even in our own history, the development of political liberalism and representative government, like the growth of technological society, was a response to the felt wishes of those who sought to escape the rigors of previous societies. Those who hark back to the values of their grandparents forget the eagerness with which these same men and women sought to create a "better world" for their grandchildren. We would find even the rigidity, complacency, and intolerance of the recent Victorian era hard to live with; the total absorption of the individual in most "primitive" societies would be even more intolerable.

However instructive the comparison of our own society with "intact" communities may be, today's problems cannot be solved by regressing to that kind of society. The new problems, the new alienations of technological society, require not regression to a romanticized past but new definitions of purpose, new forms of social organization, new goals for personal development. We must not return to the past, but transcend the present.

*The fallacy of unfinished business*—Perhaps the most potent deterrent of all to any fresh thinking about the purposes of our lives and our society is the fallacy of unfinished business—exclusive concentration on the remaining problems of productivity, poverty, education, and inequality as defined by technological values. This fallacy is most dangerous because it affects most those who are genuinely concerned with the problems of our society, critical of its achievements, impatient with the slowness of its "progress." Politically and socially, the only articulate alternative to those who would have us regress to the past is found among those who emphasize the unfinished business of technology, the "incomplete revolutions" which must be completed. From Lyndon Baines Johnson to Paul Goodman, the main thread of "progressive" thinking about American society assumes that our task is to complete our unfinished technological business.

I do not mean to deprecate this position. It is not wrong but inadequate; the evils pointed to are real and urgent. Gross prejudice and inequality are daily realities in much of America; poverty is a grinding and destructive fact to a fifth of the nation; millions do not and cannot get the minimal education necessary for an honored place in American life; it is genuinely alarming that we have not solved the problems of chronic unemployment. Nor will it be politically easy to solve these problems; the programs so far proposed only scratch the surface.

But the adequacy of this view to the problems of our society can be questioned. The "unfinished business" of technological society is, on a historical scale, increasingly vestigial, a "mopping-up operation." Revolutionary causes lose their impact when they have been largely accomplished; men are seldom stirred to arms in a cause already victorious. What is historically most salient is that *only* a fifth of the nation remains, by today's high American standards, poor. What should astound us is that *only* 30 per cent fail today to complete twelve years of education. And even in very recent American history, an unemployment rate of *only* four to six per cent would have been an unprecedented breakthrough to prosperity. Our efforts to relieve these problems should not abate; on the contrary, these efforts are still inadequate. But our technological accomplishments mean that if real "new frontiers" are to be found, they must lie beyond technology; and that if we do not now live in a "Great Society," then expanded Medicare, poverty programs, job-retraining, and anti-dropout campaigns will not suffice to create it.

Moreover, the values and instruments of technology will no longer suffice even to finish a technological society's own unfinished business. Our pursuit of quantity leads us to focus on such numerical indices of national and social success as the gross national product, the growth rate, the percentages of Americans employed, the proportion in high school, the divorce rate, the number of cars, telephones, and washing machines. We rejoice when these indices of success show us "ahead" of the Russians, and worry when our growth rate falls below theirs. But in each area of "unfinished business" in American life, our traditional techniques are inadequate. That traditional panacea, an increase in national output, no longer affects the poor, insulated from the main streams of the economy. More money poured into existing schools does not solve the problem of dropouts, whose prior problems are human and psychological, not merely educational. New technological innovations in industry are producing more, not less, chronic unemployment among the unskilled. And no matter how much we speed up the slow movement toward greater equality for Negro Americans, full citizenship cannot be achieved by traditional legal means alone. It also requires a deeper (and non-technological) effort to overcome the bitter legacies of slavery and oppression; and it may even require that we learn to recognize, accept, and enjoy the differences between white and Negro Americans that this legacy has created. In almost every area where our "technological revolutions" are incomplete, the instruments and values of technology will not alone suffice to carry us farther. Our urban sprawl, the chaos, disorganization, blight, and congestion of our society, our new alienations— all were *created* by our exploding, unplanned technological society; the technological process alone will not solve their problems.

But most important, the fallacy of unfinished business overlooks the crucial questions for most Americans today: What lies beyond the triumph of technology? After racial equality has been achieved, what then? Abundance for all for what? Full employment for today's empty jobs? More education that instills an ever more cognitive outlook?

It is all too easy to imagine a society in which the triumph of technology is complete. It would be an overwhelmingly rich society, dominated by a rampant technology and all of its corollaries—science, research and development, advertising, "conformity," secret invidiousness, overwhelming nostalgia for childhood, the dictatorship of the ego, a continuing deflection of the Utopian spirit. It would be a prosperous, ugly, sprawling society which men had learned not to see. It would have many entertainers but few artists, many superhighways but few open spaces to go to on them. It would be a science-fiction dream of automation, pre-processing, and home-care conveniences. Skyscrapers would rise ever taller and more sheer, and "developments" would burgeon outside the blighted urban cores.

Yet the central problems of today would merely be magnified. The pace of social change would increase and, without an over-all sense of direction, Americans would huddle ever more defensively in the present. For some, the romanticized stability of the past would grow more and more attractive, and this attraction would express itself more and more forcibly in political and social reaction. Life, already divided today, would be further divided tomorrow; and the vast majority of Americans, who could create no community within their own hearts, would be altogether without a home. As the pressures toward cognition grew, private escapes into irrationality, cults, and fads would flourish. The atmosphere would become ever more hostile to speculation, to idealism, and to Utopianism; the cult of efficiency, spread into human relations and industrial management, would relegate idealism and the noble dreams of youth to the hours after work or to "entertainment." In such a society the most talented would be alienated, yet they would be unable to find a positive voice; and their alienations would be, as now, self-destructive, carping, and self-defeating. To complete our incomplete revolutions, to finish our unfinished business, is therefore not enough, nor can it be accomplished by technological means alone. For their solution, the vestigial tasks of technology require values beyond technology.

## Toward a more human society

If we are to seek values beyond technology, purposes beyond affluence, visions of the good life beyond material prosperity, where are these values, purposes, and visions to be found? Must we, as many secretly fear, await the coming of some new prophet who will create, out of nothing, a new Utopian vision for Americans? Are we condemned to a continuation of technological society until some Messiah arrives to save us?

I believe the answer is closer to home. When, a century ago, Americans began to take seriously the goals of prosperity and freedom from want, these values were not created out of nothing: they had long been part of the Western tradition. What changed was that a dream of the good life previously considered beyond the reach of the ordinary man passed into his hands and was accepted as a concrete goal that could be achieved by ordinary men and women. The turning point at which we stand today requires a similar translation of already existing dreams of human fulfillment and social diversity into the concrete goals of individuals and of our society. The values we need are deeply rooted in our own tradition: we must merely begin to take them seriously.

The ideal of full human wholeness is as old as Periclean Athens. But in the course of Western history, this goal could be taken seriously by few men and women: as in Athens, only a small number of the leisured and wealthy, supported by the vast majority of their fellow citizens, attained the freedom from want which is a prerequisite for the implementation of this ancient goal. Even in the Renaissance, when the Greek ideal of full humanity was rediscovered, the vast majority of men and women were far too preoccupied by their incessant struggle against poverty, oppression, and sickness to have time for such lofty ideals. And even today, for most citizens of most nations of the world, the vision of a more harmonious integration of self, a more complete development of talent and ability, must await the attainment of more urgent goals of attaining freedom from want and oppression. Only those who have been able to conquer poverty and tyranny have energy to cultivate their full humanity.

But for those who do not want materially and are not oppressed politically, the quest for fulfillment beyond material goods becomes possible and urgent. There is in human life a hierarchy of needs, such that the higher needs are fully felt when, and only when, the lower needs have been satisfied. Just as thirsty men do not seek food, and the starved have no strength for sex, so freedom from political oppression and material want are prerequisites for any attempt to achieve a more harmonious integration of self, a fuller development of human potentials. Today, in America, and increasingly in other technological nations, these preconditions are rapidly being met: we can now begin to imagine realistically that a whole society might commit itself to the attainment of the greatest possible fulfillment for its members.

To be sure, by the quantitative and reductionistic standards of our technological era, goals like "human wholeness," "personal integration," "the full development of human potentials" are inevitably vague and imprecise. They point to the quality of individual life, rather than to quantitatively measurable entities. Partly for this reason, our knowledge of the sources of human wholeness and fulfillment is woefully inadequate, despite a half-century's systematic study of man. But we do know more than previous generations about the causes of human malformation, distortion, and blighting. Our systematic and scientific knowledge is, no doubt, no more than a confirmation of what a few wise men have intuitively known in the past. But what was heretofore the special wisdom of the sagacious few (which they often carried to their graves) is on the way to becoming communicable public knowledge. Gradually, we are learning to pinpoint the obstacles to full human growth, specifying those especially "lethal" psychological combinations of parentage and social circumstance for children, defining more adequately the antecedents of human pathology, and even at times learning how to intervene positively to foster full human development.

Yet even today, it is far simpler to list the obstacles to full human development, to personal integration, to self-actualization, than to prescribe the precise path to these ancient goals. For just as there are from birth many distinct individuals, each with his own unique genetic and environmental potential, there must remain many paths to fulfillment. Our modern search for a single definition for "maturity" and "positive mental health" that will apply to everyone is probably doomed to failure from the start. Responsiveness, activity, excitability, and even the capacity to learn are not only shaped by the environment, but partly determined by birth. "Fulfillment" depends on individual potential and on social opportunity; human "wholeness" depends on what there is to be made whole.

But though no single definition of human fulfillment is possible, some of its results can be defined. A whole man or woman has the capacity for zest, exuberance, and passion, though this capacity may often be in abeyance. An integrated man does not cease to experience tension, anxiety, and psychic pain, but he is rarely overwhelmed by it. Though all men must at times "close" themselves to that which would be subversive of their commitments, a whole man nonetheless retains the *capacity* for openness, sensitivity, and responsiveness to the world around him: he can always be surprised because he remains open to that which is alien to himself.

Above all, human wholeness means a capacity for commitment, dedication, passionate concern, and care—a capacity for wholeheartedness and single-mindedness, for abandon without fear of self-annihilation and loss of identity. In psychological terms, this means that a whole man retains contact with his deepest passions at the same time that he remains responsive to his ethical sense. No one psychic potential destroys or subverts the others: his cognitive abilities remain in the service of his commitments, not vice versa;

his ethical sense guides rather than tyrannizing over his basic passions; his deepest drives are the sources of his strength but not the dictators of his action. We recognize whole men and women because their wholeness is manifest in their lives: what they do is "of a piece."

If no unitary definition of fulfillment and integration is possible, then a society that is to support these goals must necessarily be a diverse, heterogeneous, pluralistic, and open society. And like the ideal of individual fulfillment, the goal of social diversity is one we have never seriously considered implementing. Although the ideal of political pluralism is entrenched in our liberal tradition, this ideal has most often meant the toleration of political factions, not the encouragement of the full diversity of human talents. Politically, we may tolerate lobbies and believe in political parties; but socially our goals are given by slogans like "Americanization," "the melting pot," and increasingly today "the search for excellence" defined in cognitive terms. Though we think of ourselves as a "tolerant" society, in ordinary speech we most often couple the term "tolerate" with the modifier "barely." All too often, the "tolerance" of Americans is a thin veneer over the discomfort created by all that is different, strange, and alien to them. Once, to be sure, the image of this nation as a vast melting pot suggested the noble vision that the millions of diverse immigrants who came to this shore could be welded into a single coherent nation. But today there is no menace of an America excessively fractured along ethnic, regional or class lines. The current danger is excessive homogeneity, sameness, uniformity. Already, ethnic distinctions, regional differences, even class lines have been blurred beyond recognition in a land where almost everyone lives in the same city apartments and suburban dwellings, eats the same frozen foods and watches the same television programs at the same time on the same networks. Even the current effort of some Americans who are fearful of conformity to be "different," to develop distinctive styles of consumption and life, paralleled by the attempts of advertisers and industry to promote "personalized" and "individualized" products, tends to become only another sign of the homogenization of American society.

Romantic regionalism or the idealization of ethnicity are of course not virtuous in themselves: and even if we chose, distinctions of region and ethnic background could not be naturally preserved. But there *is* an inherent virtue in the appreciation of genuine human differences and the encouragement of a new social diversity based not on region, ancestral origin, class, or race, but on the special accomplishments, potentials, talents, and vital commitments of each individual. Pluralism must be extended from politics to the individual, implemented as a concrete social goal. Human diversity and variety must not only be tolerated, but rejoiced in, applauded, and encouraged.

A society of whole men and women must, then, be a society which encourages diversity, enjoying the differences between men as well as the similarities among them. Social diversity has a double connection to individual fulfillment: not only is a diverse society a precondition for human wholeness, it is its consequence—the kind of society whole men and women choose to live in. Those who are inwardly torn, unsure of their psychic coherence and fearful of inner fragmentation, are naturally distrustful of all that is alien and strange. Those whose sense of inner unity is tenuous are easily threatened by others who remind them of that part of themselves they seek to suppress. Our "one-hundred-per-cent Americans" are those whose own Americanism is felt to be most tenuous; the bigoted and the prejudiced cannot live with the full gamut of their own feelings. And conversely, those who can still sense their shared humanity with others of different or opposite talents and commitments are those who are sure of their own intactness. The goals of human fulfillment and social diversity require each other.

Both of these ideals, I have argued, are ancient ones. They are rooted deep in our Western tradition, and they arise almost spontaneously in those whose material and physical wants have been satisfied. But it remains for us to implement these visions. These are values beyond technology, credal ideals of our civilization which we can now begin to take seriously. Probably for the first time in human history, we can move toward a fullness of life beyond a full larder, human fulfillment beyond material satiation, social diversity beyond consensus.

## The reconstruction of commitment

History is always made by men, even in an era like ours when men feel they are but the pawns of history. The inability to envision a future different from the present is not a historical imposition but a failure of imagination. It is individuals, not historical trends, that are possessed by a self-confirming sense of social powerlessness. The decision to continue along our present course rather than to take a new turning is still a decision made by men. One way men sometimes have of shaping the future is to be passive and acquiescent before it. Our collective and individual future, then, will inevitably be shaped by us, whether we choose inaction and passivity, regression and romanticism, or action, imagination, and resolve. Men cannot escape their historical role by merely denying its existence. The question is therefore not *whether* Americans will shape their future, but *how* they will shape it.

What is lacking today in America is certainly not the know-how, the imagination, or the intelligence to shape a future better than our present. Nor do we lack the values that might guide the transformation of our society to a more fully human and diverse one. Rather, we lack the conviction that these values might be implemented by ordinary men and women acting in concert for their common good. The Utopian impulse, I have argued, runs deep in all human life, and especially deep in American life. What is needed is to free that impulse once again, to redirect it toward the creation of a better society. We too often attempt to patch up our threadbare values and outworn purposes; we too rarely dare imagine a society radically different from our own.

Proposals for specific reforms are bound to be inadequate by themselves. However desirable, any specific reform will remain an empty intellectual exercise in the absence of a new collective myth, ideology, or Utopian vision. Politically, no potent or lasting change will be possible except as men can be roused from their current alienations by the vision of an attainable society more inviting than that in which they now listlessly live. Behind the need for any specific reform lies the greater need to create an intellectual, ideological, and cultural atmosphere in which it is possible for men to attempt affirmation without undue fear that their Utopian visions will collapse through neglect, ridicule or their own inherent errors. Such an ethos can only be built slowly and piecemeal, yet is it clear what some of its prerequisites must be.

For one, we need a more generous tolerance for synthetic and constructive ideas. Instead of concentrating on the possible bad motives from which they might arise (the genetic fallacy) or on the possible bad consequences which might follow from their misinterpretation (the progenitive fallacy), we must learn to assess them in terms of their present relevance and appropriateness. To accomplish this task will be a double work. Destructively, it will require subverting the methodologies of reduction that now dominate our intellectual life. Constructively, it will require replacing these with more just measures of relevance, subtlety and wisdom, learning to cherish and value the enriching complexity of motives, passions, ethical interests, and facts which will necessarily underlie and support any future vision of the good life.

Secondly, we must reappraise our current concepts and interpretations of man and society. It is characteristic of the intellectual stagnation of our era, an era so obviously different from former times, that we continue to operate with language more appropriate to past generations than to our own. Many of our critiques and interpretations of technological society, including most discussions of alienation, apply more accurately to the America of the 1880's than to the America of the 1960's. We require a radical reanalysis of the human and social present—a re-evaluation which, starting from uncritical openness to the experience, joys, and dissatisfactions of men today, can gradually develop concepts and theories that can more completely comprehend today's world. American society does not lack men and women with the fine discrimination, keen intelligence, and imagination to understand the modern world; but we have yet to focus these talents on our contemporary problems.

But above and beyond a more generous atmosphere and a more adequate understanding of our time, ordinary human courage is needed. To criticize one's society openly requires a strong heart, especially when criticism is interpreted as pathology; only a man of high mettle will propose a new interpretation of the facts now arranged in entrenched categories. And no matter how eagerly the audience awaits or how well prepared the set, only courage can take a performer to the stage. There are many kinds of courage: needed here is the courage to risk being wrong, to risk doing unintentional harm, and, above all, the courage to overcome one's own humility and sense of finite inadequacy. This is not merely a diffuse "courage to be," without protest, in a world of uncertainty, alienation, and anxiety, but the courage to be *for* something despite the perishability and transience of all human endeavors.

Commitment, I have said, is worthy only as its object is worthy. To try to "reconstruct" commitment to American society as it exists today is less than worthy, for our society is shot through with failings, failures, and flaws. It is, as the alienated truly perceive, "trashy, cheap, and commercial"; it is also, as the alienated seldom see, unjust, distorting of human growth and dignity, destructive of diversity. It has allowed itself to be dominated by the instruments of its own triumph over poverty and want, worshiping the values, virtues, and institutions of technology even when these now dominate those they should serve. Only if we can transform the technological process from a master to a servant, harnessing our scientific inventiveness and industrial productivity to the promotion of human fulfillment, will our society be worthy of commitment. And only the vision of a world beyond technology can now inspire the commitment of whole men and women.

America today possesses a vast reservoir of thwarted and displaced idealism; there are millions of men and women who sense vaguely that something is amiss in their lives, who search for something more, and yet who cannot find it. Their idealism will not be easily redirected to the creation of better lives in a better society; it will require imagination, vigor, conviction, and strong voices willing to call for many years, before we dare raise our aspirations beyond vistas of total technology to visions of fuller humanity. But for the first time in American history, and probably in the history of the world, it is conceivable that a whole nation might come to take seriously these ancient and honored visions.

In defining this new vision of life and society, we must remember the quests of the alienated. Though their goals are often confused and inarticulate, they converge on a passionate yearning for openness and immediacy of experience, on an intense desire to create, on a longing to express their perception of the world, and, above all, on a quest for values and commitments that will give their lives coherence. The Inburns of modern American life are often self-defeating; they cannot be taken as exemplars of human integration or fulfillment. But the implicit goals they unsuccessfully seek to attain *are* those of integrated and whole men—openness, creativity, and dedication. Today we need men and women with the wisdom, passion, and courage to transform their private alienations into such public aspirations. We might then begin to move toward a society where such aspirations were more fully realized than in any the world has known.

We can hope for such new commitments in the future only if men now begin to resolve their alienations by committing themselves—through the analysis, synthesis, and reform of their own lives and worlds—to the preparation of such a new society, a society in which whole men and women can play with zest and spontaneity, can work with skill and dedication, can love with passion and care—a society that enjoys diversity and supports human fulfillment.

# APPENDIX
The varieties of
alienation:
an attempt at
definition

Although formal discussions of alienation itself are largely limited to the last 150 years, the theme of alienation—of estrangement, outcastness, and loss—is an archetypal theme in human life and history. Adam and Eve were estranged from God and outcast from Eden; and since then in every tradition known, themes of irrevocable loss of former closeness abound in myth, literature, history, and life. The myth of the hero is typically a tale of the alienation and exile which precede his heroic return to his native home. The history of nations is in part a history of wandering, exile, outcastness, and the search for a homeland. The chronicle of innovation, too, involves the repudiation of established patterns and values in order to create new ones. Revolutionaries from Christ to Castro have been separated from their homes by emigration, exile, and ostracism, and have returned from their alienation in the desert or the mountains only when they could bring new doctrines by persuasion and force. In all religions, the possibility of man's estrangement from the Divine Order is fundamental; indeed, perhaps the central function of religion is to prevent this estrangement of man from God and God from man. The possibility of "alienation" is predicated on the nature of human development, of social organization, of religious thought, and of history.

The ambiguous concept of alienation has in recent years become increasingly fashionable and, partly as a result, increasingly devoid of any specific meaning. More and more, the term is used to characterize whatever the author considers the dominant maladies of the twentieth century; and since views differ as to what these maladies are, the meanings of alienation fluctuate with each writer, and often according to the moods of the same writer. One extreme reaction to the vagueness of the concept of alienation has been to suggest that alienation *is* a mysterious and inherently undefinable affliction that has overtaken modern man. Discourse about definition is therefore fruitless: one either "knows" alienation or one does not. The editor of a recent collection of writings about modern society thus argues of alienation: "A quick definition would only get in the way. It is better, far better, to begin by treating it as a mystery which will yield slowly and in its own time, to experience." Later, however, this same editor suggests that alienation *can* be defined as a failure to respond to the "beauty," the "horror," "wisdom," "pathos," and "passion" of the passages he has chosen for his anthology. And still later, he suggests that anyone who hastens to seek a definition of alienation suffers from "an advanced case of—alienation."

Though few writers approach alienation with such reverential obscurantism, equally few carry through with a clear definition of the concept. Writers like Fromm, Kahler, and Pappenheim use "alienation" to describe a variety of conditions ranging from the separation of man from nature to the loss of pre-capitalist work relationships, from man's defensive use of language to his estrangement from his own creative potential, and from the worker's loss of control over the productive process to the individual's feeling of social or political powerlessness. Of course, the purpose of such writers is to suggest that all of these different phenomena are connected, that all result from some characteristic of modern society. Yet merely to label disparate phenomena with the same tag does not establish their inner connection; it merely makes discourse difficult.

In practice, then, "alienation" has become an increasingly rhetorical and at times entirely emotive concept, often synonomous merely with the feeling that "something is wrong somewhere," and that "we have lost something important." Most usages of "alienation" share the assumption that some relationship or connection that once existed, that is "natural," desirable, or good, has been lost. The implicit rhetoric in the term is obvious when we compare "alienation" with "emancipation": both terms imply a severance of former connections, a loss of old modes of relatedness, but alienations are clearly bad while emancipations are good.

All of this makes discourse about alienation difficult. Indeed, one would be tempted to abandon the concept altogether were it not for the certainty that the same problems of definition would then crop up again with some cognate term like estrangement, disaffection, or detachment. Ambiguous terms suggest vague thinking which requires sharper distinctions—and not merely a new and equally vague synonym. While the discussion that follows does not attempt to be exhaustive (by including every sense in which "alienation" has ever been used) it is an attempt to distinguish between several distinct alienations, to give them different names, and to suggest some of the major ways in which alienations need to be defined. There are of course many ways of slicing a cake, and many ways of labeling the slices. Other distinctions than those I propose may turn out to be more useful; certainly other labels for the various forms of alienations might be substituted for those I suggest.

## Four questions about alienation

Although in ordinary speech we often speak of someone simply as "alienated," in fact we always imply he is alienated *from* something or someone. Husbands become alienated from their wives, peasants from their land, workers from their labor, men from their gods, societies from their traditional virtues. Alienation always has an object or a *focus*. For example, "self-alienation" as discussed by Fromm, Horney, and others, implies a lack of connection between an individual and some deep, vital, and valuable part of himself. Or the "alienation of the intellectual" implies his lack of commitment to the values of his society. Or the "alienation of the modern worker" points to his lack of relationship to the work process or to his own labor. And although a lack of connection in one area *may* generalize to other areas, it need not always. The alienated intellectual may be unalienated from his inner "productivity" or "real self"; the alienated worker may be at least superficially unalienated from the values of the industrial society that is purportedly alienating him. Thus, the first question to ask of alienation is, "Alienated from what?"

Secondly, the concept of alienation does not specify what alienation consists of. The rhetoric of the concept implies that something desirable, natural, or normal has been lost—that is, that a positive relationship has ceased to exist. But we need to specify what replaces the lost relationship. If a Communist becomes alienated from the Party, we do not know whether he is merely disenchanted, whether he now vehemently rejects Communism, whether he no longer cares about politics at all, or whether he blames himself for his loss of his old faith. In many cases, alienation merely implies lack of any relationship at all—detachment and indifference; but in other cases, it implies active rejection, vehement opposition, open hostility. A second question to ask of alienations, then, is "What relationship if any, has replaced the lost one?"

Thirdly, alienation can be expressed in a variety of ways. In one sense the revolutionary and the psychotic are both highly alienated from the norms and values of their society—both reject these norms and values. Yet there is a vast difference in the way their rejection is expressed: the revolutionary actively attempts to transform his society; the psychotic has undergone a regressive self-transformation that leaves his society relatively unaffected. One major way of classifying alienation is therefore according to their *mode:* e.g., whether they are alloplastic (i.e., they involve an attempt to transform the world) or autoplastic (they involve self-transformation).

Finally, alienations have different agents or sources: some are imposed while others are chosen. Merely to note that an individual is "alienated from society" does not tell us whether he deliberately rejects his society or whether it excludes him. Most of the sociological discussions of alienation that derive from Marx's work deal with imposed alienations (of which the alienated individual remains largely unaware). For Fromm or Kahler the alienated man is rarely aware that he is alienated from his work or himself. Indeed, paradoxically, the dawning of awareness of such imposed alienation usually entails the growth of a new chosen alienation from capitalist-industrialist society, and thus marks the end of self-alienation and alienation from work. To be sure, imposed and chosen alienations may be intimately connected: the rejected man may reject those who have rejected him. But often, these two forms of alienation are unrelated, as with the Black Bourgeoisie which accepts the values and norms of the white society from which it is excluded; or as with the successful alienated artist who is accepted and embraced by the very bourgeois society he repudiates. Thus, a further question relevant to a definition of alienations is "Who (or what) is the agent of the alienation?"

In brief, then, while the concept of alienation in every variation suggests the loss or absence of a previous or desirable relationship, it requires further specification in at least four respects:

1. *Focus:* Alienated from what?
2. *Replacement:* What replaces the old relationship?
3. *Mode:* How is the alienation manifest?
4. *Agent:* What is the agent of the alienation?

These four questions provide a basis for a virtually limitless number of varieties of alienation. One can be alienated from almost anything;

an enormous number of new kinds of relationships may replace the lost one; alienation may be expressed in a great variety of modes, and have a great number of agents. In fact, however, most discussions of alienation concentrate on a relatively limited number of possibilities, some of which I will discuss below. For purposes of clarity, I will reserve the term "alienation" for only one of these possibilities—for an explicit rejection, "freely" chosen by the individual, of what he perceives as the dominant values or norms of his society—and will use other terms to characterize other types of alienation.

## Some types of "alienation"

*Cosmic outcastness*—For Inburn, it will be recalled, human existence was "a short time spent in a physical world with inscrutable void on the other side," a time without inherent meaning or purpose, a time unconsciously felt to involve a "Fall," an exile from purpose, warmth, and meaning. Central to this outlook (which is common to many alienated young men) is a sense of existential outcastness, of "thrownness" into a world not made for man and indifferent to his fate. In previous centuries in Western society, this same sense of cosmic outcastness was usually expressed as a sense of religious outcastness, as a fall from grace, as loss of faith, or as an estrangement from God. In the twentieth century, however, this sense is probably best expressed in existentialism, with its denial that the world has essential meaning. Human life is in this context "absurd," lacking inherent purpose: "meaning" must be artificially manufactured by men in the process of existence. And since any one man's answers to the riddles of life are individual and private, they will often be irrelevant and meaningless to other men. Truth is subjective and solipsistic.

A sense of cosmic outcastness—of loss of connection with a divinely or metaphysically structured universe that "cares" about man—almost inevitably leads to a sense of man's estrangement from his fellow men. Since meaning does not inhere in reality itself, it must be created by each man for himself. And since men are different from each other, the meaning each creates will differ from that of his fellows. The picture of the world we create out of the raw chaos of our sensory experience will be congruent not with the true structure of reality, but with the idiosyncratic accidents of our own lives. Therefore, when two men speak, their words will not mean the same thing; what one man experiences is never identical with what another experiences. Even apparent consensus is often illusory, based upon misunderstanding and the use of the same word to describe different experiences and feelings. Men are separated from each other because no two men ever create exactly the same "truth."

This sense of alienation, of cosmic and existential outcastness, has been voiced with special urgency in our century. To be sure, the roots of this feeling lie deep in the Judeo-Christian tradition, with its emphasis on man's Fall, on original sin, and on the continual possibility of outcastness from God's grace. But during most periods of Western history, this sense of outcastness has been buried and denied within a dominant sense of shared significance—most recently, the shared significance of Christian theology and symbolism. Exceptional individuals have of course often returned to the central question of man's place in the universe and the meaningfulness of his existence; but most men have shunned this question or answered it affirmatively. Only in the last century, with the ever more rapid decline of religious faith, has a sense of cosmic outcastness become widespread.

Psychologically, it is not easy to accept the death of God (and of all the structures premised on His existence) without a feeling of deprivation and rage. Most modern accounts of man's existential outcastness —of his "thrownness" into the world, of the inherent absurdity of existence, of the difficulty in communion between men—though they are presented as "factual," also convey a resentment, anger, bitterness, and disillusion that we have seen in the philosophies of alienated students. Men never feel bitter about "facts" unless the "facts" are felt to be disappointingly different from some unstated alternative. Here the alternative is clear—a lost world view in which the universe was made for Man by a caring God, truth was objective, and men could communicate by referring to a shared objective reality. Inevitably, then, disappointment and bitterness have accompanied the progressive erosion of faith that God made the universe as the arena for man's salvation. Those who feel most outcast from the cosmos are of course those whose individual lives sensitize them to these themes: their feelings of cosmic outcastness usually parallel more personal themes of alienation. But at the same time, what they experience acutely is a problem that inevitably and increasingly affects modern men.

*Developmental estrangements*—Behind the sense of existential outcastness in alienated students we have seen another kind of "alienation" —a sense of the loss in individual life of ties and relationships that can never be re-created. These "alienations," which I will call "developmental estrangements," are crucial and salient in the lives of alienated students; but comparable if milder estrangements exist in the lives of us all. Indeed, one reason we can understand and be moved by the estrangements in the development of alienated students is because these estrangements reverberate on and activate similar themes in our own lives. For in all human development, forward growth and development means the abandonment, loss, or renunciation of what went before. Briefly to consider the universal estrangements of individual development may help to place in context the heightened estrangements of the alienated young men we have studied.

The first expulsion is from the womb. Especially in times of illness, stress, and fatigue, we all still long, if not for the prenatal state itself, then for those of its qualities which an adult can allow himself to desire—security, warmth, protection, even oblivion. The fantasies and sometimes the expressed wishes of small children clearly express their desire to be inside, protected, surrounded, and forever united with their mothers; and though adults consider such desires "regressive," we often forget that untroubled sleep gives us all much the same security, warmth, and sanctuary.

Yet the "trauma" of birth is not only a trauma but an event vitally necessary for both mother and neonate, without which neither can survive; and if all goes well the mother experiences not so much a loss as a joyous gain. For the infant, too, timely birth enables him (who would otherwise begin to waste in the womb) to enter the world and the long course of human development. For most of us birth symbolizes not so much expulsion from a desirable oblivion as the opening of a new world; and the meanings of birth are universally joyous and glad. Occasionally, to be sure, the losses outweigh the gains, as when the mother cannot bear to exchange the fetus within for the infant without, or when the newborn arrives ill-equipped to cope with the world. But what usually prevail, psychologically and physically, are the forces of forward movement.

The estrangement of birth is a paradigm for all other developmental estrangements. Just as the vitalities of the infant initially help "estrange" it from the womb, so its struggles to grow and its inborn schedules of maturation will thereafter push it to abandon old securities for new risks and possibilities. Just as the mother expels the child from her body and nurtures him in the world, so first she and then an ever widening social environment will push and prepare the child's development, sustaining and guaranteeing it when it comes. And throughout life, the chance will remain that growth will be resisted, sometimes because the way has not been well prepared, sometimes because the past retains too strong a grip, sometimes because the next stage in development is seen as impossibly unattractive, sometimes because the child's environment cannot support and guarantee his maturing. Like birth, subsequent growth can be impeded because of either too much or too little preparation: post-maturity means a wasting of the child's capacity to adapt to a new environment, prematurity means that this capacity is not yet developed. Smooth psychological development, insofar as it can exist, is above all a matter of timing and support.

The later estrangements of development follow much the same pattern. Psychologically, perhaps the most fundamental of these estrangements is the loss of the early mother-child relationship. The mere fact of physiological maturation forces a child to move from unthinking dependence on a mother not yet differentiated from the rest of the world to a more and more qualified and realistic awareness of what his mother can and will do for him, and when. This loss of symbiotic dependency comes at the same time as, and partly because of, his enormously increased powers of observation, discrimination, and conceptualization. As is usually true, the satisfactions of one period promote the very qualities that will lead to the later abandonment of these satisfactions: if all goes well, the infant abandons his infancy eagerly.

The estrangements from the womb and from infantile dependency are followed by a gradual move away from total control by parents to more and more self-control. We ordinarily think of the birth of will as an emancipation, not a loss; yet in adulthood many men and women secretly long to abandon their free will, and they often manage to bequeath its effective exercise to others—spouses, employers, and political leaders. Even in early childhood the first beginnings of will and self-control entail new responsibilities for one's deeds and misdeeds; and as all parents know, some children find it easier for a time to relinquish autonomy and responsibility to Mother. And other children, though they insist on autonomy, are for a time unwilling to pay its price of growing responsibility. These related events—the gradual development of will and autonomy, the concurrent advent of responsibility, blame, and guilt, the loss of moral innocence—constitute another universal theme in myth and literature: many religions, for example, promise relief from responsibilities and blame if one will only will the will of God.

A concomitant estrangement is the loss of the illusion of "ego-centrality"—of the belief (which many can recall from their own childhoods) that the universe was created specifically for us, and with us in its center. In Western society, at about age six, children develop the capacity to "take the point of view of the other," to see the world through another's eyes. This development is part of a larger realization, beginning in the child's immediate family circle, that his is a defined place in a world of other people with defined relationships to him. I have earlier discussed the "Oedipal" problems of alienated youths and have recounted some of the "normal" problems of this period in our society. These special Oedipal problems of American families are not universal; but in every society the child must somehow learn his place as a boy or a girl in a family of adults and eventually in the world of men and women, consigning to fantasy his wish to be (and belief that he is) all things to all men and women. He must renounce the illusion of egocentrality, abandon the fantasy of omnipotence, resign himself to being what he is—a growing child in a world of adults. Fantasies of omnipotence never die; they persist in the daydreams and nightdreams of most adults; and, suitably disguised in fairy tales and comic books, they especially delight children who have recently abandoned them. But in adult life, when such fantasies become beliefs, we rightly deem their possessors mad.

Much of what children in American society learn in school—and by the very fact of going to school—involves both an expansion of knowledge and at the same time a further estrangement—from the possibility of totally free play. This loss is seldom sudden, and in healthy men and women rarely complete: to retain the capacity to play without guilt, whether in love, recreation, or conversation, is as valid a criterion of mental health as is the capacity to work or love. Yet school does require the abandonment of *total* freedom in play, an acceptance of the requirements of work, a further accretion of responsibility, an increase in the accountability of men to their fellows. Here as elsewhere, growing up requires giving others the right to make claims—on play, time, freedom, and work. And though the acquisition of adult skills and work patterns through schooling enormously adds to the child's power and competence (and for that reason is usually prized), it entails losses as well.

In any society, the advent of adolescence involves a child in a double task: negatively, the child's awakening sexuality and the new pressures of his society call upon him to abandon his remaining ties of childish relatedness to his family, his childhood world, and his childhood self. Sexual maturation alone means that childish forms of behavior with mother, father, and siblings are no longer possible; and every society reinforces the physiological pressures of puberty with new social demands. A new relationship with family must develop, a new definition of self as an adult must emerge, be supported and encouraged by society, be incorporated in the adolescent's self-conception. The positive task of adolescence is therefore the assumption of adulthood. The adolescent must achieve or accept some new sense of himself, of his identity as an adult male or female, however that may be socially defined; he must choose, create, or accept the social role he will fill during adulthood; he must synthesize the many identifications of his childhood into one relatively coherent sense of adult identity.

The abandonment of childhood is seldom totally untroubled. Though his body and his society tell him he is no longer a child, many a youth feels consciously or unconsciously puzzled and cheated by the advent of adolescence, unwilling to accept the loss of the goods of childhood. Physical growth cannot be stopped, but psychological development can be resented or retarded; and in every community some men and women carry an undying nostalgia for childhood within an adult frame. This is "normal," predictable, and understandable, especially in societies like ours where children are well treated but much is demanded of adults; it causes special trouble only when overwhelming nostalgia for childhood is shaped into defiance and obdurate refusal of adulthood.

The estrangements of adulthood are usually less obvious to us, for most current psychologies overemphasize the visible dramas of early years and neglect the more gradual changes of adulthood. But every stage in development involves the same dialectic of estrangement and growth. Marriage entails an enormous gain in intimacy and sharing at the same time that it means a loss of freedom and irresponsibility. So, too, the birth of children requires from parents an enormous curtailment of personal self-seeking and egocentricity while it also gives them a sense of tangible connection with the future and an unprecedented expansion of themselves into their children. Especially for a man, adult work can mean tangible accomplishments, useful achievements, and even creativity; but it also involves a further increase in social responsibilities and involvedness. For men and women alike, the maturation of their children means a loss of the mutual dependence between parents and children, though at the same time it is the much desired fruition of years of effort in rearing these children. The advent of old age, with its steady physical decline and progressive loss of strength, also means gaining a new freedom from the cares and responsibilities of the rest of life. And the contemplation of proximate death can mean both the despair of life's inevitably unfulfilled potentials and the satisfactions of recalling what one has done and been.

Every stage of human development, then, necessarily involves a dialectic between estrangement from the past and growth into a future where past needs must be modified, and new needs, requirements, and satisfactions must be accepted. Most men and women find the future powerful enough not only to pull them into it but to erase any conscious nostalgia for the past. Nonetheless this nostalgia persists in some corner of all our psyches, making us unconsciously responsive to (and sometimes angrily repudiative of) the complaints of those who wish aloud to go home again.

Societies differ in the ways in which they characteristically treat their young, their mature, and their aged; and therefore societies differ in the extent to which they heighten or minimize the inevitable estrangements of growth. When the conventions of living in any society accentuate some one of the universal estrangements of human development, we can speak of a *collective estrangement,* and we will expect to find among adults symbolic expressions of nostalgia for what has been left behind. And we must recall that whatever is universal in human life, or shared by most members of the society, is always concretely manifest in unique and idiosyncratic forms in the life of any single man or woman. An estrangement that may be a minor current in one life can be a flood in another; a loss deeply felt by most of the members of a society can be barely perceived by those few whose upbringing differs from that of their fellows. An individual's development may be so idiosyncratic that he founders on the estrangements which his fellows barely remark. But just as often, a whole generation may share a similar history of personal development and therefore agree in finding the same stages painless or hard. Our conceptions of what is universal in human development are, after all, but abstractions from our understanding of many discreet individuals in many particular societies. In no man or community do we find the universal in pure form, but always as shaped by the accidents of individuality and the shared selectivities of society.

*Historical loss*—Like individual life, historical development invariably entails a dialectic between gain and loss. Most social innovations replace customs, outlooks, or technologies that are in that measure left behind; and those who are most firmly attached to what has been replaced inevitably mourn their loss. In a time like our own, when social change is rapid, worldwide, and chronic, one of the most keenly felt "alienations" is the acute sense of historical loss.

Consider, as a paradigm of historical loss, what must happen when a nomadic hunting community settles down to a pastoral life. The effects of such a change will go far beyond an alteration in the mode of subsistence. For example, as if to symbolize their dependence upon their source of economic livelihood, many predatory communities revere the very animals upon which they prey: these creatures are made the highest gods and totems of the tribe. Furthermore, in any society, children are reared so as to be able and willing to perform the society's chief tasks: in a nomadic hunting society, boys must therefore be taught to be stealthy and independent, capable of watchful vigil and strong in solitude; girls must learn to tolerate the continual dislocations of following the prey off which the community lives. The virtues of such a society are therefore likely to be the qualities of independence, solitude, craft, strength in the hunt, ability to tolerate movement, refusal to become attached to place.

If such a community suddenly shifts to the settled life of shepherds, every aspect of its existence will be profoundly affected. As men will no longer be dependent upon their hunted prey, the gods of the hunt will wane. Nor will the society any longer require the virtues of the hunter: new qualities of patience, stability, fruitfulness, care, and nurture will be required to manage domestic flocks. Settled in one location, the society can grow in size, can accumulate staples and immovable wealth, can increase in complexity. Its old gods will be abandoned; the child-rearing techniques once geared to produce resourceful nomads must give way to other techniques suited to shape men and women who will watch over their flocks.

Inevitably, then, "progress" will here involve historical losses as well, "alienations" from old modes of relatedness to nature, estrangements from old gods, the loss of traditional virtues. Men whose character fitted them well for the nomadic hunt will find themselves useless and unwanted; courage and solitary resourcefulness will now take second place to patience, co-operation and nurture; prosperity now will adhere to the domestic and the tenacious. Understandably, many men will feel profound nostalgia for the past, for the simple camaraderie of hunting life, for ancient gods and traditional virtues. And inevitably, there will be men who feel strange in their new world, guilty at what they have abandoned, who will call for a return to ancient verities, abandoned gods, and traditional ways of life.

In retrospect, such historical losses as these now seem to us more than outweighed by the social and human gains they brought: few men now mourn the nomadic life. But as we approach the present, the balance of historical loss and historical gain is harder to strike. Partly, no doubt, this is because we find it most difficult to judge what we are closest to. But lack of historical distance alone will not adequately explain the deep ambivalence with which many men of the twentieth century view the gains of our own era. For, while in every society some few men have always regretted the passing of older ways, it is indicative of our modern collective ambivalence to historical change that systematic discussions of alienations, estrangement, and historical loss have been largely confined to the past century. Many such discussions have been indirectly or directly inspired by Marx, who in his early writings made "alienation" a central concept in his diagnosis of the evils of capitalist society. For Marx, "alienation" means above all the worker's loss of control over his own labor in a capitalist economy: in factory labor, what the worker makes is no longer his own—as it was for the craftsman or the free farmer. This alienation from his labor has far-reaching consequences: the very act of working, which should be a man's fundamental mode of relationship to the world, increasingly becomes merely a way of earning his economic subsistence. Thus, the worker becomes profoundly alienated from a central part of himself: he comes to see himself as a mere commodity to be sold on the marketplace, devoid of inherent human dignity. And finally, the worker extends his view of himself to others, and all human relationships degenerate into encounters between commodities, each of which has a price but none of which has dignity.

Although the young Marx's analysis of alienation also points to man's secondary estrangement from himself and from his fellows as a consequence of his primary loss of relationship to his work, the central meaning of "alienation" for Marx comes closest to the concept for historical loss. What is lost is a "natural," "integral" connection between men and their own work—a connection seen in the peasant, the artisan, the independent craftsman. Other "alienations" follow from this first and primary estrangement. Furthermore, for Marx, alienation was imposed and not chosen; its victims were usually unaware of the extent of their separation from their work, themselves, or their fellow men. Those most profoundly affected by the historical loss of an integral connection with work were the proletariat. Paradoxically, for Marx as for most modern neo-Marxists, alienation begins to end with the awareness of alienation: only by the awareness of alienation can a worker gain the "class-consciousness" which will enable him to struggle to create a classless society where men will no longer be alienated from their labor.

*Self-estrangement*—For Marx, alienation from one's labor leads indirectly to alienation from one's self. For other writers, most notably Karen Horney, alienation from self—or what I will call "self-estrangement"—is primary and not derivative. Self-estrangement (or self-alienation) entails for Horney and her followers a lack of contact between the individual's "conscious self" and his "real self," manifest in a sense of unreality, emptiness, flatness, and boredom. The immediate origins of this condition are psychological, not social, although Horney allows that modern society may in turn encourage the psychological factors that promote self-estrangement. The individual is separated from that part of himself which is most "real," vital, and important. He is separated from his own deepest feelings, needs, and fantasies. As a result, his entire existence and his every act assume a quality of unreality: to observers, therapists, and even to himself, he seems not quite "there."

Other writers, most notably Fromm, Pappenheim, and Kahler, also use extensively a similar concept—although all agree with Marx in tracing its origins to the social conditions of modern capitalist (or industrial) society. For Fromm, for example, "self-alienation" involves a lack of contact between the individual's conscious self and his "productive" potential—the individual sees himself as a mere object among objects, and treats himself and others as commodities on the market. Self-alienation is therefore a primary characteristic of the "marketing personality;" absence of self-alienation becomes virtually synonymous with "productivity" and psychological soundness.

Despite its extensive use, the concept of self-estrangement often remains nebulous and difficult to define, partly because it presupposes a "real self" or a "capacity for productive living" which remains invisible though potential. In practice, then, self-estrangement is a term with more extensive normative connotations than empirical denotations; furthermore, one of the primary characteristics of the individual who is self-estranged is that he does not realize the extent of his separation from what is best within him. His alienation from himself is seen as largely imposed from without, either by malign psychological influences, or by the corrupting effects of capitalist society.

## Individual alienation

All of the aforementioned varieties of alienation, like most others which have been or could be distinguished, involve a loss of relationship whose agent is not the self. Furthermore, in each of these "alienations" the broken or absent relationship is replaced by no relationship at all. Throughout this book, however, I have been concerned with another variety of alienation—with alienation whose immediate agent is the self (which is "freely" chosen rather than imposed) and with alienation that involves an active rejection of the focus of alienation (rather than merely the absence of relationship with it). In particular, I have started from a study of a group of youths who articulately and deliberately reject what they see as the dominant values of American society. And although I have argued that the sources of this alienation are complex—involving psychological, social, cultural, and historical forces—the defining criterion of alienation in the sense I have used this term is the *explicit rejection of traditional American culture*. At the same time, however, I have argued that the deliberate and conscious rejection of our dominant cultural values among these students is not the only form of individual alienation. It may prove helpful, therefore, to distinguish more systematically some of the varieties of individual alienation, and to examine their relationship to each other.

## A classification of alienations and conformisms

I earlier noted four questions that must be answered in any attempt to define the meanings of "alienation." Two of these questions have already been answered with regard to what I am calling "individual alienation." First, the alienated individual is the agent of his own alienation; he chooses to be alienated; his alienation is conscious and largely egosyntonic. Second, what replaces the original or "natural" relationship is a stance of manifest rejection. Defined as a general psychological attitude, individual alienation can therefore be seen as one end of a continuum that runs from alienation (rejection) through commitment to conformism (compulsive acceptance) at the other end. Any specific attitude toward a set of behavioral norms or cultural values can, in principle, be placed somewhere along this continuum. And since we are dealing with a continuum, rather than with a dichotomy, it becomes important in each case to specify the *degree of alienation/conformism* involved. At the extreme of alienation, we would place acute psychoses, total cultural refusals, subversive and revolutionary activities, sociopathic criminality, etc. Less alienated, but still involving a rejection of central behavioral norms and/or values would be such common phenomena as non-conformity, neurosis, detachment, and social reform. And at the far extreme of conformism, we would include repressive policing activities, slavish social acquiescence, compulsive psychological conformity, Babbittry, the politics of reaction, and extreme cultural traditionalism. Closer to the center of the continuum, but still toward the conformism end, we would locate asceticism, accommodation, compliance, traditionalism, and conservatism.

These examples indicate that a classification of individual alienations merely in terms of degree of alienation/conformism is not enough. For a more adequate classification, we must return to the two remaining questions introduced in earlier pages: What is the *focus* of alienation? In what *mode* is the alienation expressed?

Although I have earlier suggested that alienation may have many foci, two of them are particularly relevant to this discussion. These are a focus on *behavioral norms* as contrasted with a focus on *cultural values*. Behavioral norms are the common social expectations about the kind of behavior that is proper, appropriate, and legal in any society. Sometimes such expectations are sanctioned by law and coercive police power: their rejection therefore involves criminality and delinquency; in other cases, social norms are sanctioned merely by social approval and disapproval, and those who violate these norms will merely be considered non-conformists. "Cultural values," on the other hand, refer not to specific expectations about behavior but to general conceptions of the desirable. Normally, the precise behavioral implications of any general cultural value require considerable specification: e.g., it is not immediately obvious what behavior should follow from accepting a value like "progress," "achievement," or "democracy."

Turning to the second question, the mode of alienation/conformism, we can usefully classify the way in which alienation is expressed according to whether it is primarily *alloplastic* or *autoplastic*. Alloplastic alienations are those expressed primarily as attempts to change the world; autoplastic alienations are expressed through the mode of self-transformation.

It now becomes possible to classify individual alienations along three distinct dimensions: *attitude* (alienation vs. conformism), *focus* (behavioral norms vs. cultural values), and *mode* (alloplastic vs. autoplastic). Figures 1, 2, and 3 indicate the possibilities created by superimposing each of these continua upon the other. Figure 1 illustrates the cross-classification of attitude and focus: a rejection of behavioral norms is termed *violation*, to distinguish it from a rejection of cultural values, or *repudiation*. Acceptance of behavioral norms is termed *conformity*, whereas acceptance of cultural values is called *confirmation*.

Figure 2 shows the cross-classification of attitude and mode. Alloplastic alienation involves *change*, whereas autoplastic alienation involves *maladaptation*. Conformism, when alloplastic, can be termed *conservation*, whereas autoplastic conformism involves *submission*.

Figure 3 shows the cross-classification of focus and mode. Combining alloplasticity with behavioral norms gives us the area of *activity*, whereas combining it with cultural values involves the issue of *ideology*. The autoplastic mode with regard to behavioral norms involves the

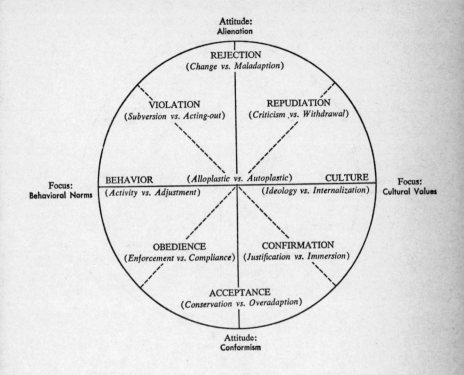

Figure I

**Attitude and Focus**

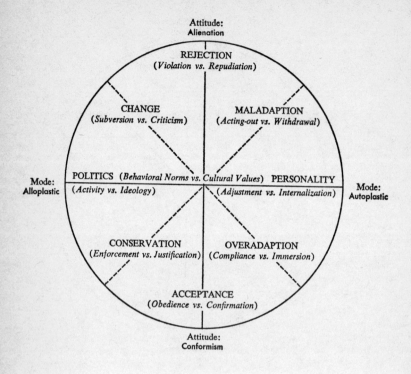

Figure 2

Attitude and Mode

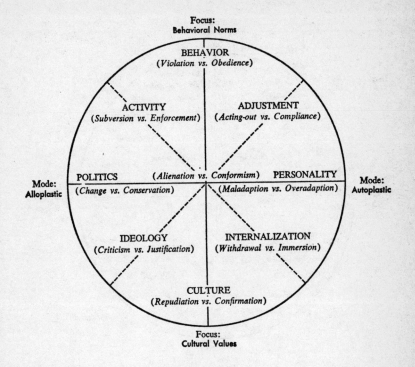

Figure 3

Focus and Mode

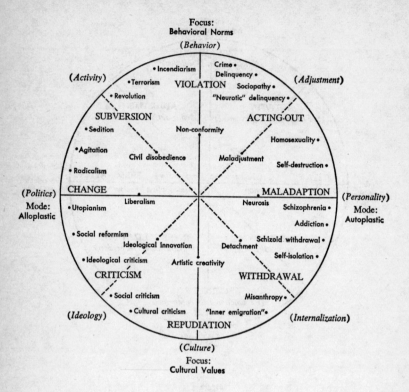

Figure 4

**Varieties of Alienation**

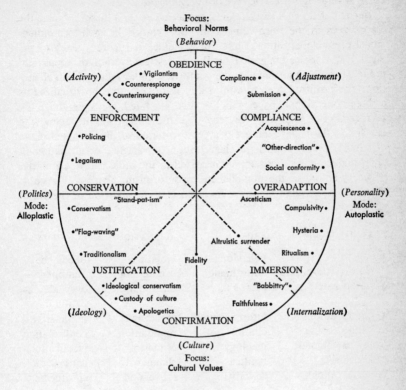

Figure 5

**Varieties of Conformism**

question of *adjustment,* whereas the autoplastic mode and the matter of cultural values gives us the area of *internalization.*

In each of the first three figures, the terms in parentheses indicate the alternatives in the third dimension not included in each two-dimensional cross-classification. Thus, for example, in Figure 3, each of the eight major issues suggested by the cross-classification of focus and mode has both an alienated and a conformist end. Figure 3, with alienation/ conformism added as a third dimension, can thus be visualized as a three-dimensional space, with the first, alienated, concepts above the surface of the page and the second, conformist, concepts below the surface of the page. Figure 4 is a representation of the alienated plane of Figure 3, and gives us a classification of varieties of alienation in eight major areas: these are summarized in the table below. Similarly, Figure 5 shows us the non-alienated, conformism, plane of Figure 3. Here, the same eight areas are involved in a classification of the varieties of conformism.

| FOCUS/MODE | AREA | ALIENATION | CONFORMISM |
|---|---|---|---|
| 1. norms | behavior | violation | obedience |
| 2. norms/autoplastic | adjustment | "acting-out" | compliance |
| 3. autoplastic | personality | maladaptation | over-adaptation |
| 4. values/autoplastic | internalization | withdrawal | immersion |
| 5. values | culture | repudiation | confirmation |
| 6. values/alloplastic | ideology | criticism | justification |
| 7. alloplastic | politics | change | conservation |
| 8. norms/alloplastic | activity | subversion | enforcement |

Figures 4 and 5 now permit us to classify specific forms of alienation and conformism according to their approximate location along the two continua of focus and mode. Thus, for example, alienation expressed in the area of behavior may involve revolution, terrorism, criminality, delinquency, non-conformity, sociopathy; whereas conformism expressed in the same area will involve such attitudes as counterinsurgency, vigilantism, submission, compliance, and accommodation. Or, to take another example, alienation that is primarily focused on cultural values may take the form of artistic creativity, "inner emigration," cultural refusal, cultural innovation, etc.; whereas conformism in the area of values will be expressed in Babbittry, faithfulness, apologetics, custody of culture, or ideological conservatism.

The classification proposed and illustrated in Figures 4 and 5 is only one of the many classifications which might be or have been suggested. For example, Talcott Parsons in *The Social System* suggests a usage of "alienation" and "conformity" that broadly parallels that proposed here, and a different way of classifying alienations. Robert Merton's widely used classification of forms of deviance and conformity provides still another way of classifying the behavioral sequelae of alienations and conformisms. Both Parson's and Merton's classifications differ from that proposed here in that they are primarily sociological, emphasizing overt behavior, whereas this classification is psychological, a classification of attitudes. A sociological and psychological classification of alienation may not overlap perfectly: two individuals with identical attitudes may behave very differently, depending upon the situation in which they find themselves.

Furthermore, this classification of alienations is a classification of attitudes and not of individuals. The same individual can, and usually does, exhibit more than one form of alienation and/or conformism; indeed, an individual may be highly alienated in one area and conformist in another. For example, although most of the alienated students described in the body of this book exhibited attitudes in the areas of repudiation and withdrawal, at least some combined extreme cultural refusal with marked neurotic trends, while others combined misanthropy and a mild tendency toward delinquency. Furthermore, any given individual may be markedly alienated in one area and markedly conformist in another: for example, the criminals studied in *The Authoritarian Personality* were markedly alienated in their norm-violating behavior; but at the same time, many were conformist in their political attitudes.

The ultimate usefulness of any effort at classification rests on its capacity to arrange observable phenomena in a way that is not only theoretically but empirically meaningful. The usefulness of this classification might be explored by attempting to answer some of the following questions.

1. Do extremely alienated individuals have common psychological characteristics regardless of the area in which their alienation is expressed? For example, rejection of paternal exemplars might be a factor of considerable etiological importance in *all* alienated attitudes among males.

2. Do individuals whose attitudes fall largely within one quadrant of Figure 4 exhibit other specific communalities: e.g., in family background, life style, life adjustment, fantasy, and ideology? For example, there is a striking similarity between the reported backgrounds of male

homosexuals and male schizophrenics. Preliminary research on the common characteristics of students active in the civil rights movement suggests a different pattern of family constellation and filial attitude.

3. When an individual whose alienation is initially expressed largely in one area of Figure 4 changes, does he tend to move to a contiguous area? For example, observers have noted the tendency of political movements to change from initial social reformism to ever more radical and active efforts to change the status quo, which may end in revolution and even in terrorism (moving, as it were, around the edge of the diagram in Figure 4). Or, to take another example, the alienated students described in this book seemed to have two major alternatives —to move toward greater maladaptation or to move toward greater involvement in society; both moves would be to contiguous areas in Figure 4. Such students seem unlikely to become terrorists, criminals, or delinquents (a move which would involve a drastic "jump" across Figure 4).

4. When an individual becomes "converted" from extreme alienation to extreme conformism (or vice versa) does the *area* of his alienation/conformism remain the same? For example, revolutionaries and terrorists who suddenly switch to a conformist position by virtue of the success of their revolution probably tend to become policemen, vigilantes, and counterrevolutionaries rather than ritualists, "Babbitts," or apologists for the new regime. Similarly, "converted" social reformers and radicals often tend to become ideological defenders of the status quo or ideological authoritarians, rather than, for example, ascetics or social conformists. It would also seem reasonable to assume that "reformed" misanthropes tend toward "Babbittry" after their reform.

5. This classification would seem to suggest that common patterns may characterize individuals in any given quadrant of Figures 4 and 5, and that these patterns may contrast sharply with those found in polar opposites on these diagrams. For example, the common characteristics of homosexuals, addicts, schizophrenics and anomic individuals should contrast in some ways with the patterns found among radicals, the civil-disobedient, the non-violent resisters, and social reformers. Or again, Figure 4 would suggest that the etiology of "acting-out" delinquency (sociopathy, juvenile delinquents, criminality) should be different in some ways from the etiology of cultural innovation, cultural refusal, social criticism and inner emigration.

In the terms proposed in this Appendix, the young men with whom this book begins are a group of *individually alienated* youths, whose alienation is manifest primarily in the areas of ideology, culture, and

internalization as criticism, repudiation, and withdrawal. Their alienation is explicit and "chosen"; its immediate *agent* is the self. Its *focus*
is on the dominant cultural values of their society; its *mode* tends to be
somewhat autoplastic. One aspect of their individual alienation is a
strong sense of *cosmic outcastness;* and the psychological roots of their
alienation lie partly in unusually intensified *developmental estrangements.* To an outsider, these youths do not appear extraordinarily self-
estranged; indeed, it could be argued that they are in closer touch with
their "real selves" or "creative potentials" than most young men their
age. Yet they have a strong sense of *self-estrangement.* And many of
the social and historical roots of their individual alienation lie in the
*historical losses* of modern technological society—the loss of a sense of
historical relatedness, the loss of traditional community and the intact
task, and, perhaps most important, the loss of a compelling positive
vision of the individual and collective future.

# REFERENCE NOTES

# Chapter 1

From the outset, it should be made clear that I am here dealing only with *one* type of alienation: namely, cultural and ideological alienation. In the Appendix, I consider in more detail the ambiguities of the concept of alienation, and point to the similarities and differences between cultural alienation and other forms of individual alienation: political, behavioral, and psychological. In *The Alienated Student* I summarize the few empirical studies of alienation that have been made. (See also M. B. Clinard [ed.], *Anomie and Deviant Behavior* [Glencoe: Free Press, 1964].) In that book, I also discuss in greater detail the empirical findings upon which the following chapters are based, the characteristics of non-alienated students, the precise selection procedures used for recruiting a small group of alienated students for intensive study, and some of the types of alienated personality found in the population I have studied. In that book, also, I deal more extensively with the methodological questions entailed in research on alienation.

Obviously, the study of a group of individuals who were selected on the basis of their *extreme* alienation cannot alone clarify the question of the prevalence of alienation in American society. However, any inquiry into the prevalence of alienation is equally impossible without a clear prior definition of the meaning of alienation and an exploration of its psychological, social, and historical concomitants in individuals who *are* clearly alienated. In Chapter 13, I consider in more detail the similarities and differences between these extremely alienated youths and the non-alienated majority of the American population.

## Chapter 2

In this chapter, as in all later chapters, names, places, and dates have been changed and other identifying information has at times been omitted or altered. Furthermore, here as in the following five chapters, I have concentrated on themes of alienation, omitting from my discussion other important aspects of personality that appeared idiosyncratic. Inburn was chosen as a "model" of alienated youth partly because his alienation is extreme, and partly because his identity could be concealed with relative ease. In Inburn, themes of alienation are unusually central; for many of the students who constitute the basis for the composite case history in subsequent chapters, alienation is a less central issue than it is for him.

Henry A. Murray's "American Icarus," pp. 615-641 in Arthur Burton and Robert E. Harris (eds.), *Clinical Studies in Personality* (New York: Harper, 1955) provided a model for this chapter. It was previously published in a different version in Robert W. White (ed.), *The Study of Lives* (New York: Atherton, 1963).

## Chapter 3

In this chapter, I have condensed and summarized materials relating to the ideology of alienation drawn from attitudinal scales and questionnaires and from written autobiographies. These materials are discussed in more detail in Chapters 2 and 9 of *The Alienated Student*.

There is of course no clear consensus as to a precise definition of "traditional American values." Gunnar Myrdal's "American Ideals and the American Conscience," pp. 3-25 in *An American Dilemma* (New York: Harper, 1944), remains one of the most useful brief summaries. Other valuable interpretations are found in Elting E. Morison (ed.), *The American Style* (New York: Harper, 1958)—in particular, the article by Clyde Kluckhohn, "Have There Been Discernible Shifts in American Values During the Past Generation?" (pp. 145-217).

## Chapter 4

In *The Alienated Student*, Chapter 3, I discuss research that indicates the lack of relationship between alienation and socio-economic or demographic variables in the Harvard College population. This research also points to the propensity of alienated students for "retroactive gloom," which casts a pall of depression over all past events. This retroactive gloom makes it virtually impossible to study the *specific* etiological factors behind alienation with non-clinical techniques: alienated students tend to agree with all questionnaire statements that suggest past misfortune. In Chapter 8 of *The Alienated Student,* I discuss in greater detail the methodological problems inherent in any attempt to separate specific background factors from this diffuse retroactive gloom.

Other researchers, studying concepts related to alienation, suggest a high relationship between low socio-economic status and high alienation. (See, e.g., Leo Srole, "Social Integration and Certain Correlaries: An Exploratory Study," *American Sociological Review* (1956), 21:709-716, or E. H. Mizruchi, "Social Structure and Anomia in a Small City," *American Sociological Review* (1960), 25:645-654. The relationship between social class and alienation is no doubt extremely complex, and studies that adequately control level of intelligence and "acquiescent response set" remain to be done.

## Chapter 5

The framework within which I interpret the development of alienation owes most to the psychosocial perspective developed in the work of Erik Erikson. See, for example, "Growth and Crises of the Healthy Personality," pp. 50-100 in *Identity and the Life Cycle* (*Psychological Issues* [1959]), and "Human Strength and the Cycle of Generations," pp. 109-158 in *Insight and Responsibility* (New York: Harper, 1964). On the specific psychodynamics of adolescent development see Erikson, "The Problem of Ego Identity," pp. 101-164 in *Identity and the Life Cycle,* and "Youth: Fidelity and Diversity," pp. 1-29 in Erikson (ed.), *The Challenge of Youth* (New York: Anchor, 1965). For an interpretation of adolescent development that places a strong emphasis on the continuing importance of the adolescent's early relationship with his mother, see Peter Blos, *On Adolescence* (Glencoe: Free Press, 1962).

## Chapter 6

My interpretation of the fantasies of alienated students owes much to the work of Theodore Lidz and his associates. In particular, I have here emphasized the critical role of Oedipal and post-Oedipal development in giving "final" form to fantasy themes that originate in earlier stages of life, and I have stressed the importance not merely of the parent-child relationship, but of the child's perception of his parent's relationships with each other. See Theodore Lidz, *The Family and Human Adaptation* (New York: International Universities Press, 1963), and Talcott Parsons and Robert F. Bales's *Family, Socialization and Interaction Process* (Glencoe: Free Press, 1955). My emphasis thus differs from the classical psychoanalytic position, which attributes greater etiological significance to "fixations" that occur in the first one or two years of life.

For a more technical discussion of the problems of interpreting fantasy productions, see Chapters 8 and 11 of *The Alienated Student*. My appreciation of the problems and rewards of the use of fantasy in psychological research owes most to Henry A. Murray.

## Chapter 7

In attempting to reconstruct the distant psychological history of alienation, I have borrowed heavily from Erik Erikson's "Reflections on the American Identity," pp. 285-325 in Erikson, *Childhood and Society* (New York: Norton, 1950). My own research, however, suggests that the mother's idealization of her father, accompanied by an explicit denigration of the relative worth of her husband, occurs more frequently and more intensely in "alienating" families than in more typical families.

In its broad outlines, the basic family constellation and developmental history that I have linked to alienation also appears related to a number of other conditions in adolescence. Thus, Lidz, Fleck, and their associates, in their studies of the etiology of schizophrenia in adolescence, often find among middle-class male patients a comparable although more extreme picture of a mother-son alliance against the father, a confusion or reversal of sex roles within the family, and a father who is unable to be "psychologically present" in a paternal role. (See references in Lidz, *op. cit.*) A similar picture of family dynamics emerges from the work of Irving Bieber and associates, *Homosexuality* (New York: Basic Books, 1962), who describe the most common pattern in families with psychoanalytically-treated homosexual sons as a "close-binding intimate" mother plus a "detached" (ambivalent, distant, or hostile) father. So, too, Erikson in "The Problem of Ego Identity" (*op. cit.*) (especially pp. 136-138) describes a similar family pattern in the etiology of acute identity diffusion among adolescents.

A precise picture of the *differential* etiology of cultural alienation, schizophrenia, homosexuality, and intense identity diffusion among middle-class male adolescents remains an important research task. The students studied here appear to differ from those described in the afore-mentioned research studies in several ways that may be crucial: one, in their ability to "intellectualize" successfully; two, in the frequent signs of a covert identification with a fantasy of what the father was like when he was young, before he was "broken by life." Impressionistically, it seems that the degree of psychological disturbance in these students was closely related to their *inability* to maintain a positive image of a father who existed before they were born. Students who had no such image appeared to be most disturbed; those who had an active fantasy of their youthful father seemed to be the most articulate and outspoken critics of American society. A similar covert identification with the unimplemented ideals of the father is suggested in two studies of politically alienated youth: Robert Coles's "Serpents and Doves," pp. 223-259 in Erikson (ed.), *The Challenge of Youth,* and Jacob R. Fishman and Frederic Solomon, "Psychological Observations on the Student Sit-In Movement," *Proceedings of the Third World Congress of Psychiatry* (Toronto: University of Toronto/McGill, n.d.). It may be that the capacity to express alienation in ideological, political, or revolutionary forms is related to an implicit identification with the lost idealism of the father.

In discussing the "search for a breakthrough" among alienated students, Ernst Schachtel's *Metamorphosis* (New York: Basic Books, 1959), has been of particular value. The importance of orientations to time has recently been stressed in the work of Robert J. Lifton (see, for example, "Individual Patterns in Historical Change," *Comparative Studies in Society and History* [1964], 6:369-383), and Florence R. Kluckhohn and Fred L. Strodtbeck, *Variations in Value Orientation* (Evanston: Row, Peterson, 1961).

## Chapter 8

In this, as in the next four chapters, my comments apply primarily to white middle-class American youth. This group constitutes the most salient and pace-setting sector of American adolescent society, and the pressures and demands that affect this sector of our society are often apparent in other groups as well. Nonetheless, were one to attempt to analyze the dominant social and historical pressures in the lives of Negro Americans, or of working-class Americans, the im-

pact and effect of these same pressures would be different. And all
of the pressures I discuss might seem trivial compared to those created
by segregation, poverty, exclusion, deprivation, and underprivilege.
Moreover, it should be clear that in these chapters I am speaking at a
very high level of generalization, attempting to describe "modal" trends
which affect each individual in a different way. The pressures and demands I am characterizing in this and the following chapters are rarely
if ever consciously experienced in precisely the same terms that I describe them. The stresses created by chronic social change, for example,
become part of what I term in Chapter 12 "the social scenery"; but
my argument is that although these pressures, stresses, and demands
can rarely be identified or precisely defined by those upon whom they
impinge most heavily, they nonetheless affect them profoundly.

Little attention has so far been given to the effects of chronic change
in advanced societies. Most studies of social change concentrate on
primitive communities in contact with more advanced societies. The social changes that result are both similar to and different from those that
occur in modern American society. Although a drastic sense of historical dislocation and social instability often results, the "goal" or "end"
of social change is usually defined by the image of the more advanced
society. Furthermore, social change in primitive societies is usually
perceived as imposed from without, and is often resented as such.
Leonard W. Doob's *Becoming More Civilized* (New Haven: Yale, 1960)
summarizes and organizes much of the available anthropological literature on social change in primitive societies.

Robert J. Lifton's studies of modern Japanese youth offer an interesting comparison with American youth, and my discussion of the need for
"historical relatedness" has been influenced by many discussions with
Dr. Lifton. Although Japan is technologically "advanced," the experience of social change among Japanese youth often appears most similar to the experience of youth in less "advanced" societies. Thus, while
the dominant temporal focus of American youth is on the present, that
of Japanese youth is frequently, in Lifton's terms, millennially "trans-
formationist" or radically "restorationist." And while young Americans
generally perceive social change as desirable and impersonally gene-
rated, Japanese youth are far more consciously ambivalent, perhaps because recent social change is seen as a result of national dishonor and
defeat. See Lifton, "Youth and History: Individual Change in Post-war
Japan," in Erikson, *The Challenge of Youth*, and "Japanese Youth: The
Search for the New and the Pure," *The American Scholar* (1961), 30:

332-344, and "Individual Patterns in Historical Change," *Comparative Studies in Society and History* (1964), 6:369-383.

In emphasizing the "unrestrained" and "unopposed" nature of social change in America, I do not wish to deny the power of the forces opposed to change. To many Americans, change often occurs too slowly, and is impeded by inefficiency and vested interests. Also, the very rate and acceleration of social change produces strong spontaneous counterreactions in the form of "restorationist" political forces, as in the Republican presidential campaign of 1964. The most vociferous opposition to "modernity" in American society comes from those who have been "left behind" characterologically by rapid rates of change; and it is quite possible that the size and vehemence of this group will increase in the future. Nonetheless, compared with other advanced societies, ours provides little planning of or brake on social change, and has few established centers of opposition to unguided technological change.

The psychological importance of rapid social change in American life has been emphasized by Allen Wheelis, *The Quest for Identity* (New York: Norton, 1958). Rapid social change is among the primary sources of social stress discussed by Talcott Parsons. See, e.g., "Social Strains in America," pp. 226-249 in Parsons, *Structure and Process in Modern Societies* (Glencoe: Free Press, 1960). Kingsley Davis was among the first to point to the effects of rapid social change on the relations between the generations. See his "Sociology of Parent-Youth Conflict," *American Journal of Sociology* (1940), 4:523-535.

An earlier version of this chapter, "Social Change and Youth in America," appeared in Erikson (ed.), *The Challenge of Youth*.

## Chapter 9

My debt to the work of Talcott Parsons is especially great in this and the next chapter. I have borrowed heavily from his analysis of industrial societies, especially as found in *The Social System* (Glencoe: Free Press, 1951) and *Structure and Process in Modern Society* (Glencoe: Free Press, 1960), especially Chapter 4. Winston White in *Beyond Conformity* (New York: Free Press, 1961) offers a parallel analysis of American society, and I am especially indebted to White's chapter entitled "Interpretation of Current Strain." Despite my great debt to Parsons, my terminology, focus, and evaluations differ considerably from his. I have preferred to use less technical terms to discuss what he labels "structural differentiation," "affective neutrality," "universalism," "achievement orientation," "instrumental activism," et cetera. My chief focus, as I have noted earlier, is upon the points at which the "structural" characteristics of American society create the greatest psychological pressure on individuals. And my evaluations of the difficulties of life in our technological society are less sanguine than those of Parsons.

The literature discussing the problems of capitalist, industrial, or "technological" society is vast, beginning with Marx, continuing through Tönnies, Weber, and Veblen, and illustrated today in the works of Mumford, Giedion, Ellul, and many others. Like the present chapter, much of this writing concentrates on the problems created by modern society. It would, however, be equally possible to explore in detail the "compensations," "emancipations," and "advances" made possible by modern society. The "shattering" of traditional community is far from complete; many men are able to find meaning—albeit a reduced meaning—in their work; and (a circumstance I discuss in more detail in the next chapter) the family and private life provide an "outlet" for many of the feelings and needs that cannot be expressed or satisfied in public life. Several recent studies have underlined the fact that "community" still exists in American life, especially among intact ethic groups and in middle-class suburban areas. See, e.g., Herbert Gans, *The Urban Villagers* (New York: Free Press, 1962) or W. H. Whyte, Jr.'s account of "The New Suburbia" in *The Organization Man* (New York: Simon and Schuster, 1956). The existence of such communities can be best understood, I believe, as survivals of an earlier way of life (as with Gans's urban villagers) or as compensations for the disintegration of more traditional community structures (as with Whyte's new suburbia). My main objective in this chapter, however, is to emphasize what seems to me the over-all direction of change in American society, rather than the many exceptions to and reactions against this direction.

The degree to which one emphasizes continuity or change in the development of any industrial society obviously depends on one's purposes, since both continuity and change are always present. Throughout the second half of this book, I have chosen to emphasize what seems to me quantitatively or qualitatively *new* about our technological society, even though this choice has often meant neglecting the many continuities that relate modern America to its past. Moreover, in discussing "technological" society, I am discussing primarily American society, for it seems misleading to consider all "industrial" societies as the same. As Lifton's studies of Japanese youth make especially clear, the impact of an industrial society upon individuals varies enormously, depending upon historical, cultural, and institutional circumstances. Thus, I have here used the term "technological" to characterize what seem to me the central tendencies of modern American society. My emphasis thus agrees with that of David Riesman in *The Lonely Crowd* (New Haven: Yale University, 1950), and in many of the essays in *Abundance for What?* (Garden City: Doubleday, 1964). An excellent discussion of the issue of continuity versus change in American society is found in the articles by Riesman, Talcott Parsons and Winston White, Seymour M. Lipset, and Leo Lowenthal in Lipset and Lowenthal (eds.), *Culture and Social Character* (Glencoe: Free Pess, 1961).

My discussion of the shattering of community owes much to the community studies ably summarized in Maurice R. Stein, *The Eclipse of Community* (Princeton: Princeton University, 1960). My discussion of the fragmentation of tasks was influenced by Daniel Bell's *Work and Its Discontents* (Boston: Beacon, 1956). Georges Friedmann's *The Anatomy of Work* (Glencoe: Free Press, 1961) and his *Industrial Society* (Glencoe: Free Press, 1955) have also been especially useful in considering the "meaningfulness" of work. My discussion of the "burden of freedom" is influenced by Erich Fromm's *Escape from Freedom* (New York: Rinehart, 1941).

## Chapter 10

This discussion of the structure and functions of the middle-class family in American society is again influenced by the work of Parsons (*Family, Socialization and Interaction Process*) and Riesman (*The Lonely Crowd*). Parsons and Lidz (*op. cit.*) both emphasize the critical importance of the family in determining the direction of ego development as well as superego development. And Riesman, of course, has been the most articulate portraitist of the new privatism and the other-directed ethic of family and fun. Unlike Riesman in *The Lonely Crowd*, however, I interpret the emphasis on family and fun primarily as a reaction *against* what seem to me the main trends in American society: the pressures and demands described in the previous chapter. Thus, although the phenomena described by Riesman as "other-direction" seem to me overwhelming in importance in modern American life, I here interpret them primarily as "outlets," "escapes," and "compensations" for the qualities of "public life." Once again, it is largely a matter of personal preference whether one chooses to emphasize how different American society in the sixties is from American society in the twenties, or how many underlying similarities the two epochs share.

Some writers argue that the "isolation" of the family in American life has been exaggerated. See, e.g., L. F. Cervantes, *The Dropout: Causes and Cures* (Ann Arbor: University of Michigan, 1965), pp. 46 ff. New patterns of companionate marriage, continuing ties with relatives in the community, the growing importance of family friends—all are said to mitigate the effects of the separation of family from wider kinship and occupational structures. My argument in this chapter is that despite such compensatory tendencies, the structural isolation of the family does make the psychological isolation of the family (and especially of the woman-in-charge-of-the-family) more probable.

The concept of "developmental discontinuities" is derived from Ruth Benedict's "Continuities and Discontinuities in Cultural Conditioning," pp. 214-223 in C. Kluckhohn and H. A. Murray (eds.), *Personality in Nature, Society and Culture* (New York: Knopf, 1948). See also the Appendix of this book for a closely related discussion of "developmental estrangements." It is crucial to distinguish between developmental discontinuities and generational discontinuities, both of which are important in modern America. Generational discontinuities ("the generational gap") are differences in the average expectable life situation of *different* individuals in different generations at the same time; developmental discontinuities are discontinuities between the average expectable demands of one stage of life and those of another stage of life for the *same* individuals as they move through the stages of life.

The special stresses and problems of women's roles in America have most recently been discussed in Betty Friedan, *The Feminine Mystique* (New York: Norton, 1963); the Winter, 1964, issue of *Daedalus;* and Ellen and Kenneth Keniston, "An American Anachronism: The Image of Women and Work," *The American Scholar* (1964), 33:355-375. The special problems of men *qua* men have to my knowledge been less frequently discussed.

In this chapter, I am in effect arguing that changes in the American middle-class family are increasing the probability that alienating family patterns will be found. In particular, the emergence of "alienated youth" is intimately related to family and occupational role definitions that lead women to "overinvest" in their children and encourage men to be physically, if not psychologically, absent from their children's upbringing. This argument, if correct, would be consistent with the observation of a comparable family constellation in the etiology of a variety of "alienated" conditions in middle-class male adolescents and young adults. (See notes to Chapter 7.)

This argument does not, however, imply that the "mental health" of children from middle-class American families is deteriorating or will deteriorate in the future. The development of new patterns of middle-class family life has resulted in fewer authoritarian and repressive families, which produce their own kinds of psychopathology. Furthermore, the enormous importance Americans attach to the proper upbringing of their children and the compensatory role of "familism" in American life both mean that American children today receive far more attention and devotion than they did two generations ago. As at many other points in this book, my argument is not that things are getting worse, but merely that they are changing; and I am underlining those trends that seem most likely to produce human problems.

## Chapter 11

The emphasis in this chapter on the critical importance of "positive myth" is derived from the work of Henry A. Murray, particularly as stated in his Introduction to Murray (ed.), *Myths and Mythmaking* (New York: Braziller, 1960). My interpretation of the role and meaning of Utopia parallels that of Karl Mannheim, *Ideology and Utopia* (London: International Library of Psychology, Philosophy and Scientific Method, 1936). See also Erikson's discussion of the psychological meaning of ideology in adolescence in "The Problem of Ego Identity," *op. cit.* David E. Apter, in his introduction of Apter (ed.), *Ideology and Discontent* (Glencoe: Free Press, 1964), discusses the relationship between Erikson's and Mannheim's usages of "ideology."

Throughout this chapter and this book, my thinking about ideology and Utopia differs sharply from that of many recent works. See, e.g., Daniel Bell, *The End of Ideology* (Glencoe: Free Press, 1960). An earlier version of parts of this chapter appeared in "Alienation and the Decline of Utopia," *The American Scholar* (1960), 29:1-40.

## Chapter 12

In using changes within psychoanalytic theory as a barometer of the most stressful demands of society, I obviously do not mean to comment on the validity or usefulness of psychoanalytic ego psychology. Most work in this field begins from Anna Freud, *The Ego and the Mechanisms of Defense* (New York: International Universities, 1946), and

Heinz Hartmann, *The Ego and the Problem of Adaptation* (New York: International Universities, 1958). For more recent thinking in this field see, e.g., David Rapaport, *Organization and Pathology of Thought* (New York: Columbia University, 1951), and recent issues of the annual *The Psychoanalytic Study of the Child*.

In this chapter, I use the term "virtue" in a sense akin to Erikson's in "The Roots of Virtue," pp. 145-167 in Julian Huxley (ed.), *The Humanist Frame* (London: George Allen and Unwin, 1961), and "Human Strength and the Cycle of Generations," *op. cit.* Erikson, however, is discussing "virtues" that he believes are required in each stage of human development, whatever the society in which the individual may live. In this chapter, in contrast, I am emphasizing social virtues, that is, the specific ego qualities most encouraged and rewarded in any given society. Developmental virtues and social virtues obviously overlap at certain points. In modern American society, for example, the virtue of "competence," which Erikson attaches to the stage of pre-adolescence, has a superordinate value throughout life, while the virtue of "wisdom," which for Erikson is associated with old age, is given little attention. Thus, the social priorities assigned to each developmental virtue may differ with social circumstance.

Throughout this chapter I am speaking of what might be termed the "preferred personality" of American society—that is, of the kind of personality organization and the ego qualities that are most encouraged and most rewarded in our society. What I term the "right" or preferred personality obviously differs crucially from the actual personality of many and perhaps most Americans. Preferred personality should be further distinguished not only from actual personality but from the articulate public social myth about desirable personality organization. These three may overlap or diverge in any given society. For example, most individuals may have personality organizations that differ both from the preferred personality of their society and from the social myth about the ideal personality organization. Furthermore, the social myth about what is desirable may not correspond to the actual handing out of rewards and punishments by the society. Most discussions of "modal personality," "national character," or "social character" do not adequately distinguish between these three aspects of the phenomenon.

## Chapter 13

Any judgment as to the extent and prevalence of alienation is obviously contingent upon the definition of alienation. In the Appendix of this book, I explore in more detail the meanings of alienation and the particular sense in which I use that term in this book. Figure 4 in the Appendix suggests a classification of the varieties of alienation, classified broadly as psychological, cultural, political, and behavioral (criminal). It should be clear, however, that in speaking of the "little alienations" of the average adjusted American, I am using "alienation" in a far more extended sense. As I state in the text, such "little alienations" never add up to the "real" alienation of a political dissident, a criminal, a psychotic, or a culturally alienated youth. These "little alienations" are related to "real" alienation in that they exhibit many of the same psychological themes that are salient in the lives of explicitly alienated individuals.

Michael Harrington's *The Other Americans* (Baltimore: Penguin, 1963,) is an excellent introduction to the problem of the rejected (who may or may not be alienated) in America. There are vast literatures on each of the forms and varieties of individual alienation, ranging from the extensive studies of psychosis and criminality to the smaller literature on cultural alienation and on the politically active (and alienated) youth largely concentrated in the students' civil rights movement. See notes to the Appendix.

Talcott Parsons, "Age and Sex in the Social Structure," pp. 218-232 in Parsons, *Essays in Psychological Theory* (Glencoe: Free Press, 1949) is the first discussion in English of "youth culture." James C. Coleman's *The Adolescent Society* (Glencoe: Free Press, 1961) provides a systematic study of youth cultures in a variety of high schools. The extent and importance of the youth culture in American life is a matter of controversy. Some writers stress the adult orientation of youth and minimize the importance of a separate teen-age culture. See, e.g., F. Elkin and W. A. Westley, "The Myth of Adolescent Culture," *American Sociological Review* (1955), 20:680-684. Others stress the power of adult society to promote conformity and "adjustment" in youth. See, e.g., Edgar Z. Friedenberg, *The Vanishing Adolescent* (Boston: Beacon, 1959). I suggest in this chapter that although the values of the youth culture are non-adult, one of the functions of the youth culture is to allow youth time and opportunity to make the transition to adulthood.

Furthermore, I emphasize that most young people themselves have a "double consciousness," partly youth-oriented, partly adult-oriented.

For a discussion of the relationship between traditional youth cultures and the students now involved in political activities, see my "American Students and the 'Political Revival,'" *The American Scholar* (1963), 32:40-64. The student civil rights movement, despite its great symbolic importance, of course involves only a fraction of one per cent of the student age group. In its current emphasis on a "single issue" (civil rights), its non-ideological approach, and its effort to implement a very traditional American value (equality), it appears consistent with many of the characteristic outlooks of American youth. As of 1965, the overwhelming proportion of alienation in American youth is expressed in private forms. The recent growth of organized discontent at Berkeley, however, suggests that private alienations may, within the next generation, be increasingly directed at public targets. As my argument in this chapter suggests, such a mobilization, if informed and reasoned, seems to me eminently desirable.

S. N. Eisenstadt's *From Generation to Generation* (Glencoe: Free Press, 1956) provides an instructive cross-cultural analysis of age-graded adolescent sub-cultures, of which the youth culture is of course one. Parsons' current views on the state of American youth and youth culture can be found in "Youth in the Context of American Society," in Erikson (ed.), *The Challenge of Youth.*

## Appendix

Since the meanings of "alienation" are so diverse, the entire literature on deviance, psychopathology, political rebellion, withdrawal, and criminality, in addition to much writing on personal misery and unhappiness, is often considered relevant to the understanding of alienation. For two anthologies which, by not defining alienation unequivocally, are able to include a highly heterogeneous selection of writings about the problems of the modern world, see Gerald Sykes's two-volume anthology, *Alienation* (New York: Braziller, 1965), and Eric and Mary Josephson (eds.), *Man Alone: Alienation in Modern Society* (New York: Dell, 1962). Despite the diversity of their collection, the Josephsons provide an excellent discussion of the meanings of "alienation" in their Introduction.

Neo-Marxist writings on alienation generally start from Karl Marx's *Economic and Philosophic Manuscripts of 1844* (Moscow: Foreign

Languages Publishing, 1959). Among the most noteworthy of such writings are Erich Fromm, *The Sane Society* (New York: Holt, Rinehart and Winston, 1955), Erich Kahler, *The Tower and the Abyss* (New York: Braziller, 1957), and Fritz Pappenheim, *The Alienation of Modern Man* (New York: Monthly Review, 1959). The trajectory from the works of the young Marx to those of the older Marx and the varying interpretations of Marxist thought are discussed by Daniel Bell in "Two Roads from Marx: The Themes of Alienation and Exploitation in Socialist Thought," pp. 335-368, in Bell, *The End of Ideology* (Glencoe: Free Press, 1960). See also Fromm, *Marx's Concept of Man* (New York: Ungar, 1961). Lewis Feuer, "What is Alienation? The Career of a Concept," *New Politics* (1961), pp. 1-19, also discusses the origins and development of "alienation." Frank Lucente, "Alienation in Hegel and Marx," *Viewpoint* (1964), 5: 29-38, discusses the similarities and differences in Marx's and Hegel's concepts of alienation. One proposed classification of the meanings of alienation can be found in Melvin Seeman, "On the Meaning of Alienation," *American Sociological Review* (1959), 24: 783-791.

On the psychological use of "alienations" see Karen Horney, *Our Inner Conflicts* (New York: Norton, 1945), *The Neurotic Personality of Our Time* (New York: Norton, 1937), and *New Ways in Psychoanalysis* (New York: Norton, 1939). See also the symposium, "Alienation and the Search for Identity," in *The American Journal of Psychoanalysis* (November, 1961). Among the many writers who connect alienation with personal maladaptation and psychosis, see, for example, Burt Kaplan's introduction (p. xi) to *The Inner World of Mental Illness* (New York: Harper and Row, 1964). My own studies of alienation began from the work of Henry A. Murray and Anthony Davids. This and other empirical studies of alienation are summarized more fully in *The Alienated Student.*

The definition of "individual alienation" proposed in this Appendix is comparable to the discussion of alienation and "alienative need-dispositions" by Talcott Parsons in *The Social System* (Glencoe: Free Press, 1951) especially Chap. VII, "Deviant Behavior and the Mechanisms of Social Control." See also Robert Merton's "Social Structure and Anomie," in *Social Theory and Social Structure* (Glencoe: Free Press, 1957). Richard A. Cloward and Lloyd E. Ohlin, *Deliquency and Opportunity* (Glencoe: Free Press, 1960) specifically discuss "the process of alienation," defined as "a process of withdrawal of attributions of legitimacy to established social norms." In the terms I use in this Appendix, Cloward and Ohlin are discussing primarily alienation from behavioral norms, which results in crime and delinquency. Similarly, Merton's distinction between "means" and "ends" in the aforementioned essay can be loosely translated into my distinction between a focus on behavioral norms (means) and a focus on cultural values (ends). Political alienations are discussed in these terms by Parsons, *op. cit.*, Chap. XI.

Discussions of "cosmic outcastness" are legion. A useful summary of the views of existentialist philosophers is found in F. H. Heinemann, *Existentialism and the Modern Predicament* (London: Adam and Charles Black, 1953), especially Chap. X, "Alienation and Beyond." Hannah Arendt in *The Human Condition* (Chicago: University of Chicago, 1958) discusses "world alienation" as a characteristic of the modern age (see especially Part VI, "The *Vita Activa* and the Modern Age"). The relationship between existential (and presumably unremediable) alienation and socially induced alienations is discussed by Heinemann, *op. cit.*, Pappenheim, *op. cit.*, the Josephsons *op. cit.*, and Helen Merell Lynd's comments in *The American Journal of Psychoanalysis* (November, 1961).

The literature on "cultural alienation," with which I am primarily concerned in this book, is relatively sparse compared to writings on other varieties of alienation. See, however, Francis J. Rigney and L. Douglas Smith, *The Real Bohemia* (New York: Basic Books, 1961), or Lawrence Lipton, *The Holy Barbarians* (New York: Messner, 1959) and Norman Mailer, "The White Negro," pp. 337-359 in *Advertisements for Myself* (New York: Putnam's, 1959). There are a number of popular anthologies of the writings of the "Beat Generation," e.g., Gene Feldman and Max Gartenberg (eds.), *The Beat Generation and the Angry Young Men* (New York: Citadel, 1958).

Also relevant to a discussion of "cultural alienation" is much of the writing on the role of the intellectual and the artist in modern society. See, for example, Julien Benda, *The Betrayal of the Intellectuals* (Boston: Beacon, 1955), George B. De Huszar (ed.), *The Intellectuals: A Controversial Portrait* (Glencoe: Free Press, 1960), or Daniel Bell's spirited defense of alienation as the proper attitude of the social analyst in his introduction to *The End of Ideology*. For one discussion of alienation as portrayed in literature, see Robert E. Jones, *The Alienated Hero in Modern French Drama* (Athens, Ga.: University of Georgia, 1962). Here, again, virtually the entire literature discussing the romantic and modern image of the artist is directly or indirectly relevant to the understanding of cultural alienation.

My discussion of "developmental estrangements" in this chapter leans heavily on unpublished lectures of Erik H. Erikson at Harvard in 1960-1962. For a brief discussion of the historical relativity of "alienation," see Erikson's Preface in Erikson (ed.), *Youth: Change and Challenge* (New York: Basic Books, 1963).

# SELECTED
# BIBLIOGRAPHY

I have listed here only those works that were of greatest usefulness in the preparation of this book.

BELL, DANIEL. *The End of Ideology*. Glencoe: Free Press, 1960.

————. *Work and Its Discontents*. Boston: Beacon, 1956.

BLOS, PETER. *On Adolescence*. Glencoe: Free Press, 1962.

EISENSTADT, S. N. *From Generation to Generation*. Glencoe: Free Press, 1956.

ERIKSON, ERIK. *Childhood and Society*. New York: Norton, 1950.

————. "Identity and the Life Cycle," *Psychological Issues* (1959), Vol. 1, No. 1.

————. *Insight and Responsibility*. New York: Harper, 1964.

————. *Youth: Change and Challenge*. New York: Basic Books, 1963.

FROMM, ERICH. *Escape from Freedom*. New York: Rinehart, 1941.

————. *The Sane Society*. New York: Rinehart, 1955.

GOODMAN, PAUL. *Growing Up Absurd*. New York: Random House, 1960.

————. *Utopian Essays and Practical Proposals*. New York: Vintage, 1964.

HARTMANN, HEINZ. *The Ego and the Problem of Adaptation*. New York: International Universities, 1958.

HAUSER, STUART T. *Alienation and Patterns of Estrangement* (ms). 1962.

JOSEPHSON, ERIC and MARY (eds.). *Man Alone: Alienation in Modern Society*. New York: Dell, 1962.

KAHLER, ERICH. *The Tower and the Abyss.* New York: Braziller, 1957.

LIDZ, THEODORE. *The Family and Human Adaptation.* New York: International Universities, 1963.

LIFTON, ROBERT J. "Individual Patterns in Historical Change," *Comparative Studies in Society and History* (1964), 6:369-383.

————. *Thought Reform and the Psychology of Totalism.* New York: Norton, 1961.

LIPSET, SEYMOUR M., and LOWENTHAL, LEO (eds.). *Culture and Social Character.* Glencoe: Free Press, 1961.

MANNHEIM, KARL. *Ideology and Utopia.* London: International Library of Psychology, Philosophy and Scientific Method, 1936.

MARX, KARL. *Economic and Philosophic Manuscripts of 1844.* Moscow: Foreign Languages Publishing, 1959.

MORISON, ELTING E. (ed.). *The American Style.* New York: Harper, 1958.

MUMFORD, LEWIS. *Technics and Civilization.* New York: Harcourt, Brace, 1934.

MURRAY, HENRY A. (ed.). *Myths and Mythmaking.* New York: Braziller, 1960.

PAPPENHEIM, FRITZ. *The Alienation of Modern Man.* New York: Monthly Review, 1959.

PARSONS, TALCOTT. *The Social System.* Glencoe: Free Press, 1951.

————. *Structure and Process in Modern Societies.* Glencoe: Free Press, 1960.

PARSONS, TALCOTT, and BALES, ROBERT F. *Family, Socialization and Interaction Process.* Glencoe: Free Press, 1955.

RIESMAN, DAVID. *Abundance for What?* Garden City: Doubleday, 1964.

————. *The Lonely Crowd.* New Haven: Yale University, 1950.

SCHACHTEL, ERNEST. "On Alienated Concepts of Identity," *American Journal of Psychoanalysis* (1961), 21:120-127.

————. *Metamorphosis.* New York: Basic Books, 1959.

STEIN, MAURICE R. *The Eclipse of Community.* Princeton: Princeton University, 1960.

*Symposium on Alienation and the Search for Identity.* American Journal of Psychoanalysis (1961), Vol. 21.

WHEELIS, ALLEN. *The Quest for Identity.* New York: Norton, 1958.

WHITE, WINSTON. *Beyond Conformity.* New York: Free Press, 1961.

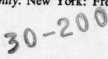